Agriculture in China's
modern economic development

Agriculture in China's modern economic development

NICHOLAS R. LARDY
Associate Professor of Economics
Yale University

CAMBRIDGE UNIVERSITY PRESS

Cambridge
London   New York   New Rochelle
Melbourne   Sydney

Published by the Press Syndicate of the University of Cambridge
The Pitt Building, Trumpington Street, Cambridge CB2 1RP
32 East 57th Street, New York, NY 10022, USA
296 Beaconsfield Parade, Middle Park, Melbourne 3206, Australia

First published 1983

Printed in the United States of America

Library of Congress Cataloging in Publication Data
Lardy, Nicholas R.
Agriculture in China's modern economic development.
1. Agriculture and state – China.   2. Agriculture –
Economic aspects – China.   3. Food supply – China.
4. China – Economic policy – 1976–   .   I. Title.
HD2098.L37   1983   338.1'0951   82-23555
ISBN 0 521 25246 6

Contents

v

Appendixes

Tables, figures, and maps

Tables

Preface

This study arises from an effort to understand several paradoxes in Chinese agricultural development. The first of these is the puzzling intertemporal path of output and productivity growth. Even after recovering quickly from the disruptions of the civil war by 1952, agricultural growth continued to be rapid from 1953 through 1957, when there were few industrial inputs used in farming and little evidence of technological change. After the mid-1960s technical change was impressive. Due to considerable investments in water control in the 1950s and the development of a chemical fertilizer industry in the early 1960s, China independently developed and began to disseminate high-yield short-stalk rice varieties on a significant scale several years prior to commercialized production of comparable varieties developed by the International Rice Research Institute in the Philippines. By 1977 these fertilizer-responsive high-yield varieties were cultivated on 80 percent of all China's rice area, while adoption was limited to about 25 percent elsewhere in Asia. Significant though less rapid technical innovations were achieved in the development of new varieties of wheat, corn, sorghum, and some other crops. Paradoxically, however, the rate of growth of cereal production from the mid-1960s to 1977–78 was no more rapid than or even somewhat below the pace of development in the First Five-Year Plan (1953–57). Even more surprising, calculations of total factor productivity in agriculture reveal that the costs of additional units of agricultural output actually rose after the mid-1960s, whereas they had fallen in the 1950s – a path precisely the opposite from what one would expect based on the evidence on technical progress. Since 1977 or 1978 growth has accelerated and productivity improved markedly, but on the basis of technology that previously had been widely used.

A second paradox is the persistence between the mid-1950s and mid- to late 1970s of chronic malnutrition and low income in a significant share of the rural population despite a doubling of per capita national income between these two periods. Although trends in per capita national income are an unreliable guide to changes in either the level or distribution of personal income in market economies, it has been believed that one of the strengths of

China's socialist system is its capability to distribute broadly income gains and to provide basic needs for all members of society.

Finally, and in some ways most puzzling, is the paradox of Mao Tse-tung. He was willing to inflict enormous political, economic, and personal hardship on the Chinese population during the Cultural Revolution (1966–77), in what he perceived to be an effort to reduce the bureaucratic power of the entrenched state apparatus and the Chinese Communist Party. At least in rural China, however, the stultifying hand of the bureaucracy was strengthened during those years, inhibiting growth and efficiency in the allocation of resources. Moreover, while Mao led a rural-based Party to power on the premise of improving the welfare of the peasantry, in retrospect many of the policies pursued by the Party after 1949 appear to have fundamentally undervalued agriculture and have left a large share of China's rural population enmeshed in extreme poverty even today.

My attempt in this study to resolve these paradoxes draws on three complementary interests. The first, which grows out of the field of comparative economic studies, is my interest in understanding the extent and implications of the use of nonmarket mechanisms for determining the structure of current production and the allocation of investment resources. Thus this study of agriculture has objectives similar to *Economic Growth and Distribution in China*, which focused on the consequences of bureaucratic allocation of industrial investment (Lardy 1978a). The second, which grows out of the field of international trade theory, is my interest in the productivity gains associated with the increasingly specialized production that occur during the course of economic development. Third, and closely related to the first two, is my interest in further understanding the economic implications of China's vast size and economic heterogeneity.

The paradoxical intertemporal path of output and productivity growth is explained by the coincidence of technological change and increased use of bureaucratic forms of resource allocation in agriculture after 1965. As the predominantly price- and market-oriented agricultural development policies of the First Five-Year Plan and the first half of the 1960s were replaced with quantity planning closely guided by state cadres, the efficiency of resource allocation declined, offsetting the productivity gains usually associated with the use of improved seed varieties and modern inputs such as chemical fertilizers and electric- and diesel-powered irrigation equipment.

The paradox of the persistently large proportion of China's rural population living in chronic poverty despite rapid growth of national income may be explained in a trade-theoretic framework. Cropping patterns were distorted and internal trade in agricultural products reduced during the quantity-planning regime that emerged after 1965. A drive to achieve local self-sufficiency in cereal production meant comparative-advantage cropping was increasingly abandoned and marketing and interregional trade in agricultural products suppressed. A decline in marketing opportunities impoverished peasants who traditionally had depended on the market both for the sale of their specialized noncereal crops and the purchase of a large share of their cereal consumption requirements.

The paradox of Mao also may be explained in this framework. His tragedy, in my view, was his failure to recognize that increased use of the market was the most effective counter to bureaucratic power, particularly in agriculture. Unfortunately, at least by the mid-1960s, Mao perceived himself as the great enemy not only of the entrenched bureaucracy but of the market as well. Thus he initiated the Cultural Revolution that led to the repression of rural markets and private plots and to the emergence of a decreasingly commercialized, more subsistence-oriented agriculture.

Mao's successors understand the costs of rejecting the use of prices and markets in agriculture. Thus they have sought to enhance the use of the market and reduce the interference of the state and Party bureaucracy in agricultural production. Initial efforts to raise productivity through price incentives and increased trade have met with some success. Yet these efforts have been resisted by lower-level bureaucrats who well understand that the price mechanism threatens their power far more than political upheaval. Furthermore, even leaders at the highest levels remain divided over agricultural development policy. Some support a further extension of the role of the market in order to raise productivity and peasant welfare. Others implicitly view the rapid growth of agricultural production since 1978 as providing a new opportunity to return to the imbalanced growth strategy of the past. They eschew the use of markets in agriculture, not because they fail to recognize the positive influence of markets on productivity, but because they fear greater reliance on markets will undermine the ability of the central government to sustain an investment structure emphasizing producer goods.

In the course of completing this study I have incurred many debts. The initial stages of the research were undertaken in Hong Kong at the Universities Service Center. Its director, John Dolphin, librarian, Lau Yee-fui, and other staff members all contributed to making my stay there most productive. Most of the research, however, was based on materials in the East Asian Collection of Sterling Memorial Library at Yale University. There Mr. Anthony Marr, the curator of the Chinese Collection, was unfailing in his efforts to help me keep abreast of the vast flow of new periodicals that began to emanate from China after 1978. Roger Thompson, a graduate student in Chinese history at Yale, provided unstinting support in exploiting these materials.

Students in my class on Chinese economic development at Yale, who were first exposed to many of the ideas contained in the study, aided me enormously through their queries and comments in improving the clarity of the exposition as the manuscript began to take shape. I revised drafts of several of the chapters on the basis of critical observations by seminar participants at Brown University, the University of Chicago, Columbia University, Harvard University, the University of London, the Stockholm School of Economics, the University of Toronto, the University of Washington, and Yale University. A draft of Chapter 3 was presented at a conference on "Agricultural Development in China, Japan and Korea" sponsored by the Academia Sinica in Taiwan in December 1980. Part of a draft of Chapter 4 was presented at a workshop convened at Cornell University in May 1979, "Agricultural and Rural Development in the People's Republic of China." Participants at both of these meetings made useful suggestions for revisions. I wish also to thank the individuals from the Institutes of Economics, Agricultural Economics, and Finance and Trade of the Chinese Academy of Social Sciences and from the Ministry of Agriculture who met with me to discuss my research during visits to Peking in June 1978 and again in June 1982.

I received encouragement and comments from many quarters. Michel Oksenberg and Thomas Rawski subjected the entire manuscript to careful scrutiny and assisted me immeasurably. Robert F. Dernberger, Robert Evenson, D. Gale Johnson, Deborah Davis-Friedman, John Michael Montias, Dwight Perkins, T. W. Schultz, Mark Selden, T. N. Srinivasan, Lee Travers, Kenneth R. Walker, and Brian Wright each read one or more chapters and provided incisive comments and advice. John Philip Emerson gave freely of his vast knowledge of problems of Chinese statistics and was unfailing in his willingness to provide copies of many of the unique holdings of the Foreign Demographic Analysis Division of the United States Bureau of the Census.

The American Council of Learned Societies supported my research in Hong Kong during the first half of 1978. The Henry F. Luce Foundation subsequently provided a generous multiple-year grant for additional research time, travel, research assistance, and other forms of support without which this study could not have been completed. Louise Danishevsky and Paula Saddler typed successive drafts of chapters, defying the trade-off between speed and accuracy.

NICHOLAS R. LARDY

New Haven
February 1983

A note on romanization. I have adopted a mixed system of transliterating Chinese into English. For provinces and major cities I use traditional postal system spellings that are more familiar to most readers. For other place names (such as counties and prefectures), personal names, and other Chinese terminology I use Wade–Giles rather than Pinyin because scholarly bibliographical tools such as library card catalogs, biographical dictionaries, gazetters, and so forth are organized alphabetically by Wade–Giles romanization.

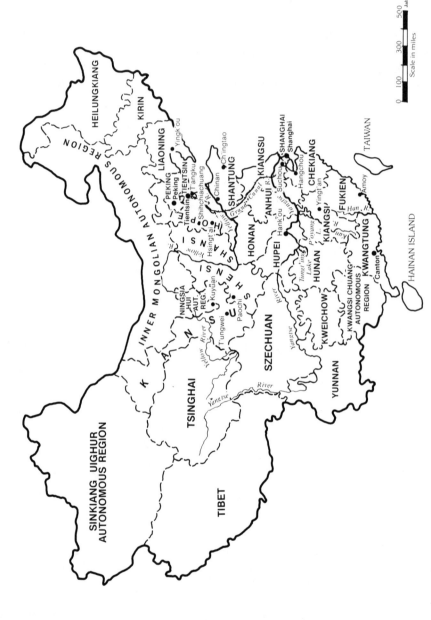

Map 1. The provinces of the People's Republic of China

1

The role of agriculture

Economic development in China accelerated rapidly after 1949. Excluding rapid postwar recovery, real per capita output tripled in the three decades between 1952 and 1981 (Table 1.1).[1] This is in marked contrast to the first half of the twentieth century, when there was no sustained per capita growth (Perkins 1975b).

Accelerated growth has been accompanied by far-reaching changes in the structure of output. The share of national income originating in industry rose from 18 percent in 1952 to almost 50 percent in 1979, while agriculture's share shrank from 60 to less than 40 percent. As industry's share more than doubled, its composition also shifted markedly. Because of a dramatic increase in the rate of capital formation, the share of producer goods in industrial output grew from about a third in 1952 to well over half by the late 1970s, primarily reflecting the rapid growth of machinery and metal products (Yang Chien-pai and Li Hsüeh-tseng 1980, 20). This pace of structural transformation far exceeds that experienced by today's advanced industrial countries during comparable periods of economic development (Kuznets 1971).

Paradoxically, although the pace of growth and the structure of output have changed dramatically since 1949, the population and the composition of the labor force remain predominantly agrarian. Although official data on the urban population (Table 1.2) are based on a changing definition and thus must be used with caution, China's development since 1949 has nonetheless been accompanied by an unusually slow pace of urbanization.[2] The urban population grew rapidly from 1949 through 1957 and explosively during the Great Leap Forward of 1958–1960.[3] Since then strict controls on rural–urban migration enforced by the Ministry of Public Security, combined with massive campaigns to resettle urban residents in the countryside, particularly in the early 1960s and again in the late 1960s, have curtailed urban population growth. Between 1952 and 1979 the labor force almost

1

Table 1.1. *Size and composition of China's national income, 1949–79*

	National income		Population (Millions)	Per capita national income index (constant prices)	Sector of origin (%)				
	Billions of yuan, current prices	Index (constant prices)			Industry	Agriculture	Commerce	Construction	Communication and transportation
1949	35.8	100	541.67	100	—	—	—	—	—
1952	58.9	169.8	574.82	160.0	18.0	59.2	15.8	3.0	4.0
1957	90.8	259.8	646.53	217.5	29.2	49.2	13.0	4.4	4.2
1965	138.7	335.1	725.38	250.2	—	—	—	—	—
1975	250.5	653.5	919.70	384.9	—	—	—	—	—
1978	301.1	778.7	958.09	440.2	—	—	—	—	—
1979	335.0	828.2	970.92	462.2	45.9	38.8	7.9	3.8	3.6
1980	366.0[a]	885.4	982.50	489.2	—	—	—	—	—
1981	388.0	912.0	996.22	496.9	—	—	—	—	—

Notes: National income is measured in the Chinese net material product concept, excluding some services originating in the non-material-producing branches. The index of national income in constant prices is a composite, linking an index of national income in 1949–57 measured in 1952 constant prices, in 1957–70 in 1957 constant prices, 1970–80 in 1970 constant prices, and 1981 in 1980 constant prices. Sector of origin data for 1952 and 1957 apply to national income measured in constant 1952 prices and data for 1979 apply to national income measured in constant 1970 prices. Since agriculture prices increased relative to industrial product prices between 1952 and 1970, the long-run pace of structural change shown above is substantially less than would be shown if the composition of output were measured in 1952 prices for all years.

[a]Originally reported as 363.0 billion yuan. Revised figure released April 1982.
Sources: National income and population – State Statistical Bureau (1980b; 1981c, VI-4; 1982a). *Sectoral composition* – 1952 and 1957; Ishikawa (1965, 76); 1979; Yüeh Wei (1981, 47).

doubled to 406 million. However, agriculture absorbed two-thirds of that increase, and consequently its share of employment only shrank from about 85 to 75 percent of the total. Although the industrial labor force more than quadrupled, its share of the labor force in 1979 was only 13 percent, remarkably small compared to the share of national income originating in industry.[4] In short, the sharply declining trend in the product share of agriculture has been accompanied by an unusually small reduction in its share of the labor force. Consequently, in terms of structure of output China resembles a relatively industrialized country, although its labor force structure is similar to that of some of the world's least developed economies.

The dichotomy between the structure of output and the composition of the labor force raises several major issues for understanding Chinese economic development since 1949. First, whereas industrial development is the main determinant of the growth of gross domestic product, changes in the level of personal income for most Chinese are determined by the pace of agricultural development and changes in the prices farmers receive for agricultural products relative to the prices of products they purchase. To what extent has rapid growth of output raised living standards, particularly for the peasantry?

Second, why has the pattern of growth been so skewed, particularly during the Maoist era, up to 1977 or 1978? While industrial output between 1952 and 1978 grew at an annual rate of 11.3 percent, agriculture grew at only 2.3 percent and cereal output at only 2.4 percent (Yang Chien-pai and Li Hsüeh-tseng 1980, 183; Table 4.2).[5] Since population growth averaged 2.0 percent over this period, the margin for improvement in food consumption has been rather modest for an economy in which per capita gross domestic product in constant prices has tripled. Indeed, although China's industrial growth accelerated markedly after 1949, it appears that agricultural growth did little more than keep pace with the expansion of the population, just matching the performance of agriculture in the previous six centuries (Perkins, 1969). The slow pace of agricultural development has been explained primarily by China's land-short resource endowment. While China's population grew by two-thirds between 1952 and the late 1970s, the quantity of arable land shrank by more than 10 percent (Table 1.3).[6] Land reclamation programs between 1957 and 1977 brought an additional 17 million hectares into cultivation, but that was more than offset by 27 million hectares of arable land used for building roads, housing, factories, and so on (Wang Chia-liang, Chang Yüeh-jung, and Chang Ch'iao-lung 1982). Thus arable land per capita was reduced by half between 1952 and 1979 (Table 1.3).

Arable land per agricultural worker also declined by half between the early 1950s and the late 1970s. While the man/land ratio has been growing in

Table 1.2. *Population and labor force composition, 1949–79 (year-end)*

	Population			Labor Force				
	Total (millions)	Urban (millions)	Percentage	Total (millions)	Agricultural[a] (millions)	Percentage	Industrial[b] (millions)	Percentage
1949	541.67	57.65	10.6	—	—	—	—	—
1952	574.82	71.63	12.5	207.29	173.17	83.5	12.46	6.0
1957	646.53	99.49	15.4	237.71	193.10	81.2	14.01	5.9
1965	725.38	101.70	14.0	286.70	233.98	81.6	18.28	6.4
1975	919.70	111.71	12.1	381.68	294.60	77.2	48.09	12.6
1977	—	—	—	386.62	292.67	75.7	48.10	12.4
1978	958.09	119.94	12.5	398.56	294.26	73.8	50.10	12.6
1979	970.92	128.62	13.2	405.81	294.25	72.5	53.40	13.2

[a]Agricultural labor force data exclude employment in rural small-scale enterprises managed by the commune level or above but include such workers at the brigade level. In 1978 and 1979 brigade enterprise employment was about 16 million, about 5 percent of the agricultural labor force. Comparable data for earlier years are not available. Employees of state farms (359,000 in 1952, 440,600 in 1957, 2.6003 million in 1965, 4.8171 million in 1975, and 4.8100 million in 1979) are included in the agricultural labor force.

[b]Includes commune but not brigade industry. Industry includes mining, manufacturing, and electric power.

Sources: State Statistical Bureau (1981c, VI-3–VI-4; 1982b, VIII-3–VIII-4); Ministry of Agriculture Policy Research Office (1980, 36; 1982, 85); Agricultural Yearbook Compilation Commission (1981, 4); International Bank for Reconstruction and Development (1981, A:170).

Table 1.3. *Population–land balance, 1952–79*

	Arable land (millions of hectares) (1)	Population (millions) (2)	Arable land per capita[a] (ha) (3)	Arable land per agricultural worker (ha)[b] (4)
1952	107.9	575	.19	.62
1957	111.8	647	.17	.58
1965	103.6	725	.14	.36
1975	99.7	920	.11	.34
1979	99.5	971	.10	.33

Note: ha = hectares.
[a]Column 1 divided by column 2.
[b]Column 1 divided by agricultural labor force data from Table 1.2.
Sources: Arable land – State Statistical Bureau (1960, 128; 1981c, VI-3); Ministry of Agricultural Policy Research Office (1982, 9). *Population* – Table 1.1.

virtually every developing country in Asia since the 1940s, the increased pressure of population on the land has been most intense in China. The number of workers per hectare of arable land grew about 2.5 percent annually from the mid-1950s to the mid-1970s, while the rate was 0.7 percent in India, 1.1 percent in Bangladesh, and 1.4 percent in the Philippines (Hayami and Kikuchi 1982, 40). At the end of the period there were 3 farm workers per hectare of cultivated land in China compared to 2.3 in Bangladesh, 1.6 in Indonesia, 1.1 in the Philippines, and 1.0 in India.

In short, the pace of agricultural development in China must be viewed against the increasingly stringent land constraint. Under conditions of unchanging agricultural technology increased supplies of labor applied to fixed land area can be expected, via the inexorable law of diminishing returns, to produce successively smaller increments of agricultural output.

An alternative to the diminishing returns hypothesis, or at least a complement of it, is that China's leaders have pursued a growth strategy that placed priority on industry and depressed the rate of growth of agriculture. The central objective of development policy has been to accelerate the pace of industrial development. That, in turn, may be related to China's defense policy. The leadership since 1949 has shared the view that China's historic military weakness had made her highly vulnerable to external pressure. Thus they sought to create a heavy industrial base that would support a modern military establishment. The policy pursued was not, however, a long-run-optimal strategy for maximizing the rate of industrial growth. Such a strategy would recognize the positive interactions between industrial and agricultural development. In some periods the policy of maximizing the growth of industry in the short run, even at the expense of other sectors, may reflect the increased salience of potential external military threats. But even after recognizing that policy has been shaped by strategic considerations, as well as by purely economic criteria, it appears that Chinese strategy has undervalued systematically the contribution that agriculture could make to modern economic growth.[7]

As will be shown in detail in Chapter 3, the state has allocated extremely modest investments either directly to agriculture or to the branches of industry that produce modern inputs for agricultural production. Moreover, the state's high indirect taxation of agriculture has curtailed reinvestment of internal resources within the farm sector. Consequently farm assets per agricultural worker remain extremely low. Thus the lagging performance of agriculture may be the consequence of an agricultural policy that has tended to be myopic and extractive rather than developmental.

Although industrial growth has been impressive in some ways, one thesis of this study is that a strategy of genuinely concurrent development of industry and agriculture could have led to equally rapid growth of national income at lower resource costs and with significantly greater improvements in the welfare of the peasantry. Underinvestment when the pace of technical change in agriculture increased in the mid-1960s provides an example. Investment in agriculture was reduced just when its rate of return was rising due to new opportunities provided by new seed varieties, particularly rice. Skewed investment allocations increased the share of investment in industry, where the rate of return was lower than in agriculture and declining. That distortion of investment allocation reduced the rate of growth of the economy below that which could have been achieved.

Moreover, the state's negative interventions in the agricultural sector have not been limited to reducing its share of investment. State policy frequently has inhibited the efficient use of even the modest resources remaining within agriculture. Periodic efforts have been made to reduce specialization in production and marketing of agricultural products. Although the political origin of these campaigns may be complex, their economic effects are straightforward: declining efficiency of resource use and, for given investment allocations, slower growth.

The low rate of investment in agriculture and policy-induced distortions in resource utilization ultimately were reflected in the level of personal incomes, particularly of the peasants. Average incomes have grown quite slowly, particularly during periods of maximal bureaucratic intervention in resource allocation in the countryside. Moreover, distortions of resource allocations have left a large share of the peasantry enmeshed in extreme poverty. Although China sometimes has been perceived as following a basic needs strategy, the extreme poverty and deprivation of a large segment of the peasantry after two or more decades of rapid growth may be similar to what some regard the characteristic fate of peasants in the early stages of development of many now developed countries (Hobsbawm 1980).

Historical perspective

Prior to 1949 China was predominantly agrarian. A nascent industrial sector existed but consisted predominantly of food-processing and textile industries that were linked tightly to agriculture. In 1933, the prewar year for which the most comprehensive estimates are available, the output of factories, mines, and utilities formed only about 3 percent of gross domestic product. And of factory output, more than 75 percent consisted of cotton, silk, and woolen textiles and food processing such as rice milling, sugar refining, oil pressing, and cigarette manufacturing (Liu Ta-chung and Yeh Kung-chia 1965, 146). Transport, commerce, and, to a lesser degree, finance also were connected closely with agriculture. Only mining and utilities, a small share of factory output, trade, and finance, and an even smaller share of government services could be said to be truly independent of agriculture.

Despite the small share of output originating in the modern sector, agriculture had supported successfully an ever-growing population. The population grew from 65–80 million at the beginning of the Ming dynasty (1368–1644) to 540 million by the middle of the twentieth century (Perkins 1969, 16). Moreover, the best evidence suggests that only slightly more than half of that incremental population was supported by simply expanding sown area within an otherwise unchanging agriculture (Perkins 1969, 33). Although still traditional by the usual criteria that farmers' knowledge about factors they use had not changed for generations and net savings on a per capita basis was quite low (Schultz 1964), Chinese agriculture had become increasingly sophisticated.

Increased sophistication was not evident in mechanical technology. Although improvements were made in the design of water pumps, mechanical technology largely was unchanged from the fourteenth to the middle of the twentieth century. Increased complexity, however, was evident in patterns of cropping and marketing and in the introduction of new fertilizers that allowed greater intensity of cultivation. Indeed, in the absence of major innovations in mechanical technology, changes in the pattern of cropping were the primary source of technical change during the Ming (1368–1644) and Ch'ing (1645–1911) dynasties (Ho Ping-ti 1959, 169). These changes, summarized below, appear to have been sufficiently rapid to offset what otherwise would have been diminishing returns induced by long-run growth of population exceeding the growth of cultivated area.

Changes in cropping patterns were stimulated primarily by increased population and the opportunities created by the introduction of improved seed varieties and new crops from abroad. These changes facilitated population growth that was increasingly more rapid than the expansion of cultivated land. The best known of these improvements was early-ripening rice (Ho Ping-ti 1956). The introduction of early-ripening varieties from central Indo-China occurred in the Sung dynasty (960–1126) when the seeds were first planted in southeast China. Within two centuries these varieties were grown widely in Chekiang, southern Kiangsu, and Kiangsi, as well as in Fukien. During the Ming dynasty early-ripening varieties diffused to large parts of the Southwest, as well as to central China, especially the present-day provinces of Hupei and Hunan. Early-ripening varieties were a particularly important source of increased grain output for two reasons. First, their shorter growing period allowed the development of double-cropping of rice in central China. Second, because their water demand was less than that of traditional rice varieties, early-ripening varieties allowed the spread of rice cultivation to higher lands with less adequate water supplies (Ho Ping-ti 1959, 171).

The introduction of new crops such as corn, peanuts, and potatoes led to equally far-reaching changes in cropping systems. Peanuts were the first American food plant introduced into China. Initially cultivated in the early part of the sixteenth century in the Southeast, they were soon grown in the lower Yangtse region. Widespread adoption in the lower and central Yangtse area and in the Southwest occurred in the eighteenth and early nineteenth centuries, and by the latter half of the nineteenth and early twentieth centuries peanut cultivation had spread to Hopei, Honan, and Shantung in north China. Because peanuts could be grown in poorer-quality sandy soils, they were widely adopted in the sandy loams north and south of the lower Yangtse and along the southeast coast. Although they were sometimes grown in rice districts because their nitrogen-fixing nodules enhance soil fertility, peanut cultivation often was adopted more rapidly in poorer mountainous districts where specialized production contributed to a marked rise in peasant incomes (Ho Ping-ti 1959, 183–5).

Corn was introduced in the sixteenth century into both the inland Southwest and coastal Southeast (Ho Ping-ti 1955). By the late eighteenth century corn had become a principal food crop in mountainous regions of the Southwest and a century later was grown widely in the North China Plain.

The introduction of the Irish potato to China a century after corn reveals a similar innovative response by Chinese farmers. The crop became widely cultivated in peripheral areas of the Szechuan Basin and in the Han River drainage in the first half of the nineteenth century and in poorer districts of the loess high plain in Kansu and Inner Mongolia and in the Northeast a half-century or more later (Ho Ping-ti 1959, 189).

Adoption of new crops was not limited to food crops but included tobacco, cotton, and other economic crops. American cotton varieties were introduced in the late nineteenth century and quickly displaced traditional Asian varieties. Tobacco, introduced in the late Ming period, was adopted rapidly in regions well suited to its cultivation and provides "one of the best examples of the extent to which self-sustaining agriculture had given way to specialized commercial farming in many areas" (Ho Ping-ti 1959, 203–4).

As this brief summary suggests, the cultivation of each new crop was not distributed uniformly across the agrarian landscape, but tended to be concentrated in areas of comparative advantage. Thus expanded cultivation of new crops naturally was accompanied by increased specialization in production and rising rates of marketing. Specialized production, of course, had emerged long before the introduction of new crops from North America in the sixteenth century. In the T'ang dynasty (618–906) there were large interregional markets in rice and staple commodities (Elvin 1973, 166–72; Shiba 1975, 29–30). That trade apparently accelerated in the twelfth and thirteenth centuries when regions of the southeast coast where sugarcane and other cash crops were of increasing importance became dependent on surplus rice produced in the Yangtse Delta, Canton Delta, and the central Kan River Valley (Elvin 1973, 129, 170; Evelyn Rawski 1972). By the first half of the seventeenth century the lower Yangtse Delta was no longer a rice-surplus region, but had become dependent on rice grown in Kiangsi, Anhui, and especially in present-day Hunan and Hupei (Chuan and Kraus 1975, 59; Perkins 1969, 144; Rozman 1973, 130). The lower Yangtse area shifted from a rice-surplus to a rice-deficient area because of the increasing share of farmers producing mulberry leaves (for silkworms), cotton, and other nongrain crops and a rising rate of urbanization. Despite significant local cotton production in Kiangsu, by the seventeenth and eighteenth centuries the textile industry in the lower Yangtse was dependent on raw cotton produced in Shantung, Honan, and present-day Hopei (Elvin 1973, 213; Ho Ping-ti 1959, 201–2). Long-distance exchange of cotton and grain between north and central China was based on comparative advantage in production and relatively low-cost water transport, both via coastal routes and the Grand Canal, built initially during the Sui dynasty (589–617) and greatly lengthened and improved during the Ming. Parts of the North China Plain produced cotton at lower cost in terms of grain output forgone than central China. It was profitable to market cotton and import cereals from the Yangtse area.

Increased cultivation of commercial crops was facilitated by trade in beancake fertilizers made from soybeans. Imports of beancake into cotton-growing regions in the Yangtse Delta from Honan and Shantung were significant by the sixteenth century and became even more important with the opening of the Manchurian trade in the late seventeenth century (Elvin 1973, 214). Soybean cake imports into the southeast coast from both Manchuria and north China were also critical for the development of sugarcane cultivation. That trade accelerated in the latter half of the nineteenth century when coastal steamers replaced junks as the major carriers of beancakes (Brown 1981, 451).

The expansion of specialized production and interregional as well as international trade in agricultural products was stimulated further by railroad development after 1895. Following China's defeat in the Sino–Japanese War (1894–95) foreigners extracted railway concessions from a weakened Ch'ing dynasty, primarily in northeast and north China. Three major foreign lines, consisting of almost 2,400 kilometers of track, crisscrossed the Northeast (Manchuria) and linked Chinan in central Shantung with the port city of Ch'ingtao. Elsewhere Chinese-controlled rail lines, constructed with the assistance of European loans and engineers, linked Peking with both Hank'ou in central China and the Russian-controlled (later Japanese-controlled) South Manchurian Railroad in the northeast.

The development of this new rail network led to specialized production of vegetables, fiber- and oil-bearing crops, as well as grain in north China (Meyers 1980, 145). After the 1890s soybeans and peanuts and their oils, hides, meat, cotton, and tobacco became important exports through the ports of Ch'ingtao and T'angku (the port of Tientsin) that had become linked by rail with agricultural regions of north China (Myers 1970, 197–9). More specialized production and higher marketing rates increased land productivity and allowed increased urbanization in north China (Perkins 1969, 154).

John Lossing Buck's observations of rural China in the late 1920s and 1930s are consistent with the hypothesis that income-maximizing behavior by farm households had led to complex cropping systems, considerable specialization in production, and significant commercialization. In his study of a sample of 2,866 farms in seven provinces in the late 1920s Buck found that an average of 53 percent of the value of farm output was sold off-farm. In the localities sampled in Anhui, Chekiang, Fukien, and Kiangsu the marketed share of output was more than three-fifths of the total (Buck 1930, 196). Complete specialization in a single crop was rare, probably because of rising costs and risk aversion, but in some counties as much as 84 percent of all output was marketed.

Not all Chinese peasants were as heavily involved in commercialized farming as those in Buck's study. His sample excluded large areas that were far less market-oriented. Even within the north, central, and eastern provinces included in his study, his sample of farms was drawn more than proportionately from those favorably located vis-à-vis transportaion systems. However, even after accounting for that sample bias, it seems likely that the rate of marketing of farm products had increased between the end of the Ch'ing dynasty in 1912 and the Japanese occupation of Manchuria in 1931.

Peasant responsiveness to new production and marketing opportunities challenges the view that Chinese agriculture was stagnant after the fourteenth century. Although farm machinery may have changed little, that is not the only measure of technological change. Peasants responded positively to opportunities created by the availability of improved seed varieties, new crops, new fertilizers, improved transport, and rising urban demand. In most respects the behavior of Chinese farmers appears to be consistent with the view advanced by Theodore W. Schultz and others that peasants respond efficiently to new production and marketing opportunities (Popkin 1979; Schultz 1964).

The hypothesis of an economically dynamic agriculture does not imply rising real per capita farm income. The evidence suggests rather that the long-run trend of farm consumption and income was unchanged (Perkins 1969). But there is little empirical support for the hypothesis, based on the classical formulations of Ricardo and Malthus, that diminishing returns in agriculture led to declining consumption either after the late eighteenth century, as suggested by Mark Elvin (1972, 170), or after the end of the nineteenth century, as suggested by Robert Dernberger (1975, 26). China appears to support Ester Boserup's (1965) hypothesis that long-run agrarian development can be stimulated by population pressure. The trend of per capita farm income may be stagnant for a long period although the response to changed opportunities is dynamic.

One further potential misunderstanding should be clarified. Although the level of per capita farm income over the long run appears to have changed little, the level in normal years was well above subsistence. Although the rate of investment in 1933 was quite low, Carl Riskin has shown that the portion of national income produced above the average consumption level of the laboring population was in excess of one-fourth of net domestic product. More than two-thirds of the surplus was produced by farmers (Riskin 1975, 74). Thus the absence of modern economic growth prior to 1949 is not easily attributable to a stagnant agriculture producing at or just above subsistence. The explanation must address the issue of why that large pool of resources was not mobilized for investment purposes.

Agriculture in China's socialist development strategy

The Chinese Communist Party came to power in 1949 committed to the transformation of China into a modern economic state. The core of the Party's vision was a vast acceleration in the pace of industrial development. The immediate tasks in 1949, however, were somewhat more prosaic: restoring the war-damaged production structure and curtailing the hyperinflation inherited from the Nationalist government. Once these objectives were achieved in the early 1950s, attention shifted to the design of a longer-run economic plan.

Among the most critical aspects of that plan was the role envisaged for agriculture. Western economists frequently conceive of agriculture's role in economic growth as including product, market, and factor contributions (Kuznets 1961). Product contribution refers simply to the growth of output within agriculture. It is usually assumed that the long-run opportunities for growth in the "modern" sector of the economy (i.e., modern industry, transport, etc.) substantially exceed those in agriculture so that the latter's share of total product will fall. Yet since agriculture's initial share is large, it typically will be the source of a significant share of incremental output of the economy, even if its growth rate lags well behind that of industry.[8]

Models of modern economic growth usually give considerably more emphasis to agriculture's contribution to growth through what Kuznets refers to as market and factor contributions. That is not surprising because premodern economic growth consists entirely of agriculture's product contribution, whereas the onset of modern growth is inevitably accompanied by a qualitative change in the role of agriculture. Through interrelationships with the rest of the economy in product and financial markets, agriculture becomes a critical contributor to growth. The market and factor contributions of agriculture discussed by Kuznets occur through these interrelationships.

Market contributions to growth occur through product markets. Agriculture provides food for a growing urban labor force and at the same time provides a growing market for domestic manufactures, both consumer goods and industrial inputs used in agriculture production. As development proceeds the rate of marketing of agricultural output invariably rises and the share of gross incomes that farmers spend on purchased inputs for farming rises. Farmers also purchase, rather than produce for self-consumption, an increasing share of their consumption goods. Although both agricultural marketings and farm purchases of production inputs as a share of net domestic product decline as growth accelerates outside agriculture, the rise of marketings relative to farm production and the flow of modern sector inputs facilitates growth. First, marketing facilitates increased specialization on which productivity improvement and all modern economic growth is dependent. Second, the flow of new factors to agriculture facilitates the transition from traditional to modern agriculture. Retarded market development reduces specialized production and inhibits the flow of modern inputs that raise farm productivity.

Agriculture's factor contributions are both human and financial. Labor contributions are both direct and indirect. Agriculture may contribute workers for industrial employment where per worker productivity is greater than in agriculture. That may be referred to as the direct effect. The indirect effect on industrial development is the investment in upbringing and training embodied in migrants to industry. Investment in human capital in agriculture determines the quality of an important part of the nonagricultural labor force (Kuznets 1961, 119).

The financial form of agriculture's factor contributions is even more important than the human form in most development models. In the early stages of modern economic growth, according to most theories of development, a significant flow of savings from the agricultural sector will help to finance investment outside agriculture. Given adequate development of product markets for the sale of agricultural output and financial markets for the transfer of part of the savings from agricultural income to nonagricultural investments, agriculture may serve as an important source of funds for nonagricultural investment. If such transfers are not made by owner–cultivators, they may occur through the portion of taxes, rent, and interest payments that flow to recipients outside of agriculture (Johnston and Kilby 1975, 315). The presumption, implicit or explicit, in most approaches is that the marginal rate of return to investment in agriculture is lower than in the nonagricultural sector, inducing a net flow of funds out of agriculture. Of course, in a dynamic model in which technical change raises the rate of return to agricultural investments in some period, the optimal flow of resources may be into rather than out of agriculture. The presumption over the long run is, however, that resources will flow to industry, where the growth potential and rates of return are higher (Johnston and Kilby 1975, 316).

Implicitly, until now, I have been considering a closed economy. Agriculture's role in an open economy is more complex because some of the functions customarily assigned to agriculture directly may be fulfilled indirectly via international trade in agricultural commodities. Moreover, in the open economy setting, designing policy to maximize agriculture's contribution to the nonagricultural sector is more complex, for there are now tradeoffs among the various contributions discussed above (Myint 1975). For a country with a strong international comparative advantage in manufactured goods, food requirements may be met through imports rather than through agriculture's market contributions to urban food supply. Initial import substitution policies may increase the demand of the whole economy for domestically manufactured goods, but most of this incremental demand may arise in the nonagricultural sector since import substitution policies generally turn the domestic terms of trade against the farm sector, ceteris paribus reducing farm incomes and thus curtailing farm sector demand for goods produced by the modern sector. In that case the international market substitutes for agriculture as the source of demand. That pattern is most likely to occur in the case of an open economy that is small enough so that its increased demand on the international market does not raise prices of food relative to those for its manufactured exports. Korea in the postwar period may be an example (Mason 1980, 210–13). Alternatively, for a country with a comparative advantage in agricultural products, the optimal strategy may require that for a long period of time the savings of the agricultural sector be reinvested intrasectorally rather than transferred to industry.

Although agriculture's contributions to modern growth may be conceptualized as occurring in product, market, and factor forms, their empirical measurement is difficult (Kuznets 1961, 104–5). Agriculture is part of an interdependent system, and what happens within it and its interactions with other sectors depend on changes in the rest of the system. Even measuring part of agriculture's contributions, namely factor contributions via financial markets, has been undertaken successfully for only a very small number of countries. Despite this shortcoming, the framework remains a useful one provided that the degree of openness is specified and the tradeoffs among alternative contributions are clarified.

Models that focus on intersectoral resource flows are frequently characterized by the degree to which they are balanced or imbalanced. Unfortunately, these terms are used by different writers with widely varying meanings.

Balanced growth may be a well-specified concept as in the surplus labor model of John C. H. Fei and Gustav Ranis, where it is defined to include the sectoral allocation of investment resources and rates of productivity growth in agriculture and in industry that lead simultaneously to the maintenance of a constant real wage in industry, no change in the relative prices of industrial and agricultural products, and the full absorption by industry of the laborers released by productivity growth in the agricultural sector (Fei and Ranis 1964, 214–19). Other authors, whose models are somewhat less restrictive than the dualistic economy models, specify balanced growth less rigorously. Nevertheless, the central characteristic is that agriculture is not regarded as simply a resource reservoir that supplies labor, food, and financial savings to the nonagricultural sector, but as a major component of a dynamic growth process. In this view of balanced or concurrent development the objective of development strategy is not simply the transfer of resources from a static agriculture, but achieving, via investment and technological progress within agriculture, a "rate and pattern of agricultural output expansion in the agricultural sector that will promote overall economic growth and structural transformation and take full advantage of positive interactions between agriculture and other sectors" (Johnston and Kilby 1975, 133). Such an approach is frequently as concerned with improvements in welfare and the distribution of income within the farm sector as with agriculture's contribution to nonagricultural growth. In terms of policy, advocates of concurrent growth argue that an overvalued exchange rate and other import substitution policies that tend to move the terms of trade against the agricultural sector – both because they depress the prices of farm exports and because they raise the prices of manufactured inputs such as fertilizer and machinery – inhibit the growth of agricultural output, farm incomes, and farm savings and investment. Moreover, these and other price-distorting policies encourage a high level of capital intensity in manufacturing, reducing the growth of employment opportunities outside agriculture.

Not surprisingly, Mao Tse-tung and other leaders of China over the last three decades were not fully conversant with Western theoretical models of modern economic growth. Yet at least portions of Mao's own analysis basically were congruent with Western models. Mao not only recognized the distinct forms that agriculture's contribution could take, but was an early advocate of a balanced growth strategy. In his 1943 report "On Coalition Government" Mao acknowledged both the market and factor contributions of agriculture. "It is the peasants who constitute the main market for China's industry. Only they can supply foodstuffs and raw materials in great abundance and absorb manufactured goods in great quantities." The peasantry was envisaged as the source of industrial workers. "In the future, additional tens of millions of peasants will go to the cities and enter factories" (Mao Tse-tung 1943, 250). Mao recognized the critical role of agriculture's financial contributions to industrialization, yet his policy was not primarily extractive but developmental. He warned as early as 1942 against the mistake of what he called "draining the pond to catch the fish" (Mao Tse-tung 1942, 114), a theme to which he would return almost two decades later in his critique of Soviet agricultural development policy.

After 1949 Mao's attitudes toward agriculture evolved considerably, primarily because of the elevation of the priority of the heavy industrial sector (Mao Tse-tung 1956, 285; 1957, 419). He still recognized that agriculture served as a major market for industrial goods and seemed to support, at least in principle, a policy of concurrent growth. Yet in practice, Mao sought to achieve agricultural growth primarily through organizational changes and to accelerate industrial development through a high level of state investment expenditures, financed largely through direct and indirect taxes on agriculture (Mao Tse-tung 1955, 197). Unfortunately, the organizational changes Mao promoted vastly increased the role of the bureaucracy in Chinese farming, leading to the most dire consequences.

This study is an analysis of the role of agriculture in China's modern economic growth. It seeks to examine two closely related issues. The first, taken up in Chapter 2, is: To what degree has China's system of socialist agricultural development preserved or inhibited the dynamism that characterized agriculture prior to 1949? In economic terms, how have the institutional arrangements, particularly the system of planning prevailing since 1949, affected allocative efficiency? Chapter 2 is centrally concerned with how the government's price and marketing policy has influenced the allocation of inputs among alternative crops and the rate of marketing of farm products.[9] Using a trade-theoretic framework, I explore the extent to which policy has influenced the evolution of specialized production along lines of comparative advantage.

The second major issue is: To what extent has Chinese development policy undervalued agriculture? Has development strategy, in some economically meaningful sense, been imbalanced, biased toward the urban, industrial sector? This book advances two criteria for judging balance. The first is based on purely positive economics – a comparison of marginal returns to investment in agriculture and industry. On this criterion growth is imbalanced if the marginal rate of return on investments in agriculture systematically exceeds that in industry. When this condition exists, efficiency in resource allocation and the rate of growth of gross national product would be increased by reallocating investment resources to agriculture, at least up to the point where the marginal rates of return on investment in the two sectors were equalized. Issues related to this criterion are explored in Chapter 3.

A second criterion for judging balance, the rate of growth of income of the peasantry, is advanced and evaluated in Chapter 4. That chapter focuses on two closely related issues. First: Has development policy overemphasized investment at the expense of consumption? And: Given the consumption investment choice made by the central leadership, has policy contributed to or alleviated urban–rural income and consumption differentials over time? Imbalance in this chapter can only be judged subjectively – on the basis of values articulated by the Chinese leadership, by one's own particularistic standard, or by the experience of other developing countries. Chapter 4 also analyzes how agricultural development policy has influenced the distribution of income within the farm sector.

The final chapter summarizes the major findings of the book and analyzes the prospects for fundamental reform of agricultural policy and for greater use of price and market mechanisms in agriculture.

2

Planning and allocative efficiency

The purpose of this chapter is to evaluate how the evolution of farm institutions and the system of agricultural planning affected the growth of output and productivity in agriculture since the Chinese Communist Party rose to power in 1949. Most analyses assume that, with the obvious exception of the late 1950s when producing and accounting units were so large that the connection between individual effort and reward was tenuous, production units allocate resources efficiently, much as might occur with profit-maximizing behavior by farm households in a market economy. The agricultural sector is presumed to produce the maximum potential output given the prices set by the state for farm products and for current inputs, the constraint imposed by available supply of land, and farmers' labor–leisure preference. The size of collective units and the methods for selecting team leaders and for distributing collective income all have been thought to facilitate efficient resource allocation (Parish and Whyte 1978, 117; Perkins 1975a, 350; Thomas Rawski 1979, 140).

These analyses, however, have focused on the internal organization of collective agriculture and virtually have ignored the larger institutional setting in which collective farm units operate. Most critically, they have not considered either the constraints imposed by the planning system on farm-level production decisions or the nature of the markets in which farm units sell their output and purchase both consumption goods and farming inputs. This chapter and the one that follows focus on how changes in these external relations of collective units have contributed to variation in the efficiency of resource allocation in Chinese agriculture since 1949.

Oscillations between indirect and direct planning have had a major effect on the rate of growth and composition of aggregate farm output and the efficiency of resource allocation. Indirect planning (*chien-chieh chi-hua*) relies essentially on state manipulation of credit, procurement contracts, taxes, and prices. State procurement prices are the major policy instrument

18

used to influence the growth and composition of farm output as well as deliveries to state procurement agencies. Indirect planning dominated from 1949 through 1955 or 1957, was readopted in 1960–61 and pursued through 1965, and has begun to reemerge since 1977 as the predominant form of agricultural planning. Indirect planning is characterized by greater use of price incentives to stimulate aggregate agricultural output, as reflected by substantially improved terms of trade for the agricultural sector; more sophisticated manipulation of relative agricultural procurement prices to influence the allocation of land, labor, and other current inputs among alternative crops; greater freedom of agricultural production units to specialize in production based on their comparative advantage; rising rates of marketing based on both state purchases and flourishing rural peasant markets; larger and more efficient rural credit markets; and larger and more secure private plots.

The use of prices to influence the allocation of resources by no means implies that the national plan is not initially conceived in explicit quantity terms. Planners' output objectives are formulated in quantity terms, and producing units are required to fulfill procurement targets specified in quantity terms. But since procurement prices are set with the objective of stimulating the relatively voluntary delivery of these products, peasants are relatively less constrained by indirect than by direct planning. In short, peasant producing units (initially farm households, subsequently agricultural producer cooperatives and production teams, and more recently again farm households) engage in relatively unconstrained maximization of net revenues.

During periods of indirect planning, which come the closest to fulfilling the conditions necessary for the efficient allocation of resources, agriculture has grown most rapidly and total factor productivity generally has risen, although modestly. Overall growth is more rapid and occurs across a broad range of products, including grains, economic crops such as cotton, sugar, and oil-bearing seeds, and aquatic, animal husbandry, and forestry products. Rapid output growth is accompanied by increased specialization in production along lines of regional and local comparative advantage and by rising rates of public and private marketing of farm products.

The second approach to agricultural planning, which the Chinese refer to as direct planning (*chih-chieh chi-hua*) or production planning (*sheng-chan chi-hua*), is essentially planning of total farm output in quantity terms. That was first attempted in 1956, again during the Great Leap Forward (1958–60), and prevailed during 1966–77. Production planning is characterized by the imposition of detailed sown area and output targets and specific cropping patterns by higher-level authorities on production units. There is little use of price incentives to encourage output growth under production planning since output targets are presumed to be attainable through direct commands to producing units. The level of agricultural prices, relative to industrial product prices, tends to stagnate when direct planning predominates. Furthermore, there is a more static pattern of relative crop prices since the allocation of sown area, at least in theory, is determined by plan, not relative profitability. The central authorities set targets with the objective of increasing output rather than net farm income. Consequently labor and other inputs are used more intensively than under price planning. In short, inputs tend to be applied well beyond the point at which marginal costs are equal to marginal revenue with a consequent loss of farm income. Because periods of production planning generally coincide with political swings to the left, manifestations of "capitalism" in the countryside, such as private plots and rural peasant markets, generally are suppressed or eliminated. Rural credit usually is curtailed in quantity and allocated more by political than economic criteria. There is also pressure to enlarge the units of production and accounting, to move toward what is referred to as a higher level of socialism.

When production planning has tended to dominate agricultural planning, divergence from the conditions required to assure efficient resource allocation is substantial. Increased inefficiency is reflected in lower rates of growth of output and stagnation or decline in total factor productivity. Equally important, output growth tends to be concentrated in a few major grain crops that are the object of considerable central-level attention, while the growth of economic crops and aquatic, animal husbandry, and forestry products lags. These phenomena arise for several distinct reasons. First, when production planning has dominated, the state has provided inadequate price incentives for the production of more labor-intensive economic crops. Second, the high costs of gathering and processing information and the limited resources of planners, whether at the center or some lower level of the hierarchy, mean inevitably that planners are unable fully to take into account local variation in soil, climatic, and other conditions. Thus the cropping pattern chosen by planners generally is not optimal from the point of view of producers. Third, the pressure for larger producing units has reduced the connection between individual effort and reward, magnifying the shirking problem characteristic of agricultural cooperatives. Finally, the longest period of production planning coincided with an explicit policy goal that all regions or even localities achieve self-sufficiency in the supply of basic cereals, regardless of whether that coincided with the region's natural comparative advantage. When local self-sufficiency in cereals is a policy objective, many production units are forced to move along their transformation surfaces between grain and nongrain crops away from the point at which the marginal rate of transformation in production is equal to the relative price of grain and nongrain crops. That movement away from the efficient production point increases costs of production and reduces agricultural productivity. Moreover, as the marketing rate of agricultural products declines, both because public procurement is reduced deliberately and private marketing opportunities are curtailed, the income of producers is reduced since the gains from trade are lost.

The systematic divergence from allocative efficiency when the quantity mode of control is utilized is consistent with the theoretical literature on the choice between price and quantity controls in a planned system. Martin Weitzman's seminal article on prices versus quantities and subsequent work have shown that the conventional a priori preference for price control is not theoretically justified (1974). Under some conditions social welfare will be greater if quantity controls are used. But as is shown below, the case for price controls is quite strong for the control of agriculture.

The theory of price and quantity control

The primary objective of economic planners in centrally planned socialist systems is to control the output of producers in a manner that maximizes the planners' social welfare function. In theory, for the simplest case of a single output produced by a single firm, the planner must choose between the use of a quantity or price directive to control production. The producer is presumed able to meet a goal expressed in terms of physical units of output or to behave as a profit maximizer, producing up to the point where the marginal cost of production is equal to the price set by the state. In a world, depicted in Figure 2.1, where the central planner knows with certainty both the firm's production function and thus marginal cost schedule $E(MC)$ and the social welfare function and thus the marginal benefit schedule MB, the choice between price and quantity controls is trivial. The central planner will maximize social welfare either by setting the output target $\hat{q}$ or by setting the price $\hat{p}$. Either control will equate marginal benefit and marginal cost, thus maximizing the difference between total benefits and total costs and achieving the highest social welfare possible.

Once uncertainty is introduced, the choice between price and quantity control is more interesting. Uncertainty could arise either because the underlying production function is not fully known or, perhaps somewhat more plausibly for the case of agriculture, because the production function is known but depends on the state of the environment that prevails during the

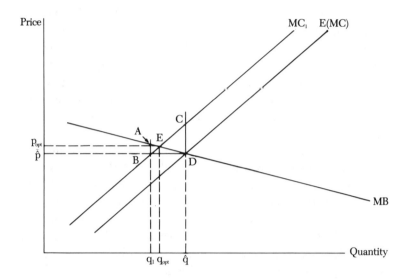

Figure 2.1. Price versus quantity controls under uncertainty.

plan. Alternatively, uncertainty could be introduced in the social welfare function. The social welfare function may be uncertain because of imprecise knowledge of the actual benefits of specific levels of production or because benefits may depend on random variables that cannot be foreseen or controlled. In either case, central planners are presumed to have to issue their price or quantity target prior to the time that the values of the random variables become known.

The underlying problem is quickly illustrated in Figure 2.1, where for the moment uncertainty is presumed to arise only on the production side. The issue is to determine whether quantity or price control more closely approximates the optimal position where social welfare is maximized (Yohe 1977, 216). Assume initially that the planners prefer production targets and set $\hat{q}$, where expected marginal cost $E(MC)$ equals marginal social benefit MB, but that an unforeseen costly state of nature, perhaps a drought, occurs. The higher costs of producing any given level of output are reflected in MC_1, lying above $E(MC)$. In a market system the producer would fix output at q_{opt} because the equilibration of marginal cost and marginal benefit at the point E would maximize profits. The market price would be p_{opt}. Under central planning with production targets, assuming $\hat{q}$ is actually produced, social welfare will be less than in the market case. Production will occur at C, where marginal costs exceed marginal social benefit by the amount CD.

The cost of quantity control is the triangle ECD, the sum of the amounts by which marginal costs exceed marginal benefits for each unit produced beyond the optimal quantity, q_{opt}.

Alternatively, if the planners had selected the price target $\hat{p}$, where expected marginal costs equal marginal social benefit, social welfare would also be below the market outcome because output would be q_1, where price equals marginal cost. But at q_1 the marginal social benefit of additional units of output exceeds by AB the marginal cost of production, even under the less favorable state of nature that prevails. The sum of the excess of marginal benefits over marginal costs for the number of units produced less than q_{opt}, or ABE, represents the welfare loss incurred under price controls when a state of nature unforeseen by the planners occurs.

The choice between price and quantity controls depends on which leads to an outcome that more closely approximates the competitive market outcome q_{opt}. I assume that costs preclude the use of contingent controls in which either price or quantity targets for each possible outcome of the random variables in the production function are specified in advance. Such contingent orders would always be preferred to either form of a single-value target since they could always be designed to duplicate the competitive market outcome (Yohe 1977, 214 15). The choice of single-value control depends on the relative (absolute) slopes of the marginal social benefit and marginal social cost curves. When the marginal cost curve is steeper the use of price controls is preferred because the area ECD will exceed ABE, indicating that the social welfare loss under price control is less than the loss would be under the quantity control. On the other hand, when the marginal benefit curve is more steeply sloped, the quantity control will provide a socially preferred outcome since ABE will exceed ECD (Montias 1976, 223–4).

The logic of this choice is quite straightforward. When the marginal cost curve is relatively flat, wide variations in the level of output have little effect on unit costs. The quantity control will thus be preferred because under price control, shifts of the marginal cost curve would lead to wide swings in the level of output that, in turn, would lead (since the marginal benefit curve is relatively steep) to a disparity between marginal benefit and marginal cost and a level of social welfare below the free market case. Alternatively, when the marginal cost curve is relatively steep, as in Figure 2.1, the output variation under price control, induced by shifts in the marginal cost curve, is desirable because cost-side efficiency gains achieved through output variation far outweigh the benefit-side losses.

When this simplest world is an agricultural one, there is a presumption that price control is the preferred policy instrument in a relatively low per capita income planned economy. That is, the absolute slope of the marginal cost curve probably exceeds that of the marginal social benefit curve and the covariance of the shifting schedules is unlikely to offset the superiority of price control. The marginal benefit curve is likely to be flat because when the level of per capita consumption is low, one would not expect the social benefit of incremental units of agricultural output to decline sharply. Nor are agricultural products required in fixed proportions with nonagricultural products. Thus the value of incremental units should not fall sharply, as conceivably could be the case if agricultural products were highly complementary in consumption with other products. The high degree of complementarity of certain components for military end use products frequently is thought to provide a theoretical basis for the use of quantity controls over the production of these items during wartime (Montias 1980, 14–15).

On the other hand, the marginal cost curve is likely to be relatively steep. In the course of any specific planning period most inputs are available only in fixed quantities so that the cost of incremental units of output would rise. In the short run the pace of technological change is slow, providing little alleviation of rising marginal costs. Both the fixed supplies of current inputs and the slow pace of technical change suggest that the incremental cost of producing additional units of output would rise moderately rapidly within any single planning period.

Of course, uncertainty may arise on the benefit side, slightly complicating the analysis above. Naturally output would be invariant under either $\hat{p}$ or $\hat{q}$ if uncertainty arose only on the benefit side. If the marginal cost curve does not shift, the profit-maximizing producer faced with a single-valued price target will not alter the level of production in response to a shifting marginal benefit curve. However, when both cost and benefit schedules have random elements, the covariance of the shifts in the cost and marginal benefit schedules will affect the choice between price and quantity controls. If there is a positive covariance between shifts of the two schedules, the advantage of price control would be enhanced since, if the two curves shifted outward (inward), reduced (increased) costs would induce a higher (lower) level of output just when the benefit of any given level of output had increased (decreased). Alternatively if the covariance was negative, then under $\hat{p}$ less (more) would be produced when more (less) output was socially desirable, undermining the advantage that $\hat{p}$ enjoyed by virtue of the relative slopes of the marginal benefit and cost schedules (Yohe 1978, 233).

But it is unlikely that a negative covariance of shifts in the cost and benefit schedules would erode significantly the comparative advantage of price control, at least for a relatively large country. Conceptually, one would expect that the underlying planners' preference function would be relatively stable and that stochastic elements would have a second-order magnitude effect on the position of the benefit curve. For example, the marginal benefit of domestically produced agricultural products could shift upward if poor weather elsewhere in the world led to an unanticipated increase in cost of meeting some portion of consumption requirements from international sources. Or if the country was a net exporter of agricultural products, increased prices of agricultural exports caused by poor weather elsewhere could also shift the marginal benefit curve upward. But for a large country such as China net trade in agricultural products is a small share of production. Thus even comparatively large unanticipated world price fluctuations would have a modest effect on the position of the marginal benefit curve. On balance, even though China's large size ensures extremely diversified agricultural production conditions, stochastic elements in China's agricultural production function make variation in the position of the marginal cost curve more important than shifts in the benefit function. Given the likely relative slopes of these two functions, I postulate a priori that price rather than quantity controls would lead to a higher level of social welfare.

The model postulated is admittedly highly simplified. But adding additional elements of realism to the analysis – such as multiple producers and several products – does not reverse the comparative advantage of price control. The advantage of using price control when there are many producers arises both because of the costs of information gathering and processing necessary under quantity controls and because of the superiority of price controls when stochastic elements influence the position of the cost and benefit curves. In theory the advantage of equalizing expected marginal costs for all producers could be achieved under quantity as well as price control. Quantity targets could be set so that ex ante marginal production costs were equalized across all producers. As a practical matter, it is extremely costly to gather and process the information necessary to set appropriate $\hat{q}_i$ for over 5 million production teams, even when targets are set at the lowest level of the state administrative network.[1] In short, the planners are unlikely to be able to set $\hat{q}_i$ such that marginal benefit and marginal cost are equated. Equally significant, even if such optimal $\hat{q}_i$ could be established costlessly, only the price control mechanism assures that ex post or realized marginal costs will be equal across all producers when random variables cause unanticipated shifts in marginal cost curves.[2] Inequality of marginal costs means, of course, that a higher level of output could be achieved through a more efficient allocation across producers of the fixed supplies of factors of production. Generally the larger the number of producers, the greater the comparative advantage of the price control mode in achieving allocative efficiency.

The multiple-good case is somewhat more complex since one must consider whether the goods are complements in consumption and whether the goods are produced independently or jointly (Yohe 1976). Analysis of both the production and consumption sides depends critically on the covariance of the two outputs under price control. In industrial production the random elements affecting the level of output of any pair of products might be independent, so that the output level of the goods would vary independently. For agriculture under uncertainty, random elements affecting the level of output of the two goods will include at least one element, weather, that affects the cost of production of both goods simultaneously. Although weather variations may affect the relative cost of production of various crops differently, weather fluctuations, except for special cases, probably shift the marginal cost curves in the same direction for all crops grown in a given locale. Thus under price controls the covariance in the level of output of any pair of crops $Cov(q_1, q_2)$ will likely be positive. When the weather is (un)favorable, output of both crops will (fall) rise, although not necessarily by the same proportion.

For those pairs of crops that are produced independently, the analysis of the multiple-good case is a simple extension of the single-good case discussed previously. The comparative advantage of price control is the sum of the advantage for each good considered separately.

When agricultural products are produced jointly, the comparative advantage of price control will be eroded if, as is usually the case, the products are substitutes in the joint production process, that is, if $C_{12} > 0$. When stochastic events lead, for example, to a decrease in production of both outputs under price control, substitution on the production side $(C_{12} > 0)$ means that the induced effect of decreased output of the second good is to lower the marginal cost of producing the first good. That induced effect partially offsets the effect of the initial stochastic event so that the optimal production point for the first good lies closer to the initial intersection of the marginal benefit and the expected marginal cost curves. Naturally the relative disadvantage of the quantity mode of control is thus reduced. Despite this erosion of the advantage of price control in this case, as a general proposition price controls will remain the preferred instrument of control for two reasons. First, most agricultural products are produced independently so the erosion does not arise. Second, even in the case of joint production, unless the two goods are extreme substitutes in production (i.e., $C_{12} = 1$) so that the final marginal cost curve for good 1 was unchanged, the price mode would retain a comparative advantage over the quantity mode.

The effect of multiple goods on the marginal benefit or social welfare function should also be added to the model. On balance most agricultural products must be regarded as gross substitutes in the social welfare function – the availability of more of one commodity tends to reduce the marginal benefit of the last unit of a second commodity. Continuing the assumption that $Cov(q_1, q_2) > 0$, the advantage of price controls is again somewhat diluted when two goods are substitutes in consumption. When $B_{12} < 0$ and $Cov(q_1, q_2) > 0$, increases in q_2 that would occur as a result of better weather, for example, will indirectly reduce the marginal value of units of the first product just when its output is also increasing. But as in the case of joint products, although an initial price advantage may be reduced when $B_{12} < 0$ and $Cov(q_1, q_2) > 0$, substitution in consumption normally will not cause the quantity mode to dominate the price mode of control.

In summary, under a broad range of conditions, one a priori expects social welfare will be greater when price rather than quantity targets are employed in the agricultural sector of a planned economy. The superiority of price control stems from two distinct sources. First, price control allows producers to adjust their production level in response to stochastic events that influence their production costs. Given reasonable assumptions about the relative slopes of the marginal cost and marginal benefit curves, that adjustment leads to an outcome with a higher level of social welfare than can be achieved by quantity controls. Second, and probably more significant, when the number of producers is large, it is unlikely that planners will be able to gather and process enough information to identify the level of output at which expected marginal cost equals marginal benefit for each producer. When there are in excess of 5 million production units, as there were in Chinese agriculture for much of the 1960s and 1970s, this second source of inefficiency probably overwhelms the first.

The theoretical model presented above assumes that the planners' objective is to set $\hat{q}$ such that expected marginal cost equals marginal benefit However, in some periods $\hat{q}$ has been set in China with a somewhat different objective – to achieve local self-sufficiency in cereal production. The prices-versus-quantities framework can also be used to analyze this policy.

Self-sufficiency

In theory, self-sufficiency could be achieved through either cost or price control. Assume the state set the domestic price $\hat{p} = p_1$ and production was initially at q_1 in Figure 2.2, where the marginal cost of production is equal to p_1, but domestic consumption was at the point $q_1 + M$, where M represents imports. This approximately captures China's position in the mid-1960s when imports of cereals averaged 5 to 6 million tons per year (metric tons throughout). National self-sufficiency then could be achieved either by setting $\hat{q} = q_2$ or by raising $\hat{p}$ to p_2. Under the quantity regime rationing would have to be tightened to reduce consumption from $q_1 + M$ to q_2. Under the price regime the higher price would cut consumption to q_2. In either case imports would be eliminated and the cost of self-sufficiency would be the difference between the cost of importing the quantity $q_2 - q_1$ and the cost of increasing domestic output by the same amount. For an open economy in which the initial domestic and world grain price are equal at p_1, the cost of self-sufficiency is simply the area ABC. From a national point of view allocative inefficiency is introduced because the domestic cost of producing beyond q_1 exceeds the world price p_1. Thus allocative inefficiency arises regardless of whether the state uses quantity or price control to achieve its goal.

An extension of this argument can be made when self-sufficiency is attempted on a subnational basis. Assume that initially regions with a comparative advantage in cereal production have surplus grain that they trade internally with regions specialized in raising other agricultural products. At the equilibrium position with no trade restrictions and ignoring transport costs, the marginal costs of production of cereal and other products are equalized across regions. When internal trade is restricted, each region must increase its output of products for which it does not have a comparative advantage. Grain-deficient regions increase their output of cereals while surplus regions increase their production of other crops, but each incurs marginal costs of production that are substantially higher than in the initial situation of unrestricted trade.[3] In terms of Figure 2.2, the cost of achieving self-sufficiency in cereals on a subnational rather than a national basis is substantially greater than the area ABC, which represents the cost of achieving self-sufficiency nationally only if incremental output is produced in the lowest-cost region. Moreover, the magnitude of allocative inefficiency increases as the administrative level (size of geographic region) at which it is sought is lowered (decreased) because the gains from specialized production and trade are increasingly squeezed out. But self-sufficiency, not the use

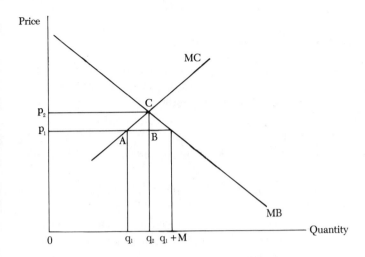

Figure 2.2. Self-sufficiency via price and quantity controls.

of quantity controls per se, is the true cause of increased inefficiency in production.

Yet the use of quantity rather than price controls has several important implications. First, the use of quantity controls shifts the burden of attempting to achieve self-sufficiency from the state to the peasantry. The area ABC, the cost of self-sufficiency, simply represents a tax imposed on peasant producers. Second, the use of quantity controls in China tended to obscure the high cost of attempting to achieve self-sufficiency. An increased indirect tax burden on the peasantry was far less salient to the central leadership than the substantially increased domestic budgetary outlays that would have been required to raise output through price incentives.[4]

Third, since self-sufficiency was imposed at a local rather than a national level, the costs of the policy were borne unequally by different regions. Because of the higher marginal cost of grain production beyond the point of initial equilibrium in deficit regions, as state supplies of basic commodity grain were reduced (at least in per capita terms) higher costs were incurred to produce foodgrains locally. Peasant incomes in cereal-deficient regions declined relative to incomes of peasants in regions with a comparative advantage in grain production since their pattern of production relative to the pattern of consumption, in which grain has a heavy share, was more specialized.

The evolution of planning in Chinese agriculture

The evolution of agricultural planning is a complex subject that cannot be treated in detail within the confines of the present chapter. My intention is not to provide a chronological history but rather mainly to establish the pattern of oscillation between price and quantity planning since 1949 and to trace the implications of these shifts for allocative efficiency. This will be done primarily by focusing on the role of prices and markets within agriculture.

Prior to the formation of higher-stage cooperatives in 1956, control of agriculture by the state was by necessity indirect. Following land reform in the early 1950s, over 100 million farm families cultivated their own land, and the state had no direct means of controlling their production decisions. To meet the objectives of increasing farm output and raising the marketed share, the state relied primarily on price incentives. After the onset of the Japanese invasion and continuing through the conclusion of the civil war in 1949, agricultural prices had fallen substantially relative to industrial products, contributing to a reduced rate of marketing. After 1949 the state moved quickly to restore private commerce and allowed relative agricultural prices to rise in the market. Initially in 1950 the state purchased and controlled less than 10 percent of marketed agricultural output (Perkins 1966, 44), and the prices of agricultural goods rose rapidly in the market, both in absolute terms and relative to the prices of industrial products (Lardy 1978a, 177). By 1953 state purchases constituted slightly in excess of 50 percent of total farm marketings, and relative farm prices had risen almost 25 percent relative to 1950. After the autumn of 1953 when compulsory grain procurement was instituted, however, the mix of price incentives and coercion used to induce increased deliveries to the state was altered. The state did not use its growing market power to move relative prices against the agricultural sector as the Soviets had in the early 1920s and again in the First and Second Five-Year Plans (1928–37), However, relative farm prices rose only 10 percent between 1953 and 1957 (Lardy 1978a, 177) as the state share of agricultural marketings rose to more than three-quarters. The point of this brief summary is not to suggest that there did not remain some considerable degree of extraction of surplus from agriculture via relative prices, but to suggest that the state, to stimulate both production and marketing, allowed the terms of trade of the farm sector to improve. However, the pace of improvement slowed dramatically after 1953 when compulsory delivery quotas for grains were instituted.

Not only did the state insure that farm product prices rose on average; it also, as early as 1950, began to manipulate the relative prices of individual crops in order to achieve the desired composition of farm output (Perkins 1966). The objective was to restore the prewar production levels of important commercial crops such as cotton, peanuts, and jute. To ensure recovery the state raised the relative prices of industrial crops. Prices of the major grain crops were still largely market-determined, so state intervention took the form of guaranteeing, in advance of planting, a fixed ratio between the prices of industrial crops and the major grain crop of each region. These were critical ratios because specialized producers of commercial crops naturally had to purchase significant portions of their food requirements, particularly grains. The state rather than the private market was increasingly the source of these cereals, so the price ratios set by the state effectively determined the terms of trade for growers of commercial crops. Guarantees of the cotton/grain price ratio were introduced in 1950, and guarantees for other fiber crops, tea, tobacco, and some oil-bearing seed crops were introduced in subsequent years (Perkins 1966, 39–40).

In retrospect, this use of price incentives was a relatively efficient means of stimulating the production of some nongrain crops. As the cotton/grain price ratio was raised in 1950 and 1951, the cotton/grain sown area ratio, the absolute cotton sown area, the output of cotton, and the cotton marketing rate all rose. When the relative price of cotton was held unchanged in 1952 and reduced in 1953 the ratio of cotton to grain sown area fell. The sown area ratio recovered, however, when relative cotton prices were raised in 1954 and held stable in 1955. The state reinforced price incentives with favorable credit policy through advance purchase contracts that provided interest-free working capital to cotton producers. In the early to mid-1950s first individual farmers and subsequently mutual aid teams responded in an economically predictable fashion to the changing set of price incentives offered by the state. Farmers in this respect seem to have changed little from the pre-Communist period when they operated in a relatively competitive market economy (T. Rawski 1977).

Traditional periodic rural markets were the major mechanism of private commerce in the early 1950s, as they had been in the lower Yangtse since the time of the transition between the T'ang and Sung dynasties (Shiba 1975) and over a much broader area during the Ming and Ch'ing dynasties (Skinner 1964–65). When the system of planned procurement and planned sales of grains was initiated in the fall of 1953, peasants, after fulfilling state purchase quotas, nominally still were allowed to sell surplus grain either in state grain markets or, for small (unspecified) amounts, within the countryside (Government Administrative Council 1953a). Private grain marketing, however, was restricted and private millers were no longer permitted to purchase grain freely on the market or to sell grain products privately but were subject to the direct administration of the Ministry of Food and its local purchase and sale agencies. Moreover, traditional grain markets in cities and in market towns were converted to "state grain markets" (Government Administrative Council 1953b). Government regulation was needed to insure that quotas for grain taxes and compulsory sales were met prior to sale of grain on the market. Thus products subject to "planned purchase," such as grain, or "unified purchase," such as cotton, generally could not be sold freely in rural markets, whereas the marketing of other products, particularly sideline and subsidiary items, was restricted less, particularly prior to the socialization of most private commerce in 1955. Consequently, the magnitude of grain transactions in rural periodic markets was curtailed substantially, from about 7 to 8 million tons annually in the early 1950s to 2 to 3 million tons by 1954–55 (Eckstein 1977, 117; Ishikawa 1967b, 42). Restrictions on rural markets were eased somewhat in the last half of 1956, and private grain sales increased to a level of from 4 to 6 million tons, the equivalent of 10 percent or more of state grain procurement and taxes.

Periodic rural markets facilitated specialization in production within local marketing areas, reinforcing the larger macro regional specialization facilitated by state-controlled commerce in rural areas. According to Ch'en Yün, the highest-ranking member of the Communist Party dealing primarily with economic work, who in the fall of 1956 also was named minister of commerce, peasant households with more than 200 million members regularly bought and sold grain in rural markets. These included households with 30 to 40 million members who partially specialized in crops other than grain, an average of 40 million members who had temporary grain shortfalls due to adverse weather, about 50 million members of grain-deficient households (a chronic condition due to family size, income, and other factors), and 12 million who were engaged in animal husbandry, fishing, forestry, salt production, or rural transportation. Peasant households with at least another 100 million members both bought and sold grain – for example buying and selling grains of different types or buying and selling at different times of the year (Ch'en Yün 1955, 52). Thus perhaps as many as half of China's peasant households were involved in commercial grain market purchases – buying grain either from the state or on rural markets.

Data on foodgrain marketings mirror the extensive peasant involvement in grain purchases and sales. Although information published on peasant grain sales frequently is specified incompletely, three types of data support the hypothesis that state policy during this period led to increased commercialization and facilitated specialized production.[5] First, the rate of marketing, defined to include deliveries to the state, taxes paid in kind, and market sales, averaged 30 percent during the First Five-Year Plan, except in 1956 when markets were closed for part of the year (Table 2.1).

Although this share is low relative to commercialized agriculture in developed countries, it represents an increase over the prewar years 1930-37, for which John Lossing Buck's (1937) data can be used to estimate a marketing rate of 23–26 percent.[6] The marketing rate for grains probably rose by more than a comparison of 23–26 percent with 31 percent for 1953–57 would suggest. First, Buck's surveys were biased geographically toward areas with better transportation where the marketing rates were probably above average. Second, Buck's data are for private farming based on households, whereas by 1956 almost all Chinese agriculture had been reorganized into higher-level producer cooperatives and collectives with an average of 150 households per unit. Income payments to members were predominantly in kind, so a share of transactions that previously would have been channeled through rural periodic (i.e., nonstate) markets was internalized within the larger production units.

Moreover, as state procurements and taxes displaced market sales, a significant portion of state-controlled grain was resold in the countryside, facilitating specialized production of nongrain crops. Resales to farmers rose from 9.3 million tons in 1953 to 11.7 million tons by 1957 (Table 2.1). Each year 5 million tons or more of these state resales were in areas of specialized economic crop production that lacked adequate supplies of foodgrains (Sun Wei-tsu 1958, 26).

Finally, restoration of at least the degree of commercialization prevailing in agriculture prior to the outbreak of World War II was reflected in significant interprovincial grain flows. In 1950 the northeastern provinces exported 1.03 million tons of grain, Szechuan 200,000 tons, and areas along the Chekiang–Kiangsi and Canton–Hank'ou railways 300,000 tons to the rest of China (Wu Shuo 1957, 22). In 1951 the Northeast exported 785,000 tons of wheat to east and north China; the central–south provinces exported a third of a million tons of grain to the North and Northwest. Three hundred thousand tons of flour were moved interprovincially in east China to alleviate localized food shortages due to flooding; Szechuan exported 27,000 tons of rice to Shanghai; and north China exported 15,000 tons of coarse grains to provinces in east China ("Grain allocation...").

Table 2.1. *Foodgrain marketings*[a], *1952–81*

	Taxes and procurement[b] (millions of tons) (1)	Total marketings		Resales[e]	
		(millions of tons[c]) (2)	As percentage of output[d] (3)	To rural areas (4)	To peasants (5)
1952	27.8	39.03	28.7	—	—
1953	41.5[f]	43.05	31.1	17.1	9.3
1954	45.1	50.89	30.0	23.2	—
1955	43.0	47.54	31.1	18.2	—
1956	41.7	40.22	25.1	23.0	—
1957	39.8	45.97	28.4	—	11.7
1958	55.7	51.83	31.2	—	—
1959	55.9	64.12	45.5	—	—
1960	42.8	46.54	39.1	—	—
1961	—	36.55	29.9	—	—
1962	32.1	32.42	24.4	—	—
1963	—	37.00	—	—	—
1965	—	39.22	24.3	—	—
1966	44.9	41.42	23.3	—	—
1967	—	41.38	22.9	—	—
1969	—	38.45	22.0	—	—
1970	—	46.49	23.3	—	—
1972	—	38.54	19.3	—	—
1975	—	52.62	22.3	—	—
1976	49.4	49.15	20.7	—	—
1977	47.2	47.67	20.3	—	16.3
1978	46.5	50.73	20.1	—	15.3
1979	53.9	60.10	21.8	—	—
1980	49.0–50.0	61.29	23.0	—	—
1981	54.3–55.4	68.46	25.4	—	—

[a]Measured in terms of trade grain, which includes rice and millet in processed form but other grains in unprocessed form (original weight) (Sun Wei-tsu 1958, 24). Includes grains, tubers (at grain equivalent weight), and soybeans and other legumes.
[b]Quantities are for the procurement year, July 1 of the listed year to June 30 of the following year in the 1950s and April 1 to March 31 in the 1970s and 1980s. Includes taxes in kind and state purchases from domestic production but excludes grain purchased in international markets. Also excluded is grain delivered by peasants to the state in exchange for the right to repurchase the equivalent quantity of grain at a later date or for the right to purchase a different type of grain. For this purpose the state issued "exchange grain certificates" (*t'iao-chuan liang-cheng*) (State Council 1955, 161). Later the grain taken in by the state for these purposes was referred to as "exchange purchases" (*huan-kou*) and was still to be excluded from the official data on "state-procured grain" (*kou-jia cheng-kou ti liang-shih*) (Chang Min-ju and Hsü Shu-keng 1981, 217). To my knowledge, no data that reflect the magnitude of this category of transactions have been published. Estimates of taxes and procurement for 1980 and 1981 are subject to some unknown error since the figure for 1980

Notes to Table 2.1 (*cont.*)
reflects procurement only through the end of February 1981, one month before the
end of the grain procurement year.

*c*Quantities are for the calendar year. In addition to the regular procurements of
grain by the state this series appears to include sales of grain in rural periodic
markets, direct sales by farmers to city dwellers in urban farmers' markets, state
procurement at negotiated prices, and purchases on the market by military units,
mass organizations, commune and brigade enterprises, and state organizations other
than grain purchase agencies.

*d*The tonnage in column 2 as a percentage of total output (Agricultural Yearbook
Compilation Commission 1981, 34) converted to trade grain weight at a ratio of .83.
The ratio varies from year to year due to the changing composition of cereal output
but the variation is quite small, even over the long run. On the basis of data on
foodgrain taxes and purchases reported by the Ministry of Agriculture Policy Research Office (1980, 29–30) both in terms of original and trade weight, ratios of .827
for 1957 and of .837 for 1977 can be derived.

*e*Chinese sources provide two inconsistent series for resales. The first series was
attributed to the State Statistical Bureau and specified to be measured in trade
weight, including soybeans (Data Office Statistical Work 1957b, 32). Chou Po-ping
(1957, 3) provided a similar series for 1954–56 measured in terms of original weight
that is consistent with that series. T'an Chen-lin (1957, 106), member of the Party
Secretariat, provided a series for rural resales in 1953–56 that was measured in fine
grains, excluding soybeans, and on a calendar year rather than a grain year basis. It,
too, after appropriate adjustment, is consistent with the first series. It has usually
been assumed that these resales were primarily to peasants. But all three sources
specify resales as being to "rural areas" (*kung-ying nung-ts'un* or *hsiao-hui nung-
ts'un*) and contrast them with "sales to urban areas and the military" (*kung-ying
ch'eng-shih ho chün-tui*). Chou's separate discussion of a survey divides the rural
population (*nung-ts'un jen-k'ou*) purchasing grain from the state into three categories: poor peasants (*p'in-nung*), peasants mainly growing commercial (nongrain)
crops (*i chung-chih ching-chi tso-wu wei chu-yeh ti nung-min*), and the nonagricultural population (*fei nung-yeh jen-k'ou*). The data contained in the second series,
published in 1980, are specified as "resales to the agricultural population (*fan-hsiao
kei nung-yeh jen-k'ou*) or as "sales to agriculture" (*nung-yeh hsiao-shou*) and are
contrasted to "sales to the nonagricultural population" (*fei nung-yeh hsiao-hui*). Thus
I believe that the data on resales published in the 1950s are inclusive of the nonagricultural population living in rural areas, including state employees in transportation;
services such as education and health; party cadres; rural handicraftsmen; and so on.
The more recent data appear to be of narrower scope. The size of the nonagricultural
rural population in 1980 can be estimated as the nonagricultural population of 160
million (Li Ssu-heng 1981, 56; Special Commentator 1981) less an urban population
of about 135 million (estimated from Table 1.2) or about 25 million. These people are
not directly engaged in collective agriculture and derive their consumption of cereals
through the state rationing system, just as do urban residents.

*f*Given as 39.2 by Chang Li-fen (1980, 30). The reason for the discrepancy in the two
figures is not clear. Chou Po-ping, writing on state foodgrain procurement and
resales in the journal of the Ministry of Food in 1957, stated that "the statistical data
from the middle of 1953 to the middle of 1954 are incomplete and should be omitted
from our discussion" (1957, 3). Perhaps 39.2 million tons represents a revised estimate for the 1953 grain year. Alternatively, because 39.2 is compared with 1978, it
could represent an estimate of grain taxes and state purchases on the basis of the procurement year prevailing in the late 1970s and in the 1980s (see footnote *b*, above).

Interprovincial transfers continued through the First Five-Year Plan, both because of the central government's efforts to alleviate localized grain shortages due to flood or drought and because the increasingly developed transportation network made such transfers feasible and less costly. Although provinces with surplus grain sought to retain their output for local use, they usually were not successful. At a Central Finance and Economics Work Conference in 1953 the provincial delegates, after lengthy debate, were unable to construct a workable plan of grain transfers, largely because surplus provinces objected to upward revisions of their export targets. The issue was referred to Premier Chou En-lai for a decision. Chou, at the urging of Ch'en Yün, ruled that such transfers of cereals must be under the exclusive control of central government and that the quantities would be subject to adjustment, on at least an annual basis, in order to be able to respond to regional variations in output (Teng Li-ch'ün 1981, 3–4). Subsequent to that decision, in the grain year 1953–54 the quantity of grain transferred was almost three times that of 1950–51. Exports from the Southwest alone totaled 750,000 tons (NCNA December 13, 1954). Throughout the First Plan some provinces, notably Szechuan and Heilungkiang, were net exporters; some, such as Hopei, were net importers; others exported or imported only episodically when harvests were unusually good or depressed due to floods or drought. Still others simultaneously exported and imported

Notes to Table 2.1. (*cont.*)

Sources: Column 1 – 1952, 1958, Sha Ch'ian-li (1959); *1953–56*, Data Office Statistical Work (1957b, 31); *1957*, Ministry of Agriculture Policy Research Office (1980, 30),ʹ Liang Hsiu-feng (1981b, 20), Liu Sui-nien (1980, 23); *1959*, Liang Hsiu-feng (1981b, 20); *1960, 1962*, Liu Sui-nien (1980, 28); *1966, 1976*, Chang Li-fen (1980, 29); *1977*, Ministry of Agriculture Policy Research Office (1980, 30), *1978*, Chang Li-fen (1980, 30); Lin Kang, (1981, 22); *1979, 1980* – an estimate of 53.9 million metric tons is supported by three separate sources. Purchases in 1980 of "more than 49 million metric tons" between April 1, 1980 and February 28, 1981 were 3.88 million tons less than the same period of the previous grain year (NCNA April 20, 1981), implying 1979 was more than 52.88 to 53.88 million metric tons; procurement in the two years between 1977 and 1979 is reported to have risen 6.5 million tons (Liang Yen 1981, 24); finally, procurement was reported to be "65 million metric tons or one-fifth of output of that year" (Chan Wu and Liu Wen-p'u 1982, 56); since 65 million tons is 19.6 percent of reported output measured in terms of original weight, 65 millions tons is certainly measured in original weight; in trade weight that is 53.95 million metric tons; *1981*, based on reported 10.8 percent increase over the previous year (State Statistical Bureau 1982a).
Column 2 – State Statistical Bureau (1982b, 341).
Column 4 – Data Office Statistical Work (1957b, 32).
Column 5 – Chang Li-fen (1980, 30), Ministry of Agriculture Policy Research Office (1980, 30).

to adjust the composition of grain consumption. Shantung, for example, usually exported 10 to 15 percent of its wheat but imported coarse grains (Sun Ching-chih 1957, 127). The volume of interprovincial transfers typically rose in years of widespread national disasters, such as 1954, but was less in years of excellent harvests such as 1955.

Although interprovincial transfers to meet famine relief needs rose in years of poor harvests, such transfers fell short of meeting all needs. As a result localized food shortages continued to stimulate rural–urban migration, despite the efforts of the Ministry of Internal Affairs to curtail and prohibit such migration. In the spring of 1957 a ministry report revealed that in the preceding half-year a half-million peasants had left famine-struck rural areas in favor of towns and cities in the hope of finding urban employment (Hoffman 1974, 88). Efforts to improve famine relief efforts and to prohibit urban factories from hiring these workers were of only limited success.

Interprovincial transfers of grain in the 1950s seem to have been significantly greater than in the 1930s. Based on Dwight Perkins's research I estimate that interprovincial transfers of grain averaged about 2.1 million tons – 1.3 percent of output in 1930–36 (1969, 159; Table 2.1). For the four years from 1953 through 1956 provincial exports (including an average of 2.0 million tons annually to international markets) averaged 7 to 7.5 million tons, almost 5 percent of total production (Chu Ching-chih 1958, 14, 17). Even if we exclude grain destined for international markets, interprovincial transfers in the First Plan were 3.2 to 3.6 percent of production, more than twice the estimated share for the 1930s.[7]

After the formation of higher-stage agricultural producers' cooperatives in the winter of 1955–56, the stage was set for the first attempt at more direct planning. Articles in the journal of the State Planning Commission, *Economic Planning*, and other publications announced the intention to shift away from price planning toward quantity planning (Liu Hsien-kao 1957). Direct planning was to be based on explicit sown area and output targets drawn up at the national level and then disaggregated and passed down the administrative hierarchy to provinces, then counties, and ultimately to producer coops. The new system was to have been put into effect in 1956, but it is difficult to judge to what extent such a far-reaching change could be implemented so quickly.[8] Many of the collectives were no more than paper organizations, hurriedly created by local cadres in response to higher-level pressure to demonstrate success in the "socialist high tide" movement.

In many provinces direct planning of sown area and the imposition of certain production techniques were attempted. In 1956, for example, the state forced cooperatives to purchase over a million of the infamous double-wheel, double-bladed ploughs (State Statistical Bureau 1960, 171). Although it previously had been used with some success in areas of dryland farming in the North, the plough in 1956 was forced on collectives in central and southern China where it was virtually useless in paddy rice cultivation. At this time also provincial and county-level authorities dictated specific planting densities for rice, irrespective of varying local conditions (Walker 1968, 421). "The planning system was over-centralized to the point where collectives merely mechanically carried out orders from above, especially those received from the *hsien* (county) authority" (Walker 1968, 424).

Production incentives also were undermined partially by the excessively large size of collectives that were formed during the winter of 1955–56. Collectives, averaging 150 families, replaced lower-stage cooperatives, which were smaller, more voluntary associations averaging from 20 to 25 families. The collective's large size diminished the connection between work and reward.

The collectivization of agriculture also coincided with the "socialist transformation" of most remaining private commerce to state ownership and control and a concomitant squeeze on the remaining rural private activities, particularly household sidelines. That reduction in opportunities to market private output and to earn income from other private activities was an important source of peasant discontent. Fei Hsiao-t'ung, China's best-known anthropologist, after returning in May 1956 to a Kiangsu village he had first studied in 1936, criticized this aspect of collectivization in the brief liberalization period known as "the hundred flowers," stating that it had depressed peasant income (Fei Hsiao-t'ung 1957).

The excessive centralization in the "high tide" of collectivization quickly became apparent at the center, leading to pressure for modifications. In the summer of 1956 the state sanctioned the reopening of rural markets, most of which had been closed in the wake of collectivization and the transformation of private commercial activities (Ch'en Yün 1956b, 29). In September the Eighth Party Congress discussed the desirability of reversing the trend of substituting direct for indirect methods of planning as well as specific improvements in procurement prices, discussed further below. Subsequently the Chinese Communist Party Central Committee and the State Council jointly issued a directive calling for a gradual move away from production planning toward purchase planning (1956).

Such an adjustment seems to have been made or at least attempted. In 1957 the purchase plan at the local level included seventeen products. The specification of quotas for delivery of products allowed peasants some freedom to follow their comparative advantage in specialized production once procurement plans were fulfilled. "The advantage of replacing the current agricultural production plan with the purchase plan for agricultural products is that the agricultural producer cooperatives can arrange their production according to their own needs after having fulfilled the state purchase quotas" (Liu Hsien-kao 1957, 33). The switch to procurement planning, which really represented a formal return to the pre-1956 methods of price planning, was to have been carried out in 1957. But local officials were not always enthusiastic about that reform, preferring to exercise direct bureaucratic control made possible by the formation of agriculture producer cooperatives. An official of the Department of Agriculture in Chekiang, for example, while recognizing quantity planning could "lead to production being divorced from reality," argued that the switch to procurement planning should be gradual and that production planning be retained for nongrain crops (Yeh Chün 1957).

Rural markets remained open in most areas in 1957 and the volume and scope of transactions broadened. While that reinforced the trend toward price planning, it simultaneously undermined the ability of the state to purchase grain. Originally the "free markets" established in the summer of 1956 were intended for native and subsidiary products not subject to planned or unified purchase by the state. The scope of these markets quickly expanded, however, to include grain, cotton, oil-seed crops and other commodities subject to state purchase. By the end of 1956 *Economic Planning* carried articles supporting the role of the free market but proposing that grain, oil seeds, and cotton be excluded from the market and that state price controls on some other commodities be instituted (Sun I-min 1956, 18–19). Not until August 1957, however, were regulations issued prohibiting the market sale of grains, oil-bearing crops, and cotton (State Council 1957b). Surplus grains could be sold only to state purchase agencies or, in some unspecified locales, in state-controlled grain markets of the type that initially had been created in 1953. Even so, grain taxes and procurement fell in 1957, largely because of an expansion of sales in rural periodic markets (Table 2.1).

Clearly price planning was far from optimal during these years. Ma Yinch'u, a leading nonparty intellectual, criticized the government's price policy in the 1950s, arguing that policy makers undervalued the role of prices in allocating resources. He was critical particularly of the failure of the government to provide adequate price incentives for the production of nongrain crops and pigs (Walker 1964, 171–7). Officials at the highest level essentially echoed Ma's critique. Ch'en Yün at the Eighth Party Congress stated that the prices of some products had been set too low, inhibiting their production (1956a, 170). Ch'en expressed particular concern that the production of pigs had declined since collectivization in 1955. Costs of raising pigs had gone up considerably since the peasants no longer retained the byproduct of rice milling, bran, which traditionally was fed to pigs. Ch'en suggested that a 15 percent increase in the state purchase price would be appropriate (Ch'en Yün 1956c, 15). Li Hsien-nien, the Minister of Finance, was equally specific. State procurement prices for tung and tea oil in the fall of 1956 were lower, relative to grain, than in the prewar period. Procurement prices for rapeseed, peanuts, tea, silk, and pigs were also low, relative to production costs, encouraging production of other crops, particularly grain and cotton, according to Li. In some cases levels of output were still below the prewar peak. The prices of all these products, he argued, should be adjusted upward to stimulate production (1956, 210–11). Clearly Ch'en and Li, as well as the chairman of the State Planning Commission, Li Fu-ch'un, envisaged price planning as a central element of control of agriculture (Li Fu-ch'un 1956, 291–2). On September 29, two days after the Congress adjourned, the State Council promulgated a directive increasing the price of rapeseed relative to wheat from 50 to 70 percent, depending on region (State Council 1956). In early 1957 the purchase price for pigs was raised 13.89 percent (State Council 1957a).

On balance, then, prices played an important role in providing incentives and influencing the allocation of resources among alternative crops. Substantial restrictions were placed on private marketing after 1953, and an initial attempt was made to introduce direct planning in 1956. These restrictions on the profit-maximizing behavior of the peasantry, while substantial, appear to have been modest in comparison to state interventions in subsequent periods. While they impinged on the efficient allocation of resources in agriculture, total factor productivity in agriculture rose, and the expansion of total agricultural output (measured by net value) exceeded the growth of grain output, reflecting an increasingly diversified mix of output.

The use of price incentives to influence the allocation of resources within the agricultural sector as well as to stimulate marketing of agricultural products distinctly differentiates Chinese development policy from that of the Soviet Union during its First Five-Year Plan (1928–32). It is frequently argued that there were strong parallels in Chinese and Soviet policy in their respective First Five-Year Plans, and that China really did not begin to evolve a distinctive "model" of development until the late 1950s. While there may be an element of truth to that generalization, it obscures important differences in their respective agricultural sectors. Chinese agricultural policy was, in fact, much more like that of the New Economic Policy period (1921–28) than the Soviet First Plan. The latter was characterized by extensive reliance on sown area and output targets and even specification of farm practices (Schoonover 1979, 88).

The commune movement and the Great Leap Forward

It was not really until the Great Leap Forward (1958–60) that the government abandoned the use of prices and markets as an instrument of resource allocation in agriculture. Nonstate markets for agricultural commodities were shut down in the fall of 1958 and private plots were eliminated in many regions. Ma Yin-ch'u came under a barrage of criticism for his advocacy of greater use of the price mechanism in agriculture. Control of resource allocation within communes was concentrated in the hands of lower-level state cadres. Peasants' rights to determine their patterns of cropping and the allocation of output (after meeting state procurement targets) were all but eliminated. Production planning was endorsed at the Sixth Plenum of the Eighth Central Committee of the Communist Party in December 1958 by its "Resolution on Several Issues Concerning People's Communes." That decision stated that "the production, exchange, consumption and accumulation of the people's communes must all be included in the state plan" (Wang Keng-chin 1959, 16). Production planning, overlaid with an element of political frenzy, reached its zenith. Moreover, it was at that time that the phrase "take grain as the key link," reflecting the philosophy of local self-sufficiency, first was articulated. Perhaps reflecting that emphasis, interprovincial transfers of grains were curtailed by 1½ million (metric) tons in 1958 compared to the previous year (Kao Yü-hsing 1959, 5).

Although a partial retreat from the extreme centralization of power at the commune level was under way from late 1958 until the fall of 1959 when the Leap entered a new upsurge, concentration of decision-making power in the countryside in bureaucratic hands was still more extreme than at any time prior to 1958. Moreover, local cadres forcefully implemented Mao Tse-tung's 1959 dictum "planning is primary, prices are secondary" (Kao Ping-k'un and Wang Huai-yang 1979).

In the late 1950s central planners and local cadres played a more direct role in the allocation of land between grain and nongrain crops. As central planners received inflated reports of grain and cotton output in the summer and fall of 1958 and the communization movement accelerated, the central planners in Peking restructured the country's cropping patterns and increased the rate of investment. The initial estimate of the 1958 harvest, published in the December Communiqué of the Sixth Plenum of the Eighth Central Committee, was 375 million tons of grain and 3.5 million tons of cotton, almost double the 1957 output of 195 million tons of grain and more than double the 1957 output of 1.64 million tons of cotton. These inflated estimates were not published entirely for external consumption. Ch'en Yün in a 1962 speech to the State Council acknowledged that economic planning for 1959 had been premised on the validity of the 1958 agricultural output figures (Ch'en Yün 1962, 161). Consequently, planners directed a 5 percent reduction in total sown area in 1959 and assigned a larger share of this smaller area to industrial crops. There appeared to be no subsequent need for reevaluation of planned reduction in grain sown area since the final grain output figure, released in April 1959, confirmed the 375-million-ton harvest. Only some time later after the achievements of the Leap were challenged by P'eng Te-huai, Ch'en Yün, and a few others did the political leadership accept the reality that output data had been vastly exaggerated. In the fall of 1959 at the conclusion of the Lushan Plenum of the Eighth Central Committee the communiqué included revised crop estimates of 250 million tons of grain and 2.1 million tons of cotton – 33 and 40 percent less than previously announced. But by the time the revised estimates became available internally, it was too late to change the 1959 plan. The rate of investment exceeded 43 percent, the urban labor force grew explosively, the crop sown area was 10 percent less than in 1957, and the share of land sown to economic crops rose to a level higher than that of any other year of the 1950s (State Statistical Bureau 1982b, 138). The most recent 1958 output figures – 200 million tons of grain and 1.7 million tons of cotton – were released in 1979 and 1981.[9] Grain output in 1959 fell to 170 million tons. The decline of 25 million tons compared to 1957 is explained by the reduction in grain sown area, since unit yields in 1959 were the same as in 1957 (Agricultural Yearbook Compilation Commission 1981, 35). Thus the usual excuse for declining grain output during the Leap, poor weather, does not appear relevant as an explanation of events in 1959. Planning errors appear to have been far more important.

Planning errors were widespread at the local level as well. Ch'en Yün's investigation of a commune in Ch'ingp'u County is one of the more interesting accounts available (Ch'en Yün 1961b). Ch'en was intimately familiar with the area since it was his native place, he had participated in the peasant movement there in 1927, and he had followed local developments closely after 1949. In his investigation in early 1961 he found that, following the formation of Hsiaocheng People's Commune in the region, cadres had issued arbitrary and inappropriate production orders. Double-cropped rice was promoted at the expense of the traditional rice–broad beans cropping pattern. Although double-cropping raised total rice output from 4.35 to 6.0 tons per hectare, peasants had opposed the change since it reduced their incomes. Double-cropping required more use of seedling beds, not taken into account in the per hectare yield calculations. The seed requirements were more than three times as great since the seeding rate for early rice had to be increased to offset the low survival rate incurred from transplanting early when the weather was cold, and double-cropping of rice precluded the fall planting of broad beans. These three additional costs more than offset the value of the incremental rice yield achieved through double-cropping. Moreover, peasants incurred higher costs for current inputs – notably fertilizer and labor – associated with double-cropping of rice. Although Ch'en recognized that there were some localities in which increased double-cropping was profitable, its arbitrary spread over wide areas where it was not appropriate had imposed substantial costs on Chinese peasants.

This account by Ch'en of the failures of production planning at the local level during the Great Leap Forward is fascinating, for it foreshadows many of the problems of production planning that recurred after 1966, discussed further below.

The poor harvests in 1959 combined with excessive state procurement, followed by an even more depressed 1960 cereal crop, initiated the devastating famine of the early 1960s, discussed in Chapter 4.

The return of price planning and the market, 1961–65

In response to the crisis in food consumption and agricultural productivity, the government moved to restore production incentives and curtail production planning. As early as the summer and fall of 1959 rural markets were reintroduced in some provinces. By September the Chinese Communist Party Central Committee and State Council (1959) sanctioned reopening of rural markets on a national scale. Although continued low-level bureaucratic constraints inhibited the restoration of these standard market exchanges, 40,000 rural markets had been reestablished by 1961 (Ho Cheng and Wei Wen 1962, 12), and a year later one-quarter of total rural commodity transactions were in rural markets (Kuan Ta-t'ung 1961, 16).[10] Private plots also were reinstated in 1959 (Ch'en Yün 1959, 94). By 1961 the Party moved the level of accounting and production decision making from the brigade to the team level (equivalent to the lower-stage agricultural producers cooperatives of 1955), raised procurement prices, and abandoned production planning below the county level. These latter changes, although implemented with a lag, were initially reflected in the "Urgent Directive on Rural Work" (the "Twelve Articles") in November 1960 and in the May 1961 "Draft Regulations on the Rural People's Communes" (the "Sixty Articles") and subsequently were endorsed at the Tenth Plenum of the Eighth Central Committee (Chinese Communist Party Central Committee 1962a, 704; 1962b, 198–9).

Policy adjustments were not limited to institutions, but included increased resources for agriculture, through increased state investment and rural credit (both discussed in Chapter 3), a 20 percent increase in 1961 and 1962 in the prices paid to peasants for agricultural products, and a one-third reduction, from 15 to 10 percent, in the agricultural tax rate (Keng Chien-hua 1981, 17; Liu Chou fu 1979, 30).[11] Price increases included a 25 percent increase for cereal crops in 1961 (Liu Sui-nien 1980, 28). The state's more active use of price policy appears to have included deliberate adjustments of relative agricultural product prices as well. Between 1957 and 1965 state purchase prices of peanuts, oilseeds, and tobacco rose relative to cereals while the relative prices of cotton, hemp, sugarcane, sugar beet, tea, eggs, hides, and wool declined by varying amounts (State Statistical Bureau 1981c, VI-24). These adjustments were made in the first half of the 1960s.

Moreover, at the same time, procurement planning provided more opportunity for peasants to respond to changes in relative prices (Liu Jih-hsin 1961) and the Party, as a matter of policy, encouraged a more diversified output mix (Chinese Communist Party Central Committee 1962b, 201). Thus the output of economic crops grew far more rapidly than that of foodgrains in the three years 1963–65. Foodgrains grew 6.7 percent annually on average in 1963–65, whereas cotton output grew 40.9 percent, oil crops 21.1 percent, jute 28.4 percent, sugarcane 57.3 percent, sugar beet 80.3 percent, tea 10.7 percent, live pigs 18.6 percent, and fish products 9.3 percent (all average annual rates) (Yü Kuo-yao 1980a, 29). Part of this rapid growth of nongrain crops, fish, and meat simply reflected the depths to which the output of these items had fallen during the economic crisis. However, by 1965 per capita production of meat, cotton, sugarcane, and sugar beet exceeded the previous peak levels of 1957, whereas per capita grain output was still more than 10 percent below the 1957 level. Thus recovery from the devastating effects of the Great Leap Forward was not limited to food-grains, but included fiber and oil crops, animal husbandry, and fish products.

Moreover, it appears that the simultaneous rapid growth of grain, economic crops, and animal husbandry was based on specialized production and increased internal trade flows. Ch'en Yün, when shortages of cereals were most acute, argued that a policy of local grain self-sufficiency would be counterproductive. Further reductions in the area sown to noncereal crops in grain-deficient areas would be unwise since that would mean the state would no longer be able to supply nongrain products to cereal producers. They, in turn, at the margin would reallocate land to grow more noncereal crops to replace, even at higher cost, products they previously obtained through trade. That would reduce the quantity of grain delivered to the state (Ch'en Yün 1961a, 123-124). Implementation of the specialization policy supported by Ch'en Yün and embodied in the "Sixty Articles" was reflected in the development of "high and stable yield grain areas" (Donnithorne 1967, 432, 490). Regions with good water control and other characteristics that gave them a comparative advantage in grain production were to specialize in cereals. Commercial crop production was also to be concentrated in areas of comparative advantage. The objectives of the strategy were to raise the efficiency of resource allocation and to increase the rate of marketing. Modern inputs for agriculture, particularly chemical fertilizers, were to be allocated to those regions where rates of return were higher, thus increasing the efficiency of resource use (Ch'en Yün 1961c, 112–13). These regions were to become the source of a disproportionately large share of grain and commercial crops, such as cotton, that were procured by the state.

It is difficult to measure the success of the policy of specialized production. State taxes and procurement by 1966 exceeded the average absolute level of the First Plan although total marketings, including private sales, as a share of output still were depressed (Table 2.1). Resales to farmers rose (Chang Li-fen 1980, 30), suggesting that state policy facilitated specialized production. Provincial grain exports in 1965 were 4.7 million tons (Chang Li-fen 1980, 30), less than the average in 1953–56 but almost certainly an increase over 1961 or 1962 (Table 2.2). The recovery in output and specialized production also is suggested by rising total factor productivity in agriculture during 1960–66 (Tang 1980a, 28).

Table 2.2. *Provincial grain "exports," 1930–79*

	Exports (millions of tons) (1)	Production (millions of tons) (2)	Share of national grain production (%) (3)
1930–36 (avg.)	2.9–3.8	168.4	1.7–2.3
1953	7.85	143.5	5.5
1953–56 (avg.)	7–7.5	153.3	4.7
1965	4.70	168.1	2.8
1978	2.05	262.1	.8
1979	3.13	285.6	1.1

Notes: For the 1930s Perkins estimates exports and production on a net basis, exclusive of soybeans, and in original weight, as 1–1.5 and 160 million tons, respectively. To make these data comparable to those for the Communist period I have added soybean production and exports (primarily to international markets) and converted his estimates of net interprovincial flows to a gross basis. For the Communist period exports are gross and total production includes soybeans and is measured in terms of trade grain. Exports for the 1950s include soybeans and are almost certainly measured in terms of trade grain weight, and I assume the same is true for data for 1965, 1978, and 1979. If exports in these three years are measured in unhusked weight, the percentage figures in column 3 would be somewhat lower – 2.4, .7, and .9 percent, respectively. Data in column 1 include grain destined for international as well as domestic markets. In the 1930s soybean exports ranged from .75 to 1.7 million tons annually. In 1953–56 international exports averaged 2.0 million metric tons annually, while exports (including soybeans) in 1965, 1978, and 1979 were 2.1, 1.7, and 1.5 millions tons, respectively (State Statistical Bureau 1982c, VIII-47).
Sources: Perkins (1969, 159, 279), Chu Ching-chih (1958, 17), Lin Kang (1981, 22), Li Ssu-heng (1981, 56).

Production planning, 1967–77

After 1966 agricultural policy fundamentally shifted in the direction of production or quantity planning. Advocates of production planning charged that procurement targets sometimes were unfulfilled, which could be avoided if production were planned directly (Wang Hsiang-ch'un, Chiang Hsing-wei, and Ch'en K'un-hsiu 1965, 34). Moreover, increased direct planning, while subject to many local variations, generally coincided with a sharp political shift to the left that drastically reduced private plots and again curtailed rural periodic markets in most of China. These policies were embodied in the Tachai model of agricultural development that was popularized during the Cultural Revolution (Tsou, Blecher, and Meisner 1982, 270). But they were foreshadowed by proponents of production planning who argued that direct state control of agriculture was necessary to prevent a "spontaneous tendency toward capitalism" (Wang Hsiang-ch'un et al. 1965, 36). A closely related policy objective was to achieve foodgrain self-sufficiency for China, its provinces, and lower-level administrative units. While most of these elements of the policy shift were noted outside China when they occurred, the full significance of the changes, suggested by several important types of evidence, is clear only in retrospect.

The first was the curtailed use of price incentives either to stimulate production or to influence the composition of output. Second, significant shifts inconsistent with the hypothesis of unconstrained peasant net-revenue-maximizing behavior occurred in the allocation of sown area. These shifts, which were the result of the drive to achieve grain self-sufficiency, reduced specialization and the rate of marketing, led to increased inefficiency in the use of inputs, and reduced the rate of growth of farm income below the growth of agricultural output.

Procurement prices for most grains were raised in 1966 and then, according to officials of the General Commodity Price Bureau, were unchanged for twelve years (Chi Lung and Lu Nan 1980, 46; Hu Chang-nuan 1979, 63; NCNA October 31, 1979). Data in Table 3.4 show that the index of prices of all farm products procured by the state rose from 162 in 1966 to 169 in 1977 (1952 = 100), an increase of only 4 percent, less than four-tenths of 1 percent per year.

Relative stagnation in the overall purchase price index was accompanied by a passive relative price policy. Unlike the 1950s, when the state adjusted relative prices of some important agricultural products every year or two, after 1966 there appears to have been little effort to influence the composition of output by manipulating relative farm prices. Beginning in 1965 procurement prices of most economic crops changed little for more than a decade. The price of cotton rose 3 percent, tobacco 1 percent, pork 3 percent, tea 6 percent, and so on (State Statistical Bureau 1981c, VI-26). Rather than using price incentives, the state sought to regulate the composition of output through production planning. The critical policy instrument became the sown area and output targets for individual crops that were transmitted downward to production units. The increase in grain purchase prices in 1966, however, reduced the relative price of cotton and most other commercial crops, and these lower relative prices were sustained for more than a decade thereafter (Ch'en P'o-yuan and Wang Min 1978; Li Te-pin 1979, 5; Yü Kuo-yao 1980b).

The decline in the relative prices of major economic crops after 1966 was particularly inappropriate because it coincided with a rise in the relative costs of producing these crops. Diffusion of hybrid corn and more fertilizer-responsive rice varieties tended ceteris paribus to reduce the per unit costs of cereal production. Cotton and other commercialized crop production technologies, on the other hand, do not seem to have benefited from significant technical change. The decline in relative profitability of economic crops had several important repercussions. First, although sown area targets inhibited the reduction in sown area that would have occurred under indirect or price planning, it was difficult to ensure plan fulfillment. Sown cotton area, for example, consistently was below the planned level during this period (Li Te-pin 1980a, 52; Mei Fang-ch'üan and Hsü P'ei-hsiu 1979). Second, although the state did exert some control over sown area, it could not prevent production teams from reducing the application of labor and other current inputs in crops with declining profitability. In the view of Ma Yin-ch'u, this inability of the state to control directly the allocation of current inputs among crops underlay the importance of relative state procurement prices (Ma Yin-ch'u 1958, 268). Third, production of economic crops became more dispersed and less efficient. Dispersion was due to both the objective of raising foodgrain self-sufficiency at the local level and the declining profitability. For example, areas that specialized in cotton in the 1950s prior to the Great Leap Forward and again in the first half of the 1960s resisted specialized production as its profitability declined. Higher-level cadres found that they could meet cotton sown area targets in the aggregate only by forcing each of the production units under their jurisdiction to accept a small portion of the target (Li Te-pin 1980a, 52). Dispersion of production thus reduced specialized production and made it more difficult to raise productivity and yields.

Grain self-sufficiency and comparative advantage

From 1949 through 1957 regions with resource endowments that gave them a comparative advantage in animal husbandry or in the cultivation of economic crops were encouraged to specialize. As discussed above, the state encouraged specialization not only through price and credit incentives, but also through the supply of basic foodgrains to producers of economic crops. Prior to 1958 this supply was achieved through a combination of public and private marketing. Between 1953 and 1956 almost half of all grain collected by the state through taxes and procurement was resold in rural areas (Table 2.1) As the remarks of Ch'en Yün, quoted earlier, make clear, a significant portion of that rural state marketing activity facilitated specialized production of noncereal crops.

Although the institutional arrangements were different, China's experience through the middle of the 1950s was a further evolution of patterns of specialization that, as pointed out in Chapter 1, had begun to emerge centuries earlier. Moreover, in this respect agricultural development in China parallels agricultural modernization in Europe and the United States in which increased regional specialization was an important source of productivity growth from the late Middle Ages and the mid-nineteenth century onward, respectively (Fisher and Temin 1970; Slicher van Bath 1963, 14, 170, 271).

After 1965, specialized production gradually and with significant interregional variation was abandoned in favor of a policy of local foodgrain self-sufficiency. Rural areas were still allowed to produce economic crops or raise animals, but only after they had achieved basic self-sufficiency in foodgrains. The impetus for the change appears to have come from Mao Tse-tung. The ideology of self-sufficiency was incipient in the formation of communes in the late 1950s. Each unit was to be largely self-sufficient with its own food-processing plants, small-scale industries, and social service system. The vision of self-contained rural communities evaporated in the collapse of the Great Leap Forward experiment. Mao's economic scheme was widely perceived to have failed, and his influence on economic policy making waned.

Yet Mao remained profoundly antagonistic to the concept of specialized production based on comparative advantage. Initially that view appeared to be a rejection of specialization on an international basis. Mao, in his notes on the Soviet textbook *Political Economy*, attacked comparative advantage. Commenting on the text statement that "each country [should]...develop its own manpower and material resources to develop its own most advantageous natural and economic conditions.... The respective countries would not need to produce goods that other countries could supply," Mao wrote flatly, "That is not a good idea" (Mao Tse-tung 1960, 102). Perhaps this rejection of international comparative advantage stemmed from his earlier criticism of the Soviet view that China remain dependent on imports of machinery and equipment in exchange for exports of certain agricultural products. Mao's critique, however, extended to China's domestic economy as well (Mao 1960, 102). Perhaps Mao naïvely thought that by requiring each region to be self-sufficient he could eliminate foodgrain imports from the West. China's shift from a net exporter to a net importer of cereals coincided with the end of the Great Leap Forward. Perhaps Mao wished to eliminate this internationally discernible sign of the failure of his strategy. In any case Mao argued that not only should China seek national self-sufficiency but that it was dangerous for any area of China to depend on grain supplied by other provinces (Mao Tse-tung 1960, 103).

Thus in Mao's view the policy of self-sufficiency was to apply at both the national and provincial level. Fortunately for the welfare of the population and the development of agriculture, Mao's views on economic matters tended to be ignored, at least prior to the Tenth Plenum in the fall of 1962. Although he continued to promote the concept of local self-sufficiency, for example at a 1964 work conference of the Party's Central Committee (Lieberthal 1976, 211), grain imports from the West continued and, as discussed above, specialized production was encouraged at least through 1965.

But in a March 1966 speech to an enlarged meeting of the Politburo of the Central Committee, Mao took up the topic with greater urgency. The dependence of north China on grain from the South was the specific target of his attack (Mao Tse-tung 1966, 638). There were several reasons Mao's ideas apparently were ignored less easily after 1965. First, following the Tenth Plenum, Mao, through the Socialist Education Campaign (1963–65), had laid the foundation for reestablishing his predominance over China's political system in a movement that would come to be known as the Great Proletarian Cultural Revolution. His withdrawal from economic policy making, which had followed the failure of the Great Leap, was coming to an end. Second, the concept of local self-sufficiency was one element of a military strategy postulated on a war of attrition fought by decentralized, self-sufficient regional forces (Lieberthal 1976, 243). The leadership presumably initially was concerned that the war in Southeast Asia might spill over into China and, after 1968 when military clashes occurred on the Sino–Soviet border, feared a Soviet invasion in the North. The creation of regions that could survive even if cut off from neighboring provinces and regions became an official policy goal.

The policy of local self-sufficiency was not simply exhortative but also reinforced by powerful policy instruments. First, the state reduced the share of foodgrain that it purchased or collected in taxes. In 1966, before the self-sufficiency policy was effectively underway, state procurement and taxes had surpassed the average of the First Plan and as a share of output were equal to the 25 percent average of 1956 and 1957 (Table 2.1). In the following decade procurement and taxes grew extremely slowly and in 1976 through 1978 averaged less than 48 million tons, up less than 10 percent compared to 1966. Since grain production had increased by over a third, the share of output distributed directly by the state through the Ministry of Food declined from about 25 to 20 percent. Moreover, the comparison of procurement and taxes in 1976–78 with 1956–57 understates the decline in marketing because private grain sales in the 1950s and presumably in the first half of the 1960s averaged several million tons per year, adding several percentage points to the share of foodgrain output that was "marketed," whereas private grain sales from 1966 through 1978 officially were prohibited and probably quite small. This is reflected in the third column of Table 2.1, which shows the broad definition of marketing declining from 30 percent during the First Five-Year Plan (excluding 1956, when markets were closed for part of the year) to 20 percent in 1976–78.

Not only was the share of foodgrains procured by the state in 1977 and 1978 substantially smaller than in the First Plan, the quantity of grains resold to the agricultural population grew only by a third between 1957 and the average of 1977 and 1978 while the agricultural labor force over the same period grew almost 70 percent (Table 1.2). Since the total quantity of marketed grain reflects largely the extent of urbanization, changes in the quantity of grain sold to peasants are a more accurate reflection of the extent to which marketing policy facilitates specialized production.

Interprovincial transfers of grain, an important component of the policy of the 1950s facilitating specialization, also were curtailed substantially. By 1978 provincial exports had declined to less than 1 percent of production compared to 4.7 percent in 1953–56 and 2.8 percent in 1965 (Table 2.2). If grains, predominantly rice and soybeans, destined for international markets are excluded from interprovincial transfers, the decline is even more dramatic – to .1 percent in 1978 compared to 3.4 percent in 1953–56 and 1.5 percent in 1965. Equally significant, interregional trade in cereals as a share of output was lower than in the 1930s when transfers exclusive of international trade were 1.3 percent.

The virtual collapse of interprovincial cereal markets is borne out by more detailed provincial data for 1978. Rice exports from major producing regions with large surpluses were astonishingly small. Hunan, with a population of about 51 million and cereal production (80 percent rice) in excess of 21 million tons (Agricultural Yearbook Compilation Commission 1981, 101; Hu Ch'iao-mu 1980, 103–4), was one of the highest per capita producers of cereals. Per capita output was 401 kilograms or 83 kilograms over the national average. Yet its rice exports were only 500,000 tons (Kwangtung Economics Society 1981, 195) or 2.4 percent of output. Other surplus producing provinces exported even less than Hunan. Hupei, where per capita production in 1978 was 380 kilograms (Agricultural Yearbook Compilation Commission 1981, 101; Hu Ch'iao-mu 101–2) exported only 300,000 tons (Kwangtung Economics Society 1981, 195) or 1.7 percent of production. Kiangsu and Chekiang, where per capita production was about 400 kilograms, exported 350,000 and 100,000 tons, respectively – about 1.5 and .6 percent of production.

Agricultural tax policy reinforced self-sufficiency. During the 1950s there had been a gradual tendency to allow the payment of the agricultural tax in cash or crops other than grain, thus drawing peasants into specialized commercial crop production. Peasants in cotton-producing areas delivered cotton rather than grain to meet their tax obligations. In 1955, 8 percent of the agricultural tax was paid in cotton (Chao Kuo-chün 1960, 200), a significant share for a crop that occupied only about 4 percent of sown area. By the late 1960s and well into the 1970s the state was more insistent on payment in grain. That posed a significant additional constraint on producing units since the agricultural tax in the mid-1970s amounted to about 13 million (metric) tons, almost one-third of all grain procured by the state. Since grain could not usually be purchased on rural markets, that reinforced the necessity for all regions to grow grain.

The pattern of growth after 1965 reflects the grain self-sufficiency policy and the declining profitability of commercial crop production. In the five years from 1966 through 1970 grain output increased at an average annual rate of 4.5 percent, while nongrain crops and animals, except for tea, grew at lower rates: cotton 1.7 percent, oilseed crops .6 percent, sugarcane .1 percent, sugar beet 1.2 percent, live pigs 2.3 percent, aquatic products 1.3 percent, and tea 6.2 percent (Yü Kuo-yao 1980a, 29). That reversed the pattern of growth during 1963–65 when price-oriented planning prevailed.

The consequence of attempted self-sufficiency was declining allocative efficiency within agriculture and, as will be discussed in Chapter 4, declining per capita consumption of many noncereal foods. Increased inefficiency is most evident in regions of northwest China that had a significant comparative advantage in the production of meat and other animal products. By the late 1960s these regions were forced to devote increased resources to grain production. Pasture lands were brought under the plow despite the lack of water resources adequate for growing field crops and high probability of increased wind erosion. In many cases the grain yields achieved on these lands were less than a tenth of the national average and were obtained only at the expense of reduced production of high-valued animal products.

Pursuit of increased grain production was not confined to predominantly pastoral regions but extended the areas previously specializing in nongrain crops, such as peanuts, oil-bearing seeds, cotton, and tobacco. Consequently the area sown to these crops in regions with a significant comparative advantage frequently was reduced. Increased inefficiency, however, was not confined to regions that were grain-deficient. While some regions were initially more than self-sufficient in grain, reduced opportunities to purchase nongrain crops from other regions led these grain-surplus regions to increase the share of their land allocated to producing sugar, oil-bearing crops, and so forth as compared with the era of freer trade. Because the yields of these crops were relatively low, that reallocation reduced allocative efficiency.

Thus the strategy of the first half of the 1960s of encouraging rapid growth and high rates of marketing of grain in the "high and stable regions" was undercut. As will be discussed in Chapter 5, the marketing rates in many of these regions in the late 1970s, when marketing and specialized production had undergone something of a revival, were still surprisingly low. Although output of some economic crops continued to expand, specialized production was reduced. The pattern of production of many economic crops became increasingly dispersed, and an increasing share of output originated in regions that did not enjoy an initial comparative advantage. The opportunity cost of increasing the output of nongrain crops in these grain-surplus regions, measured in terms of the grain output foregone, was frequently several times as high as in grain-deficient areas. Despite the tendency for sown area of economic crops to expand in grain-surplus areas, the aggregate area sown to some economic crops, particularly cotton, peanuts, and oil-bearing seeds, was reduced.

Unfortunately, it is not possible to measure precisely the aggregate costs of these enforced shifts toward a less efficient use of resources. With complete provincial time series data on the allocation of sown area and other inputs to each agricultural activity, on the full spectrum of agricultural outputs, and on the volume of interprovincial trade in each product, it would be possible to estimate the aggregate costs of divergence from the comparative advantage cropping patterns that existed in the mid-1950s. Conceptually the problem is similar to estimating the costs of restrictions on international trade. These estimates usually are based on a Heckscher–Ohlin framework that implicitly assumes production technology is everywhere the same and that comparative advantage is determined by relative factor endowments. The procedures, however, assume that the production function for each good within each country is homogenous of degree 1. The costs of divergence from an optimal pattern of international exchange arise only because as trade shrinks each country is obliged to employ more of its relatively scarce factor in the production of its noncomparative advantage product, that is, the good that uses its scarce factor relatively intensively. Increased self-sufficiency raises the domestic price of the noncomparative advantage good because domestic production of the good requires large quantities of the home country's scarce factor of production. Although this source of increased costs is not trival, this estimation procedure ignores interregional variation in production conditions. In short, production functions vary from place to place since they are dependent on differences in climate and other natural factors that can't be traded on the market. As production moves away from the initial free trade equilibrium, marginal production costs rise rapidly. The higher the marginal cost of grain output in pastoral regions of the Northwest or of wheat production in cotton-producing regions of north China, for example, the greater is the opportunity cost of reducing interregional trade.

With sufficient data one could estimate supply functions for major agricultural products by province and, given time series data on interprovincial trade flows, estimate the opportunity costs of reduced trade. Even if this were possible, it would represent only a start on the problem at hand. First, these estimation procedures would not account for losses in productivity due to the undermining of production incentives. As previously pointed out, this is crucial because of the pressure for equalitarian forms of income distribution, constraints on private production activities, and the absence of adequate price incentives that tended to accompany periods of constraints on trade. Even an augmented model used to measure the costs of increased regional self-sufficiency under conditions of inelastic supply would have to assume implicitly the continuity of the underlying production and incentive framework. Clearly this would be inappropriate for the period under consideration.

A second shortcoming of the hypothetical estimate is that much of the increased inefficiency stemmed from changes in the intraprovincial patterns of production and exchange. These changes would not be taken into account. In short, more detailed analysis of producing units, usually production teams, is required. Only a few studies of production teams based on field research in China have been undertaken. It would be difficult to generalize on the basis of such a small sample, even if it had been drawn at random. Moreover, most of the case studies have been of units that in critical respects are atypical.[12] Thus they are not a reliable basis on which to form a judgment on aggregate allocative inefficiency. Consequently, my analysis is based on an a priori theoretical framework and more aggregate data.

Animal husbandry

China has more than 250 million hectares of grasslands where animal husbandry traditionally has been the chief form of agricultural activity. While meat production was largely for self-consumption, these regions exported animal products such as wool and hides and imported manufactured goods and sometimes grain. Documentation of the attempt to force these regions to

become self-sufficient in foodgrain is difficult because provincial-level reporting is seldom the ideal geographic unit for analysis. Animal husbandry
regions in northwest China, such as Inner Mongolia and Kansu Province,
also contain rich cropping regions in the Yellow and Wei river valleys where
grain yields and marketing rates are relatively high.[13] Much of the trade that
facilitates specialization is thus intraprovincial and rarely reported in sources
available in the West. Most data are compiled and reported for provinces or
autonomous regions.

One case of enforced grain self-sufficiency occurred in Inner Mongolia, a
sparsely populated north China province. Crop and animal husbandry development had proceeded rapidly from 1949 through 1967. In 1956, a year
of unusually good weather, Inner Mongolia's per capita grain production
ranked second only to Heilungkiang. Animal husbandry also flourished during the 1950s – production grew 9.2 percent per year from 1949 through
1958 (NCNA December 3, 1978). The region was a major wool producer,
and the region's First Five-Year Plan included a large woolen goods factory.
Although husbandry output fell during the late 1950s and early 1960s, it
subsequently recovered, and growth between 1959 and 1968 still averaged
2.9 percent per year.

After resources were shifted into grain production in the late 1960s, the
output of animal husbandry products fell at an average annual rate of
four-tenths of 1 percent between 1969 and 1978. Ironically, emphasis on
grain production does not appear to have succeeded in raising per capita
grain output in Inner Mongolia compared to the 1950s. Long-term comparisons are hazardous for two reasons. First, grain output is highly variable
due to weather conditions, so comparisons are extremely sensitive to the
particular initial and end years selected. Second, in 1971 and 1979 Inner
Mongolia's boundaries, unlike most other regions, were subject to major
realignments. Thus long-term comparisons are not always for the same geographic unit. Output per capita reached a peak in the 1950s of 519 kilograms
of unhusked grain per capita in 1956 (Chou Hui 1980), while the low point
was 321 kilograms in 1957, still about 5 percent above national average. Per
capita output in 1978, when the population of the region was slightly less
than that at year end 1957 since its 1971–78 area was shrunk, is said to have
declined "considerably" compared with 1956. That suggests per capita output is unlikely to have been much above the average of the First Plan, 425
kilograms. But the significance of this is difficult to judge since Inner Mongolia's 1978 area was so much less than its 1957 area. Output in 1979, after the
region's boundaries were realigned to approximately those of the 1950s, was
only 275 kilograms per capita and grew little in 1979–81.[14] Thus on average

in 1979–1981 Inner Mongolia's per capita foodgrain output was about half the average of the First Plan. That is more meaningful than the comparison of 1978 with 1956 since it is not based on the peak output of the 1950s and because Inner Mongolia's boundaries after 1978 are roughly comparable to those of the 1950s. On the other hand, part of the long-term decline may be due to adverse weather conditions in the late 1970s. However, the magnitude of the drop is so large that there is little doubt that even on a weather-adjusted basis per capita grain output in the late 1970s was substantially below the average of the 1950s. Rather than ranking above average in per capita grain production, the region now ranks near the bottom.

A similar situation developed in Sinkiang, where animal husbandry and foodgrain production both declined after the mid-1960s. Grain and animal husbandry production expanded at an average annual rate of 8 and 6 percent, respectively, from 1949 through 1966. But grain production and animal husbandry both declined between 1967 and 1977 (Wang Feng 1978). Grain production reached a peak output of 3.34 million (metric) tons in 1966, almost two-thirds above 1957, but stagnated between 1966 and 1975. Output was 3.145 million tons in 1975, 5 percent less than in 1966. Animal herds also declined by 10.3 percent between 1965 and 1978 (Cheng Po-ch'üan 1980).

It is clear why grain output failed to keep pace with population growth in Inner Mongolia and Sinkiang. Annual population growth in these two regions between 1957 and 1980 averaged 3.3 and 3.7 percent, respectively, compared to the national average rate of 1.9 percent.[15] The rapid rates of population growth reflect both the relaxed birth control efforts in minority-populated areas (both Inner Mongolia and Sinkiang are autonomous regions) and the forced resettlement of millions of urbanites in these regions. Since most of those resettled had few farming or animal husbandry skills and brought with them no fixed assets, it is perhaps not surprising that the massive resettlement program reduced output per worker.[16] Moreover, the self-sufficiency policy induced a shift of resources away from comparative advantage in animal husbandry and other economic crops that not only reduced further productivity per worker but may have contributed to the modest character of grain output growth. Declining output of animal products, sugar beets, and edible vegetable oils reduced peasant food consumption and their cash income. That, in turn, made it difficult for peasants to purchase the inputs necessary to sustain grain production. In some places the need for purchased inputs was increasing since smaller animal herds reduced the supply of organic fertilizer (Ku Chien-p'eng and Ku Chung-ch'eng 1980). Over the longer run, as pasture areas ill suited to grain production came under the plow, particularly in Inner Mongolia, substantial soil erosion set in, ruining not only pasturelands but reducing cropped area below the initial level.[17]

But a fully satisfactory explanation of declining grain output in pastoral regions will have to await a detailed analysis of intraregional production patterns and population growth.

It is possible to provide a more satisfactory analysis of trends in specialized production for several commercial crops.

Cotton

Before World War II China was one of the world's major cotton producers, and cotton was by far China's most important nonfood crop. Prior to the Japanese invasion average annual output was about 800,000 (metric) tons (Shen 1951, 308) and net imports about 75,000 tons (United States Department of Agriculture 1972, 15, 17). Output was depressed during the war but recovered in absolute terms to the peak prewar level by the early 1950s. Through the manipulation of the cotton/grain price ratio and the institution of advance purchase contracts, the government encouraged the expansion of cotton sown area from 2.77 million hectares in 1949 to 5.8 million hectares in 1957 (Appendix 1). By 1957 production was twice the prewar peak, and imports proportionately were less. Cotton was grown in reportable quantities in nineteen provinces in 1957, but in only eight provinces – Hopei, Hupei, Honan, Shantung, Shansi, Shensi, Kiangsu, and Sinkiang – was the share of sown area devoted to cotton significantly greater than the national average. These eight provinces accounted for 80 and 82 percent of China's cotton sown area and production, respectively, in 1957.

When indirect planning predominated the allocation of land was consistent with the principle of comparative advantage. In theory, comparative advantage should be measured according to relative cost per unit of output. Because the requisite data on input usage by area and by crop are not available I continue to use a Ricardian perspective and measure comparative advantage by relative land productivity. This procedure is analogous to MacDougall's use of labor productivity data to test the Ricardian model's ability to explain trade patterns between the United States and the United Kingdom (1951). Internationally the validity of that approach depends critically on competitive international markets in which exporters of the same product from different countries face the same international price. One could easily imagine that in an underdeveloped agrarian economy with inadequate transport, product markets might be fragmented, resulting in sub-

Table 2.3. *Provincial specialization in cotton production, 1957*

| | Cotton sown area | | | | |
	Thousands of hectares (1)	Percentage of total regional sown area (2)	Cotton yield (kg/ha) (3)	Grain yield (kg/ha) (4)	Cotton/grain yield ratio (3) ÷ (4)
National	5,775	3.7	284	1,460	.19
Hopei	969	8.5	324	1,100	.30
Hupei	583	8.0	390	1,990	.20
Shansi	343	6.7	287	863	.33
Sinkiang	114	6.5	447	1,660	.27
Honan	875	6.4	205	1,030	.20
Kiangsu	671	6.2	284	1,380	.21
Shensi	321	5.7	322	1,170	.28
Shantung	767	5.6	236	1,110	.21

Notes: Grain yields are calculated inclusive of soybean sown area and output.
Sources: National – State Statistical Bureau (1960, 119, 128, 129), Ministry of Agriculture Planning Bureau (1958, 32). *Provincial* – *Columns 1, 2,* Central Intelligence Agency (1969) for all provinces except Kiangsu, for which that source reports data inclusive of Shanghai municipality; for Kiangsu, Chin Chi-ming (1959, 245); *Column 3,* calculated from column 1 and output data in Committee on the Economy of China (1969); *Column 4,* calculated from sown area data reported in Central Intelligence Agency (1969) and grain output reported in Walker (1977b, Table 1).

stantial interregional price variation. Profit-maximizing producers presumably would allocate a relatively large share of their land to a crop if its local price were sufficiently high, even if its yield was relatively low. In China, however, all producers of the same crop face uniform state procurement prices.[18] Thus, interregional variation in the share of land allocated to cotton or other crops during periods of price planning should reflect underlying differentials in the relative physical productivity of land, not interregional price variation. For cotton, I need only distinguish between cotton-growing areas in north China where the predominant alternative crop was wheat and cotton regions in central China provinces where the alternative was rice or millet.

Table 2.3 shows cotton sown area, cotton yields, and grain yields for the eight major cotton-producing regions in 1957. Efficiency in the allocation of resources is suggested by the concentration of production in regions that have a strong comparative advantage in cotton relative to the dominant alternative of foodgrain production. In each of these provinces the ratio of cotton to grain yields shown in the last column of the table exceeded the national average. Most notable is Hopei Province, which in 1957 had the largest absolute sown area, the highest share of land sown to cotton, and the highest yield of cotton relative to grain of any province.[19]

The economic rationality of large-scale production of cotton appears dubious only for Hupei and Kiangsu. Their relative cotton/grain yield ratios are not significantly above the national average. But these are the only central China provinces in the table, and their cropping patterns vary considerably from the north. Since the cotton/rice and cotton/millet–barley price ratios were 40 percent higher than the cotton/wheat price ratio, specialization in cotton was profitable in both Hupei and Kiangsu where rice and millet, respectively, were the predominant grain crops even though the average cotton/grain yield in physical units was lower than in the north.[20]

Efficiency in resource allocation among provinces, not surprisingly, was made possible by specialized intraprovincial production, particularly on the North China Plain. In Hopei, for example, in 1957 80 percent of the cotton was grown in four areas in the southern and central portions of the province (Sun Ching-chih 1957, 62). This broad area is east of the Peking–Hank'ou Railroad and south of the east–west rail line between Shihchiachuang and Techou. The Grand Canal delineates the eastern boundary between Hopei and Shantung in this area before continuing north to Peking through Hopei at Techou. The four areas were Luanch'eng and Chao counties southeast of Shihchiachuang; Ch'engan and Wuan counties, in South Hopei near the city of Hantan, on the north–south rail route; Tungkuang and Wuch'iao counties in T'ienching Prefecture, just north of the east–west rail line and on the Grand Canal; and Nankung and Wei counties in the southeast part of the province. In these eight counties cotton occupied more than a third of sown area compared to 8.5 percent for the province as a whole. The share of cotton sown area was highest in Ch'engan County – 51 percent. Cotton had been a major crop in this area since the Ming dynasty (1368–1644), and specialized cotton production flourished there in the early part of the twentieth century. In Luanch'eng County, for example, a rise in the price of cotton relative to grain in the first decades of the century increased the share of land sown to cotton to 70 percent by 1930 (Myers 1970, 67).

Cotton production in Shantung was concentrated in the northwestern prefectures adjacent to the cotton-producing regions of Hopei. Cotton sown area there was 65.6 percent of the whole province and occupied more than 30 percent of the sown area in Linch'ing, Hsiachin, and Pin counties, and in P'utai, a village near the Pin County seat. Most of these areas were known historically for specialized cotton production (Sun Ching-chih 1957, 131).

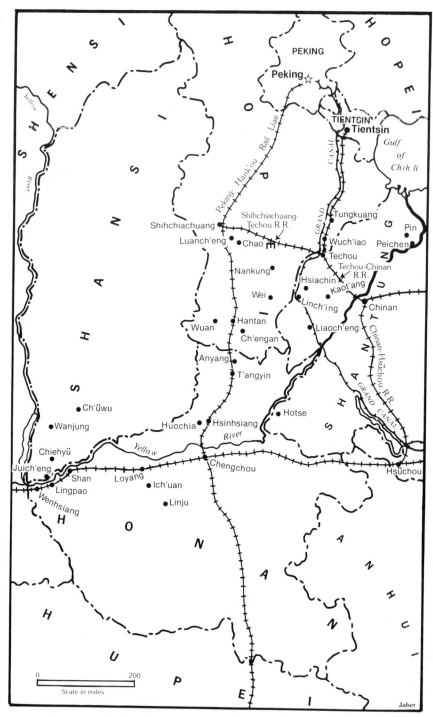

Map 2. Areas of specialized cotton production on the North China Plain.

Northern Honan, near the cotton-growing regions of Hopei and Shantung, was another region of specialized production. Cotton occupied 15 to 20 percent of total crop area in T'angyin, Hsinhsiang, Huochia, Shan, Lingpao, Ich'uan, and Linju counties and areas near the city of Loyang and exceeded 30 percent in Anyang County and in Wenhsiang (Sun Chingchih 1957, 164). Cotton production in Shansi was concentrated in the southern counties of Chiehyü, Wanjung, Juich'eng, and Ch'üwu, where it occupied between 20 and 30 percent of sown area (Sun Ching-chih 1957, 107).

In Kiangsu cotton production was concentrated in Nant'ung and Yench'eng prefectures in the eastern coastal portion of the province, as it had been since the 1930s (Hu Huan-yong 1947). Soil salinity in the eastern portion of these two prefectures is relatively high, making cotton, with its ability to withstand salinity better than other crops, a comparative advantage crop. In 1957 over 30 percent of the sown area in these two prefectures was sown to cotton (Sun Ching-chih 1959b, 34).

Specialized cotton production was made possible by trade. Some of that trade was intraprovincial. But a significant portion was interprovincial, particularly for the north China producers, continuing a pattern existing since the seventeenth century, discussed in Chapter 1. Hopei, the largest producer, exported 40 percent of its cotton to other regions, primarily Shanghai (Sun Ching-chih 1957, 58). Honan and Shantung were also major cotton exporters.[21] Exports from Honan on average exceeded 40 percent of production (Sun Ching-chih 1957, 160), and Shantung's exports in some years of the 1950s reached as high as 75,000 (metric) tons, also about 40 percent of production (Shantung Science Commission 1981). Shansi, another important north China cotton producer, was also a large exporter to east China (Sun Ching-chih 1957, 105). As will be detailed further below, with the exception of Shansi Province, per capita grain production in these north China provinces was relatively low and north China as a whole was an importer of cereals. Even Sinkiang, which was geographically distant from main textile regions, exported significant quantities of its cotton to as far away as Shanghai as early as 1954 (NCNA July 30, 1954).

More data are necessary to test the the hypothesis that the allocation of land increasingly diverged from the principle of comparative advantage, but both quantitative and qualitative evidence suggest that the pattern of cropping by the mid-1970s was far less efficient than twenty years earlier. The Chinese have published a complete time series of national cotton sown area and yields since 1949 (Appendix 1), but provincial data are far less complete, particularly for the years prior to 1978. Moreover, a satisfactory test of the hypothesis would have to rely on prefectural or county data since increased dispersion of cotton production within provinces may be as significant a source of increased inefficiency as declining cotton area in provinces with a comparative advantage in cotton production. Such data are available only for Shantung. They are analyzed in Chapter 4 Nationally, cotton sown area in 1977 and 1978 averaged 4.85 million hectares, a decline of 16 percent compared to 1957. Yield of ginned cotton rose 53 percent. Yet cotton sown area fell by relatively larger proportions in the north China provinces that initially had a substantial comparative advantage in cotton production. Between 1957 and 1977 sown area fell 58 percent in Hopei, the province enjoying the strongest initial comparative advantage in cotton. In 1979 sown area in Shansi was down more than a third compared to 1957. Over the same period cotton sown area fell 39 percent in Honan (Appendix 2).

Not all of the measurable changes in cotton production since the 1950s appear irrational. In Sinkiang, which has a strong comparative advantage in the production of cotton, particularly highly valued long-staple varieties, cotton sown area expanded almost 30 percent between 1957 and 1978. In Liaoning, a region with no comparative advantage, cotton sown area was reduced 80 percent by 1978 (Appendix 2). On balance, however, the data suggest increased inefficiency in the allocation of land to cotton production between 1957 and 1977 or 1978.

A major source of increased inefficiency was the drive, after the mid-1960s, to reduce the chronic dependence of north China on imports of grain from other provinces. Yet modest grain imports in north China had facilitated specialized commercial cotton production since the seventeenth century, a pattern that continued during the 1950s. Hopei could allocate 8.5 percent of its sown area (more than twice the national average) to cotton and be China's major cotton supplier in the 1950s only because the state supplied, on average, over 1 million (metric) tons of foodgrains per year, slightly over 10 percent of provincial production, to help meet basic cereal consumption requirements of peasants who were engaged in production of economic crops, primarily cotton but also peanuts, edible oil seeds, and so on (Sun Ching-chih 1957, 59; Walker 1977a, 571).[22]

Honan and Shantung, perhaps because their comparative advantage in cotton production was less than Hopei's, allocated a smaller share of their sown area to economic crops. On balance they were self-sufficient in cereals in 1953–57, although they each were net importers in some years (Walker 1977a, 571). Shansi was a net grain exporter – about 8 to 10 percent of its production was supplied to other provinces in the North China Plain, most probably Hopei Province (Sun Ching-chih 1957, 103).

Although foodgrain self-sufficiency in north China is not complete, dependence on external food supplies was reduced. Shantung imported 40,000 tons annually for several years prior to 1975 (Cheng Shou-lung 1980, 24), although it was a net exporter on average in 1970–78 (Liu Hsüan-huo et al. 1982, 22). Honan, too, was on average a net exporter of cereals in 1970–78. Hopei imported grain in 1971–74, 1976–78, and 1980 (Li Pin, Lu Yung-ch'ing, and Wang Feng-wen 1981), but the volume was reduced to an average of 80,000 tons per year in 1970–78, substantially less than in the 1950s (Liu Hsüan-huo et al. 1982, 22). Shansi Province, which had been on average self-sufficient in foodgrains in the First Five-Year Plan, imported grain in twenty-one of the twenty-four years between 1955 and 1978. Imports, however, were modest, averaging only 140,000 tons per year (Li Wen-chin and Chia Chih-shan 1981, 37–38).

Although the magnitude of inward transfers relative to local grain production declined in the 1970s compared to the 1950s, increased self-sufficiency in cereals in north China was achieved only at the expense of declining area and output of cotton, edible vegetable oils, and other noncereal crops and, at least through the early 1970s, declining average per capita foodgrain consumption, compared with 1953–57 (Walker 1977a, 580). The main cost of self-sufficiency in cereals was in cotton production. Cotton sown area was reduced by more than 1 million hectares or almost 40 percent in Hopei, Honan, and Shantung between 1957 and 1977–79.[23]

As a consequence of these acreage shifts, in the late 1970s north China ceased to export cotton. Production was below the raw material demands of the textile plants in the region, and despite transfers of cotton from central China and imports from North America, textile production was far less than the capacity of the factories in Tientsin, Hantan, and other textile centers in north China. In Shantung, for example, prior to 1980 provincial cotton output was sufficient to supply only 40 percent of the raw material required to operate local textile mills. In Shansi in 1978 local production supplied only 57 percent of the province's cotton textile raw materials (Li Wen-chin and Chia Chih-shan 1981, 39). It is unlikely that Hopei could be in a different position since cotton output had suffered a long-term decline, reaching a low point in 1977 when output was 68 percent less than in 1957 (Niu Jo-feng 1979). Although north China cotton production began to recover in the late 1970s, as late as 1979 Hopei, Shantung, and Honan imported over 200,000 tons of cotton with imports in Shantung of 68,000 tons (NCNA January 21, 1981; Pai Ju-ping 1982, 16).

Increased dispersion in cotton production may be as important a source of inefficiency in production as declining sown area in comparative advantage provinces. That hypothesis, however, is difficult to test because of the difficulty of finding appropriate time series data. By 1977–78 cotton was grown in more than 1,200 of China's 2,100 counties. However, in only 340 counties did cotton sown area occupy more than 10 percent of cultivated area (Ts'ai Yüan-yüan 1979, 32). There were more than 700 counties where cotton sown area was very small (less than 3,300 hectares) and yields less than half the level achieved in the few counties where production was most specialized. The lack of external food supplies is the primary cause of dispersed production. According to a member of the Chinese Academy of Sciences, specialized production would be greatly facilitated by seeking cereal self-sufficiency within units as large as a county rather than on the basis of each producing unit (Mei Fang-ch'üan 1982).

From the national perspective the decrease in specialized production of cotton after 1966 led to stagnant cotton output, declining productivity in cotton production, declining per capita cotton cloth consumption, and vast imports of cotton from abroad. While grain output grew rapidly, cotton production grew less than 10 percent between 1966 and 1973. Output declined annually thereafter, reaching a low in 1977 when production was 13 percent less than 1966, the peak year of production in the 1960s, and only 25 percent above the output of 1957 (Appendix 1). Because production is far less than aggregate demand even at the relatively high prices of finished cotton goods, cotton cloth remains strictly rationed, as it has been since the mid-1950s. Average per capita consumption declined from 8.3 meters in 1956 to 7.6 meters in 1976 (P'ei Yüan-hsiu, Liu Ping-ying, and Li Ping-chang 1980). Even sustaining lower levels of per capita cloth consumption of a growing population and increased textile exports required a steady rise in raw cotton imports. Net imports averaged less than 45,000 and 100,000 tons annually in the 1950s and 1960s, respectively, but grew steadily after 1970, averaging over 320,000 tons per year between 1972 and 1978. In 1979–80, when China became the world's largest importer of raw cotton, the volume averaged 770,000 tons (United States Department of Agriculture 1972, 30, 38; 1979, 23; 1981, 31).

Sugar

Sugar traditionally has formed an unusually small portion of the Chinese diet, and nonfood uses of sugar are modest, so the area devoted to its production has been and will continue to be small. Nevertheless, sugarcane and sugar beets are interesting crops to examine because their demanding production conditions can be met efficiently in only a few regions. Moreover, in the prewar period, about 70 percent of China's sugar was produced

Table 2.4. *Provincial specialization in sugarcane and sugar beet production, 1957*

| | Sown area | | Raw cane, beet yield (tons/ha) | Grain yield (kg/ha) | Cane, beet/grain yield ratio |
	Thousands of hectares	Percentage of total			
Cane					
National	267	.17	38.9	2,700	14.4
Kwangtung	117	1.53	42.6	1,800	23.6
Fukien	25	1.05	49.9	2,060	24.3
Kwangsi	37	.87	22.3	1,440	15.5
Yunnan	20	.51	38.1	1,600	23.8
Szechuan	41	.31	41.5	2,080	20.2
Beet					
National	159	.10	9.4	1,070	8.8
Heilungkiang	114	1.60	9.5	1,020	9.3
Kirin	34	.74	6.5	1,270	5.1

Notes: The national grain yield in the top part of the table is for rice since sugarcane is grown in tropical regions where the predominant alternate crop is rice. Provincial grain yields, however, are for aggregate grain output. Since rice yields are higher than in other grains, this introduces some bias to the comparisons of cane/grain yield ratios in the provinces with the national average. This bias is not significant for Kwangtung and Fukien, where more than 70 percent of grain area was sown to rice, and for Kwangsi, where 60 percent of grain area was sown to rice. It is more severe in the southwest provinces, where only 30–40 percent of grain area was sown to rice. Adjustment for this would reduce the comparative advantage of Yunnan and Szechuan sugar production considerably by the measure of the table. The national grain yield in the sugar beet portion of the table is a weighted average of wheat, millet, sorghum, corn, and soybeans, the predominate alternate crops in beet-producing regions.
Sources: National – State Statistical Bureau (1981c, VI-10–VI-11).
Provincial – *grain yields,* calculated from sown area data in Central Intelligence Agency (1969) and grain output data in Walker (1977b); *sugarcane sown area and yield,* Kwangtung – Sun Ching-chih (1959a, 25), Fukien – Sun Ching-chih (1959a, 120), Kwangsi – Sun Ching-chih (1959a, 74, 78), Yunnan – Sun Ching-chih (1960, 531), Szechuan – Sun Ching-chih (1960, 34); *sugar beet sown area and yields,* Heilungkiang – Sun Ching-chih (1959c; 398, 403), Kirin – Sun Ching-chih (1959c, 221).

in Taiwan – a source that was not available after 1949 (Shen 1951, 236). Because of the loss of Taiwan supplies, the expansion of area sown to both cane and beet in the 1950s was more rapid than for most noncereal crops. The major regions of comparative advantage in the 1950s were in the Northeast (Kirin and Heilungkiang) for sugar beets and the South (Fukien, Kwangtung, and Kwangsi) and Southwest (Yunnan and Szechuan) for sugarcane (Table 2.4).

Production of the two principal raw materials for making sugar in 1957 was far more concentrated than cotton. The share of sown area devoted to sugar production in major producing regions, while still small, ranged up to sixteen times the national average. In 1957 the two leading beet-producing provinces accounted for over 90 percent of the sown area and the five highest-yielding cane-producing regions accounted for 90 percent of the national sown area and output. In the absence of data on production cost by crop and region, and since all cane (beet) producers faced the same sugarcane/rice (sugar beet/grains) price ratio, comparative advantage is assumed to be measured by the ratio of sugarcane or sugar beet yield to grain yield, relative to the national average.

The provincewide physical yield ratios shown in Table 2.4, however, are a less reliable guide to comparative advantage than they are for cotton, since sugar is a minor crop in terms of its share of sown area and its production is more concentrated in a few counties with a decided comparative advantage within producing provinces. In short, the relative yields facing sugar producers within provinces are reflected very imperfectly by the provincial data.

The importance of intraprovincial specialization based on comparative advantage as a source of allocative efficiency is best illustrated for Fukien, the province with the strongest comparative advantage in sugarcane production in 1957. In the 1950s Fukien's sugarcane area expanded rapidly, by 1957 reaching a level almost 60 percent greater than 1936 and more than four times 1949 (Table 2.5). Sugarcane production increasingly was concentrated in five counties in Chinchiang Prefecture. By 1957 four of these counties, Hsienyu, P'ut'ien, Nanan, and T'ungan cultivated half the sugarcane area and produced two-thirds of the province's sugarcane. Hsienyu was the leading producer, as it was in the thirteenth century (Elvin 1973, 129). Sugarcane yields were 84 tons per hectare – more than twice as great as in the remainder of the province – allowing the county to produce 45 percent of the raw cane of the entire province (Hsü Chien-p'ing and Shih Wei-liang 1980, 17). The county's strong comparative advantage in cane production was matched by the allocation of its sown area. Cane was cultivated on 17 percent of the county's sown area in 1957, a manyfold multiple of the provincewide average of 1.05 percent (Table 2.4).[24] Refineries in Hsienyu processed almost half of the sugar produced in Fukien (Hsü Chien-p'ing and Shih Wei-liang 1980, 17).

Allocative efficiency was dependent on extraprovincial markets for sugar and for cereal supplies. Sugarcane production in central coastal Fukien was well established as early as the Ming dynasty when Fukien's sugar was sold

Map 3. Areas of specialized sugarcane production in Fukien Province.

in Southeast Asian markets as well as throughout the Chinese empire (Evelyn Rawski 1972, 48). Even prior to the Ming dynasty, the great southward migration of population had led to population densities in the southeast coast far in excess of what could be supported on the basis of rice cultivation alone. Central coastal Fukien, where sugarcane, mulberry leaves (for silkworm production), and other nongrain crops were grown, depended on cereal imports from the Yangtse Delta, the Canton Delta, and the central Kan River Valley as early as the twelfth century (Elvin 1973, 170). Dependence on external sources of rice persisted in the eighteenth and nineteenth centuries (Perkins 1969, 142–8; Chuan and Kraus 1975). Interregional trade accelerated in the latter half of the nineteenth century when steamships entered the coastal trade. There was a lively export of sugar from southeast ports to Hank'ou in central China, Shanghai in the east, and Tientsin in the north. Sugar was even shipped to the treaty port of Newchang (Yingk'ou) in Liaoning after it was opened in 1861 and traded for beancake, which was shipped to south China where it was used as a fertilizer, especially in sugar-

Table 2.5. *Fukien Province sugar production and export, 1936–81*

	Sown Area (thousands of hectares)[a] (1)	Production[b] Cane (2)	Refined (3)	Yields of cane (tons/ha) (4)	Exports of refined sugar to rest of China (thousands of tons)[c] (5)
1936	15.9	522	60[d]	32.8	—
1949	5.7	150	15	26.2	—
1957	24.8	1,236	94	49.9	—
1967	22.6	—	180	—	100
1976	25.3	900[e]	112	39.5	22
1978	—	2,750	331.8	—	—
1979	41.3	3,255	324.2	78.8	—
1980	41.2	3,512	372.7	85.2	180
1981	43.2	3,881	385.0	89.8	—

[a]Sown area is the area harvested in the year listed; planting actually occurs the previous year.

[b]Output data are for the crushing year which in Fukien starts in December of the preceding calendar year and goes through the end of April or beginning of May. Thus the row for 1967 shows production in the crushing year extending from December 1966 through May 1967. The sugar content of the cane reaches a peak in January–March in Fukien.

[c]Exports are exclusive of refining by-products and other products manufactured from sugar, such as candy.

[d]For 1937, the prewar peak level of output of refined sugar.

[e]Quantity of sugarcane pressed; output data not available for 1976. The quantity pressed is usually 85–90 percent of the quantity produced.

Sources: Column 1 – *1936, 1949, 1957,* Sun Ching-chih (1959a, 120, 128); *1967, 1979, 1980;* Fukien Provincial Academy of Agricultural Sciences, Sugarcane and Hemp Institute (1980, 23), Wang Ch'eng-hsuan (1981); *1976,* NCNA (January 13, 1980); *1981,* NCNA (January 21, 1981), Wang Ch'eng-hsuan (1981).

Column 2 – *1936,* Sun Ching-chih (1959a, 120); *1949, 1957,* calculated from data in columns 1 and 4; *1976,* NCNA (May 27, 1980); *1978,* Fukien Provincial Service (September 24, 1979); *1979–81,* Fukien Provincial Statistical Bureau (1981, 1982).

Column 3 – *1949, 1957,* Fukien Provincial Academy of Agricultural Sciences, Sugarcane and Hemp Institute (1980, 23), Sun Ching-chih (1959a, 128); *1967,* Fukien Province Department of Agriculture (1980, 24), Hsiao Hui-chia and Chang Jui-san (1980); *1976,* Hsiao Hui-chia and Chang Jui-san (1980), Hsü Yi-ming and Ch'en Ming-hsing (1980); *1978,* Fukien Provincial Service (September 24, 1979); *1979, 1980,* Fukien Provincial Statistical Bureau (1981); *1981,* Ho Hsi-lan and Ch'en Yang-ts'ung (1981), Fukien Provincial Statistical Bureau (1982).

Column 4 – *1936, 1957,* Sun Ching-chih (1959a, 120); *1949,* Fukien Provincial Academy of Agricultural Sciences, Sugarcane and Hemp Institute (1980, 23); *1976, 1979–81,* calculated from data in columns 1 and 2.

Column 5 – *1967,* Fukien Province Department of Agriculture (1980, 24); *1976, 1980,* Fukien Province Department of Agriculture (1980, 24), Hsiao and Chang (1980, 2).

cane production. Coastal areas of Fukien, where 92 percent of the province's sugarcane was grown, continued to depend on external sources of grain throughout the First Plan (Sun Ching-chih 1959a, 143–4).

The expansion of sugarcane and other economic crops was facilitated by improved transport links. Fukien was devoid of rail development prior to 1949. By April 1957 the province was linked to the main rail network at Yingt'an in Kiangsi by service from Amoy on the southern coast adjacent to Chinchiang Prefecture. A year later a line to Fuchou, the provincial capital on the central-northern coast, was completed (Shabad 1972, 96, 172, 178).

After a drop in sugarcane output in the early 1960s, production in Fukien responded rapidly to the price incentives and increased marketing opportunities that, as discussed above, had reemerged by 1962–63. As shown in Table 2.5, by the 1966–67 refining season output of refined sugar was 90 percent greater than in 1957–58, and exports to the rest of China reached 100,000 tons, 55 percent of production.

In the ensuing decade, however, production declined dramatically as incentives were reduced and marketing opportunities diminished. Most critically, because the state no longer guaranteed grain supplies to peasants in sugar-producing regions, current inputs were allocated increasingly to grain production, causing raw cane yields to plunge. By 1976, although the sown area had increased slightly, cane production had declined more than a quarter compared to 1957 and refined sugar production fell almost 40 percent compared to 1967. Far more significant from the point of view of comparative advantage and allocative efficiency, in a decade the quantity of exports fell almost 80 percent to 22,000 tons and the share of output exported from the province fell from over half to under 20 percent.

Declining production was arrested beginning in 1976–77 when an explicit policy of specialized sugar production was initiated. The new policy was unusual because it predated by three or four years the national policy of reintroducing specialized cropping and provides some indication of the magnitude of allocative inefficiency introduced when marketing was curtailed. Beginning in 1976, the central government supplied Fukien annually with 100,000 tons of grain that the province, in turn, sold to specialized cane producers to ensure adequate grain supplies (Hsiao Hui-chia and Chang Jui-san 1980). Under that system, for each ton of sugarcane sold to the state in excess of a fixed target, production teams were given the privilege of buying, at the quota purchase price, 125 kilograms of unhusked grain. For the province as a whole the target was 984,000 tons of cane (Fukien Province Department of Agriculture 1980, 24).[25] Furthermore, in 1978 cane producers were assured better access to both fertilizers and refined sugar. For every ton of cane sold to the state, the quantity of fertilizers that they had the right to purchase was increased from 15 to 25 kilograms. Sale of 1 ton of cane was also tied to the right to repurchase 10 kilograms of refined sugar. Peasants were exempted from paying the state tax on 1½ kilograms of this sugar per capita and could trade any portion of this sugar for grain at a ratio of 1:2, or for additional fertilizer at a ratio of 1:1.[26] Under these incentives, cane producers purchased outright or bartered with their excess refined sugar 717,500 tons of grains in the first five years of the new system. Average per capita grain purchases in specialized cane-producing regions were 75 kilograms annually. These purchases, plus additional local grain production, attributed to the allocation of some part of the incentive fertilizers to grain fields, raised annual per capita grain consumption in cane-producing regions from an average of 150 kilograms prior to 1976 to 250 kilograms in 1979 (Hsiao Hui-chia and Chang Jui-san 1980).

The assurance of adequate grain supplies has led to increased specialization and a remarkable resurgence of sugar production in Fukien. Raw cane production more than tripled between 1976 and 1980, both because yields almost doubled and sown area increased by three-quarters. Moreover, by 1980 exports of refined sugar from the province, 180,000 (metric) tons, were more than eight times the quantity of 1976 and even vastly surpassed the level of 1967. The share of sugar exported rose from 19.6 to 48.3 percent.

Fukien's episodic freedom to pursue patterns of production and trade consistent with the principle of comparative advantage is mirrored in the experience of Hsienyu County, shown in Table 2.6. In 1957 Hsienyu accounted for over a fourth of the province's sugarcane area. Hsienyu, like Fukien as a whole, experienced a sharp decline in sugarcane production in the early 1960s. Sown area and yields by 1962 had declined 40 and 60 percent, respectively, compared to 1957. Refined sugar output was less than a fourth the level of 1957. But as national grain production rose above crisis levels and price incentives and market opportunities for sugar producers were restored, sugarcane sown area and output resurged. By 1966 refined sugar output had quintupled compared with 1962 and, more significantly, exceeded the level of 1957. However, after 1966 production fell drastically as markets for refined sugar and external sources of foodgrains disappeared. In three years cane production and refined sugar output in the county fell by 60 and 50 percent, respectively.[27]

In 1972, in an effort to restore production, peasants in Hsienyu County were given the opportunity of purchasing from the state 7.5 tons of grain for each hectare of grain land converted to cane production. It is difficult to know whether this policy was effective since no sown area data for 1972–74

Table 2.6 *Hsienyu County sugar production, 1949–82*

	Sown area (thousands of hectares)	Production (thousands of tons)		Yields of cane (tons/ha)
		Cane	Refined	
1949	—	—	12.4	—
1957	6.7	562.8	45.2	84.0
1962	3.9	134.6	10.9	34.5
1966	9.9	677.7	54.9	68.1
1969	5.1	285.3	27.5	56.0
1972	—	294.7	38.4	—
1973	—	415.5	53.4	—
1975	5.8	—	40–50	60–75
1976	—	355.3	40.9	—
1977	8.1	522.2	63.2	64.2
1978	—	—	>70	75.0
1979	8.1	—	>80	82.5
1980	8.6	821.9	102.3	95.3
1981	8.7	—	—	—
1982	9.3[a]	—	—	—

[a]Planned area.
Sources: Hsü Chien-p'ing and Shih Wei-liang (1980, 17–18, 20), Hsü Ya (1981, 19), Fukien Provincial Service (January 19, 1979), Hsü Tzu-hsin (1982).

are available. Production of cane and refined sugar rose 41 and 39 percent, respectively, in 1973. The decline in production after 1973 is attributed by Chinese sources to the failure to tie the bonus to sugarcane production and to a reduction in the bonus to 6 tons and then by 1975 to 5.1 tons for each hectare of land converted (Hsü Chien-p'ing and Shih Wei-liang 1980, 20). Again, because the requisite data are lacking, that hypothesis is difficult to test. In any case by 1976 production of sugarcane and refined sugar were 14.5 and 23.5 percent, respectively, below the level of 1973, and still well below the historic 1966 peak levels (Table 2.6).

The welfare consequence of this long-run divergence from the principle of comparative advantage was low peasant income and consumption. In sugar-producing regions in Hsienyu County per capita cereal consumption in 1975 was only 145 kilograms (Hsiao Hui-chia and Chang Jui-san 1980). That was below the national poverty standard for rice areas. As will be discussed in Chapter 4, 200 kilograms of unhusked rice is considered the minimal annual consumption standard for avoiding malnutrition.

The depression of peasant income and consumption was perhaps inevitable given the long-standing dense population on the southeast coast. Although rice yields were among the highest in all of China, arable land in the late 1970s in Hsienyu was only .03 hectare per capita (Hsiao Hui-chia and Chang Jui-san 1980), about two-thirds less than the national average (Table 1.3). Such a dense population for centuries had been sustained primarily on the basis of specialized production of high-value crops such as sugarcane.

Sugar production and peasant welfare in Hsienyu improved substantially following the introduction of the policy of specialized sugar production in 1976. Between 1975 and 1977 sugarcane area expanded by half, to occupy more than a third of the county's cultivated land, recovering to and exceeding the area of 1957 for the first time since 1966. By 1980 unit yields increased almost half and production of refined sugar was almost twice the level of 1966. Increased productivity raised incomes and welfare. Between 1975 and 1979 annual cereal consumption of peasants producing sugar in Hsienyu almost doubled to 270 kilograms, substantially above the poverty line and more than 10 percent above average national cereal consumption (Hsiao Hui-chia and Chang Jui-san 1980; Hsü Chien-p'ing and Shih Wei-liang 1980, 21).

Hsienyu is an interesting case study because the magnitude of dependence on cereals supplied by the state can be measured. In the crushing year 1979–80 the county purchased 82,000 tons of grain from the state (Hsü Chien-ping and Shih Wei-liang 1980, 21). Although I do not know total grain output, the magnitude of these purchases can be gauged in per capita terms since the population of the whole county was 720,000 (Hsiao Hiu-chia and Chang Jui-san 1980). Even ignoring the nonagricultural population and peasants not engaged in sugar production, purchases amounted to 114 kilograms per capita. In short, most of the increase in average cereal consumption in Hsienyu depended on the revival of internal trade in grain – in this case via state-controlled channels.

Equally important, rising peasant income and consumption were achieved without a significant increase in the price of sugarcane relative to rice, the predominant grain grown in Fukien.[28] The increased share of land allocated to sugarcane is a function of the increased supplies of grain offered for sale to cane producers and the freedom to follow comparative advantage cropping – not an increase in the relative price of sugarcane. Thus the large increase in income and consumption may be interpreted as a pure allocative efficiency gain achieved through a restoration of marketing and comparative advantage cropping.

Renewal of specialized production of cane in the other major producing regions – Kwangtung and Kwangsi – was delayed until 1980 and 1981, respectively. Thus the growth of sugar output and improvements in allocative efficiency were inhibited for four or five years after marked gains were initiated in Fukien. Nationally, cane sugar yields in 1978 were 38.5 tons per hectare, down slightly from the level of 1957 (Chinese Academy of Sciences Economic Geography Research Office 1980, 223). Although yields were up substantially in Fukien, in marked contrast unit yields in Kwangtung in 1979 were still below the level of 1957.[29] The growth of cane sown area in Kwangtung in the latter half of the 1970s was modest compared to Fukien, and sown area remained 20 percent below the level of the mid-1960s. The supply of raw cane was so low that Kwangtung's refineries in 1980 operated at only 70 percent of capacity (Liang Chao, Liu Hsiao-t'ieh, and Li P'u-mi 1981, 27; Wang Chien-ming, 1980) and the share of output exported from the province had fallen from 60 percent in 1957 (Sun Ching-chih 1959a, 34) to less than 40 percent (NCNA August 21, 1981).

The contrast in performance between Fukien and the other major producing provinces is explained by the failure to encourage specialized sugar production in high-yielding regions. In Kwangtung in both the 1950s and 1970s the highest-yielding area was the Pearl River Delta. Cane yields in this region were about two-and-one-half times the national average. Yet in 1977 area sown to sugarcane in Foshan Prefecture, in the heart of the delta area, was less than in 1957. Sown area was said to be particularly low in counties such as Toumen (within Foshan) and P'anyü (a part of Foshan in the 1950s but subsequently subordinate to Canton Municipality) that had a strong comparative advantage in cane production. Not until August 1980 did Kwangtung adapt a program of specialized production similar to the one in effect in Fukien since 1976 (Reporter 1981).

The consequences of slow growth of specialized production in Kwangtung and Kwangsi relative to increasing domestic demand are evident both in the allocation of land and in China's pattern of foreign trade. By the late 1960s provinces that previously had relied on sugar purchased from other provinces had begun to grow sugarcane or beet because external supplies were shrinking (Hsiang Nan 1980; Yü Yu-hai and Chou Ch'uan 1980). Significant amounts of sugarcane were grown in Anhui and Shansi in the late 1970s where yields were, respectively, less than one-third and equal to one-fourth of those in Fukien. Sugar beet production also was initiated in areas of Kweichow and Szechuan where yields were low and significant production had not been undertaken in the 1950s. Unit yields in these two areas within the Southwest in 1979 were only a third the level of sugar beet yelds achieved in Kirin Province. Not only are cane or beet yields low in provinces such as Anhui, Shansi, Kweichow, and Szechuan, but the sugar content of the raw material is less and sugar refining is less efficient.

Given the shrinkage in the external supplies of sugar, diversion of land from grain to sugar in these localities was a perfectly rational strategy. In effect, the real price of sugar had risen relative to grain so some adjustment was appropriate. From a national perspective, however, such reallocations distorted internal resource allocation and reduced social welfare since the marginal cost of sugar production in these regions substantially exceeded that in traditional sugar-growing areas.

As in the case of cotton, intertemporal variation in the efficiency of resource allocation domestically is reflected in the pattern of China's sugar trade. China's net imports of sugar in the 1950s were modest, less than 50,000 tons annually. In the early 1960s net sugar imports skyrocketed, averaging over 800,000 tons in 1960–62.[30] As domestic production recovered imports fell steadily, reaching a trough of 29,000 tons in 1965. Subsequently imports jumped to an average of 240,000 tons in 1968–69, and over 425,000 tons in 1970–76, reaching a peak of 1.7 million tons in 1977. Because domestic sugarcane and sugar beet production accelerated after 1977 (see Table 4.4), net imports declined. They averaged 1.2 million tons annually in 1978 and 1979 – equivalent to more than 50 percent of domestic production, and fell to an average of 750,000 tons in 1980 and 1981, about one-fourth of domestic output (United States Department of Agriculture 1972, 27, 35; 1979, 17; 1981, 31; 1982, 28).[31]

Oilseed Crops

The allocation of resources in the production of soybeans, peanuts, and oil-bearing seeds such as rape and sesame up to the mid-1950s also appears to have been relatively efficient. It is difficult to show that the pattern of production was consistent with the principle of comparative advantage since the production of these crops is more widely diffused than either cotton or sugar. Moreover, crops such as rape are planted as overwintering crops, so the yield ratios shown in Table 2.7 are a poor measure of comparative advantage. But the regional distribution of peanuts, sesame, rapeseed, and soybeans in the mid-1950s was similar to that prevailing in China's competitive agriculture of the 1930s, so I presume that the degree of distortion induced by collectivization in the mid-1950s was modest.

Oilseed production collapsed in the early 1960s in response to the crisis in cereal production. Sown area declined by 40 percent and output fell even

Table 2.7. *Provincial specialization in peanut, oilseed, and soybean production, 1957*

| | Sown Area | | | Grain | |
	Thousands of hectares (1)	Percentage of total (2)	Yield (kg/ha) (3)	yield (kg/ha) (4)	Yield ratio (3) ÷ (4)
Peanuts					
National	2,542	1.6	1,012	1,460	.69
Shantung	685	5.0	993	1,112	.89
Honan	229	2.2	783	1,027	.76
Hopei	220	1.9	—	1,100	—
Sesame					
National	942	.6	331	1,460	.23
Honan	396	2.9	—	1,027	—
Hupei	206	2.8	510	2,047	.25
Rapeseed					
National	2,308	1.5	385	1,460	.26
Kweichow	252	8.0	330	2,050	.16
Kiangsi	343	6.3	248	1,780	.14
Yunnan	184	4.7	405	1,600	.25
Szechuan	354	2.7	780	2,080	.38
Soybeans					
National	12,748	8.1	788	1,530	.51
Heilungkiang	1,514	21.2	1,116	1,240	1.04
Kirin	907	19.7	1,280	1,260	1.02
Liaoning	730	14.8	1,051	1,650	.64
Shantung	1,882	13.9	1,018	1,330	.76
Anhui	1,036	10.3	795	1,450	.54
Honan	1,107	8.0	1,339	1,030	1.30

Note: For all sections of the table, except soybeans, grain yields are calculated inclusive of soybean sown area and output.

Sources: National – Ministry of Agriculture Planning Bureau (1958).

Provincial – Sown area data: Central Intelligence Agency (1969) except soybean area in Shantung assumed to be the same as 1956. *Yields:* peanuts, calculated from sown area data in column 1 and output data reported in Chen Nai-ruenn (1967, 350, 356); sesame, Sun Ching-chih (1958, 24); rapeseed – for Kiangsi, Sun Ching-chih (1958, 126), for Kweichow, Szechuan, and Yunnan, Sun Ching-chih (1960, 252, 34, 531, respectively); soybeans, calculated from sown area data in column 1 and output data reported in Walker (1977b, table 2).

more, 55 percent, since current inputs were diverted to grain production.[32] Production began to recover after 1962 and by 1965 unit yields had recovered completely to the level of the 1950s. But since sown area did not recover fully, production in 1965 was still less than 1957 (Table 4.4). Peanut sown area, for example, fell from over 2.5 million hectares in 1957 to 1.2 million hectares in 1961 but had partially recovered to over 1.8 million hectares in 1965 (Chinese Academy of Sciences Economic Geography Research Office 1980, 211).

The recovery, however, was truncated by the policy emphasis on foodgrains after 1965. Peanut sown area fell between 1965 and 1970 and as late as 1977 was 10 percent and 30 percent, respectively, below the level of 1965 and the average of 1955–57 (State Statistical Bureau 1982b, 140). Yields also stagnated over the same period, partially because a smaller share of current inputs was allocated to peanut production and, as will be discussed below, less efficient distribution of sown area. Consequently, aggregate output of edible vegetable oils declined by 5 percent between 1957 and 1977 (Table 4.4). As will be discussed below, that squeeze reduced oil consumption despite increase in edible vegetable oil imports. Since China was a major exporter of these products in the 1930s and exports continued in the 1950s, there is reason to suspect that reducing domestic oil production to accelerate grain growth was a fundamentally uneconomic choice, given the relative international prices of the two alternative crops.

Even this uneconomic strategy does not appear to have been well implemented. Violation of the principle of comparative advantage occurred domestically as well as internationally. Some regions with comparative advantage in oilseed production were the source of a declining share of national output after the 1950s. As production in comparative advantage regions was curtailed, it was difficult to maintain yields, despite the availability of increasing quantities of chemical fertilizers. Yields for all oilseeds were roughly stagnant between 1965 and 1975–1977.

Peanuts, the single most important source of edible vegetable oil in China, provide one example. The North China Plain was the major area of peanut production in the latter half of the nineteenth century. China was the world's largest producer by the 1930s and the major world exporter. Exports continued in the 1950s – both of peanuts in the shell and of peanut oil – based largely on production in north China. During the period of price planning in the 1950s oilseed production appears to have been consistent with comparative advantage. As shown in Table 2.7, Shantung in 1957 had the largest absolute sown area, the highest share of its sown area allocated to peanuts, and a strong comparative advantage in peanut production, judging from the high yield relative to grain. Exports of peanut oil from the province reached a peak of 150,000 tons in the 1950s (Cheng Shou-lung 1980, 23), about a third of provincial output. Honan and Hopei were also large producers. In 1956 and 1957, on average, slightly over half the national peanut sown area was concentrated in the three North China Plain provinces. Other provinces – for example, Hupei in central China – had higher absolute yields, but these were more than offset by the higher opportunity costs of peanut production so that the share of area sown to peanuts was 1.0 percent, far below that of Shantung.

By the late 1970s the allocation of sown area was less efficient than in the 1950s. Total peanut sown area in the North China Plain in 1978 was only half of the level of 1957 (Liu Hsüan-huo et al 1982, 23). In Shantung sown area declined by almost 40 percent between 1956 and 1978, while in Honan sown area declined by more than half between 1957 and 1979 (Agricultural Yearbook Compilation Commission 1981, 108). The area sown to oilseeds in Hopei also declined substantially between 1955, the peak year of the 1950s, and 1977. Area sown to summer grains, which in north China are directly competitive with peanuts as well as cotton, expanded from 2 million hectares in 1966 to 2.9 million hectares in 1974 and 3.84 million hectares in 1976 as part of the drive for foodgrain self-sufficiency (Li Pin, Lu Yung-ch'ing, and Wang Feng-wen 1981).

Reductions in peanut sown area in high-yielding provinces obscure important additional distortions in the intraprovincial allocation of land. In Shantung, for example, peanut production in the 1950s was concentrated in counties with land ill suited to grain production, frequently because of lack of water and rugged, mountainous terrain. Incremental grain production in these areas was particularly costly.

Production of sesame also was distributed rationally in the mid-1950s but sharply curtailed by the mid-1970s. Honan traditionally was the largest producer of sesame, the source of a food flavoring as well as the highest-quality, most expensive cooking oil in China (Shen 1951, 263). Specialized production and provincial export in Honan continued in the 1950s. Area sown to sesame in 1953 was 39 percent of the national total, and this rose to 42 percent by 1957. More than 40 percent of production was consumed outside the province (Sun Ching-chih 1957, 162). Hupei was another strong comparative advantage producer of sesame both before World War II and again as production recovered during the First Plan. Only 15 percent of the oil purchased was consumed locally; 25 percent was transferred to other provinces, while 60 percent was exported to international markets (Sun Ching-chih 1959b, 26). Anhui was the third largest producer of sesame in the 1950s with most of the sown area concentrated in Fouyang Prefecture in the northwest part of the province (Sun Ching-chih 1959b, 79). By the mid-1970s sesame sown area was down dramatically in the most efficient producing regions. In Honan, for example, the 1977 sown area had fallen by more than 50 percent to 185,000 hectares (NCNA October 29, 1978).

Rapeseed, China's second most important source of edible vegetable oil, was concentrated in the Southwest and to a lesser extent in Kiangsi in central China. In 1957 Szechuan was the highest-yielding and strongest comparative advantage producer and grew about 30 percent of the country's entire rapeseed crop. It was, not surprisingly, the largest supplier of rapeseed oil to other provinces (Sun Ching-chih 1960, 40). Kweichow was the country's second largest producer in the mid-1950s, indicating a high degree of specialization since the province's sown area is among the smallest of all provinces. The major producing region was Tsuni Prefecture in the northern part of the province. Kweichow, too, was a major rapeseed oil exporter (Sun Ching-chih 1960, 117). Yunnan's rape production was only slightly less than Kweichow's, and a large share of the processed oil was exported from the province (Sun Ching-chih 1960, 521).

Throughout the Southwest, area sown to rapeseed and other economic crops was depressed in the aftermath of the Great Leap Forward. But that shrinkage was reversed after 1962 when specialized production again was encouraged. In Yunnan, for example, the area sown to economic crops grew by almost two-thirds between 1962 and 1965 (Liu Shih-chiang 1980, 31–2). Rape sown area, however, had not recovered fully to the level of the 1950s. After 1965, emphasis on foodgrains led to a continuous squeeze on the area sown to rape and peanuts in Yunnan. By 1978 both sown area and production had declined by more than half compared to 1957. In 1978 production had fallen to 1.7 kilograms per capita compared with 4 kilograms in 1965. By 1978, although Yunnan had become a net importer of vegetable oils from other provinces, per capita consumption had declined. Imports in 1979 of 5,000 tons were quite small compared to the 33,000-ton decline in production between 1965 and 1978. But they were used almost exclusively to feed Yunnan's nonagricultural population and comprised fully half of their supply (Fu Shih-min 1980, 70). Data for Kweichow are sparse, but there also the peak level of output was achieved in 1966 and was not surpassed again until 1978.

In the late 1960s Szechuan provincial authorities, as part of the broad national policy of emphasizing foodgrain production, began to push a triple-cropping pattern of wheat–rice–rice. Since rape traditionally had been planted as a winter crop in conjunction with a single crop of midseason rice in the summer, it was displaced in the new cropping pattern. In 1977, when triple-cropping of grain reached its peak, the area devoted to rapeseed production was marginally less than in 1957. After Chao Tzu-yang became the first party secretary of the province in late 1975 and personally took the initiative to reduce the bureaucratic pressure for triple-cropping, rapeseed sown area began to rise (NCNA September 27, 1978). Between 1976 and 1980 rape area rose by 100,000 hectares to total 430,000 hectares (NCNA June 25, 1978; Szechuan Provincial Service May 21, 1980). That plus improved production incentives led to rapid growth – rapeseed output doubled in the province between 1976 and 1980 (Szechuan Statistical Bureau 1980; 1981).

Output of soybeans, another high-value oil-bearing crop, fell dramatically during production planning. Soybeans were a major export crop before the war – in 1938–40 sown area was 63 percent of the world total. Prior to the war China regularly supplied 90 percent of world soybean exports – 750,000 to 1.7 million tons of soybeans and 50,000 to 125,000 tons of soybean cakes. Although soybeans were cultivated widely, China's dominant position in the world market was made possible by the spectacular rise of soybean production in Manchuria after the area was opened to Han Chinese colonization in 1860 (Eckstein, Chao, and Chang 1974). Output was depressed during World War II, but grew rapidly between 1949 and 1952. Although national output failed to recover to the prewar level, the Northeast did reemerge as the predominant source of soybeans during the First Plan. Its share of production was over a third, rising to a peak of 36 percent in 1957 – comparable to its average share of 38 percent of national output in 1931–37. As is shown in Table 2.7, the northernmost provinces of the Northeast – Heilungkiang and Kirin – were major producers, with the highest share of sown area, a strong comparative advantage, and the largest output. Significant concentrated production in the North China Plain, including the Huaipei area of Anhui, also was based on comparative advantage. Specialization facilitated a high rate of marketing, about 50 percent, and a resurgence of exports to international markets that averaged 1.05 million tons in the First Plan (State Statistical Bureau 1982, VIII-47; Wu Leng 1980, 30).

Soybean production declined beginning in 1958. In 1965, sown area and output were 33 and almost 40 percent less, respectively, than in 1957. Sown area declined continuously after 1965, reaching a low point of 6.7 million hectares in 1976 (Wu Leng 1980), 22 percent less than 1965 and only 52 percent of the 1957 area (Agricultural Yearbook Compilation Commission 1981, 348–9). Because of a slightly rising trend in yields after 1965, total output grew slowly despite declining sown area. But growth was very slow and in 1976, although production was up 8 percent over 1965, it was a third less than in 1957. The decline in output between 1957 and 1976 of almost all of the leading producers exceeded the national average. Production in Kirin and Liaoning dropped by 50 percent or more, in Shantung by 70 percent, and in Anhui by 40 percent. Hopei and Honan, also leading producers in the 1950s, suffered output declines of 40 and 60 percent respectively between 1957 and 1976 (Wu Leng 1980, 29). Only Heilungkiang, among the most efficient producers, appears not to have had a disproportionate decline in soybean production.

Because production was dispersed more widely, the marketing rate for soybeans was halved to 25 percent. Lower production and less marketing led, not surprisingly, to reduced exports. China's share of the world soybean market had fallen from the prewar level of 90 percent to 1 percent by 1976. Net exports to the world market in 1978 were only 190,000 tons, less than a fifth the level of the First Plan (Wu Leng 1980, 30).

Because soybeans have been treated since 1958 as a cereal crop rather than a source of edible vegetable oils for statistical, planning, and procurement purposes, declining production cannot be attributed simply to the emphasis on grain production (Yang T'ing-hsiu, 1981b). Rather, the dismal performance seems to be the result of inadequate economic incentives and bureaucratically determined cropping practices. After 1958 soybeans were accepted in meeting procurement targets on the same basis as grain. Since procurement targets were specified in terms of weight and failed to reflect the higher value of soybeans, and since absolute grain yields exceed those for soybeans, even in specialized regions, that policy stimulated a shift of sown area out of soybeans. Soybeans frequently were intercropped with corn – a practice that depressed yields by 20 to 30 percent because of the competition for sun and other resources. By the 1970s it was no longer economical to grow soybeans in many areas and sown area targets for the crop were underfulfilled.

Curiously, Heilungkiang was the only province to escape the trend of declining soybean sown area and production. Data for the 1950s through 1976 are not available, but sown area in 1977 was less than 5 percent below the level of 1957 (Central Intelligence Agency 1969; Heilungkiang Provincial Service December 14, 1978) and yields in 1979 were 1.1 (metric) tons per hectare, the same as 1957 (Agricultural Yearbook Compilation Commission 1981, 107). The sustained production of soybeans may be due to the unusually large role of state farms in the province and the province's grain surplus status. China's state farms lost money in every year from 1967 through 1978 (Ts'ai Hsin-i 1981). Since the losses of these farms were subsidized by the state budget, through the Ministry of State Farms and Land Reclamation, and workers were paid wages rather than sharing net revenues of the producing and accounting unit as in collective agriculture, the absence of economic incentives did not lead them to cut soybean sown area. In 1978, for example, fully a third of the province's soybean area was under the management of state farms (Heilungkiang Provincial Service, December 14, 1978; August 14, 1979).

Moreover, Heilungkiang had the highest level of per capita cereal production and was a major exporter of cereals during the 1950s.[33] There was no need to shift acreage into corn or wheat in order to become self-sufficient.

As in the case of cotton and sugar, the irrational allocation of domestic resources depressed the output of oil-bearing seeds far below the level that could have been achieved with the same level of current inputs. Consequently per capita consumption of vegetable oils in 1978 was one-third less than in 1957 (Liu Fang-yü 1980, 20). Even reduced consumption standards were made possible only through significant imports from abroad. Although China was a large net vegetable oil exporter in the 1950s and continued modest exports into the early 1970s, the pursuit of regional self-sufficiency led to initial net imports by the mid-1970s. By the late 1970s China was one of the world's largest importers of refined vegetable oils and soybeans.

Vegetables

Enforcement of grain self-sufficiency was not limited to remote animal husbandry regions of the Northwest or grain-deficient areas of the North China Plain. It extended even to periurban areas where farmers historically had specialized in the production of high-value vegetables for the urban market and had depended on foodgrains purchased in rural markets or from the state. But these sources of grain were curtailed in the late 1960s and early to mid-1970s, and many suburban communes had to shift sown area and current inputs into grain production (Editorial 1980; Ku Wei-chin 1979; NCNA November 8, 1979; Myers 1978, 324).

Reductions in vegetable sown area attributed to the policy that vegetable producers also be self-sufficient in grain supplies were widespread, but it is impossible to estimate the reduction in vegetable sown area. Reductions are usually reported to have occurred for only a few years in the early to mid-1970s. One indicator of the downward pressure on vegetable area is the expansion of sown area after the reintroduction of specialized production in the late 1970s. In Shanghai, for example, vegetable sown area expanded by more than a fourth in 1977–79 (NCNA November 8, 1979).

Although aggregate data on vegetable production have not been published, vegetable supplies in many cities appear to have been shrinking in the 1970s. However, it is difficult to determine if reduced sown area was a significant source of these problems, since declining relative purchase prices and inadequate state marketing arrangements further discouraged vegetable production (Chang Kuang-yu and Ch'iu Yung sheng 1980; Sun Yu-ch'i 1979). Consequently, vegetable production in the late 1970s was said to be inadequate to meet demand and attempts to meet demand from more distant production locations increased transportation costs and increased losses due to spoilage (NCNA February 2, 1979).

Triple-cropping of grain

The imposition of irrational, inefficient cropping patterns was not limited to regions specializing in nongrain crops. Even areas with a comparative advantage in grain did not always escape the losses associated with production planning. The most widely known case was the imposed expansion of triple-cropping beginning in the late 1960s. By the mid-1960s grain yields in several highly productive double-cropping regions had reached a plateau. Within these regions, however, there were smaller areas that successfully had pursued triple-cropping. That pattern typically included double-cropped rice followed by an overwintering crop of wheat or barley. Total yield in these small areas was higher than in double-cropped regions. Moreover, triple-cropping in these regions had been adopted voluntarily, suggesting that it led to higher peasant incomes as well. Triple-cropping appeared to present a solution to the stagnation of cereal output in double-cropped areas.

Expansion of triple-cropped area frequently led to increased inefficiency because it was undertaken when the sole criterion for judging the success of local cadres was the level of grain unit yields achieved per year and when, as discussed above, overwhelming emphasis was placed on grain production. Enormous pressure was brought to bear on local cadres to raise yields irrespective of whether or not the increase in costs (given the price structure) entailed with greater intensity of cropping more than offset the value of increased output. In many areas pressure for increased output led to a rise in production costs as a share of the value of output, declining factor productivity, and lower farm incomes than under the older, well-established patterns of double-cropping. That development is not surprising since, under conditions of short-run rising marginal costs, the pressure for increasing output will lead to production at a point where marginal costs exceed marginal revenue and where net income is less than would be achieved under unconstrained maximization of net revenues.

The best evidence of the imposition of triple-cropping comes from Kiangsu and Szechuan provinces, although it also appears to have been a source of inefficiency in central China, along the Yangtse River, and elsewhere in the Southwest. In the rich Yangtse River Delta area of Suchou Prefecture in Kiangsu Province the multiple-cropping rate expanded by 30 percent between 1966 and 1976 as a result of the spread of triple-cropping, which was limited to 15 percent of cultivated area in the prefecture in 1966. Expansion of triple-cropping was made possible by growing early rice as a third crop on 200,000 hectares of additional land. Over the decade grain output grew by 20 percent, from 3.05 to 3.70 million (metric) tons or by 1.9 percent per year (Chi Pu 1979; Hsiung I 1979; Li Erh-huang 1979; Lu Shih-chien 1979; Yang Jui-ch'un and Cheng Li-chih 1979).

Expanded multiple-cropping increased physical output, seemingly consistent with the state's objective. But greater output led to neither an increase in the share of grain output delivered to the state nor increases in peasant-foodgrain consumption or net farm income, even in the short run. First, to shift from a rice–wheat to a rice–rice–winter grain cropping pattern it was generally necessary to substitute barley for wheat as the winter crop. Because barley matures more rapidly, its substitution for wheat makes it physically possible to subsequently cultivate two rice crops. But the milling rate of barley is 15 percent less than that for wheat, and the value of the milled product is less than wheat flour. In Suchou 100,000 hectares of wheat land were converted to barley production between 1970 and 1976, and although the summer grain harvest increased by 8,915 tons, the output value declined by 8.468 million yuan because of the lower value of barley. The opportunity costs of the change in cropping pattern were greater than this since the increased supplies of fertilizer used and the improvements in drainage would have yielded a greater return if they had been used to grow wheat. Second, the triple-cropping pattern necessitates planting early indica rice, which yields 4 to 5 percent less polished rice than late rice varieties. Furthermore, when the additional seed requirements for the third crop were taken into account (all output data are inclusive of seed), in many areas the advantage of triple- over double-cropping became marginal at best.

The share of output delivered to the state declined from 39.2 to 34.0 percent over the decade. The absolute quantity of foodgrains purchased by the state rose by 60,000 tons, but the value of purchases declined because reduced quantities of high-value wheat and japonica rice more than offset the increased purchases of low-value barley and indica rice (Yang Jui-ch'un and Cheng Li-chih 1979).

Peasant foodgrain consumption also declined. The average per capita quantity of unmilled grain distributed in Suchou increased by only 1 kilogram over the decade when triple-cropping was adopted widely, but consumption of processed grain declined because of the lower milling rates of the grains required for the triple-cropping system. In many areas the increased purchased inputs required for triple-cropping also led to a reduction in net per capita farm income.

Over the longer run triple-cropping based on double-cropped rice had other disadvantages. Soil quality of triple-cropped fields deteriorates rapidly due to compaction that affects yields of both wheat and rice. The use of chemical fertilizers must be at least doubled because nitrogen is released more slowly due to the low temperatures prevailing in the period of early rice cultivation and the lack of time for adequate drying of the soil. Continuous cultivation required by triple-cropping also increases the vulnerability of crops to insect infestation. Finally, in areas where nitrogen-fixing green manures (azolla) had been planted as an overwintering crop to enhance soil fertility, the early planting date for the first rice crop required plowing under these nitrogen-fixing plants well before the optimal date. Consequently, green nitrogen-fixing manures were grown on a declining share of the cultivated land.

Although per capita food consumption declined only marginally in Suchou, the drive to increase triple-cropping in Szechuan beginning in the early 1970s contributed to a major agricultural crisis by the mid-1970s. Szechuan in the 1950s was China's largest producer of single-crop midseason rice, planted after the harvest of an overwintering crop, such as wheat or rapeseed, and harvested in the late fall (Central Intelligence Agency 1969). As early as 1955 the multiple-cropping rate in the province exceeded 1.5. But in most parts of the province a short day length, low temperatures, and excessive autumn rains make it difficult to add a second crop of rice to this well-established double-cropping pattern (Fei Hsiao-t'ung, 1979, 62; NCNA August 4, 1974). For example, in the Ch'engtu Plain, the major area where the expansion of triple-cropping was attempted, the last day on which it is considered safe to plant late rice is a full two weeks earlier than in Suchou Prefecture in Kiangsu. These limitations had prevented any significant increase in multiple-cropping. The multiple-cropping indexes in the province in 1957 and 1973 were identical (Central Intelligence Agency 1969; NCNA December 6, 1973).

Despite these limitations, meetings were held in late 1973 and in 1974 to promote double-crop rice production to expand the triple-cropped area (NCNA December 6, 1973, August 4, 1974; Szechuan Provincial Service November 9, 1974). Party cadres at these meetings insisted that the success of some localities in triple-cropping could be generalized over a wide area. The area of early rice was increased by more than a third in 1974. Much of this was followed by late rice and then an overwintering crop. Successful expansion of triple-cropping would have required substantial increases in the supply of labor, fertilizer, and most other inputs, but most of these inputs were in short supply. As a result, the net incremental output achieved through triple-cropping was small. Gains achieved through a second crop of rice were offset by a decline in yields achieved on overwintering crops and on the lower yields of late rice compared to midseason rice that had been cultivated previously, since only marginally increased inputs were spread over three rather than two crops. Costs per unit output rose and peasant incentives were reduced.

The consequence of the imposition of an irrational cropping pattern was a marked change in the production of foodgrains. Because production data for the first half of the 1970s have not been released, it is difficult to know how severe the crisis was. Food "shortages" are first said to have appeared in 1974. But the full extent of the crisis was evident in 1976 when, for the first time, the central government had to supply 600,000 (metric) tons of foodgrains from other provinces to avert widespread famine in Szechuan (NCNA September 27, 1978). That was a marked change from the First Plan when Szechuan's grain exports, 8.25 million tons or 1.65 million tons per year, were the largest of any province (Donnithorne 1970; Li Ssu-heng 1981, 56; Sun Ching-chih 1960, 26), and perhaps even from as recently as the mid-1960s when the province is said to have been a large net exporter (Fei Hsiao-t'ung 1979, 59).

The province's change from a large net exporter to a significant importer was not surprising given trends in production. By 1976, the first year for which data are available after 1966, production was only 24.85 million tons, 12 percent above 1966. Far more significant, output was only 7 percent or 1.6 million tons more than in 1957, whereas the population over the same period increased by a third, from 72.1 to 95.7 million (NCNA March 10, 1980; Szechuan Statistical Bureau 1980; Walker 1977b, 4).

In December 1975 Chao Tzu-yang, who subsequently became China's premier, became first secretary of the Szechuan Provincial Communist Party Committee (NCNA September 27, 1978). He launched a full-scale investigation of the province's agricultural situation, visiting more than a hundred counties in the province. In 1976 Chao proposed the restoration of the traditional wheat–rice double-cropping system. In 1977 double-cropped rice acreage was reduced by 266,000 hectares. Triple-cropped area continued to decline in 1978 as production team autonomy gradually was restored. By

1977–78 the cropping pattern was similar to the mid-1950s, with about a quarter-million hectares of double-cropped rice area, down from a peak of two-thirds-million hectares in 1975. While grain sown area was reduced in 1976–79, output rose by 29 percent, over 7 million tons, the level of per capita foodgrain availability of the mid-1950s was restored, and modest exports resumed in 1979 (Li Ssu-heng 1981, 56). Moreover, output of oil-bearing crops increased by three-quarters, cotton by a third, sugarcane by 100 percent, and so forth (Szechuan Statistical Bureau 1980). While it is not possible fully to disentangle the causes of this marked recovery, it appears that the reversal of an irrational cropping pattern, the gradual (though still not complete) restoration of team level autonomy in production decisions, and provision of more adequate incentives were more important than the increased flow of modern inputs after 1976.

The costs of production planning

In aggregate terms the costs of increased inefficiency arising from decreased specialization and the imposition of ill-conceived cropping patterns are suggested by the sharp increase in costs as a percentage of the gross value of farm output and by declining factor productivity in 1967–77. Evidence on costs comes from farm surveys and on aggregate data, both of which show that costs rose after 1965. Rising costs as a share of farm output, however, reflect both increased inefficiency and an increased indirect tax burden in the form of increased sales of overpriced farm inputs by the state to the collective sector. It is impossible to separate these two causes. The burden of increased indirect taxes in the form of price manipulation will be discussed in Chapter 3.

Three major farm surveys were undertaken in 1976–78 (Chiang Hsing-wei 1980). The first study of 2,162 production teams revealed that grain yields had risen a respectable 35 percent from 1.74 (metric) tons per hectare in 1965 to 2.37 tons per hectare in 1976. But during the same period, production costs rose 54 percent. A second major survey of 1,296 teams in 1976 is less satisfactory because it does not establish the level of costs in the mid-1960s. By 1976, however, production costs for six types of grain were found to be 11.6 yuan per 50 kilograms of output while the purchase price of grain was only 10.74 yuan per 50 kilograms. Net losses were 7.4 percent of costs. A similar situation prevailed in 1977 in 302 teams where cotton was grown; the average cotton procurement price was 2 percent less than production costs.

In these cost calculations labor is included at a constant accounting price, probably the national uniform standard of .80 or .87 yuan per day, that is

Table 2.8. *Nonlabor costs as a percentage of gross farm output, 1957–79*

Year	Percentage
1957	26.5
1965	27.3
1974	31.9
1975	33.6
1976	35.5
1977	35.7
1978	34.4
1979	33.6

Notes: Nonlabor costs include production costs (seeds, chemical fertilizers, insecticides, costs of irrigation and mechanized plowing, repair of farm implements, purchases of some hand tools, etc.); management fees (office expenses such as stationery, pencils, forms, and management fees paid to higher administrative levels); and other expenditures (interest, losses on materials in storage, etc.) (Chang Min-ju and Hsü Shu-keng 1981, 205–6). It is exclusive of depreciation.
Sources: Ministry of Agriculture Policy Research Office (1980, 102–4), Agricultural Yearbook Compilation Commission (1981, 382, 383), Chia Hsiu-yen (1979, 15), Li Ch'eng-jui and Tso Yüan (1979, 8–9), Yüeh Wei (1981, 47), Wang Chen-chih and Wei Yün-lang (1980, 7).

closely tied to the value of a day's labor in the base year of the calculations (Yao Hsien-kuo 1981, 109). Thus when costs exceed income, producing units do not incur operating losses, but the value of a day's labor, internal reinvestment, or collectively provided consumption decline. For example, the value of a labor-day declined by 20 percent to .56 yuan in the first survey cited above.

The national data, shown in Table 2.8, confirm the rising cost trend shown in the farm surveys and support the negative assessment of the productivity performance of agriculture after 1965. Whereas costs as a share of farm output were roughly constant during the period of price planning of the 1950s (Ishikawa 1965, 56), they rose after 1965. Costs as a share of output were 26.5 percent in 1957 and 27.3 percent in 1965, but then rose to a peak of 35.7 percent in 1977. The implications of this are quite far-reaching. While the official data on gross value of output, measured in constant prices, show agriculture grew at an average annual rate of 3.7 percent per year between 1965 and 1977 (State Statistical Bureau 1982c, VIII-9), that rate of growth is upward-biased. When growth is measured on a net (value-added) basis, farm output in this twelve-year period grew only 35 percent, not 50 percent as the gross value data show. In per capita terms the gross value data show an average 1.5 percent annual growth, whereas the net value data show virtual stagnation, four-tenths of 1 percent annually. Moreover, as will be discussed in Chapter 3, Chinese cost procedures account inadequately for depreciation and thus understate the increase in costs, since the farm sector's capital stock has grown since the mid-1960s. A proper cost accounting might show no growth or even a slight decline in per capita net farm output between 1965 and 1977.

The reemergence of price planning since 1977

Far more salient to the Chinese leadership than rising production costs, which largely were borne by the peasantry, were the soaring outlays of scarce foreign exchange for imported agricultural commodities and a crisis in food consumption in the mid-1970s. Bulging imports of grain, edible vegetable oils, sugar, and cotton exceeded U.S. $2.5 billion by 1978, absorbing over a fourth of foreign exchange earnings (U.S. Department of Agriculture 1981, 30). Despite growing imports, the food situation was less favorable than during the mid-1950s. As will be discussed in Chapter 4, average caloric intake was still below the level of the mid-1950s, and the distribution of food may have become somewhat more unequal. Those developments were due to reduced per capita production of critical nongrain crops and the combination of increased regional production disparities and declining rates of marketing and interregional grain transfers.

The policy response to the rising share of food products in the import bill and to the crisis of food consumption and productivity was to shift toward the use of price planning. That shift in policy coincides with the political reemergence of individuals such as Ch'en Yün, a critic of the Maoist approach to agricultural development and a leading advocate of price planning and increased marketing and specialization during the 1950s. Ch'en, of course, was one of the major architects of the renewed emphasis on price incentives and marketing in the early 1960s (Lardy and Lieberthal 1983).

Although important elements of production planning remain and there is also important regional variation in the pace of change; on balance there has been a fundamental change. Many of the elements of the shift toward price planning have been widely noted, whereas others are somewhat more subtle and less widely noticed outside China. They include increased use of price incentives, greater freedom for production units to choose their cropping patterns, and a resurgence of private marketing of agricultural and subsidiary products in both rural and urban areas. Moreover, private plots have been reinstituted and expanded, and production incentives have been strengthened by reducing the size of production units. In most regions farming is now carried out under variants of the "responsibility system" in which farm households or small groups of households contract with the production team to meet specified production goals.

Price incentives

The pivotal element of the new policy was the first increase in state procurement prices for major farm products in twelve years. The price increases carried out beginning in 1978 were marked by four characteristics. First, they were substantial, raising procurement prices in 1981 to an average of 42 percent above 1977 (Table 3.4). The official price level of manufactured goods sold in rural areas rose only 3 percent, so that the terms of trade faced by the farm sector rose 38 percent in four years.[34]

Second, the state's price adjustments were not uniform across crops. For the first time in more than a decade the state in 1978 cautiously but systematically began adjusting relative farm prices in an attempt to influence the composition of output. Prices were increased in 1978 for cotton, rapeseed, and animal husbandry and aquatic products (Appendix 3; NCNA July 1, 1979). There also was a major price increase for soybeans.[35] These price changes preceded the more widely publicized price increases of 1979 that covered eighteen major product categories, including all cereal crops (State Council 1979; State Statistical Bureau 1979b). The response to increased procurement prices in 1978, reflected in Table 2.9, was an increase in the area sown to cotton, oil-bearing seed crops, and soybeans. This analysis is not meant to imply either that changes in acreage were solely a response to changes in relative prices or that the peasants fully adjusted to the new set of prices in a single year. Area sown to cotton and other noncereal crops is still subject to centralized planning and control. Moreover, because marketing of cereals, both public and private, still was depressed, many producers of economic crops could not purchase the cereals that would allow them to take full advantage of the new relative prices. Policy, however, differed with the previous decade or more in two respects. First, the central government consciously used price incentives as one policy instrument to achieve desired changes in cropping patterns. Second, the state improved the access of growers of commercial crops to cereals for their own consumption.

In 1979 quota procurement prices were raised 15 percent for soybeans and cotton, 20 percent for grains, and 25 percent for oilseed crops (Appen-

Table 2.9 Cropping patterns, 1976–81 (millions of hectares)

	Grain				Economic Crops						
							Oil seeds				
	Total	Rice	Wheat	Soybeans	Total[a]	Cotton	Total	Peanuts	Rapeseed	Sugarcane	Sugar beet
1976	120.74	36.22	28.42	6.69	—	4.93	5.79	1.84	2.35	.54	.36
1977	120.40	35.53	28.07	6.84	13.47	4.84	5.64	1.69	2.22	.51	.35
1978	120.59	34.42	29.18	7.14	14.47	4.87	6.20	1.77	2.60	.55	.33
1979	119.26	33.87	29.54	7.25	14.77	4.51	7.05	2.07	2.79	.51	.33
1980	117.23	33.88	28.89	7.22	15.92	4.92	7.93	2.34	2.84	.48	.44
1981	114.95	33.30	28.30	8.02	17.56	5.19	9.13	2.47	3.80	.55	.44

[a]Excludes vegetable sown area.

Sources: Agricultural Yearbook Compilation Commission (1981, 34, 35, 97, 348), State Statistical Bureau (1982b, 139, 140), Wu Leng (1980, 29), Chan Wu and Liu Wen-p'u (1982, 28).

dix 3). Again the responses seem rational. The relative profitability of cotton and cotton sown area both declined marginally compared to 1978. Oilseed production became more profitable relative to other crops, and sown area expanded significantly in 1979, beyond the already larger 1978 sown area. Although the procurement price of grains rose relative to cotton, it was reduced relative to oil crops, and grain sown area declined, although by proportionally less than cotton. Most of the decrease in grain sown area, as discussed further below, was due to a reduction in the area of double-cropped rice.

In 1980 and 1981 the state continued to manipulate relative crop prices, raising procurement prices for cotton, sheep- and goatskins, jute and ambary hemp, timber, raw lacquer, and tung oil in 1980 (State Statistical Bureau 1981a, 17) and for soybeans, tobacco, and vegetables in 1981 (State Statistical Bureau 1982). These price changes had predictable effects on allocation of land, output levels, and marketing rates. Since grain prices were unchanged in 1980, the relative profitability of cotton again rose, as it had in 1978, and sown area expanded. In 1981 tobacco and soybean sown area rose 48 and 11 percent, respectively (State Statistical Bureau 1982b, 139–40). As will be discussed in Chapter 4, cotton acreage continued to rise in 1981, though its relative price was unchanged. That was due to an increase in domestic trade that led to an increase in the supplies of cereals in traditional cotton-producing regions.

Furthermore, in 1980 the state began to revise payment practices in a manner that effectively raised further prices of farm products subject to above-quota purchase. Prior to 1980 all deliveries during the year by production units were credited at the basic procurement price. Not until the end of the year were peasants paid the premium for the above-quota portion of deliveries. Because large deliveries to the state of winter wheat, early rice, rapeseed, and so on are made in the late spring or early summer, production units in most regions had to wait several months for the premium payments on deliveries. Under the new system estimates are made of deliveries from the fall harvest and producing units are paid at time of delivery for that portion of the delivery of summer grains that is expected to fall ultimately into the above-quota category (NCNA June 3, 1980; Wen Shao-hsing 1981, 223). The new system was tried on an experimental basis in 1980 and approved for general use beginning in 1982 (NCNA June 7, 1982).

The third characteristic of the price changes was their provision of increased incentives for marketing. In 1970 the state initiated uniform 20 percent premium payments for deliveries of grain above the basic "quota deliveries."[36] Because the quota delivery levels were fixed for multiyear periods, incremental marketings could be sold at the premium price, in theory providing an incentive for increasing output and sales to the state. In 1972 the premium was raised to 30 and in 1979 to 50 percent. A premium of 30 percent for deliveries of cotton and oilseeds in excess of the quota amounts also was instituted in 1979.

Finally, the state instituted a fourth price category for procured cereals – negotiated prices. That category had been used by commercial departments in the 1950s for the purchase of subsidiary agricultural products, but generally had not been used for the purchase of grain crops. Once a producing unit has fulfilled tax levies, quota purchase targets, and over-quota purchase targets, it may sell additional amounts at prices determined by mutual agreement with the state. Negotiated prices appear to be closely related to market prices prevailing in newly reestablished rural periodic markets, discussed below.

Production unit autonomy and specialized production

Price incentives alone could be expected to have little effect on the decisions of producing units unless production planning was relaxed. In 1978 a campaign to enhance the decision-making powers of production teams was initiated. That shift was accompanied by a rediscovery of the principle of comparative advantage and encouragement of specialized production. The goal of achieving regional self-sufficiency in foodgrains was somewhat relaxed, at least in the short run; state procurement of foodgrains for resupply to rural areas specializing in commercial crops increased somewhat; and private marketing has flourished with the reopening of rural markets. Evidence of these changes is suggested by changes in cropping patterns, both among and within provinces, that have been under way since 1978.

The most notable change in cropping patterns is a marginal shift from grain production to commercial crops such as sugar, cotton, and oil-bearing seeds in many regions. That shift in the allocation of sown area, stimulated by increases in prices of commercial crops relative to cereals and better production and marketing incentives, resulted in a more balanced pattern of agricultural growth. Grain output increased 15 percent in four years (1978–81), but the growth of other crops accelerated relative to grain, reversing the trend of 1966–77: oilseed output rose 154 percent, sugarcane and beet output by 67 and 159 percent, respectively, and cotton output by 49 percent (State Statistical Bureau 1979a; 1980a; 1981a; 1982). Thus the pattern of growth in 1978–81 confounded the Maoist view that presumed commercial crop production would expand only at the cost of grain. Grain and commercial crop production both have expanded markedly.

On balance changes in the composition of sown area suggest that production teams have greater freedom to choose their own cropping patterns, taking into account relative profitability. The best example is shrinkage of double-cropped rice area.[37] Nationally 1976 was the peak year of rice sown area (State Statistical Bureau 1982b, 139). Chao Tzu-yang's policies in Szechuan, when he was first party secretary, led to large reductions in early rice sown area in 1977 and 1978. On almost half this land a single crop of midseason rice replaced the previously sown double-cropped rice. Elsewhere in Szechuan rice paddy land was converted to dryland grain crops or industrial crops. Early rice planting was reduced by almost 300,000 hectares in Kiangsu Province between 1976, when the peak of 867,000 hectares was reached, and 1979, when the area was 600,000 hectares (Kiangsu Provincial Service 1979; NCNA August 24, 1976). In many areas of Kiangsu farm incomes were raised by reverting to traditional double-cropping patterns involving only a single crop of rice. In Suchou Prefecture double-crop rice area fell from 267,000 to 136,000 hectares between 1976 and 1981 and triple-cropping declined from 86 to 46 percent of sown area (Sun Ming 1982, 33). Nationally rice sown area declined 2.92 million hectares, about 8 percent, between 1976 and 1981 (Table 2.9). Double-cropping of rice has been reduced in areas where either climatic conditions or resource constraints make it uneconomic compared to alternative patterns of land use.

Most of the changes in cropping patterns that can be documented, like the case of sugar discussed above and other examples discussed in Chapter 4, are consistent with the hypothesis of greater specialization along lines of comparative advantage. Oil-bearing seed and sugarcane and sugar beet sown area grew most rapidly in high-yielding areas – peanuts expanding most rapidly in Shantung and Honan, rapeseed in Szechuan, sunflower seed in the Northeast and Inner Mongolia, sugar beets in Heilungkiang, sugarcane in Fukien. For sugarcane, although sown area expanded rapidly in regions of comparative advantage, national sown area changed little because sown area in non–comparative advantage regions declined. These regions earlier had initiated or expanded their sugar area because of inadequate supplies from specialized producers in comparative advantage regions (Chang Ch'iao-ling 1981).

Although changes in sown area among provinces are most readily identifiable, equally significant reallocations within provinces also have taken place. Since the cropping area in many provinces exceeds 5 million hectares and

occurs across heterogeneous growing conditions, these changes are fundamental, raising the efficiency of farming inputs. In Hopei and Shantung the
proportion of cotton area grown in the prefectures with the greatest comparative advantage in cotton production has risen. High-yielding rice-growing
areas in Kwangtung are contracting for grain–oil exchanges with areas within
the province that have a comparative advantage in oilseed production. A few
of these changes are analyzed in greater detail in Chapter 4.

Marketing

Increased specialization is, of course, possible only if the state ensures supplies of cereal crops to regions producing nongrain crops and of nongrain
products to areas specialized in grain production. Provision of adequate
grain supplies to growers of sugar, cotton, and other noncereal crops has
improved, but may still constrain specialized production. Although state
policy explicitly encourages specialization, the rate of marketing of foodgrains
through state channels has increased only modestly in response to the new
incentives for increased deliveries to the state. The small increase in public
marketing can be explained by the preference of peasants in some regions to
sell commodities on periodic markets, where prices are well above even the
state's over-quota purchase prices (discussed in Chapter 3); a reduction in
state procurement quotas as a relief measure in China's poorest counties
(discussed in Chapter 4); and an inability of the state commercial system to
purchase more grain both because of constrained storage and processing capacity and a lack of incremental budgetary support that such purchases
require, given the commitment to stable urban retail prices (discussed in
Chapter 5).

   Although publicly marketed grain has grown slowly, reopening of rural
periodic markets facilitated an increase in specialized production. The quantities of grain sold in these markets are significant. In 1979 and again in 1980
private sales were 5 million (metric) tons (NCNA March 2, 1980; Ministry of
Food Research Office 1981, 13). Although that is less than 2 percent of
output, it is about 10 percent of the grain collected as taxes or procured by
the state as quota and over-quota deliveries and 33 percent of resales.[38]
Although little, if any, of this grain would enter long-distance transport,
increased private local marketing of grain and industrial crops and sideline
products facilitates specialized production within local markets.

   In addition to reopening rural periodic markets, the state has expanded
the number of long-term commitments for the delivery of state-procured
grain to regions of specialized agricultural production. The first example,

the supply of 100,000 tons of grain annually to Fukien Province beginning in 1976, as discussed earlier, led to significant growth of specialized production. It appears to be a model for similar subsequent arrangements.

In August 1980 the State Council, China's highest governmental organization, approved a five-year commitment of 225,000 tons of state-procured grain per year to Hainan Island for sale to producers of tropical crops and plants (T'ang Chen-yang and Wang Chang-hu 1980). The island, with an area of 34,000 square kilometers and a 1980 population of 5.4 million, in the 1950s was a major producer of rubber, coffee, coconuts, pepper, sisal, and other important economic crops. The share of cultivated land allocated to economic crops rose from 4 percent in 1953 to 19 percent in 1956 when policy emphasized specialization along lines of comparative advantage (Sun Ching-chih 1959a, 58). The island was China's largest source of natural rubber, produced predominantly on state rubber farms. The staff and workers of these rubber plantations and a large portion of the rest of the rural population depended on cereals supplied by the state from external sources. The island was a net importer of foodgrains throughout the First Plan. In 1954, for example, imports were 130,500 tons, equivalent to 18.1 percent of the island's grain production (Sun Ching-chih 1959a, 58).

During the first half of the 1970s, however, farmers on Hainan were compelled to reduce their dependency on cereals supplied by the state. Economic crops were neglected and in many areas rubber tree plantations were destroyed to expand the area sown to rice.

The commitment of 225,000 tons of grain per year is substantial relative both to the island's 1979 production and to its population. For example, 225,000 tons is 26 percent of the 970,000 tons of grain produced on the island in 1979 (T'ang Chen-yang and Wang Chang-hu 1980). It is sufficient to provide the basic cereal consumption of about 1 million people. Moreover, the state has supplied the increased credits necessary to finance the expansion of state rubber plantations. Communes on the island also have altered their cropping patterns, sowing more area to sugarcane, oil-bearing crops, and medicinal herbs.

The central government made a similar if somewhat smaller long-term commitment to Shensi Province to accelerate production of cotton and rapeseed. The province has been guaranteed an annual inflow of grain of 160,000 tons and, in turn, will sell this grain in regions of specialized production (NCNA August 27, 1980). In the late 1960s and 1970s because of the emphasis on local self-sufficiency in food grains, cotton production was increasingly dispersed away from comparative advantage regions within the province and output declined. Although cotton sown area was not expanded, beginning in 1980 cotton production was concentrated in Tali, Lint'ung, Weinan, and Hua counties (in Weinan Prefecture) and in Hsienyang municipality (in Hsienyang Prefecture) all in east–central Shensi. Cotton production on 19,000 hectares of sown area in thirteen other lower-yielding counties was eliminated. Similarly, rapeseed production expanded by 20,000 hectares in the Hanchung Basin and in the counties within Paochi Prefecture (NCNA August 27, 1980).

Finally, the state cautiously has permitted long-term trade contracts between specialized producers both within and between provinces. These barter contracts appear to be arranged apart from the long-term commitments made by the central government. High-yielding sugarcane areas in Fukien, Kwantung, and Kwangsi trade sugar for grain produced in high-yielding grain-growing areas in the Yangtse River Delta. In a sharp departure from past administrative practice, in which interprovincial trade was all tightly controlled by the central government, these exchanges appear to be arranged by mutual direct agreement between lower levels of the administrative hierarchy. Many of the barter contracts are intraprovincial in nature and entered into by units as low as communes. Yangyung Commune, situated predominantly in sandy soil in Tienpai County, Chanchiang Prefecture, Kwangtung Province, agreed in 1980 to barter 500 tons of surplus peanuts with grain-producing communes in four counties in Kwangtung – two in Chanchiang and two in Foshan Prefecture. That exchange allowed the commune to expand its peanut sown area to 58 percent of its cultivated area and to raise consumption of cereals, which it was unable to do under the self-reliance policy (Chou Yung-shen and Wu Han-piao 1980). Not all of the barter arrangements involve agricultural products on both sides of the transaction. Tsinghai, a major animal husbandry region in the Northwest, has agreed to supply wool and animal hides to Shanghai in exchange for technical assistance from China's most advanced industrial center (NCNA July 31, 1980). Chekiang in both 1980 and 1981 contracted to barter 50,000 tons of rice and 2,000 tons of edible oil in exchange for 1 million tons of coal from Shansi. Chekiang has bartered its rice for chemical fertilizer from Foshan Prefecture in Kwangtung (NCNA June 22, 1980).

Summary

Variation over time in the willingness of the Chinese Communist Party to allow the peasantry greater freedom to choose their own patterns of production rather than following the dictates of Party cadres at higher levels appears to reflect a fundamental debate. Those who rejected the more liberal course of relying on relative prices to influence cropping decisions did so only in part out of a failure to appreciate the magnitude of the potential efficiency gains that such a course offered. At least equally important was their view, whether stemming from a desire to ameloriate China's long-run industrial and military backwardness or to improve China's intermediate-run strategic position, that heavy industrial development was the central priority. In this view it was inevitable that the state play a major role in extracting resources from the agricultural sector not by price incentives but through indirect taxation and forced deliveries of agriculture's product into state hands. Of course, policy making was not usually as rational as this perspective implies, since not all participants in the debate saw the tradeoff in these terms. There were some for whom the major elements of policy were ideologically motivated. Periodic markets in the countryside for this group undermined the most fundamental claims of the superiority of the socialist system that they were seeking to establish. Unconstrained private profit seeking, in this view, would only lead to a replication of the rural economic and social ills against which the revolution was in some measure fought.

The relationship between the debate on the forms of organization and motivation of the peasantry and the broader development issues just referred to is implicit in the following chapter, which examines variations over time in the intersectoral allocation of resources.

3

Prices and intersectoral resource transfers

A central aspect of the role of agriculture in modern economic growth is its market and factor contributions. One of agriculture's market contributions, its provision of food to the urban sector, was analyzed partially in the previous chapter. This chapter focuses on agriculture's factor contribution to growth, particularly its role in financing industrialization. Although Western scholars have intensively studied China's agriculture, little work has been undertaken on intersectoral resource flows. With the notable exception of two pioneering works by Shigeru Ishikawa (1967a, 1967b), most published studies treat the subject cursorily, usually assuming that the slogan "agriculture first" implies that agriculture was a significant net beneficiary from intersectoral resource flows, especially after the crisis of 1959–61.

The purpose of this chapter is not to determine the magnitude of intersectoral flows at specific times since the end of the civil war, but to ask whether development policy has been balanced on the basis of the first criterion proposed in Chapter 1: Has the intersectoral allocation of investment resources equalized the marginal rate of return to investment in agriculture and industry? Alternatively the focus could be formulated in terms of whether policy has maximized successfully the interactions between agriculture and other sectors of the economy.

Conceptually there are several ways that the issue of balance might be addressed. The simplest would be to compare the marginal rates of return on investments in the two sectors. A marginal rate of return on agricultural investments persistently higher than the return in industry, on this criterion, suggests an imbalanced growth strategy. A reallocation of resources would raise the rate of growth of the economy as a whole. When, as for China, data on these marginal rates of return are not available, one alternative is to compare the incremental capital output ratios in the two sectors. If, over an appropriately defined period, the ratio is higher in industry than in agriculture, the returns to industrial investment have been lower than in agriculture. The validity of either approach, however, depends on the contributions of each sector to output growth in the other sector being reasonably measured by the product market transactions discussed in Chapter 1. If, for example, raw cotton is undervalued in these product markets, then the rate of return on investment in cotton production will be understated. The validity of the Chinese price structure as a measure of relative costs or scarcity cannot be assumed, but requires detailed investigation. Here, too, analysis is handicapped by a shortage of data, but this chapter reports some preliminary evidence.

Conceptually there are two methods for measuring intersectoral resource transfers: via either commodity or financial accounts. The problem is analogous to international economics. In an ex post accounting framework a surplus of commodity exports over imports must be offset by a capital outflow, whereas a trade deficit is financed by a capital inflow. Agriculture, in this framework, is the equivalent of a country trading with the rest of the world – the nonagricultural sector. A flow of resources out of agriculture is simply an agricultural trade surplus. The excess flow of goods must be financed by transfers of financial resources to the nonagricultural sector either through the private investment decisions of landlords or others who control the agricultural surplus or through government tax and expenditure policy. The net real resource flow may be measured in either product or financial markets.

In most empirical studies of intersectoral resource flows agriculture is defined to be inclusive of all economic activities of farm families, including subsidiary and handicraft production, rather than to be simply the raising of agricultural products. That definition focuses the net resource flow analysis on the prospects "for mobilizing resources out of the traditional sector into the emerging modern sector" (Ishikawa 1967a, 295). In the present chapter I prefer to expand somewhat the scope of agriculture to include that portion of rural small-scale enterprises that are operated by brigades and communes. At the same time at certain points it is useful to exclude state farms from the analysis. This definition is both broader than agriculture, functionally defined, yet, in a sense, narrower since it excludes state farms. At the same time it is considerably narrower than "rural" since it excludes a whole range of nonagricultural rural activities carried out by units other than collective enterprises. Thus conceptually the focus becomes the flow of resources between collective agriculture and the state rather than between agriculture and industry or between rural and urban areas. However, there is a large overlap among these definitions.

This definition of agriculture has certain conceptual advantages and also proves empirically useful since published data frequently reflect administrative arrangements, particularly the form of ownership, rather than function. Rural collective enterprises have become increasingly important since the 1960s. They are major employers of industrial, transport, and construction workers. They repair agricultural machinery and perform other tasks directly relevant to crop production, as well as engaging in subcontracting work for urban state-owned enterprises. Since they receive some investment funds from the state, pay significant taxes to the state, and, at the same time, reinvest some of their profits directly into agricultural activities (narrowly defined), collective enterprises are an integral part of the flow of resources between the state and collective agriculture.

State farms, on the other hand, usefully are excluded from the scope of agriculture, at least in the analysis of the sectoral allocation of investment in the latter portion of this chapter. State farm workers are salaried employees, drawing fixed wages comparable to other state workers, and receive many of the same benefits as urban state employees – free medical care, state-funded retirement programs, subsidized food, and so forth. Moreover, financially state farms are operated in a manner similar to state industrial enterprises. Their profits (losses) are submitted to (absorbed by) the state budget, and investment funds are provided almost entirely by budgetary grants. This is in sharp distinction to collective agriculture where incomes are derived from a division among workers of net revenues left after production costs, taxes, and certain other deductions are made from gross income; where benefits provided to workers are relatively small; and where investment funds are derived primarily from internal accumulation and interest-bearing bank loans.

Unlike the Soviet Union, however, state farms in China are a rather small share of the agricultural sector by most measures. In 1979 some 2,047 state farms employed less than 5 million workers, less than 2 percent of the national agricultural labor force (Table 1.2); cultivated 4.357 million hectares, about 4.4 percent of the national total (Table 1.3); and produced 7.04 million tons (metric tons throughout) of cereals (Agricultural Yearbook Compilation Commission 1981, 18–19), 2.1 percent of the national total (Table 4.1).[1] They are, however, important producers of some crops such as fruit, tea, and rubber. For example, about 80 percent of China's rubber plantations are under the state farm system. Moreover, although there are state farms in every province and autonomous region as well as in China's three major municipalities, state farms are concentrated geographically in more remote and border regions such as Heilungkiang, Sinkiang, and Inner Mongolia, where land reclamation activities are particularly important.[2] But because in aggregate terms state farms produce such a small share of the value of agricultural output – less than 3 percent in 1979[3] – it was not necessary to differentiate them from collective agriculture in the discussion of price and quantity planning in Chapter 2.

Conceptually the measurement of intersectoral resource flows by the analogy with international economics can be adapted to the definition of agriculture just outlined. But there are other problems. Both the commodity flow and financial approaches omit part of agriculture's labor contributions to nonagricultural growth. Between peak agricultural seasons, peasants work not only on local small-scale irrigation and land improvement projects, which are a form of internal reinvestment within agriculture, but also on large-scale state construction projects. Participation in these projects frequently is induced by political mobilization rather than by paying workers their reservation wage. Since, as will be discussed below, a significant portion of the benefits of these large-scale projects accrues to the nonagricultural sector, the usual measures of intersectoral resource flows understate agriculture's contribution to other sectors. Investigation of the magnitude of such labor transfers, however, lies outside the scope of this study.

Moreover, a shortage of data impedes the measurement of nonlabor resource flows. Even during the 1950s, when data were relatively more plentiful than in the following two decades, some basic data series were not available, and there is insufficient information concerning the coverage and definition of those series that were published. For example, even the construction of the commodity trade accounts for the 1950s depends on several assumptions (Ishikawa 1967b, 32–4). Estimates for the same period based on savings transfers and financial flows arising from factor services and current transfers are even more problematic since data on net receipts of wages by farm households and on private financial transfers are unavailable. For more recent years the magnitude of state investment in rural commune and brigade industries is not known. Fortunately, the Chinese State Statistical Bureau in 1979 resumed publication, after a twenty-year hiatus, of annual statistical communiqués and in 1982 published a statistical yearbook with time series data reaching back to 1952 for many important parameters for evaluating intersectoral resource transfers.

Despite better data there remain exceptionally troubling valuation problems. Since the early 1950s administrative means rather than market forces have determined the price structure. Since prices have been set largely to generate industrial profits, and thus government revenue, rather than to allocate resources, there is some presumption that the government has distorted relative prices of agricultural and industrial products. Ishikawa grappled with this problem but finally made his estimates on 1952 prices, which he felt were more meaningful than the alternative of a prewar (1936–37) price base.

Yet a number of questions regarding the price structure remain unresolved. The first concerns the appropriate base year. Some authors have criticized the use of 1952 as a base year since farm prices relative to manufactured goods prices were depressed by about 30 percent compared to 1936–37, the immediate prewar period (Data Office Statistical Work 1957c; Li Te-pin 1979). Others have argued that even the prices of the mid-1930s are inappropriate for analyzing intersectoral relations because by 1936–37 relative farm prices had been declining for five to ten years (Hu Chuang-nuan 1979; Li Te-pin 1980b). The second problem concerns the procedures for compiling price indexes. As will be discussed below, there is reason to doubt the utility of the official index of prices of manufactured goods sold in rural areas.

Remaining shortcomings in the data make it necessary to use several partial approaches to examine intersectoral commodity flows and to analyze the degree to which development strategy was imbalanced. I begin with a discussion of intersectoral resource flows measured by the commodity flow approach since the data for this are relatively more complete. That approach leads directly and naturally to the issue of the relative prices of industrial and agricultural products. I conclude with a partial analysis of financial flows, as part of an effort to examine the sectoral composition of investment. In that analysis I look at state budgetary investment in agriculture, investment financed through loans, and farmers' self-investment financed from retained earnings.

Intersectoral commodity flows

Professor Ishikawa's reconstruction of the trade account for the farm sector for 1953 and 1956 is shown in Table 3.1. His calculations show that Chinese agriculture sustained an export surplus only through 1952. By 1953, the outset of the First Five-Year Plan, agriculture had become a net recipient of resources from the nonfarm sector. Subsequently the sector's trade deficit grew, not only in absolute terms but also as a share of the value of farm output. Moreover, the growing deficit in the trade account measured in current prices occurred while the terms of trade for agriculture were improving; that is, prices of farm exports were rising more rapidly than prices of farm imports. Expressing the 1956 data in constant 1952 prices substantially increases the net inflow to agriculture. Its exports in value terms are

Table 3.1. *Ishikawa's estimate of intersectoral resource flows, 1953 and 1956 (billions of yuan, current prices)*

	1953	1956
Farm exports (total)	17.04	19.55
Taxes in kind	2.58	2.59
Sales to state and on free market	14.46	16.96
Farm imports (total)	18.51	24.07
Household purchases	17.32	22.89
Government current expenditures	.53	1.00
Government investment expenditures	.66	1.18
Balance of trade surplus (deficit)	(1.47)	(4.52)

Source: Ishikawa (1967a, 300).

reduced almost 20 percent, while imports are reduced only 1 percent. The net result is a 7-billion-yuan inflow to agriculture in 1956, of which about two-thirds was due to real flows while one-third was due to the invisible or terms-of-trade effect.

Changes in trade flows since the 1950s

Farm exports. Although it is difficult to extend the data in Table 3.1 to the 1960s and 1970s, some of the major components of the farm sector trade accounts for the 1950s and for 1977–79 are displayed in Table 3.2.

Farm exports consist of the agricultural tax, collected predominantly in grain, and state purchases of cereals and other agricultural commodities. In quantity terms the tax (including the surtax) was relatively stable from 1951 through 1957, averging 18.6 million (metric) tons. By 1978 it had declined to a little more than 13 million tons, and it fell further to less than 11 million tons in 1979 in the wake of the Third Plenum decisions to reduce the agricultural tax in China's poorest regions. In current prices the agricultural tax (including the surtax) rose from about 3.2 billion yuan in 1951–57 to 4.7 billion yuan in 1977. But since the price of grain increased by 65 percent over this period (Appendix 3), in constant prices the value of the tax declined more than 10 percent compared to the average of 1951–56. The declining quantity of tax collections, combined with the growth of farm output, underlies the frequently repeated claim that the tax fell from 12 percent of agricultural output in 1952 to 4.4 percent in 1978 (Keng Chien-hua 1981, 17; Lardy 1978a, 178). However, as will become clear below, this direct agricultural

Table 3.2 *Agricultural tax and state grain purchases, 1950–79*

	Agricultural Tax[a]		State grain purchases (millions of tons of foodgrains)[d]	Purchases and taxes (millions of tons of foodgrains)[d]
	Value (millions of yuan)[b]	Quantity (millions of tons of food grains)[c]		
1950	2,293	13.5	—	—
1951	3,073	18.1	—	—
1952	3,299	19.4	—	27.8
1953	2,943	17.1	22.3	41.5
1954	3,182	18.6	24.3	45.1
1955	3,270	19.2	21.5	43.0
1956	3,110	18.3	21.2	41.7
1957	3,346	19.7	17.7	39.8
1958	3,260	—	—	55.7
1959	3,300	—	—	55.9
1977	4,680	—	—	47.2
1978	4,140	13.2	31.7	46.5
1979	3,390	10.8	41.8	53.9

[a]The agricultural tax excludes other taxes levied in rural areas such as the animal husbandry tax, the slaughter tax, the land registration or deed tax (relevant only in the early 1950s), industrial and commercial taxes levied on handicraft and processing activities of individual peasants, rural handicraft cooperatives, and (in the 1970s and 80s) collectively run brigade and commune rural enterprises. In 1950–57 these other rural taxes were .56, .96, .48, .65, .59, .47, .42, and .36 million yuan. In 1978 and 1979 taxes on collectively run enterprises were 2.20 and 2.26 billion yuan. For the years through 1957 both the value and quantity measures include the local agricultural surtax, which varied between 5 and 15 percent of the basic tax. The year-by-year breakdown of the total tax between the basic tax and the surtax is given in the original source. For 1958 and 1959 the tax revenues shown are exclusive of the local surtax. The surtax for those years was 15 percent (Li Ch'eng-jui 1959, 321). The data for 1977–79 include the surtax, but the rate appears to have been smaller than at any time in the 1950s, and by 1979 the surtax may have been abolished. The 540-million-yuan reduction in taxes in 1978 was specified to have included a 36-million-yuan reduction in the agricultural surtax. Moreover, the 746-million-yuan or 18 percent reduction in agricultural taxes in 1979 included a further unspecified reduction in the surtax. In at least one province, Kwangtung, the surtax of 5 percent was abolished in 1979 (Kwangtung Provincial Service February 10, 1979). Since the authority to levy surtaxes and to control their magnitude usually is under the unified control of the Ministry of Finance, that may indicate that the agricultural surtax was abolished nationally in 1979.
[b]In current prices, for the calendar year listed.
[c]Measured in terms of fine grain. The physical quantity listed for each year is for the procurement year, as defined in Table 2.1.
[d]Includes taxes, in kind, quota purchases, and over-quota purchases, but excludes purchases at negotiated prices. Measured in trade grain, as defined in Table 2.1. Thus columns 2 and 3 do not sum precisely to column 4.

tax is only part of the tax burden of collective agriculture, and a rather small one at that.

As soon as the system of compulsory sales to the state was introduced in 1953, state purchases of grain doubled.[4] In the First Five-Year Plan, purchases exceeded the agricultural tax as the major export item from the farm sector. By 1978 and 1979 purchases were more than two-and-one-half times the grain tax, and the margin between the two was expanding in response to the increased absolute sales offered by the peasantry in the wake of the price changes discussed in Chapter 2.

The data on purchases and the agricultural tax collected in kind reveal the very slow growth of farm grain exports between the mid-1950s and 1977 or 1978. The tax expressed in terms of grain was substantially less than in the mid-1950s, and state purchases grew by an amount sufficient to increase the flow of cereal exports to the state in 1977 and 1978 by only 10 percent over the level of the mid-1950s.

Farm imports. While taxes and state grain purchases grew quite modestly between the mid-1950s and mid-1970s, farm imports soared. The growth is reflected both in the value of farm purchases and in inventories of farm machinery and other equipment. Mechanical equipment was only 1.65 million horsepower in 1957 but rose to 14.94 million in 1965 and 101.68 million by 1975. The inventory of medium and large tractors, for example, was less than 15,000 in 1957 but increased to 73,000 in 1965 and 345,000 by 1975. Smaller garden tractors were not even produced in the 1950s. The inventory was only 4,000 in 1965 but soared to 600,000 by 1975. Similarly large increases were registered in powered irrigation equipment. At the end of the First Plan the inventory of power-driven irrigation equipment was only 564,000 horsepower. By 1965 it had reached 9.07 million and by 1975 more than 48.67 million (State Statistical Bureau 1981c, VI-12).

The increased use of chemical fertilizers and electric power after the early 1960s is also well known. The First Plan included only three chemical fertil-

Notes to Table 3.2 (*cont.*)

Sources: Columns 1 and 2 – 1950–57, Li Ch'eng-jui (1959, 156, 192, 193); 1958–59, Li Hsien-nien (1959, 22; 1960, 14–15); 1977–79, Reporter (1980c), Ministry of Agriculture Commune Management Bureau (1981c, 26).
Column 3 – Column 4 less agricultural taxes, expressed in terms of trade grain; the conversion factor from fine to trade grain is 1.12.
Column 4 – table 2.1, column 1.

Table 3.3. *Farm sector transactions with the state, 1949–81 (millions of yuan, current prices)*

	Producer goods purchased by agriculture	State purchases of agricultural commodities[a]	
		First series	Second series
1949	670	—	—
1950	730	8,000	—
1951	1,030	10,500	—
1952	1,410	12,970	9,010
1953	1,920	15,320	—
1954	2,500	17,360	—
1955	2,820	17,800	—
1956	3,700	18,400	—
1957	3,260	20,280	17,650
1962	6,030	—	16,170
1965	8,020	—	27,420
1970	12,920	—	31,400
1975	22,470	—	41,460
1977	25,850	—	—
1978	29,370	—	46,000
1979	32,400	—	58,680
1980	35,000	—	67,700
1981	—	—	76,470

[a]There are two series for state purchases of agricultural commodities by the state. The data for 1952 and 1957 show that the two series are not comparable, but the source of the discrepancy is not known.
Sources: State Statistical Bureau (1960, 168, 170; 1980a; 1981a, 17; 1981c, VI-20; 1982a), Ministry of Agriculture Policy Research Office (1980, 43), Special Commentator (1981), Agricultural Yearbook Compilation Commission (1982, 326, 330).

izer plants. Consequently in 1957 the industry supplied only 151,000 tons of chemical fertilizer (nutrient weight) or 1.35 kilograms per hectare of farm land. Following increased domestic investments and major complete plant imports, both in the early 1960s and the first half of the 1970s, domestic production of chemical fertilizer grew to 1.73 million (metric) tons in 1965 and more than 5.25 million tons in 1975. Rural electric power consumption, including the amount used by farm households, rose from 140,000 kilowatts in 1957 to 271,000 kilowatts in 1965 and 1,831,000 kilowatts in 1975 (State Statistical Bureau 1981c, VI-15).

The growing flow of industrial inputs into farming is reflected in the value series on the producer goods supplied to agriculture shown in Table 3.3.

These inputs were modest indeed in the 1950s. They did not surpass 3 billion yuan until 1956, when they were the equivalent of 16 percent of the farm sector's gross income from sales of commodities to the state and only 5 percent of the value of total industrial production. But producer inputs to agriculture expanded following the adoption of the "agriculture first" policy in 1961, ratified at the Tenth Plenum of the Eighth Central Committee in 1962. The value doubled between 1962 and 1970 and doubled again by 1977. By 1978 producer goods supplied to agriculture were more than 60 percent of the farm sector's gross income from sales of commodities to the state.

The contrasting pattern of slowly increasing grain exports and rapidly rising farm imports appears to support the common Western view that Chinese agriculture by the mid-1960s had become a large net recipient of resources from the nonfarm sector. In this view, whatever contribution agriculture had made to nonfarm investment in the 1950s was rapidly reduced as the state shifted investment priorities to favor agriculture to facilitate recovery from the devastating effects of the Great Leap Forward (Perkins 1975a).

Two additional issues must be examined before this hypothesis can be sustained: exports of agricultural commodities other than grain and trends in the relative prices of agricultural and nonagricultural products.

Analysis of state purchases of nongrain products in the mid-1970s is critical to any discussion of intersectoral resource flows, since by 1978 grain comprised only 24 percent of the value of state purchases of agricultural commodities.[5] State purchases of cotton did rise from 1.38 million (metric) tons in 1957 to 2.21 million tons in 1978. On the other hand, purchases of edible vegetable oils declined sharply from 1.337 to .982 million tons over the same period (Ministry of Agriculture Policy Research Office 1980, 39–40). In 1979 state procurement of oils rose to 1.310 million tons but still was less than the 1.572 million tons sold to the state in 1955 – the peak procurement year of the 1950s (Agricultural Yearbook Compilation Commission 1981, 327). The most comprehensive measure of farm sector exports consists of the two series for the value of state procurement of agricultural products (Table 3.3). In current prices farm sector exports as measured by the second series increased from about 18 to 46 billion yuan between 1957 and 1978. Measured in constant 1952 prices, using the official price index (Table 3.4), farm sales to the state increased by 80 percent in twenty-one years. That increase was achieved by increasing the share of some economic crops, such as cotton, sugarcane, and sugar beet, purchased by the state, and by increased purchases of subsidiary farm products.[6] Thus simply in quantity or constant price terms it is not true that farm sector exports stagnated between 1957

Table 3.4 *Agriculture's terms of trade, 1952–81*

	Index of purchase prices paid to farmers[a] (1)	Index of prices of manufactured goods purchased by farmers[b] (2)	Farmers' terms of trade (1) ÷ (2)
1952	100	100	100
1956	116.6	100.4	116.1
1957	122.4	101.6	120.5
1958	125.1	99.4	125.9
1962	161.9	114.7	141.2
1965	155.0	107.3	144.5
1966	162.0	102.6	157.9
1977	168.8	99.5	169.6
1978	173.5	99.5	174.4
1979	211.8	100.2	211.4
1980	226.9	101.1	224.4
1981	240.3	102.8	233.8

[a]The index of purchase prices paid to farmers is a weighted average of prices received by farmers in sales to the state, including quota purchase prices, over-quota prices, and negotiated prices. It does not reflect prices of transactions on rural periodic markets.
[b]Including both consumer and producer goods.
Sources: State Statistical Bureau (1960, 173; 1981a, 17; 1982a), Agricultural Yearbook Compilation Commission (1981, 376–77), Chi Lung and Lu Nan (1980, 45–46).

and 1978. And as will be shown below, the invisible transfer or price effect may have become an increasingly important transfer mechanism after the mid-1950s.

Price effects

Western observers, including myself, have relied on official price indexes to analyze both prices farmers receive (state purchase prices) and prices farmers pay for manufactured goods. These price indexes, shown in Table 3.4, suggest that peasants have benefited from a significant long-run improvement in prices of agricultural products they sell relative to industrial products they purchase (Lardy 1978a, 176–8). Over a little more than two-and-a-half decades prices received more than doubled while the prices of products purchased, except for a rise in the early 1960s, remained stable. These price trends imply that, for any given pattern of intersectoral commodity flows expressed in current prices, agriculture's real net outflow (inflow) would actually be sharply decreasing (increasing) over time. In particular, in many analyses it has been thought that changes in relative prices substantially raised the real flow of resources into the agricultural sector after some point in the mid-1950s or by the mid-1960s at the latest (Perkins 1975a, 365).

My own view is now different, for several reasons. First, since the share of agricultural output sold to the state is low and for one major commodity, grain, has declined compared to the 1950s, the effect on peasant incomes of higher prices has been attenuated. As shown in Chapter 2, the share of grain output marketed through state channels declined from about 25 percent in 1956 and 1957 to under 20 percent by 1978. Moreover, while declining, a significant share of that grain is delivered to the state at a zero price since it is taxes paid in kind. Deliveries of grain to the state for which peasants were paid in 1978 composed less than 13 percent of output.

Second, the incremental income accruing to the peasant sector through higher procurement prices is partially eroded by the higher prices that peasants have had to pay for grain they purchase from the state. The degree of erosion clearly depends on the change in the price level and the share of grain resold. The former subject rarely has been considered by outside observers, but an accumulation of evidence suggests that in contrast to urban areas, where grain has been sold at a stable nominal price for more than thirty years, the price of grain resold in the countryside is tied to the quota procurement price, which has more than doubled.[7] The rise in the price of resold grain thus offsets the incremental income gain from higher purchase prices for that share of deliveries that is resold. As discussed in Chapter 2, whereas resales grew slowly after 1957, in 1978 they accounted for half the grain sold to the state (Tables 2.1, 3.2). Thus in the short run for the farm sector as a whole, prior to 1979 doubling the average procurement price of grain would increase the value of the grain harvest by only 6–7 percent.[8] Peasants could gain from higher prices in the longer run through increased specialization, productivity, and marketing, particularly since that would allow them to sell a rising share of their output at above-quota premium prices. But as already discussed in Chapter 2, state policy inhibited these developments between 1965 and 1978, mitigating the effect of higher prices.

Finally, and by far the most important, although the index of farm purchase prices (column 1 of Table 3.4) within the limits just analyzed is meaningful, I no longer believe that the official index of prices farmers pay for industrial products is a useful analytic tool. That judgment is based on several factors. First, the Chinese have never disclosed the weights used in the construction of the index. Knowledge of the nature of the index is important because the paucity of price observations at the farm level for machinery, fertilizers, and so on has made it impossible to construct independent price indexes. The weights are critical because of the changing mix of industrial products sold in rural areas. In the 1950s manufactured goods sold in rural areas were predominantly consumer goods, since few agricultural producer goods were manufactured. But as discussed above, after the early 1960s the industrial sector produced tractors, pumps, chemical fertilizers, insecticides, electricity, and other products that were purchased by the agricultural sector in growing quantities.

It has never been clear how the prices of these new products were reflected in the official index of prices of industrial goods sold in rural areas. An index of prices of producer goods sold in the countryside declined by 7.6 percent between 1952 and 1977 (Wang Hai-tu and Sun Lien-ch'eng 1979, 7). But the price of several of the more important items declined more dramatically. An official of the State Commodity Price Bureau, for example, stated in 1978 that prices farmers paid for farm machinery, chemical fertilizers, and pesticides were 48 percent lower in 1977 than in 1952 (NCNA, July 22, 1978). The constancy of the index of prices of all manufactured goods sold in the countryside while the prices of major commodities declined dramatically suggests it is a Laspeyres index, constructed with base year weights. Since few producer goods were sold to farmers in 1952, large reductions in their prices would be expected to lead to very small changes in the index of manufactured goods sold in the countryside. On this view the official index might be thought to understate the real improvement in the terms of trade of the peasantry, since the share of producer goods in total farm purchases has risen over time.[9]

Yet this interpretation does not withstand careful scrutiny. Many of the producer goods sold in the countryside today were not produced in China in 1952 or were imported in such minuscule quantities that they might not have been included in the index in the base year. Thus a Laspeyres index based on 1952 prices would not reflect price declines of the many commodities that entered production from the late 1950s through the mid-1960s. The alternative – a given year weight or Paasch-type index – is actually more widely used in China (Fang Ping-chu 1962). A given year weight index should reflect a rapid reduction in prices in recent years since producer goods would be weighted with the larger given year share in sales to farmers rather than the tiny base year weights. The constancy of the overall index of industrial goods prices sold in rural areas from 1966 through 1979, however, would be possible only if there was an increase in the prices of manufactured consumer goods sold in the countryside that fully offset the decline in producer goods prices. Yet there is no evidence that such an increase in consumer goods prices occurred. Thus it seems unlikely that the index in column 2 of Table 3.4 is of the Paasch type.

The most plausible alternative is that the index of manufactured goods is based on a narrow range of commodities that were sold in the countryside in significant quantities in the early 1950s. That view is supported by an article in a journal of the Chinese Academy of Social Sciences that states that the index is based on the prices of cotton cloth, refined sugar, refined salt, kerosene, and matches, and specifically excludes agricultural machinery, insecticides, and chemical fertilizers (Yang Chien-pai and Li Hsüeh-tseng 1980, 36). Given its limited coverage, the value of this widely used official index of prices of manufactured goods sold in rural areas is doubtful. In particular, it no longer can be used to support the contention that the level of indirect taxes embodied in the prices of industrial products and paid by the peasantry has been stable.

In the absence of reliable price indexes that might be used to evaluate comprehensively the trends in the terms of trade that farmers face in their transactions with the state, I propose to examine the relative price issue through three separate approaches. The first focuses on the price of modern industrial products used in agricultural production. Prices of these products are evaluated both by comparison with their domestic costs of production and by comparison of the ratio of prices paid by farmers for these products to the prices they receive for major agricultural products sold to the state with price ratios prevailing in other countries or in international markets for similar product pairs. Since many governments intervene to influence prices of agricultural outputs or inputs and because comparisons involving nonhomogenous inputs such as machinery are difficult, relative prices in other countries are an imperfect standard for evaluating the Chinese price structure.

The second approach is to compare the prices farmers receive for products sold to the state with those that prevail in alternative markets, that is, rural periodic markets. That comparison is impossible for the Cultural Revolution decade since rural marketing activities were suppressed in many regions, cereal and oil crops generally could not be sold legally even where markets remained open, and price observations for the few remaining markets are extremely scarce. But at the Third Plenum of the Eleventh Central Committee the Party endorsed the resumption of private marketing activities by farmers. Moreover, the state began to publish price data for transactions in these markets, so it is now possible to compare government and market prices.

Analysis of these price differentials, for reasons explained in some detail below, is also difficult. Thus a third approach to the relative price issue proves useful. This is an examination of the profitability of consumer goods, such as textiles, and processed foods, such as refined sugar, that are manufactured with raw materials supplied to state factories by collective agriculture.

Relative prices of agricultural producer goods

Chemical fertilizer is an example of an agricultural producer good that is overpriced relative to both domestic production costs and international standards (T'ung Ta-lin and Pao T'ung 1978b). A modern imported large-scale plant in Heilungkiang, for example, has production costs of 150 yuan per ton of urea. The profit markup by the producing factory is 200 yuan, leading to an ex-factory price of 350 yuan. The markup at the distribution stage is 100 yuan, leading to a sale price at the farm level of 450 yuan per ton.

The profit rate for the producing factory is over 130 percent of production costs. Of the 100-yuan markup over the ex-factory price, 64 yuan is to cover distribution, marketing, and working capital costs, 16 yuan is profits earmarked for the provincial government, and 19 yuan is profits for the commercial system. Total profit is thus 235 yuan per ton, 109 percent of production and distribution costs. Since Chinese accounting procedures understate the costs of fixed capital, the true economic profit is less than the financial profit that this cost structure generates. But even if we take this into account, the rate of return on capital invested in these plants is quite high.[10]

The high rate of profit on the production and sale of nitrogen fertilizer is confirmed by our second standard, the relative prices of nitrogen and rice in China compared with those in other countries. That relative price comparison is one of the most frequently made in agricultural economics since chemical fertilizer is usually the most important purchased current input in Asian agriculture and because both fertilizer, when adjusted for nitrogen content, and paddy rice are reasonably homogeneous products. The comparison is complicated by the Chinese government policy of purchasing rice and other major farm commodities in a multiple-price system, since that means several nitrogen/rice price ratios can be calculated. Analytically it is most appropriate to use the marginal price (i.e., over-quota or negotiated price) of rice to calculate the nitrogen/rice price ratio when analyzing the efficiency of utilization of inputs. But the average price received for rice is probably most appropriate to use in the examination of intersectoral resource flows.

In comparative terms, shown in Table 3.5, the nitrogen/paddy rice price ratio in China was relatively high throughout the 1960s and 1970s.[11] In 1976, for example, before the 1979 price increase for paddy rice, the average relative price of fertilizer in China was the highest of any country in Asia,

Table 3.5. *Ratio of nitrogen to paddy rice price for Asian economies, 1965–69 and 1976*

	1965–69	1976
Bangladesh	—	1.93
Burma	8.31	1.81
China[a]	8.90	4.39
India	1.97	2.23[b]
Indonesia	—	2.48
Korea	1.47	1.42
Philippines	3.38	3.56
Sri Lanka	1.44	2.04
Taiwan	3.23	.78
Thailand	8.10[c]	4.08

[a]For 1976 the price of a kilogram of nitrogen in the form of urea was .978 yuan: (450 yuan per ton of urea × 1,000 kg/ton) ÷ .46 kg of nitrogen/kg of urea. The quota purchase price of rice (a weighted average of japonica and indica varieties) was .1962 yuan per kilogram (Appendix 3). Due to sales at the over-quota premium of 30 percent, the average sale price was 13–14 percent over the quota price (Chang Ch'un-yin 1979, 71) or about .223 yuan per kilogram. In 1965 the ex-factory price of urea was 54 percent higher than in 1976. I presume that the ratio between the farmgate and ex-factory price (1.29:1) was unchanged between the two years. The quota purchase price for rice in 1965 was .1694 yuan per kilogram (Appendix 3). There was no system of premiums for over-quota sales in 1965.

Nitrogen purchased in the form of ammonium sulfate (20.8 percent nitrogen) is more expensive than for urea, and the price was unchanged between 1955 and 1978–80. The price ratio for nitrogen in this form was 13.7 in 1957, 11.1 in 1965, and 8.6 in 1976. The decline in the ratio is due entirely to the rising average purchase price for rice.
[b]For 1974.
[c]For 1970.
Sources: Johnson (1978, 205), for all countries except China; T'ung Ta-lin and Pao T'ung (1978b); Agricultural Yearbook Compilation Commission (1981, 380); Lardy (1982b).

including Thailand, where a rice export tax depressed the domestic price of paddy rice relative to the international price. The relative price of nitrogen in China was more than twice as high as in Bangladesh, Burma, and Sri Lanka, twice the price in India, and almost six times the price in Taiwan. Even for Chinese producers who sold part of their output at the 30 percent premium, the marginal relative price of fertilizer, 3.8 units of rice, exceeded all countries but Thailand.[12]

Although the relative price of fertilizer declined by 50 percent in China between 1965 and 1976 (Table 3.5), the price remained high. Since state sales of urea produced in the thirteen large-scale ammonia-urea complexes imported in 1972–74 grew significantly after 1975 while the price of urea was unchanged, the high price constituted a substantial indirect tax on the agricultural sector.[13]

Since a significantly lower fertilizer price might have led to excess demand in the short run, a substitution of the relative international price for the relative domestic price may not have been warranted. Yet there probably was excess supply of chemical fertilizer at the prices prevailing prior to 1979. That was evident not in the accumulation of unsold stocks, as would be the case in a market economy, but in bureaucratically determined levels of input usage that were in excess of those warranted on the basis of economic returns. County and lower-level bureaucrats had a particular incentive to specify levels of chemical fertilizer usage far higher than optimal on purely economic criteria since their performance was judged more on the basis of absolute yields achieved than the efficiency of resource use.[14] Thus many production teams were supplied with arbitrarily high quantities of fertilizer, the cost of which the state deducted from their revenues, and so that level of chemical fertilizer usage became a fixed cost. By 1979–80, when there had been some restoration of the rights of production teams to determine their own cropping patterns and levels of input usage, some units substantially reduced the quantities of fertilizers that they used.[15] That suggests that the government manipulated the grain/fertilizer price ratio to transfer resources out of agriculture.

If excess supply was limited to a few localities rather than a general phenomenon and if production units had more discretion over the level of their input usage levels than the above description implies, then the sustained disparity between the domestic and international price relatives suggests that state policy of overpricing chemical fertilizers and underinvesting in additions to capacity not only transferred real resources out of agriculture but also depressed the long-term rate of growth of farm output. Historically, allocating a larger share of domestic investment resources to expand chemical fertilizer production capacity would have allowed the state to reduce the relative price of fertilizer more rapidly without creating excess demand.[16] A more rapidly declining relative price would have stimulated peasants to increase the application of fertilizer more rapidly than actually occurred, leading to faster growth of agricultural output.[17] The actual share of investment resources allocated to chemical fertilizer and other agricultural producer goods will be discussed further below.

Other modern inputs, particularly farm machinery, also appear to be overpriced relative to agricultural products when judged against relative prices in other countries. Comparisons of relative prices of machinery are always difficult because of potentially large quality differences in seemingly similar machinery products manufactured in different countries. One recent comparison may convey some order-of-magnitude sense of the price relatives. A conventional 20-horsepower Japanese tractor sells for the equivalent of 5.5 tons of rice, whereas the equivalent 28-horsepower Chinese "East Is Red" model sells for 35.5 tons of rice (Chia Hsiu-yen 1979, 15; Yang Chien-pai and Li Hsüeh-tseng 1980, 37). That comparison, of course, is distorted because the Japanese government maintains the price of rice at roughly three times the world level. Even after we discount for the inflated rice price in Japan the relative price of the Chinese model is just over twice the world price.[18]

Some Western observers have pointed out that many Chinese plants manufacturing agricultural machinery and other modern agricultural inputs achieve low or even negative profit rates. Thus by the first standard suggested above, domestic production costs, prices may not be high. In my judgment, even if the rural small-scale industrial sector could be shown to achieve low financial profits, that does not imply that the inputs they sell to agriculture are underpriced or in any meaningful sense subsidized by the state. This view is based on an analysis of both the state-run and collectively run portions of rural small-scale industry.

In the state-managed sector the proliferation of prefectural and county-level plants precludes gaining most of the economies of scale that are essential to the efficient production of power-driven agricultural machinery (Wong 1981, 13–15). For example, the low volume of output in handtractor plants in the latter half of the 1960s and in the 1970s contributed to excessive production costs. Because of the large number and specialized character of the machine tools required to produce the thousand-plus components they contain, the production of handtractors is characterized by significant scale economies (Wong 1981, 14). The attempt by Chinese plants to produce internally most if not all of the large number of required parts rather than relying on subcontractors meant that, except for perhaps ten plants located in or near urban centers, "all were operating at levels substantially below their break-even points" (Wong 1981, 15). In Wong's judgment, "the effort to set up handtractor manufacturing facilities in over 100 of the 190 odd prefectures resulted in a tremendous waste of capital" (1981, 15). The large financial losses incurred by state-operated farm machinery plants reflect the drive for local autarky in production as well as mismanagement of the production process, not underpricing of inputs at the farm level.

Not all state-managed small-scale plants are unprofitable. Some, such as the county plants producing ammonium sulfate, that sell their output pri- marily if not exclusively to the collective agriculture, are profitable. The cost per unit of nutrient is even higher than the state-run large-scale nitrogenous fertilizer plants discussed above. But the bureaucratic process for allocating inputs assured these plants of a guaranteed market, even though agricul- tural producers try to resist accepting these inputs in favor of the less overpriced urea fertilizer.

Because the Chinese do not report separately on the aggregate profitabil- ity of state plants producing agricultural inputs, it is difficult to judge whether the sector as a whole is profitable. Moreover, low profitability may reflect a misallocation of investment resources, as in the case of proliferating plants for the production of power-driven agricultural machinery, and poor man- agement, rather than low prices paid by farmers for the output of this sector.

Evaluation of the role of collectively owned small-scale industry in intersectoral resource transfers is more difficult. As alluded to at the outset of the chapter, collective industry is an integral part of the intersectoral flow of funds. As discussed later in this chapter, collective enterprises appear to have received only modest funds from the state, relying rather on the pool- ing of resources contributed by basic agricultural accounting units from their own internal funds and the reinvestment of their own profits to pur- chase their initial machinery and subsequently to finance additions to their fixed assets. In some cases state enterprises may have provided machinery and equipment to collective units so that they could undertake certain pro- cessing activities, and in a few cases local governments provided state re- sources for the establishment of collective enterprises. But for the most part, infusions of state resources into rural industries have gone to state-owned- and-managed enterprises at the county level or above (Wong 1981, 24).

On the other hand, the state receives significant funds from collective rural enterprises both directly in tax payments and indirectly through its control of the prices at which commodities pass between the state and the collective sector. What little is known suggests the magnitude of these pay- ments may be large. Direct tax payments, for example, totaled 2.20 and 2.26 billion yuan in 1978 and 1979, respectively (Agricultural Yearbook Compila- tion Commission 1981, 366). That transfer is more than half the size of the direct agricultural tax in 1978 and 1979 (Table 3.2) and also is roughly quintuple the magnitude of all other taxes levied directly on the farm population in the First Plan (Table 3.2, footnote *a*). In addition to direct taxes, at least some collective enterprises remit "enterprise management fees" to the state that appear to be treated as a cost and are not included in the tax transfers. These fees are discussed below.

Indirect transfers through the price mechanism may also be an important element in the flow of funds between the state and collective rural enterprises, since the latter purchase capital goods and current inputs from the centrally managed state sector at artificially established prices rather than in competitive markets.

The important effect of changes in the prices of state-supplied inputs on the revenue of collectively operated enterprises is illustrated by the production of agricultural implements in Wuchiang County, Kiangsu. In contrast to power-driven equipment, which is manufactured by county- and prefectural-level state enterprises, hand-powered machines and hand tools generally are manufactured in commune- and brigade-run collective enterprises (Wong 1981, 13). Wuchiang is no exception to this general pattern since in 1980 nineteen of the twenty-three factories producing small and medium-sized agricultural implements were collective enterprises at the commune level, whereas only four were under county control. In 1980 the annual financial losses of these enterprises were 155,000 yuan, 16.5 percent of the value of output (Cheng Chung-chieh 1981, 43). The losses stem primarily from an average rise of 17.1 percent between 1965 and 1980 in the prices of raw materials purchased from the state and from increased "enterprise management fees" remitted to the state. Price increases ranged from 60 percent for cold-rolled steel and 40 percent for bamboo to 10 percent for coal. For the factories for which detailed cost data were provided, increased prices for raw materials and increased enterprise management fees accounted for from 67.1 to 100 percent of increased costs (Cheng Chung-chieh 1981,42). Although retail prices paid by peasants were not raised to cover the higher production costs, since the factories were predominantly collective the increased costs were passed on to the peasantry in the form of losses, rather than borne by the state.

In short, the comparison of relative prices of agricultural producer goods and prices received by farmers in China to price ratios for similar pairs of products elsewhere supports the hypothesis that major agricultural inputs, such as machinery and chemical fertilizer, were expensive, at least up to 1978. Low profit rates in state-owned machinery plants reflected a strategy of local production autarky leading to inefficiency and high costs, rather than modern inputs that, in any meaningful sense, were underpriced. It is not clear whether the outputs of collectively owned plants were similarly overpriced. Perhaps because there were fewer economies of scale, these products would be more efficiently manufactured and more fairly priced. These plants in the aggregate, however, were profitable and paid substantial direct taxes to the state. Moreover, the case of agricultural implements discussed here suggests that the intersectoral resource implications of changing fixed prices of inputs supplied to this sector by the state warrant more research.

Since 1978 the relative prices of agricultural producer goods have declined for several reasons. Key, of course, has been the substantial increase in the quota and over-quota purchase prices for cereals. Moreover, since the state has changed the mix – reducing the quota share and raising the over-quota share of its purchases – average prices received by farmers have increased more than an examination of the quota or over-quota prices alone would suggest. Finally, state subsidies for the sale of agricultural producer goods such as electricity and diesel fuel may have increased.

Until recently, the Chinese rarely disclosed the relative shares of quota and over-quota deliveries of cereals. However, the budgetary implications of the rise in the over-quota share of state purchases were quite important, and the size of the shares was revealed in the course of these discussions. The share of state purchases at the over-quota price was about 45 percent in 1976[19] but fell in 1977 and 1978 to about one-quarter.[20] But the new price incentives offered beginning in 1979 and the reduction in tax and quota deliveries led to a rise in the share of over-quota deliveries. This share was 32.7 percent in 1979 and by 1981 some 60 percent of the grain purchased by the state fell into the over-quota and negotiated price categories (Chang Li-fen 1980, 32; Wu Chen-k'un 1982). Thus the ratio of the average to the quota price was 1.14 in 1976, 1.08 in 1977–78, 1.16 in 1979, and at least 1.3 by 1981. Thus the rising share of premium-priced deliveries and the increase in the premium rate from 30 to 50 percent meant that the average price of grain sold to the state in 1981 was more than 40 percent greater than in 1977–78 although the quota price rose only 18 percent (Appendix 3).

Thus the ratio of agricultural producer goods prices to average prices received by farmers dropped. For example, in 1981 the average nitrogen (in the form of urea)/rice price ratio had dropped to 3.2:1, a decline of almost 30 percent from the relative average price prevailing in 1976 (Table 3.5).[21] The average nitrogen/rice price ratio remains more than twice the international level, where nitrogen in the form of urea and rice trade at a ratio of 1.4:1 or about 1:1 when rice is priced in milled form.[22]

Finally, in 1981 state subsidies of agricultural producer goods reached 4.5 billion yuan (Liu Chou-fu 1982, 34). These subsidies represent financial transfers to sales agencies that allow them, in turn, to sell diesel fuel, electricity, and perhaps other inputs to agricultural collectives at lower prices than those prevailing in sales to state enterprises. In Sinkiang in 1978 the subsidy for diesel fuel used on farms was 145 yuan per ton, reducing the price to farmers to 155 yuan per ton (Sinkiang Regional Service February 27, 1979). In Hupei the subsidy was 130 yuan per ton (Chang Kuo-fan 1980, 15). Electricity, too, is subsidized at the point of sale to the farm sector. But the subsidy of diesel fuel at a level of 120 yuan per ton was established in 1956 (Cheng Chien-ho 1982, 57), suggesting the level of subsidies provided by the state has not increased much over the long run. Moreover, in the aggregate these subsidies were only slightly more than 10 percent of the value of producer goods purchased from the state (Table 3.3).

State and periodic rural market prices for agricultural products

Because grains and vegetable oils in the late 1970s were traded legally in rural markets for the first time in more than a decade, it is possible to estimate the implicit rents embodied within the pricing system. An examination of state purchase and periodic market prices also suggests that state purchase prices, especially for cereals and edible vegetable oilseeds, were relatively low and contained a large pure tax component, particularly prior to 1978.

Of course, the difference between the state and market prices may overstate the tax component of the government purchase price. In theory there may be no tax at all since the average price received by peasants in a system combining forced deliveries to the government at below-market prices and a free market need not be less than the price that would be received in a single market in the absence of government market intervention. The average price received under a system involving a quota delivery is simply the weighted average of the price received for sales to the state and the open market price. If the latter rises sufficiently, in response to the supply withdrawn by government procurement at artifically low prices, the average price received by producers might actually be higher than in the absence of government intervention. Such an argument has been made, for example, to counter the criticism that the producer levy scheme run by the Indian government depresses prices received by farmers, undermining production incentives.

However, the rise in the average price received by producers is contingent on the separation of the market for grain consumed by the nonagricultural population into two income classes for which the price elasticity of demand differs significantly (Hayami, Subbarao, and Otsuka 1982). If government-procured cereals are supplied to the urban poor at below-market prices while the urban rich, for whom the (absolute) price elasticity of demand is considerably lower, compete for the residual supply on the open market, then the average price received by producers will be higher than under the free market equilibrium with no government intervention. In such a situation the government is able to transfer income to the peasantry and subsidize the consumption of the urban poor, all at the expense of the urban rich, without imposing the usually supposed negative production incentive effects on producers since the average price they receive does not fall.[23]

The conditions necessary to improve the distribution of income (assuming that the procurement levies are not assigned in a regressive way and that the average peasant income is less than the average income in the nonagricultural sector) with little or no efficiency loss are not fulfilled in China. Most important, the entire nonagricultural population receives cereal supplies through the public distribution system. Thus there is no segmentation of the demand for grain by the nonagricultural population such that the poor receive subsidized cereals through public distribution while the rich, for whom the price elasticity of demand is significantly lower, compete for grain supplies in a residual open market. At best, then, the average price received by producers would be just equal to the single free market price that would prevail in the absence of government intervention.

Even this condition is unlikely to prevail since the supplies of cereals provided through the rationing system are sufficiently large in quantity to almost completely satisfy the demand for cereals by the nonagricultural population. Moreover, in most of the years since 1949 urban farmers' markets have been closed or the sale of rationed commodities in these markets has been legally prohibited. Thus the volume of sales of agricultural products by peasants to the nonagricultural population has been small and composed predominantly of vegetables, poultry, and other commodities for which there are no compulsory quotas for delivery to the government.

Although a priori the institutional arrangements probably depress the average price received by producers for products subject to quota delivery, analysis of the degree of indirect tax embodied in the official procurement prices is difficult. Deliveries of many products subject to levy occur at two or more prices, and the weighted average delivery price must be used in comparison with market prices. Table 3.6 presents data on quota procurement prices and rural market prices for several grains, soybeans, and vegetable oils in the first quarter of 1980. These data show that the quota prices for wheat and corn delivered to the state are only about half the average prices prevailing in rural markets. But the state's over-quota prices are only about

Table 3.6. *Quota procurement and rural free market prices*
for agricultural products, 1980 (yuan/kg)

	Quota price[a]	Rural market prices			
		Average[b]	Anhui[c]	Kiangsu[d]	Szechuan[e]
Rice (japonica, grade 3)	.2972	—	—	—	—
Rice (indica, grade 3)	.2312	—	—	—	—
Rice (husked)	.3363[f]	.780	.544	.58	.70–.72
Wheat (grade 3)	.3296	.594	.492	.54	.53–.56
Corn (yellow, grade 2)	.2144	.396	—	—	—
Sorghum (husked, grade 2)	.2082	—	—	.46	—
Soybeans (yellow, grade 3)	.4614	—	.920	1.02	—
Edible vegetable oil (average)	2.0388	—	3.90	4.14	—

[a]Official prices are the unified national quota procurement prices; no adjustment has been made for above-quota deliveries for which a 50 percent premium is paid.
[b]Average prices prevailing at the end of March 1980 in the 206 rural markets under the administrative control of the General Administrative Bureau of Industry and Commerce.
[c]Average prices in a survey of eleven markets in north, central, and south Anhui.
[d]An average of nineteen markets during the first quarter of 1980.
[e]Prices at a market in Lengchuanyi in the eastern portion of the Ch'engtu Plain on the morning of April 29, 1980.
[f]A weighted average of japonica and indica varieties converted to husked rice, assuming losses in processing are 30 percent of the original weight.
Sources: State Statistical Bureau (1979b), NCNA (April 21, 1981), *People's Daily* (1980b).

20 percent under the market price. For rice, the comparison is more complex, since the official price is for unprocessed product (paddy), whereas the rural market price is for husked rice. A weighted average of the official purchase prices for indica and japonica rices expressed in terms of husked rice is .3363 yuan per kilogram for quota purchases and .5045 yuan per kilogram for above-quota purchases.[24] Thus for rice the rural market price was 2.3 times the state's quota price and more than 50 percent greater than the government's over-quota purchase price. The free market prices for soybeans and sorghum in Anhui and Kiangsu were at least twice the state quota price and from a third to a half greater than the marginal state over-quota purchase price.

Since, as discussed above, prior to 1981 the weighted average of quota and over-quota prices was only 10 to 15 percent greater than the quota price, the average price paid by the government in 1980 for cereals was only about half the prices prevailing in rural periodic markets.[25] Significantly, market prices in 1980 were generally lower than those prevailing in 1979 and in some cases were lower than the prices prevailing in the mid-1960s before rural markets were suppressed (People's Daily 1980b). Thus for earlier years, when quota procurement prices were at least 20 percent lower and periodic market prices were higher by an unknown amount, the implicit rents embodied in the state procurement system were greater.

There is, of course, no way to judge the representativeness of the market prices shown in Table 3.6. The national average prices are for the 206 rural markets that are under the administrative control of the General Administrative Bureau of Industry and Commerce. But in 1980 there were 37,890 rural markets (Hu Ch'iao-mu 1981, 195), and presumably there was wide interregional variation in rural market prices. Prices for wheat and rice in Anhui, Kiangsu, and Szechuan, although somewhat below the national average market prices, do reflect significant variation, even though for Anhui and Kiangsu the reported data are already averages of eleven and nineteen markets, respectively.

After 1981, as the volume of market transactions grew, the large differential between state and free market prices persisted. In March 1981 the average national free market prices for rice, wheat, and corn were .740, .594, and .362 yuan per kilogram, down 5, 0, and 8 percent, respectively, from the previous year (NCNA April 21, 1981). Increases in specialized production of noncereal crops, rising average farm income, and high income elasticity of demand apparently have shifted the demand schedule, resulting in modest changes in the average market price even as the supply schedule shifted to the right.

State extractions of grain and oils from the countryside at below-market prices do not lead directly to large state profits. Indeed, as discussed in detail in Chapter 5, the state commercial system incurs growing financial losses on the purchase and resale of grain and edible vegetable oils. The purchase of grain from the peasantry at a low price nonetheless constitutes a transfer from agriculture to other sectors of the economy, since maintaining low prices for basic foods in urban areas has been a central component of state wage policy. After 1956 labor productivity in the state industrial sector rose at an average annual rate of almost 3 percent, yet the state held real wages constant for more than two decades. That combination of rising productivity and constant or declining real wages allowed the profits of state-managed enterprises to soar from 11.4 to 49.3 billion yuan between 1956 and 1979 (Li Hsien-nien 1957, 17; Wang Ping-ch'ien 1980). The fiscal system channeled most enterprise profits directly to the state budget. A constant or declining real wage strategy, however, was predicated partly on the continued provision of basic foodstuffs to workers at low, fixed nominal prices. By 1961–62 this policy required state subsidies for the commercial sector. But over time, the real cost of the subsidy was held down by extracting grain from the countryside at low prices.

Relative prices of consumer goods based on agriculture

Not only are cereals extracted from the peasantry at a low price, but the prices of some noncereal crops are undervalued relative both to grain and to the prices of consumer goods for which they are the major input. One example is cotton, China's most important nongrain crop. The price of ginned cotton relative to wheat reached a peak in 1951 and 1952 when it recovered to the prewar level. After several further adjustments, it had declined about 10 percent by 1957 (Appendix 3). After 1957 the state reduced the relative price of cotton to a low point in 1970 when it was 35 percent less than in 1952. Following an increase in the price of cotton in the early 1970s, its relative price in 1975–77 was about 26 percent less than in 1952, 18 percent less than in 1957. In the world market, the relative price of cotton in 1976–77 was about 10 percent less than in 1951–52, but about 20 percent higher than in 1956–57.[26] Thus in the mid-1970s the cotton/wheat price ratio in China, relative to the world price ratio, declined by about one-fifth compared to 1951–52, and by one-third compared to 1956–57. The declining price of ginned cotton relative to the price of wheat, the most important commodity purchased by cotton producers, imposed a substantial and growing indirect tax burden on cotton producers.

The government reaped enormous profits from these price trends by establishing itself as the monopsonist purchaser of raw cotton and the monopolist seller of yard goods and cotton clothing, both in domestic and international markets.

The state established its monopsonist position in the purchase of ginned cotton by forbidding its sale on rural markets and increasing the share of output that it purchased from 76.7 to 97.7 percent between 1952 and 1979 (Agricultural Yearbook Compilation Commission 1981, 327). Peasants in cotton-producing regions may retain only a kilogram or less of ginned cotton annually (Chinese Communist Party Central Committee 1970; Hunan Agricultural College 1959, 97), primarily for use in padding quilts and winter jackets. Although peasants may circumvent this regulation and retain additional amounts, the sale of homespun yarn and handwoven cotton cloth in rural markets has been and remains legally prohibited (NCNA August 5, 1981). Thus marketing of cotton is more restrictive than grains and oils, which in most of the First Plan, between 1960 or 1961 and 1965 or 1966, and again since 1979 were sold in nonstate markets after compulsory quotas to the state were met. Precluding rural market sales was an essential mechanism for cutting off the supply of cotton to the native rural spinning and weaving industries that otherwise would have continued to supply a portion of rural cloth requirements at prices lower than those charged by the state. That policy effectively established the government's position as the monopoly supplier of textiles. Although the government used its increasing monopsony power, especially after 1957, to reduce the price of raw cotton relative to the price of the major commodity that it sold to cotton producers, its price-setting policy for textiles sold on the domestic market has not been studied. Evidence shown in the tabulation below suggests that the price the government set for cotton cloth relative to ginned cotton in the first half of the 1950s was higher than in the prewar period (Li Te-pin 1981a, 50).

White cotton cloth/ginned cotton price ratio

	Shantung	Szechuan
1930-36	2.53	2.16
1950-55	1.96	1.79
Relative price of cotton cloth in 1950-55 (prewar = 1.00)	1.29	1.21

This ratio is particularly useful, for it provides a measure of the purchasing power of agricultural raw materials over the finished goods produced from the agricultural product. It is less clear whether the price of textiles in the 1950s relative to other consumer goods was higher or lower than in the prewar years.

The nominal price of rationed cotton cloth has not increased since the mid-1950s, while the price of raw cotton has increased, ceteris paribus reducing the profitability of the textile industry. Declining profitability on domestic sales of textiles may have been offset by selling a growing share of output in international markets.[27] In 1952–54 cloth exports were only 2 percent of domestic production, but this share rose as the heavy industrialization program got under way in the mid-1950s. The export share rose to 7–8 percent in 1955–56, to 11 percent in 1957–58, and reached a peak of 25 percent in 1962 (Chao Kang 1977, 280). Exports to the Soviet Union were particularly important, since the complete plants they supplied, which formed the core of the First Plan, were financed with exports of textiles and other agricultural products. Textile fabric exports to the Soviet Union rose from U.S. $60 million to $440 million between 1955 and 1959, increasing from 9 to 40 percent of total exports to the Soviet Union. Even after the Sino–Soviet split in 1960, China's exports fell only gradually, since through the first half of the 1960s China repaid its cumulative debt to the Soviet Union, largely through textile exports. Textiles as a share of total exports averaged 60 percent in 1962–64 (Chao Kang 1977, 282).

Because its major input was underpriced (at least through 1978) and its products at least initially probably overpriced, the cotton textile industry has been one of the most profitable branches of industry and the single largest source of state revenues, providing in the late 1970s about 10 percent of state budgetary revenues from all sources (Ministry of Textile Industry Research Office 1981, IV-48). Since peasants provide most of the raw material and purchase about two-thirds of domestically consumed cotton, they bear the burden of state price manipulation.

A similar situation prevails in sugar refining. The state's monopsony power derives from its control of the modern sugar-refining industry and the suppression of sugar processing by "native methods." Although the state purchased only 70.1 percent of all sugarcane and beet produced in 1958, by 1978 that share had risen to 89.2 percent (Agricultural Yearbook Compilation Commission 1981, 327). In 1979 the costs of producing and retailing 1 ton of refined sugar from cane were as follows (Hsiao Chuo-chi 1980, 47):[28]

Raw material cost	314 Y
Labor and other costs	196
Total production costs	510
Profits and taxes	740
Ex-factory price	1,250
Distribution and marketing costs	290
Retail price	1,540 Y

The profit and taxes received from 2.13 million tons of refined sugar produced from cane in the 1979–80 refining season can be estimated at 1.60 billion yuan.[29] To place that number in perspective it is sufficient to point out that the state's profit on the production and sale of a single very minor food product (per capita consumption in 1979 was about 2 kilograms, and sugarcane was sown on only one-half of 1 percent of total cultivated land) was the equivalent of 30 percent of all state investment budgeted for agriculture in 1979 (Table 3.8).

The state appears to follow a similar policy in other branches of light industry, again by establishing itself simultaneously as a monopsonist purchaser of raw materials and the monopoly supplier of finished goods. The state has acknowledged that it has raised retail prices of tobacco, wine, and liquor, all products with a low price elasticity, since the early 1950s and that retail prices are "much higher than production costs" (NCNA December 8, 1979). Furthermore, while the state has lowered the prices of some consumer goods produced with industrial inputs (for example, pharmaceutical prices declined 45 percent between 1952 and 1979), the retail price of cotton clothing changed little since the early 1950s when relatively high prices for finished textile products were established (State Statistical Bureau 1981c, VI-23). Price manipulation places a disproportionate burden on the agricultural sector since it is both the major source of raw materials and the primary market for final products of the light industrial sector. Although chemical fibers, plastics, and other materials of industrial origin are of increasing importance, as shown below, as late as 1978 more than two-thirds of light industrial goods still were manufactured from inputs procured from agriculture (Yang Chien-pai and Li Hsüeh-tseng 1980, 32).

Share of light industrial products (%)

Source	1952	1957	1965	1970	1975	1978
Raw materials from agriculture	87.5	81.6	71.7	70.0	70.1	68.4
Raw materials from industry	12.5	18.4	28.3	30.0	29.9	31.6

In addition to cotton, sugarcane, and sugar beet, these inputs include tobacco, silk, hemp, ramie, other fiber crops, wool, timber for paper, hides for leather, grains for wines and liquors, as well as food crops for the food-processing industry.

Light industry as a whole – not just textiles and sugar – has been a major source of government revenue because the state has manipulated the prices of agricultural inputs and the sales prices of final goods to insure high profits. For the twenty-eight years from 1950 through 1977 enterprises manufacturing light industrial products paid profits and taxes to the state budget that were the source of 29 percent of all state budgetary revenues – a remarkable achievement given that the share of national income produced by light industry was about 13 percent in the 1950s (Ishikawa 1965, 66, 76) and rose only slightly to less than 16 percent in 1978 (Yang Chien-pai and Li Hsüeh-tseng 1980, 20). These funds were the equivalent of 70 percent of all state investment in this twenty-eight-year period. Less than 8 percent of these profits were reinvested in light industry – the bulk was used to finance investment in heavy industry.

Summary

Although much of the data required for a more definitive analysis is lacking, enough evidence exists to postulate that the state transferred significant resources out of the agricultural sector over a sustained period. That transfer contributed to a remarkable increase in the rate of investment after 1949. Whereas the ratio of gross domestic capital formation to gross domestic product was only about 5 percent in the early 1930s, by the First Plan the average rate of accumulation had reached over 20 percent.[30] Although this rate declined as a consequence of the economic crisis created by the Great Leap Forward and the withdrawal of Soviet economic asssistance in 1960, it rose again after the mid-1960s and averaged in excess of 30 percent during 1970–78, reaching a peak of 36.5 percent in 1978 (Hsü Ti-hsin 1981, 4). Agriculture's contribution to increased investment in the early 1950s was facilitated by a significant direct agricultural tax. As the direct tax burden declined it was replaced by an agricultural procurement and retail price policy that enabled the state to generate significant resources through the profits of light industry. Although changes in the terms of trade during the First Plan favored agriculture (Table 3.4), it seems that the price trends reduced the net flow of resources out of agriculture only marginally.

After the 1950s the picture is less complete. Agricultural exports declined in the early 1960s and then recovered. Net of resales to peasants, 1965 grain taxes and state purchases of 27.78 million tons were slightly less than the 28.2 million tons of 1957 (Ministry of Agriculture Policy Research Office 1980, 39). Procurement of vegetable oils was down substantially, while procurement of cotton, sugarcane, sugar beet, and pigs was greater than 1957. After 1965 procurement of grains, net of resales, grew very slowly in absolute terms. Procurement of cotton stagnated except for the bumper harvest year of 1973, and oil procurement fell. Although this pattern might suggest decline in intersectoral resource transfers, the hypothesis advanced here is that, with the exception of the early 1960s, the state continued to extract significant resources from agriculture. This was achieved through several means. First, the state did not raise agricultural purchase prices significantly between 1966 and 1978, thus largely eliminating that "leakage" from farm sector extractions measured in real terms. Measured relative to world prices, which are particularly relevant since Chinese exports remain predominantly processed food and agriculturally based light manufactures,[31] the indirect tax inherent in the system of procurement of agricultural products may have increased. Second, and probably more important, the state raised the burden of indirect taxation on the peasantry by supplying agricultural producer goods such as chemical fertilizers, pesticides, and farm machinery at prices that frequently were high relative to their domestic costs of production and relative to international prices. Thus the mechanism of intersectoral resource transfers has changed over time, with the predominant role initially played by direct taxes and subsequently by indirect taxes entailed in state transactions with the farm sector.

The effect of policies since 1978 on intersectoral resource flows is uncertain. As discussed in great detail earlier in this chapter and in Chapter 2, agricultural prices have risen substantially. Moreover, both the direct agricultural tax and the share of sales to the state at the lower quota price level have been reduced. At the same time, the farm-level prices of most agricultural producer goods and consumer goods sold by the state (with the major exception of grain resold by the state to collective agriculture) appear to have been held constant. But by international standards some major purchased inputs, such as nitrogenous chemical fertilizers, are still substantially overpriced. The evidence on machinery is less clear. Most consumer goods based on agricultural inputs still appear overpriced. But on balance the price changes have had such far-reaching implications for the state budget that one wonders whether the policies can be maintained, a subject to which we return in Chapter 5.

Sectoral allocation of investment

Was such a large-scale transfer of resources from agriculture to industry as that which occurred prior to 1979 justified economically? As previously suggested, there are at least two criteria for answering this question. An analysis based on the welfare criterion will be postponed until the following chapter. The question addressed here is whether or not the sectoral allocation of resources was economically rational. Note that this question can be answered only if we set aside the issue of time preference. That is, I simply accept, as given, that the rate of aggregate investment that was attained in various periods reflected the preferences of the leadership for consumption now versus consumption in the future. Given the time preference revealed, was the sectoral allocation of resources optimal?

Lacking data on the marginal rates of return to alternative investments, one must resort to less precise criteria. Specifically, I propose to compare the average rate of return on investments in the two sectors. Put simply, did the relatively high share of investment allocated to industry lead to a proportionately higher rate of industrial growth? Rather than comparing the capital output ratios of the two sectors directly, it proves convenient to compare the relative investment shares and growth rates of the two sectors over an appropriately defined time period. However, the criterion for balanced growth then becomes not the equality of the ratio of the investment shares and the growth rates of the two sectors but the equality of the ratio of the investment shares and the ratio of the growth rates, adjusted for the relative initial product shares of the two sectors.[32]

Data on the sectoral allocation of state investment funds and the composition of state budgetary expenditures on agriculture are displayed in Tables 3.7 and 3.8.

State expenditures for agriculture are allocated among four categories: fixed investment, working capital, current expenditures, and expenditures for financing current consumption, including rural relief and aid to poor communes (Han Po 1958). The categories conceptually are separate. For example, the funds allocated to support communes are supposed to be used primarily to finance investment such as purchases of tractors and other machinery and to develop commune- and brigade-run collective enterprises rather than to finance current consumption (Ko Chih-ta 1980, 13). In practice some of these resources may be fungible across categories, and the accounting system may miss some transfers.

Beginning in 1952, after economic recovery from wartime disruption was complete, state investment and noninvestment expenditures were biased strongly toward industry. Between 1953 and 1957 cumulative budgetary expenditures on agriculture in all categories were 10.7 percent of total budgetary expenditures. Agriculture's investment share for the twenty-five years from 1953 through 1978, 12.0 percent, was similarly modest and only one-fifth that of industry (Table 3.7). Since industry's share of national product initially was less than half that of agriculture (Table 1.1), industry's growth rate would have had to exceed that of agriculture's by a ratio much greater than the 5:1 investment ratio in order to satisfy the balanced growth criterion. Yet the rates of growth of industrial and agricultural output, measured on a net rather than gross basis and in constant prices over the same period, were 11.3 and 2.3 percent, respectively (Yang Chien-pai and Li Hsüeh-tseng 1980,183).[33] Since the ratio of industry's to agriculture's growth rate, 4.9:1, is far less than the ratio of the investment shares times the ratio of the initial product shares, there is a presumption that the allocation of resources was imbalanced. The rate of growth of national income would have been higher if a larger share of investment resources had been allocated to agriculture.

Table 3.7. *Sectoral allocation of investment, 1953–78 (billions of yuan and percentage)*

	Total	Agriculture	Industry		Heavy – of which agricultural producer goods[a]	Light
			Heavy			
1953–57	55	4.30 (7.8)[b]	25.599 (46.5)[b]		.758	3.25 (5.9)[b]
1958–62	119	14.64 (12.3)	66.627 (56.1)		3.827	6.18 (5.2)
1963–65	40	7.52 (18.8)	20.126 (49.8)		1.968	1.58 (3.9)
1966–70	91	10.74 (11.8)	52.477 (57.4)		4.773	3.66 (4.0)
1971–75	168	18.98 (11.3)	92.058 (54.8)		9.338	9.07 (5.4)
1976–78	125	15.59 (12.5)	65.783 (52.6)		7.316	—
1953–78	598	71.77 (12.0)	324.163 (54.2)		27.993	32.30 (5.4)

[a]Includes investment in agricultural machinery, chemical fertilizers, and pesticides.
[b]Figures in parentheses are percentages of total investment.
Sources: Yang Chien-pai and Li Hsüeh-tseng (1980, 31), Liang Wen-sen (1981, 12), Chan Wu (1980, 3), Liu Kuo-kuang and Wang Hsiang-ming (1980, 27), P'ei Yüan-hsiu, Liu Ping-ying, and Li Ping-chang (1980).

Table 3.8 *State budgetary expenditures on agriculture, 1953–82[a] (millions of yuan)*

	Total[b]	Fixed investment[c]	Working capital[c]	Current expenditure	Support for communes	Expenses for resetting urban residents in the countryside	Relief
1953–57	9,960	4,090	209	3,730	—	—	1,360
1958–62	28,360	12,670	1,500	6,700	4,640	30	2,230
1963–65	17,700	6,820	910	5,390	580	60	3,800
1966–70	23,040	9,840	1,300	7,110	720	1,920	1,880
1971–75	40,000	17,360	1,400	13,130	2,990	2,730	1,750
1976–77	20,780	7,400	720	6,890	2,360	1,750	1,660
1953–77	140,740	58,560	6,160	43,220	11,290	7,030	12,430
1978	14,800	4,835	—	6,080	1,620	—	—
1979	17,180	5,792		7,930	1,090	—	—
1980	14,400[d]	6,660[d]		8,210		—	—
1981	—	—		7,300[e]		—	1,090[f, g]
1982	—	—		7,610[d]		—	—

[a]Data for 1953–77 vary in minor respects from those previously published (Han Po, 1958). I have used these data because their source provides data for subsequent years that are not available elsewhere and because the broad categories correspond to those given in previously published sources. Moreover, the categories shown here are even more detailed – for example, providing information on expenditures incurred by the state in the resettlement of urban residents in the countryside.

[b]Component categories sum to slightly less than the stated total, presumably due to an unspecified residual category.

[c]Fixed and working capital investment shown here for each period sum to an amount that differs slightly from the agricultural investment series shown in Table 3.7. The source of the differences between the two series is not clear.

[d]Budget expenditure.

[e]Including rural relief.

[f]Estimated expenditure based on eleven months actual expenditure.

[g]Probably included in 7,300.

Sources: Ministry of Agriculture Policy Research Office (1980, 51–53; 1982, 105), Chang Ching-fu (1979, 31, 34), Wang Ping-ch'ien (1980; 1981; 1982), Agricultural Yearbook Compilation Commission (1981, 334).

The analysis of imbalance needs to be modified in four respects. First, the degree of imbalance was not invariant over the whole period, and the intertemporal variation is of interest in and of itself. Second, the measure of investment underlying Tables 3.7 and 3.8 requires several comments. Also, we must ask whether the data on average rates of return provide an adequate guide to the marginal rates of return on which sectoral allocation should be based. Finally, one must recognize that Chinese development policy has been determined not solely on the basis of a growth-maximizing calculus but a series of complex trade-offs between growth and other objectives. I discuss the methodological problems first and then turn to the intertemporal analysis.

The investment data reported in Tables 3.7 and 3.8 are based on the Chinese concept of "basic construction investment." That concept corresponds very roughly to gross domestic investment in that it is inclusive of depreciation and includes increases in inventories as well as additions to fixed assets. It includes all investment financed through the state budget, and thus in the state plan, but excludes most investment outside the plan such as expenditures on major repairs, investment financed from retained profits and depreciation funds of industrial enterprises, and farmers' self-investment.[34] I refer to the latter as collective farm investment because after cooperativization it consisted primarily of accumulation of collective units rather than individual accumulation. It includes purchases of capital goods (including livestock and vehicles), investment in self-prepared capital goods, and the imputed value of the labor component of rural construction (Ishikawa 1965, 180–1). Adjusting for these and other items substantially increases the share of investment allocated to agriculture, at least during 1953–57. In their comprehensive national income study T. C. Liu and K. C. Yeh (1965) estimated the shares of agricultural and industrial investment in the First Five-Year Plan as 11.9 and 40.4 percent, respectively (p. 239). The official data understate the farm share of investment, presumably because they exclude most farmers' self-investment. The official data suggest a ratio of investment of 6.7:1, whereas the Liu–Yeh estimate shows a much less imbalanced ratio of 3.4:1, both for 1953–57.

However, even on the basis of the more comprehensive Western estimate of investment, resource allocation in the First Plan was somewhat imbalanced. Industrial and agricultural growth, measured in value-added and in constant prices, averaged 18.7 and 3.8 percent per year, or a ratio of 4.9:1 (Yang Chien-pai and Li Hsüeh-tseng 1981, 106). Since the ratio of the investment shares is far less than the ratio of the growth rates times the ratio of the initial sectoral product shares, even on the broader definition investment appears to have been skewed toward industry during the First Plan.

Unfortunately, independent estimates of the sectoral allocation of investment for the 1960s and 70s have not yet been undertaken, so it is not clear the extent to which the official data for the whole period 1952–78 underestimate farm sector investment. For reasons discussed below, it is likely that the share of farm investment funds originating in the state budget in the mid-1970s was higher than in the First Plan. That is, the ratio of collective farm investment to state budgetary investment in agriculture declined.[35] Also, after 1966 state industrial enterprises retained a portion of their depreciation funds to finance investment outside the plan, whereas in the 1950s depreciation funds accrued to the Ministry of Finance.[36] Thus, compared to the 1950s the data for 1966–78 may understate the magnitude and share of industrial investment. Thus the long-term imbalance in investment shares may be greater than the 1:5 ratio between industry and agriculture reflected in the official data.

While the data in Tables 3.7 and 3.8 on state investment and current outlays for agriculture are understated because they exclude collective investment, they overstate the flow of funds into the agricultural sector as I have defined it earlier in this chapter. State agricultural investment and current expenditures include not only those for agriculture, but also for forestry, fisheries, water conservation, and meteorology. Several difficulties arise. First, a large share of total state investment resources under the agricultural heading is for water conservation (Table 3.9). For the years 1949 through 1979 water control projects absorbed 47.3 billion yuan,[37] about two-thirds of the total quantity of funds earmarked for agricultural investment. The noncapital operating expenses of the water conservation system in 1949–79 absorbed 29 billion yuan, a very large share of cumulative expenditures in the category "Current Expenditure" shown in column 4 of Table 3.8 (Agricultural Yearbook Compilation Commission 1981, 25). Although state investment projects benefit agriculture because they increase the area and improve the quality of irrigation, a share of the benefits of these projects accrues to the nonagricultural sector. Large- and medium-scale water conservation projects, in addition to serving agricultural functions, are designed to supply water to urban households, to facilitate waterborne transportation and communication, and to promote urban construction and industrial development (Ministry of Agriculture Policy Research Office 1982, 131). Supplying the consumption and industrial needs of the municipalities of Peking, Tientsin, Ch'angch'un, Shenyang, and Fushun, for example, requires

Table 3.9. *The allocation of agricultural investment*
(millions of yuan, current prices)

	Total	Cropping and husbandry	Forestry	Water conservation	Aquatic products	Meteorology
1952	583	167	2	411	—	3
1957	1,187	426	25	730	—	6
1962	1,439	502	108	827	—	2
1965	2,497	738	193	1,515	46	5
1975	3,840	855	214	2,566	170	29
1979	5,792	614	362	3,496	282	52

Source: Agricultural Yearbook Compilation Commission (1981, 41).

several tens of billions of cubic meters of water annually, all supplied by large-scale water projects financed with "agricultural investment." Similarly, the construction of small-scale hydroelectric projects in 1,500 counties, which in 1979 generated 11.9 million kilowatts of electric power, was financed partially with funds provided from "agricultural investment." These small hydrostations are a major source of power not only for irrigation pumps and other electrically powered farm machinery, but also for the development of local–state (i.e., county) industry that properly is part of the state rather than the collective sector (Agricultural Yearbook Compilation Commission 1981, 26). Investment as well as current expenditures for meteorology benefits not only agriculturalists but civil aviation and other nonagricultural bureaucracies.

The inclusion of expenditures for these diverse purposes in the categories of investment and current expenditures for agriculture reflects both the difficulty of separating the benefits of large-scale multiple-purpose water projects into functionally different categories and the bureaucratic flow of funds. The ministries of Water Conservancy, Agriculture, Forestry, Aquatic Products, State Farms and Land Reclamation, and Electric Power all began in the early 1950s as independent entities but subsequently have been subjected to periodic reorganizations, the water conservation and electric power bureaucracies being merged in 1958 under a new Ministry of Water Conservation and Electric Power, forestry as well as the state farms system sometimes being subsumed within the Ministry of Agriculture, and so on.[38] Although the evolution of these various bureaucracies has not been carefully examined, I believe that in published statistics the flow of funds to all of these organizations from the Ministry of Finance is consolidated into a single broad category.

A second adjustment necessary to calibrate the flow of funds to the broad sectoral conception outlined earlier is to separate agricultural investment, narrowly defined as in the second column of Table 3.9, and working capital and current expenditures on agriculture, shown in columns 3 and 4 of Table 3.8, into state and collective components. For the years 1949 through 1978, some 16 billion yuan of funds in these categories, a large share of the total, was allocated to state farms (Ko Chih-ta 1980, 13). Unlike collectives where investment funds are derived largely from internal reinvestment, state farms depend on state budgetary allocations to expand their fixed assets. Compared to collective agriculture, state farms are highly capital-intensive both because of their reclamation function and because of their lower man/land ratio. Although their cultivated area was only 4.4 percent and their agricultural labor force only 1.6 percent of the national totals, in 1978 they owned 12.8 billion yuan in fixed agricultural assets, more than 13 percent of collective and state agriculture assets combined. Judging from the data on agricultural investment, narrowly defined, state farms must have absorbed almost all of the investment resources shown in column 2 of Table 3.9. From both the empirical data and the form of organization of the accounts it appears that state investment used to increase the fixed assets of collective agriculture is limited to the relatively small level of expenditures carried in the category "support to communes" in the fifth column of Table 3.8.

The above analysis is not meant to suggest that investments and current expenditures for urban water supply, transportation, or state farms were not justifiable in economic terms. That is an independent question, the answer to which lies beyond the scope of this book. Rather, it is to point out that Chinese statistical practice, which lumps all of these investments and current outlays into the broad category of agriculture, vastly overstates the flow of state resources into the collective agricultural sector and thus simultaneously understates the rate of return on investment in collective agriculture.

Even if a proper attribution of the flow of benefits from multiple-purpose large-scale water projects could be used to allocate an appropriate share of what is labeled "agricultural investment," in Chinese statistics, to agriculture, appropriately defined, it would still be difficult to use these data and the growth rates of industry and agriculture as the basis for addressing the question of sectoral balance. What are required are data on the marginal rates of return to alternative investments, whereas the comparison of investment shares and growth rates implicitly compares the average rates of return. Two issues are implicitly involved. First, is it possible that the rate of return to investments in agriculture is declining so rapidly that although the average rate of return exceeds that in industry, the marginal rate is less? If the average-rate-of-return schedule for industry was rather flat compared to that for agriculture and if the rate of return for agriculture was initially higher, there could be a range in which although the average return in agriculture was higher, its marginal return would be lower. However, the incremental capital output ratio for industry increased significantly between the middle of the 1950s and the late 1970s.[39] Thus the average-rate-of-return schedule for industry is rather steep, reducing the prospect that the marginal rate of return on industrial investments is above that in agriculture. Furthermore, even if it could be shown that the marginal rate of return on investment in agriculture is less than that for industry, that could be due primarily to the rising allocative inefficiency induced by planning failures in agriculture, particularly after 1966.

The second issue is more complex. Because of systematic biases in the Chinese price structure, a critical assumption necessary to infer anything about marginal rates of return from average-return data is probably unjustified. We probably should not assume that the marginal contributions of each sector to output growth elsewhere in the economy are measured adequately by the prices prevailing in intersectoral product markets. The analysis earlier in this chapter suggests that intersectoral transactions understate the contributions of agriculture to industrial growth. Since agricultural products frequently are underpriced relative to domestic production costs or international price standards, the average rate of return on agricultural investments is downward-biased. Part of the return shows up in industrial growth and is not measured in the rate of return within agriculture. In a parallel fashion the average rate of return on industrial investment in some agricultural producer goods appears to overstate their marginal rate of return in a true economic sense. Although my earlier analysis does not measure the extent of distortion introduced by the price structure, correcting this problem increases the case for reallocating investment resources in favor of agriculture.

Finally, it is interesting to examine the composition of investment in heavy industry. Sometimes it has been suggested that the large share of budgetary investment flowing into industry, especially in the 1960s and 1970s, is explained by the rapid development of agricultural machinery, chemical fertilizers, pesticides, and so on. That hypothesis is not supported by the available data (Table 3.7). Although the priority of agricultural producer goods investment rose after the First Plan, for the years 1958–78 they absorbed less than 10 percent of heavy industrial investment. Moreover, only a small share of the rise in the producer goods share of total state investment, from 46.5 percent in the First Plan to 54.9 percent for 1958–78, can be explained by the increased allocations for chemical fertilizers, machinery, and pesticides.[40]

Long-run underinvestment in agriculture was attenuated in certain periods. Most notably in 1963–65 agriculture's share of investment and of total budgetary outlays rose substantially and the share of industrial investments was somewhat less than average. Moreover, although agricultural producer goods absorbed only 2.9 percent of heavy industrial investment or 1.3 percent of total state investment in the First Plan, those shares rose sharply after 1962, to 9.7 and 4.8 percent, respectively, reflecting the investment decisions on chemical fertilizers pushed through the Central Committee of the Party by Ch'en Yün in 1961. Agricultural investment fell sharply in the Third Plan (1966–70), and the agricultural producer goods share of heavy industry fell, but by a smaller proportion. Investment in agricultural producer goods as a share of investment rose in 1970–78, reflecting the continued development of the agricultural machinery sector and the investment in thirteen large-scale ammonia–urea complexes imported from the West. Contracts for these plants were signed between late 1972 and early 1974, and construction was complete by the end of 1978.

The decision to import large-scale ammonia–urea complexes coincided with parallel efforts to raise prices for farm products by introducing the system of premiums for over-quota deliveries of cereal on a national unified basis in 1970 and then raising the premium rate in 1972. The early 1970s was a brief interlude after the most intense phase of the Cultural Revolution (1966–69) when Chou En-lai and other conservative leaders at the North China Agricultural Conference and other meetings sought Party approval for a higher priority for agricultural development and a modification of the emphasis on grain production at the expense of other crops and other aspects of the Tachai model (Yü Kuo-yao 1980a, 29). These efforts to pursue a more moderate agricultural development policy were dissipated in a resurgence of radical political power and the renewed emphasis on Tachai as a national model, a movement that reached the apex of its influence in 1975–77 (Tsou, Blecher, and Meisner 1982, 272–7).

After the Third Plenum in December 1978 the cycle began again. Agriculture's share of total budgetary expenditures rose modestly from the 9.1 and 10.2 percent prevailing in 1966–70 and 1971–75, respectively (Ministry of Agriculture Policy Research Office 1980, 51–3) to 13.3 and 12.5 percent of the 1979 and 1980 budgets. Investment expenditures on agriculture as a share of the total also rose slightly. Finally, and most interestingly, in late 1978 the Chinese reentered the international market to purchase substantial new capacity for the production of urea, synthetic ammonia, and nitrophosphate fertilizer.[41]

The analysis above is based on state budgetary funds, but is supplemented below by examining expenditures financed by other sources: collective farm investment and bank loans. Finally, I examine the magnitude of fixed assets in the farm sector, which reflects the history of farm investment flows from all sources and provides an independent check of the order of magnitude of the investment flow estimates.

Collective farmers' self-investment

Although state budgetary expenditures for collective agriculture, with the exception of those for large-scale water projects, are relatively small, they are only one of three sources of funds. Collective farm investment and expenditure financed through bank credit must also be examined.

Farmers' self-investment, including additions to working capital, totaled 17 billion yuan in the First Five-Year Plan, or an average of 3.4 billion yuan per year (Wang Kuang-wei 1959a, 9). Shigeru Ishikawa has analyzed exhaustively the information on farmers' accumulation or self-investment for the 1950s. He found that the 17-billion-yuan total was internally consistent with data on farmers' and cooperative purchases of capital goods, survey data on farmers' investment in the form of self-prepared capital goods, and the imputed value of the labor component of rural construction (1965, 172–87).

Western economists frequently have thought that self-investment became increasingly important in the 1960s and 1970s as a consequence of the agriculture-first policy adopted at the Tenth Plenum of the Eighth Central Committee in 1962. The improvement in the farm terms of trade shown by the official data, combined with a declining direct tax burden, was thought to provide the financial resources to increase farmers' self-investment.

Although collective farm investment has risen since the 1950s, the increase was modest when placed against the growth of farm sector output. Between 1957 and 1978 total internal reinvestment, including both fixed investment and additions to working capital, was 75.1 billion yuan, an average of 3.6 billion yuan annually, little more than the average of the First Plan (State Statistical Bureau 1982b, 195).[42] In part the low average level reflects the collapse of internal farm investment during the early 1960s. Between 1973 and 1978 internal reinvestment was 39.2 billion yuan, an average of 6.5 billion yuan. But since value added in agriculture grew more rapidly than farmers' self-investment between the First Plan and the 1970s, collective farm investment as a share of value added in agriculture declined from about 10 percent to 6–7 percent.[43]

In addition to internal reinvestment by basic-level farm production units, a share of the profits of brigade- and commune-managed enterprises also are allocated to farm investment. The magnitude of these funds, 1.43, 2.63, 2.69, and 2.26 billion yuan in 1977, 1978, 1979, and 1980, respectively, is significant relative to internal reinvestment from farming operations (Agricultural Yearbook Compilation Commission 1981, 366; Editorial, 1981a). Since collectively run rural enterprises are included within my definition of agriculture, these funds should be considered analogous to internal reinvestment of income from farming activities. When this addition is made, internal agricultural reinvestment is higher, but proportionately is still less than in the 1950s. Finally, if we add profits of collective enterprises that are reinvested in rural industrial, transport, agricultural processing, and other activities, 3.09 and 4.06 billion yuan in 1978 and 1979, respectively, internal reinvestment is proportionately comparable to the First Plan.

Internal investment funds may also be evaluated relative to agriculture's labor force, cultivated land, or the financial requirements of modernized agriculture, given the Chinese price structure. Internal reinvestment from farming averaged 2.75 million yuan per county annually in 1973–78 (Chao Jung 1980, 39) or 60 yuan per hectare of cultivated land (Reporter 1980a, 11). The investment costs of modernized agriculture vary by region, depending primarily on the difficulty of providing irrigation, but are substantial. In north China, for example, investment costs for mechanization and irrigation are estimated at 3,000 yuan per hectare on the basis of actual outlays at what the Chinese refer to as "experimental points" (Tsung Han 1979, 8). In the lower Yangtse region, where water is more plentiful, costs are somewhat lower, 2,250 yuan per hectare. That level of expenditure is required to achieve what are described as relatively low levels of irrigation and mechanization. For higher levels, such as those prevailing in the area around Wuhsi in Kiangsu, where grain yields are the highest in China, expenditure levels are somewhat greater, 3,000 yuan per hectare (Reporter 1980a, 11). Based on an investigation of model units, the investment required to achieve modernized agriculture is roughly 400 million yuan per county, compared to internal reinvestment averaging 10 million yuan per year (Tu Ch'eng 1980, 19).

All of these measures of the investment costs of modernized agriculture are quite crude. They provide no precise measures of the effectiveness of irrigation or the level of mechanization that could be achieved for the specified level of expenditures. Moreover, as investment decisions increasingly reflect the profit-maximizing calculations of producers rather than the political choices of cadres, the levels of mechanization actually sought may be less than those described in the sources cited above.[44] The data presented above, however, do show that even on the broadest possible measure, internal reinvestment has not grown relative to value added in agriculture and may be modest relative to the costs of modernized agriculture, given the present prices of producer goods. Bank credit is the only other source of funds remaining to be examined.

Bank credit

Bank credit is yet a third source of funds for collective agriculture. Two central issues are examined below. First, does credit add substantially to investment financed through the state budget and collective farm investment? Second, how effectively does the State Bank and system of credit cooperatives allocate working capital to the farm sector?

Data on the year-end volume of loans outstanding to agriculture by the State Bank between 1950 and 1980 are summarized in Table 3.10. These data reflect the extent to which increases in bank credit provide potential funds for fixed investment and increases in working capital over and above those financed from the state budget and farmers' self-investment.[45] In practice about 80 percent of loans are used to finance increased working capital or fixed investment.[46] It is immediately apparent that relative to budgetary investment increased credit was a significant source of long-term investment funds prior to 1966 and since 1977. But between 1965 and 1977 loans outstanding increased by only 2 billion yuan, or an average annual amount of about 170 million yuan. Of this amount approximately 135 million yuan may have been allocated to investment.[47] By contrast, state budgetary allocations for investment and increased working capital averaged more than twenty times as much, 3,170 million yuan per year (Table 3.8). Loans outstanding actually declined between 1965 and 1975, the longest sustained period of quantity planning.

Loans were far more important prior to 1957 and after 1977. During the First Plan the investment financed from the increase in loans outstanding was the equivalent of 40 percent of fixed investment and increased working capital provided through the budget.[48] Since 1977 loans have been relatively large compared to budgetary outlays as a source of fixed investment and increases in working capital. Between 1977 and 1981 loans outstanding increased by 2,360 million yuan per year and again financed investment equivalent to about 40 percent of that provided through the state budget.

Bank loans were not an important source of funds for fixed investment or increases in permanent working capital between 1965 and 1975. But since

Table 3.10 *Agricultural credit from the State Bank, 1950–81[a]*
(millions of yuan, year-end balances)

Year	Amount	Year	Amount
1950	95	1965	7,820
1951	205	1963–65 (avg.)	7,350
1952	481	1970	8,510
1953	666	1966–70 (avg.)	8,190
1954	783	1975	7,250
1955	1,001	1971–75 (avg.)	6,070
1956	3,029	1976	9,030
1957	2,759	1977	9,820
1953–57 (avg.)	1,640	1978	11,550
1958	4,020	1979	13,674
1959	5,860	1980	17,588
1962	6,670	1981[b]	19,255
1958–62 (avg.)	5,620		

[a]Includes funds dispersed from the Agricultural Bank of China and its predecessor organization, the Agricultural Cooperative Bank, when it operated as an entity administratively separate from the State Bank, i.e., during 1951, from March 1953 until April 1957, from October 1963 through November 1965, and since February 23, 1979. When the Agricultural Bank was dissolved periodically, its operations were subsumed within the Rural Banking Management Bureau of the People's Bank (Agricultural Yearbook Compilation Commission, 1981, 170). Includes loans to state farms as well as to collective agriculture. Excludes loans from agricultural credit cooperatives.
[b]Preliminary.
Sources: Yang P'ei-hsin (1958, 32), Li Hsien-nien (1958, 4), Ministry of Agriculture Policy Research Office (1980, 53; 1982, 106–7), NCNA (July 3, 1981), State Statistical Bureau (1982b, 399).

these data do not reflect funds borrowed prior to planting but repaid after harvesting (prior to the end of the year), they tell us nothing about the provision of short-term working capital. Provision of short-term credit by the state is critical because most production teams have only modest internal working capital, and the traditional sources of credit, notably landlords and rural loan associations, were eliminated as sources of funds during land reform. A survey of 637 production teams showed that internal working capital in 1979, called "production expense funds," was only 3.24 million yuan or 28.8 percent of production costs, exclusive of labor (Sun Pu 1980). Current outlays were financed primarily by loans from banks and credit cooperatives, although in some cases teams borrowed from their own members at interest rates about three times the bank rate because of inadequate state credit facilities.

For the teams in the survey additions to working capital in 1979 from nonloan sources were quite small: 370,000 yuan, 1.2 percent of total income or 3.3 percent of cash outlays for purchased inputs. Three hundred five teams, almost half of those in the sample, made no additions to their working capital in 1979.

The undercapitalization of the farm sector is more acute than these data suggest because the Chinese measure of cost is based on a cash flow concept that accounts for depreciation of fixed assets inadequately. Provision for depreciation is made in a separate depreciation fund that, like funds for self-financed fixed investment, are deducted from gross revenues prior to the distribution of work point income to team members. Yet in 1979 financial retentions for depreciation were 225,000 yuan, only 1.4 percent of the value of fixed assets of the teams investigated. The majority of China's agricultural producing units retain no depreciation funds (Ministry of Agriculture Commune Bureau 1980). Since the actual rate of depreciation on agricultural fixed assets is unlikely to be less than 10 percent, a share of retained investment funds inevitably must be allocated for the maintenance of fixed assets. Thus whereas in theory internal investment funds should be the equivalent of farmers' net self-investment – that is, it should finance the purchase of new assets – it may be that only a portion is so used.

It must be pointed out that the picture that emerges on the basis of the survey of six hundred–odd production teams is undoubtedly unduly optimistic. Published investigations frequently are based on a sample of atypical production units. The survey discussed above is no exception. Per capita distributed collective income, a concept discussed in detail in the following chapter, averaged 126 yuan in 1979 in the surveyed teams, more than 50 percent greater than the national average (Sun Pu 1980, 12). Ninety percent of all producing units are less developed than those in the survey and probably have proportionately even less working capital and depreciation funds.

A substantial increase in the total quantity of loans in 1980 may have relieved the shortage of capital in the farm sector. In 1980 total loans of the State Agricultural Bank and of credit cooperatives were 31.0 billion yuan.[49] Most of these loans supplied short-term credit since 24.4 billion yuan of the loans were repaid and loans outstanding rose 6.6 billion yuan.[50] By contrast in 1979 total loans were only 19.4 billion yuan, of which 17.0 billion yuan was repaid (Chinese Agricultural Bank Rural Finance Research Office 1981, IV-161). Borrowed working capital thus expanded markedly in 1980.

Farm sector fixed assets

The data on farm sector fixed assets are congruent with the analysis of the magnitude of farm investment presented above. The total value of fixed assets in collective agriculture, excluding state farms, was 73.2 billion yuan in 1977 and 84.9 billion yuan in 1978 (Yang Chien-pai and Li Hsüeh-tseng 1980, 31; Ministry of Agricultural Policy Research Office 1980, 58; Tai Mao-an and Li Yu-hua 1981, 39).[51] When state farms are included, agricultural fixed assets in 1978 were 97.7 billion yuan (Agricultural Yearbook Compilation Commission 1981, 339). Although there is no single published source that describes in detail the methodology for measuring agricultural fixed assets, the scope of fixed assets is known. It is broad because it is inclusive of all assets valued at 30 yuan or more that are used for two or more years and in some regions even includes equipment such as hand-sprayers that cost less than 30 yuan but are used for many years (Liu Kuang-jung, Lui Hua-chen, and Cheng Chen-ju 1979, 44–45). But fixed assets are exclusive of the value of land (Ministry of Agriculture Policy Research Office 1982, 118) and almost certainly the value of rural housing, which is privately rather than collectively owned. Fixed assets also are exclusive of large- and medium-scale investments in water conservation projects since these remain state- rather than collectively controlled and managed. Agricultural fixed assets also excludes most machinery, equipment, and structures of small-scale rural industrial, food-processing, transport, and other enterprises that are owned by brigades or communes (that is, are collective, but not farming assets).[52] Finally, assets almost certainly are valued at original cost rather than depreciated value.[53]

Collective agricultural fixed assets are not large, either compared with the magnitude of assets in industry or in absolute terms. Fixed assets per agricultural worker in the collective sector in 1977–78 averaged 275 yuan, less than a tenth the level in industry. Fixed assets per production team averaged less than 17,000 yuan in 1977 and 1978.[54] Almost all communes visited by Westerners are model units and have innumerable tractors and pumps and a vast array of other equipment. But the total assets of the average team, which in 1977–78 had 60 workers and 20 hectares of cultivated land, would be limited to three walking tractors at the farm level prices prevailing in the late 1970s.

The evidence on assets is roughly consistent with the data on the state agricultural investment, internal farm reinvestment, and bank loans. Fixed assets in collective agriculture in 1957 were 15.5 billion yuan (Ministry of

Agriculture Policy Research Office 1980, 58), implying a growth of 57.7 billion yuan or 2,885 million yuan annually between 1957 and 1977.[55] Fixed budgetary investment during 1958–77 was 54.47 billion yuan (Table 3.8) and investment financed from increased loans 5 to 6 billion yuan. But most, if not all, of the budgetary funds were allocated to large and medium water conservation projects, state farms, and investments in state run fisheries, meteorological services, and so forth. These assets, as discussed above, are excluded from collective agriculture. State investment in collective agriculture in 1957–77 appears to have been limited to about 12 billion yuan in the category of support for communes. Thus the funds available to finance increased farming assets between 1957 and 1977 include 12 billion yuan of budgetary support,[56] 5 to 6 billion yuan in increased loans,[57] and 68 billion yuan from internal sources (State Statistical Bureau 1982b, 195), for a total of 84 to 85 billion yuan. I know little about the rates of obsolescence and scrappage of farm equipment, the amount of internal investment used to maintain existing assets, or the share of internal investment allocated to increased working capital rather than to increased fixed assets. But it seems plausible that gross investment of 84–85 billion yuan would lead to a net increase in fixed assets of about 54 billion yuan.[58]

Summary

The evidence reviewed in this chapter suggests that development policy in most of the first three decades of the People's Republic of China was imbalanced. State budgetary expenditure and investment in agriculture were modest relative to the large share of national income originating in agriculture. Moreover, stringent budgetary investment was combined with a price policy that imposed a significant indirect burden on the farm sector. Internal reinvestment in the 1970s was small – both because, as discussed in Chapter 2, distorted cropping patterns led to declining efficiency of resource use and because the high implicit taxes imposed on many transactions with the state left few resources within the farm sector.

Policy has not been uniformly imbalanced. In the First Five-Year Plan indirect taxation of agriculture was more moderate because few modern inputs were available. Thus internal farm investment was substantial. Furthermore, credit flows to agriculture were significant. Combined with the more rational cropping patterns and less constrained marketing arrangements that prevailed, the growth of output was higher than in most other periods. By contrast, 1966–77 was marked by a proportionately reduced agricultural investment share, a decline in the volume of agricultural credit supplied by the state, and increased indirect taxation through a vast increase in the flow of relatively expensive industrial inputs. Since this period was also characterized by declining efficiency of resource use, it is perhaps not surprising that the growth of output was modest, just keeping pace with population growth.

Since 1978 policy has shifted once again. State expenditures for agriculture have risen moderately, there has been an increase in the flow of state credit to agriculture and a reduction in direct tax payments, and price policy has favored farmers, compared to the recent past, in three separate ways: (1) Average prices for products delivered to the state have risen considerably; (2) a larger share of deliveries occurs at higher premium prices; and (3) some producers of cotton and edible vegetable oilseeds have been able to reap further gains from purchasing increased quantities of cereals at the quota procurement price while selling a large share of their cotton and oilseeds at the 30 percent premium above-quota prices that exist for these crops.

Changes over time in state policy toward collective agriculture not only directly influence the efficiency of resource use in ways discussed in Chapter 2 and the intersectoral flow of funds as discussed in this chapter, but also influence trends in consumption and income as well as the distribution of income in the farm sector. It is to these latter topics that the next chapter is addressed.

4

Living standards and the distribution of income

China's economy has undergone significant economic growth and structural change since the Communist Party rose to power in 1949. Yet, as shown in the previous chapter, the sectoral allocation of resources has been imbalanced, emphasizing industry, particularly producer goods, rather than agriculture. The puzzling intertemporal growth path referred to in the Preface seems to be partly a consequence of the skewed allocation of investment resources, lack of adequate price incentives for agriculturalists, and periods of increasing allocative inefficiency stemming from quantity planning and efforts to meet the goal of local foodgrain self-sufficiency. China's land-short resource endowment is a constraint on rapid growth, but one that has been compounded rather than alleviated by policy.

China's imbalanced growth strategy is evident not only in the allocation of investment resources and its relative price structure but also, as will be shown in this chapter, in the stagnation of average food consumption between the mid-1950s and the middle to late 1970s. After 1949 agriculture recovered from wartime devastation, and by 1957–58 average per capita food consumption recovered to the prewar level. In the subsequent two decades, however, the quantitative and qualitative standard of the average diet was significantly below that of 1957–58. Average food consumption surpassed the level of the mid-1950s only at the end of the 1970s, when more favorable price, marketing, and production incentives increased levels of agricultural production, particularly of nongrain crops.

Without growth in average per capita food consumption, significant improvement in the diet of most Chinese could have occurred only through a more egalitarian distribution of food. Land reform in the early 1950s, followed a few years later by collectivization of agriculture, probably improved the distribution of food in rural areas compared with the prewar period. Similarly, the introduction of rationing of cereals and edible vegetable oils in cities in 1955 improved the intraurban distribution. But in the twenty years

146

after collectivization, the production and consumption of cereals and other foods may have become increasingly uneven, with growing urban–rural as well as intrarural differentials. These increased consumption differentials are surprising, given supposed Maoist egalitarian objectives that have widely been believed to have shaped agricultural policy after the mid-1960s.

Average income and food consumption

Outsiders have made several estimates of per capita food consumption in China (Wiens 1980; Smil 1977). Although these studies have brought together fragmentary and incomplete data, a detailed analysis of changes over time in the quality and quantity of food consumption will be possible only after more production and demographic data are available. The paragraphs below simply summarize the most comprehensive estimates and point out some of their deficiencies.

The two most important sources for the 1930s are the survey of 2,728 households in 136 rural communities conducted by Buck (1937) and the Food Balance Sheets for 1931–37 (Shen 1951, 373–81). The latter, published by the Food and Agricultural Organization as part of its World Food Survey, were based on crop reports compiled by the National Agricultural Research Bureau of the Nationalist Government. Most scholars believe that both of these sources overestimate food consumption. Revised estimates produced by T. C. Liu and K. C. Yeh and by Wiens are presented in Table 4.1, together with the original estimates. Liu and Yeh as well as Wiens's estimate that average per capita intake of food in China in the early 1930s was between 2,000 and 2,100 calories per day.

Because no large-sample disaggregated consumption surveys have been published since 1949,[1] Western estimates of caloric intake for the Communist period are based on production data. Two alternative methodologies have been used. The most common is to estimate caloric intake from foodgrains and to assume that that comprises the same share of total caloric intake found in Buck's 1929–33 survey. Wiens's per capita estimate for 1957, applying that procedure to the official population and production data, is 2,053 calories per day. An alternative approach has been used by Smil (1977). He estimated total caloric supply by constructing food balance tables incorporating data on production, trade, nonfood uses (for example, grains used for seed and feed), and extraction rates for grains, vegetables, tubers, fish, and animal products. His estimate of per capita caloric intake in 1957, again based on official population and production data, is 2,057 calories per day, almost exactly equal to Wiens's estimate.

Table 4.1. *Food consumption in prewar China*

Sources	Calories from foodgrains	Foodgrain share of total calories (%)	Total caloric consumption
Buck	2,072	90	2,313
Food and Agricultural Organization/National Agricultural Research Bureau	1,771	80	2,226
Liu and Yeh	1,936	91	2,127
Wiens	1,789	90	1,998

Notes: Calories from foodgrains include those derived from grains, tubers, soybeans, and other legumes. Buck's data are for the rural population only and refer to 1929–33. The FAO/NARB data are for the total population and refer to 1931–37. Both the Liu-Yeh and Wiens data are for the total population and refer to 1933.
Sources: Schran (1969, 98), Liu Ta-chung and Yeh Kung-chia (1965, 29), Wiens (1980, 76).

The conclusion emerging from both these studies is that average daily per capita consumption in 1957 was much the same as in the early 1930s. Agricultural output and food consumption declined during the Sino–Japanese and civil wars. Although population growth accelerated after 1949 due to public health measures that quickly reduced mortality caused by parasitic and infectious diseases, grain output grew even more rapidly. The official production data for 1949 may be somewhat understated, exaggerating the pace of recovery in the early years of Communist rule. But most observers believe that by 1952 underreporting was no longer significant (Wiens 1980). Even after 1952, however, grain output grew more rapidly than population, leading to the improvement in per capita supplies reflected in Table 4.2. By 1957 both production and consumption had recovered to the prewar level. Furthermore, the majority of the population probably consumed a more adequate diet than in the 1930s because the redistribution of farmland and the introduction of rationing of grains and edible oils in urban areas reduced the skewness in food consumption.

In contrast to the positive trend up to 1957, per capita food consumption decreased after 1958. Reductions were most drastic in the crisis caused by the Great Leap Forward. The magnitude of the consumption decline and the consequent loss of life were the subject of considerable although inconclusive debate in the West. In the late 1970s and early 1980s the Chinese released important evidence revealing more clearly the scope of the disaster. On the

Table 4.2. *Foodgrain–population balance in China, 1952–81*

	Foodgrain output[a] (millions of tons)	Population (millions at year end)	Foodgrain output per capita (kg)
1952	164	575	285
1957	195	647	302
1958	200	(661–662)[c]	(303–302)
1959	170	(670–675)	(253–252)
1960	144	(659–672)	(218–213)
1961	148	(642–659)	(230–225)
1962	160	(659–664)	(243–241)
1965	195	725	268
1970	240	825	291
1975	285	920	309
1976	284	933	305
1977	283	945	299
1978	305	958	318
1979	332	971	342
1980	321[b]	983	326
1981	325	996	326

[a]Foodgrain output, in Chinese statistical practice, includes grains, tubers (at grain equivalent weight), soybeans, peas, and beans. Output and output per capita in this table are measured in unprocessed form (original weight).
[b]Originally reported as 318 million tons. Revised figure released in April 1982.
[c]Figures in parentheses are Western estimates; all other data are official.
Sources: Foodgrain output – Agricultural Yearbook Compilation Commission (1981, 34), State Statistical Bureau (1982a). *Population* – *1952, 1957, 1965, 1975, 1979*: State Statistical Bureau (1981c, VI-3), *1958–62*: (Aird, 1980, tables 7 and 8), *1970*: Ministry of Agriculture Policy Research Office (1980, 32), *1976, 1977–1979*: State Statistical Bureau (1980b, 8), *1980*: State Statistical Bureau (1981a, 20), *1981*: State Statistical Bureau (1982a).

production side, grain output dropped by 26.4 percent or more than 50 million tons* in 1960 compared to 1957, the last year of the First Five-Year Plan. The 1960 production level, 143.5 million tons, is roughly equal to 1951 output and is 12 to 16 million tons less than the most widely accepted earlier Western estimates.[2] Newly released figures for 1958 and 1962, as well as 1960, are incorporated in Table 4.2. Consumption, of course, did not fall quite so dramatically because foodgrain stocks were drawn down, grain was diverted to human use as pigs and draft animals were slaughtered, and in 1961 China became a net importer of foodgrains.[3] Despite these palliatives,

*All references to tonnage are in metric tons.

Table 4.3. *Average per capita foodgrain consumption, 1952–81 (kg)*

1952	197.5
1954	195.5
1956	204.5
1957	203.0
1958	198.0
1959	186.5
1960	163.5
1962	164.5
1965	184.0
1970	188.0
1972	173.5
1975	191.5
1976	182.8
1977	193.0
1978	196.5
1979	205.0
1980	213.5
1981	219.2

Note: Consumption in this table is measured in terms of trade grain.
Sources: Yang Chien-pai and Li Hsüeh-tseng (1980, 26), Liu Fang-yü (1980, 20), P'ei Yüan-hsiu, Liu Ping-ying, and Li Ping-chang (1980), Chan Wu (1980, 4), NCNA (April 20, 1981; March 30, 1982), Liang Hsiu-feng (1981a, 22), Chang Li-fen (1980, 29), Ministry of Agriculture Policy Research Office (1982, 207), Liu Sui-nien (1980, 30).

average foodgrain consumption fell precipitously. Per capita consumption declined 20 percent from 203 kilograms in 1957 to 163.5 kilograms in 1960 (Table 4.3). Severe food shortages continued into 1961 and 1962 because state stockpiles were drawn down in 1959 and 1960, partly cushioning the production decline. Ch'en Yün, in a speech at the time, predicted that, despite rising production, food shortages in 1962 would be acute since previously accumulated stocks were severely depleted by the middle of 1961 (Ch'en Yün 1961a, 120). Data released subsequently show no significant improvement in consumption between 1960 and 1962 (Table 4.3).

The decline in cereal consumption both reduced fertility and increased the death rate. The magnitude of population loss has now been estimated using a variety of Chinese demographic data.[4] In 1979 the Chinese released a survey of the 1975 age distribution that showed a marked deficit for the ages 15–19, the age cohort born in the crisis years. In addition, in the spring of 1980 the

Chinese published a graph indicating the number of births annually from 1949 through 1977. Using these data and the results of the midyear 1964 population survey, Aird (1980) constructed three alternative models of demographic developments in the critical years. A model that follows the above-described data most closely shows a net loss of 28 million persons in 1960–61 (from a peak population of 670 million at year end 1959 to 642 million at year end 1961) and a total population cost (measured as the sum of reduced births as well as increased mortality) of 64 million (p. 28). One of the two alternative models, the one Aird prefers, assumes that the 1975 age distribution data were constructed on the tradition of considering children one year of age at birth. That makes the peak birth rate year 1964 rather than 1963, and the level of mortality required to link the official year-end 1957 and midyear 1964 totals (given the number of births per year) is thus substantially smaller. The net loss of population on that assumption is cut almost in half, to 16 million (Aird 1980, 3). Estimates based on yet another Chinese source imply excess deaths of 16.5 million but over the four-year period 1958–61 (Coale 1981, 89).

The estimate of net population loss in Aird's preferred model is roughly consistent with data subsequently published in China. Yang Chien-pai has written that the population declined by more than 13 million from 1959 to 1961 (1981, 122). Other reports show the mortality rate rose sharply in 1959 and reached a peak of 25.4 per thousand in 1960, more than double the rate of 10.8 per thousand in 1957 (Chang Huai-tzu et al. 1981, 83; Sun Yeh-fang 1981, 3), implying increased mortality in 1960 alone of over 9.5 million.[5] The mortality rate remained relatively high in 1961, 14.4 per thousand, well above the level of the mid-1950s. Starvation deaths presumably declined sharply after 1960 since state extractions of cereal from the countryside were reduced. Information concerning the regional distribution of food shortages may have improved so that available supplies could be redistributed more effectively. But severe food shortages continued and many individuals must have succumbed to epidemic diseases after 1960 because of their deteriorating general health. It is not unusual for the death rate to remain high or even reach a peak after the most acute period of starvation has passed (Sen 1981, 55, 215).

There are some inconsistencies between the population totals and the vital rate data discussed above. The data on the annual number of births, for example, "cannot be combined with the official population totals for 1957 and 1964 without assuming crude death rates during the crisis years much higher than the official crude death rate for 1960" (Aird 1982, 182). Some inconsistencies may reflect disruption of statistical work during the crisis caused by the Great Leap Forward. Moreover, the accuracy of the 1964 population census is difficult to judge since so little information has been released. In the future additional demographic data may help to explain some of the existing discrepancies and lead to revised estimates of excess mortality. But the best evidence available suggests that prior to Aird's study, outsiders underestimated the magnitude of the famine of the late 1950s and early 1960s.

Although the magnitude of the famine is now apparent, little is known of its character. Although the sharp increase in the mortality rate coincided with a general decline in the availability of cereals and other foods, the decline in food supplies tells us little about the incidence of famine. We know very little about the differential incidence of famine deaths, either on an interregional or urban–rural basis. It is quite likely that, like other famines, the magnitude of the crisis is explained largely by factors other than the decline in aggregate food supplies (Sen 1981). Among the most obvious is that in the political environment created by the Great Leap, local officials were unwilling to report food shortages so that the central government was frequently not aware, until it was too late, of the need to redistribute food interregionally as they had done with some success in the 1950s. Indeed, at least in 1958 and 1959, the political pressures to report great agricultural success had reduced rural consumption since government procurement, based on inflated output statistics, increased significantly (Table 2.1).

The unwillingness of local cadres to report food shortages is borne out by the rural investigations carried out by two members of the Politburo of the Central Committee, P'eng Te-huai and Ch'en Yün. After the Wuchang meeting in November 1958, when the 1958 output figures of 375 million tons of grain and 3.5 million tons of cotton were announced, P'eng visited his hometown in Hunan and found that production was not soaring, as had been reported by provincial officials, and that "the masses were in danger of starving" (quoted in Li Jui 1982, 10). P'eng felt the situation so urgent that he sent a telegram to the Central Committee of the Chinese Communist Party warning that the production figures were overstated. Ch'en Yün also traveled in the countryside in the spring of 1959 pointedly choosing to visit Honan Province, where First Party Secretary Wu Chih-p'u had been credited by Mao Tse-tung with creating the first commune in China. When Ch'en made his investigation, Wu was claiming great success for Honan agricultural development. Honan, Wu claimed, had doubled its output of wheat in a single year and no longer required imported grain to feed its population. It could even export to other provinces. Ch'en, guessing that Wu's claims had no basis in fact, bore in with penetrating questions:

"What was the level of consumption of foodgrains of peasants in Honan with the lowest living standard?" "What were Honan's cereal requirements for seedgrain and animal fodder?" "How many people in the province were receiving rationed grain?" Ch'en explicitly stated that he did not want Honan to export grain and wondered whether grain procured would be sufficient to feed the urban population of the province. Ch'en was rebuffed by Honan cadres who, although unable to provide sound answers to his questions, insisted that in the event urban cereal supplies fell short, they would simply raise procurement targets in the countryside (Teng Li-ch'un 1981, 54–5).

Ch'en and P'eng, however, were unable to stem the political tide of the time. Ch'en dropped out of the political scene sometime prior to the convening of the Lushan Conference in June 1959, not to reemerge until the spring of 1961 when he became one of the chief architects of the program to extricate the country from the disastrous consequences of the Leap (Lardy and Lieberthal 1983, 15–16). P'eng was not so fortunate. At the Lushan Plenum in August 1959 he was charged with heading an anti-Party clique and effectively purged.

Despite evidence cited by Ch'en, P'eng, and perhaps others, state procurement of cereals continued at a very high level in 1959. Even in 1960, as grain production was plunging to the lowest level in a decade, procurement was proportionately well above the level of the middle of the 1950s (Table 2.1). The level of rural cereal consumption fell precipitously, by 48.5 kilograms per capita or 23.7 percent, while urban consumption was scarcely affected (Table 4.5). Though the urban population grew during the Great Leap Forward as a consequence of an increase in the labor force employed in modern industry and construction, their basic food supplies were assured by increased procurement from the countryside, a drawdown of state-controlled grain stockpiles, and, after 1960, imports from abroad.

Not only did the central government procure excess cereals from the countryside, it lacked a reliable basis for redistributing cereals interregionally to avert localized famines. Moreover, the disruption of rural peasant marketing probably reduced the ability of producers of nongrain food crops or animal husbandry products to convert their products to cereals that would provide less expensive sources of calories and probably reduced the ability of producers of fiber crops to obtain food crops at all. In short, the maldistribution of food, both between urban and rural areas and within the countryside, may have been more important than the decline in average food consumption. That hypothesis, however, needs further refinement and testing based on disaggregated data on production, trade, and consumption.

From the low point of 1960, grain output grew at an annual average rate of over 4 percent for two decades. But even at this pace per capita production did not regain the 1957 level until 1975 (Table 4.2). Despite continued imports, consumption recovered even more slowly. As late as 1978, when per capita output was well above the 1957 level, consumption of grain was still below that of 1956 and 1957 (Table 4.3). Furthermore, consumption standards remained vulnerable to a sequence of poor harvests such as occurred in 1970–72. By 1972 annual per capita consumption had fallen to 173.5 kilograms, only marginally above the depths of consumption levels in 1960. Interestingly, there is no evidence of significantly increased mortality in 1972, suggesting that in the more normal political environment then prevailing the state was more successful in redistributing cereals to compensate for local shortfalls.

Based on data on the production of nongrain foods, it is possible to estimate whether the slight decline in grain consumption between the mid-1950s and 1976–78 was offset by increased consumption of nongrain foods. The end point for these comparisons is generally 1977–78. That end point has been chosen because, although the partial return to indirect forms of agricultural planning and improved price incentives were initiated in 1978, they did not begin to have a significant effect on output levels until 1979. Furthermore, for cereal consumption it is appropriate to avoid long-term comparisons based on 1977 as the final year because adverse weather depressed output. Averages for 1977–78 are thus generally used, although 1975–77 data are used for some nongrain items.

Consumption of some important nongrain foods clearly declined over the twenty-year period. Per capita consumption of vegetable oils pressed from peanuts and from oilbearing seeds such as rape and sesame was down by a third between 1957 and 1978 (Wang Keng-chin 1979a, 37). Judgments of some other nongrain foods can be based on trends in production (Table 4.4). Per capita consumption of soybeans, an important source of protein, fell substantially since China shifted from being a net exporter in the 1950s to being a net importer by the mid-1970s, compensating for only part of the 50 percent decline in per capita production between 1957 and 1977–78. Judging from production figures, average per capita fish consumption in 1977–78 was about the same as in 1957. Consumption of sugar, fruit, and meat, however, did increase.

Increased per capita consumption of meat, fruit, and sugar must be placed in perspective. The calories supplied by these foods are dwarfed by the 80 to 90 percent share derived from grains (Yü Chin-man 1979). The lack of diversity implied by the high share of calories derived from grain is confirmed by the small quantities of nongrain foods consumed. Per capita meat

Table 4.4. *Output of nongrain foods, 1952, 1957, 1965, 1975, and 1977–81 (thousands of tons)*

	Fish	Sugarcane	Sugar beets	Oilseed crops	Tea	Fruit	Soybeans[a]	Meat	Milk, cow	Milk, goat
1952	1,670	7,116	479	4,193	83	2,443	9,500	3,385	—	—
1957	3,120	10,393	1,501	4,196	112	3,248	10,045	3,985	—	—
1965	2,980	13,392	1,985	3,626	101	3,240	6,150	5,510	—	—
1975	4,410	16,667	2,477	4,521	211	5,381	7,250	7,970	—	—
1977	4,700	17,753	2,456	4,015	252	—	7,255	7,800	—	—
1978	4,660	21,117	2,702	5,218	268	6,570	7,565	8,160	883	88
1979	4,305	21,508	3,106	6,435	277	7,015	7,400	10,624	1,070	237
1980	4,497	22,807	6,305	7,691	304	6,793	7,880	12,055	1,141	—
1981	4,605	29,668	6,360	10,205	343	7,801	9,245	12,609	1,291	—

[a]In Chinese statistical practice soybeans are treated as a grain and are included in the cereal output data reported in Table 4.2. The output of soybeans is shown here as a distinct item because of its importance as a source of protein in the Chinese diet.

Sources: State Statistical Bureau (1960, 124; 1980b, 4; 1981a, 25; 1981c, VI-10–VI-11; 1982a; 1982b, 146), Wu Leng (1980, 29), Agricultural Yearbook Compilation Commission (1981).

consumption averaged 8.4 kilograms annually in 1976–77, placing China ninety-eighth in world consumption. Per capita sugar consumption, 2.8 kilograms in 1976–77, was only a tenth the world average and below that of many developing countries (Liu Fang-yü 1980, 20). In 1978 fruit production was less than 7 kilograms per capita. Consumption of other food products was also quite small. Per capita consumption of eggs and dairy products in 1976–77 averaged 2.2 kilograms and 1.1 kilograms per year, respectively (Liu Fang-yü 1980, 20; Yü Kuo-yao 1980d; Chan Wu 1980, 4). Since adult Chinese do not consume dairy products, the average consumption figure is somewhat misleading, but milk production in the late 1970s was said to be inadequate to supplement the diets of infants and to supply the needs of several tens of millions of minority races living in China who do consume milk (Ch'in Nien 1979).

Data on some foods – for example, vegetables and poultry – are not available, so a definitive assessment of the long-term trend cannot be made.[6] But on balance, in comparing 1976–78 with the mid-1950s, it seems unlikely that increased supplies of meat, sugar, and fruit were sufficient to offset the sharp decline of edible vegetable oils and beancurd and the slight reduction in cereal consumption. Consequently, average per capita caloric intake in 1976–78 was probably somewhat below the 1957 range of 2,000 to 2,100 calories per day. Protein intake was also almost certainly lower than in the 1950s because of the sharp decline in soybean production. The shortage of soybeans in most regions continues to be a major contribution to health problems, particularly among children. Widespread anemia among children has been attributed by Chinese medical sources to protein deficiency in the diet, because anemia is widespread except in the traditional soybean-growing areas of the Northeast where beans are more readily available. In an experiment reported in one region the incidence of anemia among children was reduced from 90 to 10–20 percent within three months as a result of simply consuming bean products made from one-fourth kilogram of beans per child per month (Chinese Press Service December 4, 1981).

The quality of diet, or at least the people's perception of it, might have gone down because of the rising share of grain accounted for by potatoes and coarse grains, particularly corn, that are generally considered inferior foods. However, that does not affect caloric intake significantly because caloric values among grains do not differ much. The variety of vegetables also probably was reduced as price incentives for producing higher-quality leafy vegetables were reduced and cabbages comprised an ever-larger share of vegetable output. Average food consumption has grown sharply since

1978, in response to the agricultural development policies adopted in the late 1970s. These improvements will be summarized in Chapter 5.

Trends in urban and rural consumption and income

In most developing countries the change over time in average food consumption reveals little about variation in the share of the population that suffers from malnutrition. Slight variations in the distribution of food may more than offset the effect of changes in average food intake on the fraction of the population that is undernourished. Some observers have felt that because of its food-rationing system China was an exception to this general thesis. Yet the evidence on the efficacy of the rationing system is sparse. Since the formal rationing system is limited to the nonagricultural population, I doubt whether China is an exception to the general proposition that changes in average food consumption do not have strong implications for the extent to which undernutrition is a serious problem.

In one important dimension – urban versus rural – inequality of consumption increased between the mid-1950s and the late 1970s. For example, while average national cereal consumption declined between 1957 and 1978 by 3.2 percent (Table 4.5), rural consumption fell by a somewhat larger proportion, 5.9 percent, while urban consumption actually rose 10.5 percent. Average edible vegetable oil consumption declined by a third while rural consumption fell by more than 40 percent. Urban consumers were insulated from declining production – their consumption fell less than 10 percent. The changes in per capita consumption of cotton cloth are similar to those for grain. National average consumption fell slightly, 2 percent, but rural consumption fell by almost three times as much, again implying a substantial increase in the difference between per capita urban and rural consumption.[7]

Increased urban–rural differentials in per capita consumption of cereals, vegetable oil, and cotton cloth, in my judgment, are significant since these three commodities have been subject to rationing more consistently and for a longer period than other consumer goods. Cotton cloth is unique in that it is the only major consumer good subject to long-term coupon rationing in both urban and rural areas. A special central government agency, the Ministry of Food, with bureaus at the provincial and municipal levels and offices in many communes, closely supervised the procurement and the distribution of the key staple commodities, grain and vegetable oils. Some central ministries undergo periodic reorganization and amalgamation with related agencies, but this critical ministry had unchanging and undiluted responsibilities from the time of its establishment in the fall of 1952 until the spring of 1982 when

Table 4.5. *Urban and rural consumption of foodgrains,[a] edible vegetable oils, and cotton cloth,[b] 1957, 1960, and 1978*

	1957	1960	1978	Percentage change	
				1960/1957	1978/1957
National					
Grain (kg)	203.0	163.5	196.5	−19.5	− 3.2
Vegetable oils (kg)	2.4	1.85	1.6	−22.9	−33.2
Cotton cloth (ft)	19.5	—	19.1	—	− 2.0
Urban					
Grain (kg)	196.0	192.5	216.5	− 1.8	10.5
Vegetable oils (kg)	5.15	3.55	4.70	−31.1	− 8.7
Cotton cloth (ft)	30.0	—	—	—	—
Rural					
Grain (kg)	204.5	156.0	192.5	−23.7	− 5.9
Vegetable oils (kg)	1.85	1.45	1.05	−21.6	−43.2
Cotton cloth (ft)	17.5	—	16.5	—	− 5.7

[a]Consumption is expressed in terms of trade grain.
[b]Excluding synthetics. Including synthetics, national per capita consumption of cloth rose almost 20 percent between 1957 and 1978 with urban and rural consumption rising by more than 50 and less than 10 percent, respectively. In an earlier study (Lardy 1982a) I estimated the absolute levels of cereal consumption in urban and rural areas based on the estimated urban and rural population weights. The data presented here are taken from more recent sources and involve no estimation.
Sources: Liu Fang-yü (1980, 20), Wang Keng-chin (1979a, 37), Pao Kuang-ch'ien (1980, 2), Wang Hai-tu (1981, 63), Ministry of Agriculture Policy Research Office (1982, 207), Liu Sui-nien (1980, 23).

it was merged, along with the All-China Federation of Supply and Marketing Cooperatives, into the Ministry of Commerce.[8] Thus increased differentials in the consumption of these commodities are more significant, from the point of view of judging the success of rationing in preventing rising consumption differentials, than is rising differential consumption of pork and other foods that are procured and distributed under far less centralized and unified government agencies.

Since we lack comparable data for other years around 1978, it is difficult to rule out the possibility that 1978 was atypical and that changes between the mid-1950s and 1978 do not represent long-term trends. The tentative conclusion, however, is that the system of rationing and procurement, including large-scale grain imports from the West, which are used almost exclusively to feed cities in the North and Northeast, protected or even improved urban food standards while rural consumption declined.

The hypothesis of significant and sustained urban–rural consumption differentials is supported by anthropometric data. These data compare for urban and rural areas the height achieved by Chinese children at specific ages and the weight achieved at specific heights. The advantage of these studies is that they allow analysis based on the distribution of anthropometric statistics within the Chinese sample rather than on standards derived from studies of other societies. Unfortunately, the rural sample was drawn from suburban communes where incomes and consumption are atypically high compared to most of rural China, thus almost certainly understating true urban–rural differences. Low height for age, known as "stunting," is one of the most widely used indicators of long-term malnutrition. Even though the rural sample was drawn from prosperous suburban communes, the prevalence of malnourishment by the stunting measure was more than three times greater in rural than in urban areas. By the weight-for-age measure, malnourishment was eight times greater in rural than in urban areas. Although these measures are generally thought to reflect chronic but not necessarily severe malnutrition, they have a measurable influence on intellectual development. Even those suffering from "moderate malnutrition" fell behind their peers in Chinese schools (International Bank for Reconstruction and Development 1981, B:14–16).

China is probably the only country in modern times to combine, over twenty years, a doubling of real per capita national income (Table 1.1) and constant or even slightly declining average food consumption. Moreover, while urban–rural consumption differentials may increase during the early stages of economic development, that usually occurs while average consumption rises in both sectors but more rapidly in the nonfarm population. Rarely does rural food consumption suffer a long-term absolute decline while urban consumption rises. Thus it is hard to imagine a criterion for judging macroeconomic performance that would not sustain the judgment that Chinese growth has been imbalanced. Indeed, the discrepancy between trends in national income and food consumption is so marked that one's first reaction is to doubt the reliability of the data on which the national income or food consumption estimates are calculated.

Although the purpose of this book is not to review the plausibility of Chinese economic data, there are two important explanations of the paradox outlined above that are directly relevant to agriculture. First, the growth of national income since 1949, shown in Table 1.1, is somewhat overstated because of China's skewed price structure, discussed in Chapter 3.[9] A sec-

Table 4.6. *Per capita peasant income, 1956–81 (yuan)*

	Collectively distributed income			
	Current prices[a] (1)	Constant 1957 prices (2)	Index of constant price income (3)	Total income (current prices) (4)
1956	43.1	45.5[b]	} 100	73
1957	40.5	40.5		—
1958	41.4	40.5[b]	94.7	—
1959	37.6	—	—	—
1960	41.3	—	—	—
1961	48.1	—	—	—
1962	46.1	34.9[b]	81.6	—
1965	52.3	41.3[b]	96.6	—
1970	59.5	—	—	—
1974	65.8	—	—	—
1975	63.2	—	—	—
1976	62.8	—	—	113
1977	65.5	47.5	111.1	117
1978	74.7	52.7[b]	123.3	—
1979	84.2	—	—	—
1980	85.9	—	—	170
1981	97.9[c]	—	—	—

[a]The price system in effect since 1978 is a complex hybrid. Cereals distributed in kind to commune members continue to be valued at 1978 prices, but the portion of income distributed in cash reflects the higher purchase prices, for both grain and nongrain crops.
[b]Estimated, explained in text.
[c]Also reported as 103.7 yuan, but the higher figure, according to the vice-minister of agriculture, reflects an upward adjustment in some regions of the internal accounting price for grain distributed in kind and a drop in retained collective funds (Chu Jung 1982, 2).
Sources: *Column 1* – Agricultural Yearbook Compilation Commission (1981, 41), Ministry of Agriculture Policy Research Office (1980, 105), Ministry of Agriculture Commune Management Bureau (1981a, 117; 1981b, 13), State Statistical Bureau (1981a), Wang P'ing (1981, 120), Reporter (1982b); *column 2 – 1957*: Chan Wu (1980; 4); Hsiyang Agricultural College (1980, 222); Chang Liu-cheng (1981, 43); *1977*: Chan Wu (1980, 4); *column 3* – calculated from the second column;
column 4 – State Statistical Bureau (1981b).

ond possible explanation of the apparent paradox between rapid growth of per capita national income and stagnant food consumption is the slow growth of personal income, particularly for the rural population, which still comprises 85 percent of the total.

The most frequent measure of peasant income is "collectively distributed income," the remuneration received from collective activities. These data, shown in Table 4.6, have been cited frequently by both Chinese and foreign writers to show that farm incomes rose continuously after the mid-1950s. Two fundamental weaknesses vitiate the value of these data for most analytical purposes: they include only income from collective sources, and they measure income in current prices.

The problem of incomplete coverage of income sources may be overcome by using the data in column 4 of Table 4.6. These purport to include income from noncollective sources, what the Chinese refer to as "household sideline income" and "other income." These data show a 60 percent rise in income between 1956 and 1977 and a further 45 percent increase in the subsequent three-year period. These increases, while based on a broad definition of income sources, still are misleading as a measure of changes in peasant welfare since they are based on current prices.

The misleading character of current-price measures of collective income is immediately apparent from column 1. In 1961–62, collective income was higher than in 1956–57, whereas the real product of the agricultural sector had declined substantially. The rise in income reflects the sharply higher procurement prices instituted in 1961. Unfortunately, the Chinese have not released enough data on prices and the composition of rural consumption to allow us to construct a price deflator for either column 1 or 4 of Table 4.6. Chan Wu (1980), the Director of the Institute of Agricultural Economics of the Chinese Academy of Social Sciences, has disclosed that in constant 1957 prices the national average per capita distributed collective income in 1977 was 47.5 yuan.[10] Thus the gain in income derived from collective sources between 1957 and 1977 was not 60 percent (2.4 percent per annum) but 17 percent (.8 percent per annum). In other words, more than two-thirds of the claimed increase represents increased prices rather than real income. Long-term comparisons based on 1956 show even less real growth, since collectively distributed income was higher in 1956 than in 1957.

The high deflator for collectively distributed incomes reflects the statistical procedure used to value income in kind. A large share of the income derived from collective agriculture is not cash but grain and other agricultural commodities distributed in kind. Income distributed in cash in 1974–78 averaged only 13 yuan per commune member per year and was slightly less than in either 1957 or 1965. The share of collective income distributed in cash fell from 35 percent in 1957 to less than 20 percent in 1974–78.[11] Commodities distributed in kind are valued at quota procurement prices. Since procurement prices have increased since the 1950s (Table 3.4), the same quantity of wheat, rice, or other foods distributed in the late 1970s was valued at a much higher price than twenty years previously. Of course, the recorded increase in collectively distributed income is illusory because real consumption is unchanged. Higher prices are relevant only for output sold to the state. Since a large share of agricultural output is consumed by producing units, most of the increase in column 1 of Table 4.6 reflects rising prices. The increased income arising from the sale of agricultural products at higher prices is reflected in columns 2 and 3.

Interestingly, the implicit deflator for collectively distributed income in 1977, which is 137.9 (= 100 × 65.5 ÷ 47.5), is identical to the estimated index of state purchase prices for 1977, or 137.9 (1957 = 100), that can be calculated from the data in Table 3.4. I have followed what appears to be the Chinese practice of deflating collectively distributed income with the index of purchase prices and calculated real income for 1956, 1958, 1962, 1965, and 1978, shown in column 2.[12]

Finally, I have calculated an index of per capita collectively distributed income measured in 1957 constant prices, shown in column 3. Real per capita collectively distributed income rose 23 percent between 1956–57 and 1978. More significant from the perspective of judging alternative planning systems is the path of growth. Real per capita distributed income rose rapidly between 1962 and 1965 and almost had recovered from the crisis years by 1965. From the onset of production planning in the mid-1960s the growth of distributed collective income slowed. Between 1965 and 1977 it grew by only 6.2 yuan, one-half of 1 percent per year. The amount of income distributed in cash actually fell.

Evaluating trends in total real farm income is more difficult because the Chinese have not published price deflators for total farm income that, when applied to the data in column 4 of Table 4.6, would result in a constant-price series for total farm income. However, there are several reasons for believing that the trend in total farm income between 1965 and 1977 must have been less favorable than the constant-price collective income trend. In the production planning regime after the mid-1960s constraints on private marketing activities and reductions (or in some places elimination) of private plots curtailed the income derived from private plots and household sideline activities. Income derived from noncollective activities probably rose sharply in the first half of the 1960s when private rural marketing activities were allowed and then fell after 1966 when private plots were squeezed and the number of rural markets reduced. This may be the reason that one source states that although nominal collectively distributed per capita annual income rose 10.5 yuan between 1965 and 1976, real income fell (Hsiyang Agricultural College 1980, 222).

Thus the best evidence, taken from Chinese sources and adjusted for price changes, shows that real per capita farm income at best grew very modestly between 1956–57 and 1977, growing particularly slowly after recovering to the 1957 level in 1965. That very slow growth of farm income is consistent with changes in consumption discussed earlier. Consumption of cereals and cotton cloth, two important components of rural consumption, declined somewhat while farm income at best grew quite modestly. Moreover, as will be shown below, incomes of those employed in the state sector, the largest component of the urban population, rose significantly over the same period. That is consistent with the rise in urban food consumption and suggests that urban–rural income differentials, as well as consumption differentials, rose substantially between the mid-1950s and the late 1970s.[13]

Incomes of state employees

In contrast to the slow growth of per capita rural income between 1965 and 1976, per capita income of state employees rose substantially. That rise is not apparent in official data since these are usually for income per worker. Average income of state employees declined somewhat between 1957 and 1976–77 or between 1964 and 1976 or 1977 (Table 4.7). Thus it initially might appear that the urban–rural income gap was reduced. However, between 1964 and the mid-1970s the urban labor force participation rate increased, reducing the number of dependents per state employee from 2.4 in 1964 to 1.06 in 1978 and .83 in 1980. Thus per capita incomes in families with workers employed by the state rose 61 percent between 1964 and 1978. Moreover, official data show that the cost-of-living index for state workers and staff declined slightly between 1964 and 1978. Thus real per capita income of workers and staff members and their families rose by almost 65 percent between 1964 and 1978. During roughly the same period, 1965 to 1978, per capita distributive collective farm income rose only 27 percent. Thus the urban–rural gap widened considerably.

Naturally, this comparison is very crude and subject to certain limitations. The nature of the index used to calculate the cost of living of state employees is unknown. It may give undue weight to commodities subject to state price control and insufficient weight to commodities sold on markets less subject to price control. Moreover, state employees receive a broad array of subsidies for basic consumption goods, services, and other benefits that are not provided to ruralites. From the perspective of the state, these subsidies are cash outlays indistinguishable from wage payments, but they are not reflected in the official income figures. In 1978 these included subsidies for grain, vegetable oils, and subsidiary foods, 179.6 yuan per employee per year; for housing, for which state workers pay only a nominal 2 to 4 percent of their income, 85.3 yuan; for retirement, death, maternity, disabil-

Table 4.7. *Per capita income of state employees, 1957–80*

	Average income per employee (current yuan) (1)	Average number of dependents per employee (2)	Average per capita income, (current yuan) (3) = (1) ÷ (2)	Index of per capita income (constant prices) (4)	Income deflator (5)
1957	637	2.3	193	—	—
1964	661	2.4	194	100	100
1976	605	—	—	—	—
1977	602	—	—	—	—
1978	644	1.06	313	164	98.6
1979	705	—	—	—	100.4
1980	803	.83	439	209	107.9

Notes: The average number of dependents per worker was calculated by the State Statistical Bureau from data on the number of persons in households in which there was a state employee and on the number of workers per household. The data were collected in surveys of different size and with somewhat different coverage. The 1957 data are based on two surveys – one of 5,900 households in twenty-seven medium and large cities, and the other of 4,800 households in thirty-two cities – and was limited to state industrial workers. The 1964 survey was of 3,537 households in forty-four small, medium, and large cities and included state workers in industry, commerce, culture and education, and office organizations. The 1980 survey was of 7,962 households in forty-four small, medium, and large cities and in addition to the sectors included in the 1964 survey included construction, communications, posts and telecommunications, public utilities, science, health, and banking. I have used income data that are the reported average wages of all state employees. If the household size or labor force participation rates are not distributed randomly across households with employees in different sectors of state employment, the data in columns 1 and 2 are not completely comparable.
Sources: Column 1 – State Statistical Bureau (1982b, 426); *column 2 – 1957, 1964, 1980*: State Statistical Bureau (1981c, IV-25); *1978*: Li Ch'eng-jui and Cheng Chungchi (1982, 26); *column 4* – calculated from data in columns 3 and 5; *column 5* – State Statistical Bureau (1980c).

ity, injury, and some types of health benefits and labor insurance fees, paid by the state to the trade union system, 67 yuan; for other health benefits, 48.3 yuan; for coal for home heating, 10.1 yuan; for visiting relatives, to underwrite the travel of workers to visit their native places upon the death of one of their parents, and so on, 10 yuan; for daily transportation to and from factories and offices, 6.3 yuan; for collective welfare programs provided by the state, 84.5 yuan;[14] and for collective welfare programs provided directly through the work unit, 35 yuan. These subsidies in 1978 totaled 526 yuan per year per employee or 82 percent of the average wage (Ching Lin and Lei Yang-lu 1981, 33; Hsiang Ch'i-yüan 1981, 61; Wang Hai-tu 1981, 57).

These subsidies add considerably to disparities between agricultural and nonagricultural employees. Workers in rural collectives receive few if any of these benefits from the state. Housing for peasants is privately owned, not subsidized by the state; collective workers do not receive death, maternity, retirement, or disability payments from the state; coal for home heating is a scarce commodity in rural areas and not subsidized. Welfare programs in the countryside are modest and when they exist are rarely financed by the state. In retirement peasants depend primarily on support from their children; health care is provided via collective insurance schemes for which peasants typically pay 1 yuan per year; other collective welfare programs are financed by deductions from the net income of production teams prior to the distribution of in-kind and cash income to members. Moreover, the value of some urban subsidies is understated since the commodities, services, or benefits are allocated through work units and frequently are not available in the countryside at any price.

Finally, subsidies to urban residents have grown substantially over time. Food subsidies did not exist in the 1950s since the margin between procurement and ration prices left large profits for the Ministry of Food.[15] Subsidies for housing rent have also increased over time. Prior to 1955 rents were set to cover maintenance and replacement costs and averaged three times the rents charged in the late 1970s. Rents were lowered absolutely, first in August 1955 and again during the Cultural Revolution, while costs of construction materials and labor rose (Chang Chih-yi 1982, 41-42; Chang Tse-yü 1982, 28). By the late 1970s rents collected covered less than 25 percent of costs (Chang Tse-yü 1982, 28).[16] Tracing the origins of the other subsidy programs requires more research, but between the 1950s and 1978 the growth of rent and food subsidies alone is sufficient to have doubled the per worker value of subsidies. Thus while per worker income stagnated between 1957 and 1978, the value of subsidies grew rapidly, increasing the gap between urban and rural per capita income.

Urban subsidies, of course, are part of a broader policy that has sought to suppress wage differentials within the modern sector. Over time a larger share of the benefits of state employment have come in the form of subsidies received by all workers regardless of skill, seniority, and so forth. The value of these subsidies, however, rarely has been taken into account in comparisons of living standards of peasants and urbanites.

Income distribution in rural China

The draft of a Chinese Communist Party Central Committee report presented in a meeting in December 1978 stated that China's 1977 per capita grain production was slightly less than in 1957 and, more significantly, that more than 100 million peasants had "insufficient amounts of foodgrains" (Chinese Communist Party Central Committee 1978, 151). A Communist-controlled periodical published in Hong Kong painted an even bleaker picture, stating that "the annual foodgrain consumption of 200 million peasants in China is less than 300 jin [150 kilograms], that is to say they are living in a state of semistarvation" (Lin Shen 1979, 11). The final Central Committee report adopted in late September 1979, however, deleted the estimate of the number of inadequately fed peasants and merely pointed out that 1978 per capita grain output was only equivalent to that of 1957. Subsequent, more specific reports, however, stated that in 1978 the cereal consumption of 150 million peasants was less than 150 kilograms, less than 200 kilograms in southern rice areas (Lu Hsüeh-i 1981, 79).

Yet when net imports (not shown in Table 4.2 but averaging almost 10 million tons per year) are included, per capita grain supplies in 1976, 1977, and 1978 were greater than in 1957 or, for that matter, than in 1956 or 1958. There were official reports of localized food shortages in some years in the mid-1950s. In 1956, for example, more than 300 peasants in three counties in Kwangsi starved as a result of famine (Chou Po-ping 1957, 4). More generally, it was difficult for large areas of the North China Plain, including northern Anhui and northern Kiangsu, as well as northern Shensi to grow sufficient quantities of foodgrains. The annual incomes, including earnings from noncollective sources, of 15 percent of the peasantry were under 40 yuan per capita (T'an Chen-lin 1957). Although specialized production of noncereal crops and trade in cereals allowed peasants in many regions to raise their level of consumption and income, a significant portion of the rural population remained quite poor. Evaluation of the extent of deprivation in the mid-1970s relative to the mid-1950s is impossible because comparable data on the distribution of rural incomes in both periods have not been published. Tentatively, it would appear that two decades of collectivized agriculture failed to raise, and may even have reduced, the level of consumption of the poorest quintile of China's rural population.

One naturally must consider whether the admission of widespread malnutrition in 1976–78 is not simply an attempt to discredit the policies of the Maoist era. Perhaps rural China was not suffering deprivation as widespread as the relevations imply. How could such widespread deprivation have occurred, given the programs that were thought to have placed a floor of minimum subsistence for all members of Chinese society? After all, coupon rationing of basic staples – cereals and vegetable oils – was instituted in 1954–55 in urban areas, and peasants who cannot afford the basic ration have been allowed to borrow from their production teams (Parish and Whyte 1978, 77).

Quite simply, food rationing, as it is usually described, applies only to urban residents. There is no formal rationing system in rural China for cereals except insofar as grain taxes and quotas for the sale of grain by producing units to the state are set to allow minimum food requirements to be met. Yet we have almost no direct evidence how such quotas were set in the 1950s or how they were adjusted subsequently. Moreover, the efficacy of such a system for providing a floor on consumption is critically dependent on achieving harvests that, for each producing and accounting unit, are adequate to meet the demands of consumption and grain taxes, as well as quota and "over-quota" deliveries. For as we have seen in Chapter 2, Table 2.1, in the late 1970s the state reallocated only about 5 percent of total foodgrain production among producing units within the countryside, a decline from 1957 when such transfers amounted to 7 percent of grain production. Moreover, the sharp decline in interprovincial transfers (Table 2.2) suggests that most transfers among producing units are carried out with grain produced within each province. The decline in the marketing rate implies that intraprovincial transfers of grain have also shrunk and that redistribution of cereals after 1965 was dependent primarily on surpluses that could be mobilized within prefectures or even counties. Thus the capacity of the state to redistribute cereals to meet basic consumption needs in rural areas declined.

Redistribution of edible vegetable oils in the countryside also was curtailed. In the 1950s the state sold vegetable oils to deficient areas as part of its regular system of distribution of staples, although the quantities sold have not been disclosed. But by the 1970s, perhaps earlier, that system had vanished (Hsiyang Agricultural College 1980, 183; Ministry of Food Research Office 1981, 63). Rural vegetable oil consumption became dependent on production within each locality, leading to the more dispersed pattern of production discussed in Chapter 2 and the substantial decline in rural consumption shown in Table 4.5.

What of the demand for grain and edible vegetable oil to meet basic rural consumption needs? Here one must differentiate, at least conceptually, between demand arising from short-term fluctuations as a result of crop failures due to floods, droughts, or other natural causes and long-term trends. Analysis of short-term fluctuations is difficult because data at the appropriate level of analysis, the production team, have not been and probably never will be available. Such data might show that the year-to-year variation in output among producing units declined following the gradual spread of irrigation and drainage systems and the partial mechanization of water control and other farm operations. Aggregate national data, however, do not support such a hypothesis, at least for cereal production. Year-to-year fluctuations in output in the 1970s were not more damped than those of the 1950s (Tang 1980b, 345). As provincial data on cereal production for the 1970s accumulate, it may be possible to make a similar calculation at the subnational level. Year-to-year fluctuations in provincial output, at least when measured on a population-weighted basis, conceivably could have declined even if the aggregate national data show no dampening of fluctuations. That, however, remains speculation. And what data are available for the latter half of the 1970s show significant year-to-year fluctuation in output at the provincial level.

Success of the grain self-sufficiency policy pursued after 1965, discussed in Chapter 2, also could have reduced the demand for redistributed grain in the countryside. Although reduced specialized production of cotton, sugar, vegetable oils, and so on surely was accompanied by reduced redistribution of cereals, the relevant issue is whether the initial levels of cereal consumption in areas of specialized nongrain production were maintained. The a priori prediction, based on the theory of comparative advantage, is that they were not, and that a decline in specialized production of nongrain crops led directly to lower income and reduced levels of consumption. On balance, the evidence presented below shows that the policy of grain self-sufficiency was only moderately successful in reducing the demand for redistributed grain in areas of specialized nongrain production. Soil, climatic, and other natural conditions that favored production of noncereal crops made grain self-sufficiency a chimerical goal except to the extent it could be achieved through reductions in consumption and income.

Although in principle one would wish to base analysis of rural poverty on comprehensive data on the distribution of income at the household level, such data are not available. There are, however, data on the regional distribution of low-income rural households. In fact, these data are of considerable value in analyzing rural poverty because, as has been shown by Roll (1975), land reform in the early 1950s so reduced the degree of inequality of income within natural villages (*hsiang*) that an unusually large share of the remaining inequality arose from differences in the quality and quantity of land and other resources across villages, differences that had not been affected significantly by land reform. The formation of cooperatives in 1955–56, which collectivized private productive assets other than land (farm tools, draft animals, and so on), reinforced that trend since cooperatives rarely extended beyond *hsiang* boundaries. Thus analysis of the interregional distribution of rural income has considerable value for understanding the character of rural poverty.

Chronic poverty in rural China

In 1981 the Ministry of Agriculture released a most interesting survey of rural per capita incomes, based on average per capita team income but aggregated at the county level (Ministry of Agriculture Commune Management Bureau 1981a). The report provides unique data that can be used to measure, more accurately than previously has been possible, the magnitude of rural poverty. Moreover, it provides some basis, when used in conjunction with other information, for analyzing the causes of chronic poverty in rural China. The following paragraphs discuss these data, highlighting both their unique character and their shortcomings. I then turn to a discussion of the possible causes of chronic poverty.

The report of the Ministry of Agriculture is unique in several respects. First, it identifies the provincial distribution of all counties where average annual per capita collective income was less than two specified income levels, 40 and 50 yuan, in 1977, 1978, and 1979. Although such data previously had been available for some provinces, this source provides data for all provinces except Tibet. Second, the survey also specifies the number of counties where poverty was chronic, where annual per capita collective income was under 50 yuan in three consecutive years. Thus the list excludes counties where incomes dropped below 50 yuan in one or two years due to transitory weather factors. That is an important advantage since in any given year a significant portion of rural poverty is transient. Finally, the data have the extraordinary advantage of being the first to name the chronically poor counties. That makes it possible to look at the intraprovincial distribution of rural poverty, which was impossible with the previously available data that provided only the average per capita collectively distributed income by province.

County-level data also have limitations. First, they obscure a vast amount of chronic poverty within counties where the average level of annual per capita income was above 50 yuan in any of the last three years of the decade of the 1970s. Second, the data do not indicate the distribution of income among teams in counties where the average annual per capita income was less than 40 yuan, thus obscuring significant variation in living standards even within the poorest counties. Since, as will be shown below, some accounting units within poor counties fall far below the 40-yuan poverty line, county data understate both the magnitude of chronic poverty and the extent of absolute deprivation in rural China.

Before measuring the magnitude of chronic rural poverty in China, it is important to understand the significance of the poverty lines commonly delineated by the Chinese, 40 and 50 yuan per capita per year. First, the concept is based on collectively distributed income, presumably because that is the only rural income measure for which there is complete enumeration of income by accounting unit. Because the underlying income concept is based on collective production, it excludes income derived from production on private plots or from other household sideline production and probably excludes consumption financed by loans or by transfer payments, such as government relief.

Second, the measure includes income distributed in kind, such as grains and edible vegetable oils, when it is derived from collective production. Finally, the concept of poverty is based on a measure of absolute rather than relative income that, in turn, is closely related to the value of what is considered to be an absolute bare minimal diet. Forty yuan per capita per year is the monetary value of 150 kilograms of wheat or 200 kilograms of rice, both measured in unprocessed form.[17] These rations provide a low level of consumption. Two hundred kilograms of paddy rice, after husking, would yield roughly 140 to 150 kilograms of polished rice or the equivalent of 1,260 to 1,350 calories per day. One hundred fifty kilograms of wheat, since its milling rate is somewhat higher, would yield about 130 kilograms of flour, with a daily caloric value of about 1,200. Of course, that diet typically would be supplemented with foods purchased with earnings from household subsidiary products sold in private markets and foods (including grain) grown on private plots, the value of which is not included in collective income. In 1976, for example, average income derived from these activities was a third of income from collective sources (Chang Liu-cheng 1981, 43). Unfortunately it is not known whether that share is also typical for the poorest peasants in China.

If poor peasants derived no larger a share of their total income from private sources than the average peasant, the standard of living provided would be well under any reasonable standard of absolute deprivation. Although the diet would be supplemented above the level of 1,350 calories per day, there would be little cash income to purchase cotton and wool cloth, cotton for padding clothes, other clothing, fuel, subsidiary foods such as wine and tea, or a whole range of daily necessities such as soap and salt. Nonfood items comprised 42 percent of peasant consumption expenditures, including consumption in kind, in a sample survey in 1955 (Data Office Statistical Work 1957a, 4). Peasant families with annual per capita incomes under 50 yuan would be unable to purchase the wide array of consumer durables such as bicycles, radios, and furniture that were commonly observed by Westerners in their visits to model rural units in the 1970s.

Although data on average annual per capita collective income are only a partial measure of welfare, there is some evidence that even when they are averaged at the provincial level there is a systematic relationship between that measure of income and life expectancy. Tracing this relationship is difficult because available life expectancy data have two shortcomings.[18] First, they are provincial averages, including both urban and rural residents. Since life expectancy is higher in urban China, part of the variation by province in life expectancy reflects varying degrees of urbanization. Second, the life expectancy data are for 1973–75, whereas income data for most provinces are not available until 1978 or 1979. Although on a national basis annual per capita collectively distributed income measured in constant prices changed little between 1975 and 1978, relative provincial incomes may have changed. But even after these factors are taken into account, it would appear that life expectancy is systematically related to income. Kweichow, with the lowest average distributed collective income (46 yuan) in 1979 and, as will be discussed below, the greatest concentration of chronic rural poverty in the late 1970s, had the lowest reported life expectancy of any province, 59 years.[19] That is 6 years less than the national average of 65 and far less than for high-income provinces. Where per capita farm incomes are highest (outside of the special cases of suburban farms in Peking and the like) such as in Heilungkiang (110 yuan), Liaoning (116), and Chekiang (120), life expectancy is 68–70 years.[20] Although life expectancy is undoubtedly determined in part by the relative supplies of curative health care and preventive medicine, it is influenced by the adequacy of food intake as well, which in turn is determined largely by income. Presumably the relationship between income and life expectancy would appear even stronger if we had life expectancy data available at the county level.

Magnitude and geographic distribution of rural poverty

Table 4.8 shows the number of poor counties where average annual per capita distributed income was below 50 yuan from 1977 through 1981. The proportion of poor counties was significant but declining, from 22.5 percent in 1977, to 12.4 percent in 1979 and 9.2 percent in 1981. The number of chronically poor counties where per capita income was less than the 50-yuan poverty line throughout 1977–79 was 221, or 9.6 percent of the national total. The agricultural population of these counties was 87,870,000.[21]

However, as noted above, this approach obscures chronic poverty within counties where the average level of income was above the poverty line in any of the years 1977–79. That is a serious problem since the average county in

Table 4.8. *Number of poor counties, 1977–81*

Average per capita annual income	1977	1978	1979	1980	1981
Under 50 yuan	515	381	283	278	211
Under 40 yuan	182	97	81	—	—
Chronically poor	—	—	221	165	87

Note: Chronic poverty is defined as annual per capita distributed collective income less than 50 yuan for three successive years. Data are exclusive of Tibet.
Source: Ministry of Agriculture Commune Management Bureau (1981a, 117), Ch'en Fu-kuei (1982, 22).

the late 1970s had an agricultural population in excess of 400,000. For example, in 1977 the share of all production teams where income fell below the poverty line, 39 percent, was almost twice as large as the share of counties that were poor, 22.5 percent. In 1978 the respective percentages were 29.5 and 16.8. In 1979, when per capita grain output was at an all-time peak level and output of many nongrain crops had grown 20 to 30 percent in two years, per capita collective income was less than 50 yuan in only 12.4 percent of all counties but in 27.2 percent of all teams. In the same year per capita income averaged less than 40 yuan in only 3.5 percent of all counties but in 8.2 percent of all production teams (Ministry of Agriculture Commune Management Bureau 1981a, 117; Wang Han-chih 1980).

    Whether one uses a poverty standard of 40 or 50 yuan, somewhat more than half of all poor production teams are located in counties where the average team income is above the poverty line. These data suggest that averaging income data at the county level obscures at least half of China's rural poverty. For example, in Hsianghsitujiatsumiaotsu Autonomous Prefecture in northwest Hunan in 1979 there were 915 poverty-stricken production teams, where per capita incomes were under 40 yuan (Wu Yün-ch'ang 1980). Prior to 1949 the prefecture, a relatively remote, mountainous area, produced one-fifth of China's tung oil and in the 1950s it continued to export tung oil, tea oil, timber, medicinal herbs, and forestry products to finance its cereal imports. As self-sufficiency was emphasized, valuable forests were converted via slash-and-burn techniques to grow cereal crops. Output of tung oil fell 60 percent from 1958, the peak production year of the 1950s. A reduction by the state in the relative prices of timber and other forest products only reinforced the drop in income induced by the policy of foodgrain self-sufficiency. Yet because the average income in each of the ten counties within this autonomous prefecture was above the poverty line, the report of

Table 4.9. *Provincial distribution of chronically poor counties, 1977–79*

	Chronically poor counties			Chronically poor population	
	Number	Percentage of national total	Percentage of province's counties	Number (thousands)	Percentage of provincial agricultural population
Kweichow	43	19.6	49.4	13,730	61.1
Kansu	26	11.8	32.5	6,610	41.2
Honan	26	11.8	20.2	17,320	27.0
Shantung	24	10.9	19.7	12,820	19.7
Yunnan	23	10.4	18.0	5,480	20.0
Shensi	11	5.0	14.7	1,820	7.7
Fukien	11	5.0	15.9	4,560	22.6
Hopei	11	5.0	7.1	3,180	7.1
Anhui	10	4.5	12.3	9,440	22.4
Shansi	8	3.6	7.2	1,180	5.8
Sinkiang	8	3.6	9.4	1,110	16.3
Kwangsi	5	2.3	5.8	1,620	5.4
Kwangtung	3	1.4	2.8	1,650	3.9
Ninghsia	3	1.4	16.7	920	32.4
Chekiang	3	1.4	4.3	1,340	4.2
Kiangsu	2	0.9	2.7	1,980	4.1
Szechuan	2	0.9	0.6	1,630	1.9
Inner Mongolia	1	0.4	1.2	60	0.4
Kiangsi	1	0.4	1.1	1,420	5.4
Total	221	9.6	9.6	87,870	11.2

Notes: Chronic poverty is defined as per capita distributed collective income averaging less than 50 yuan in each of three years 1977–79. Tibet was not included in the original source.
Source: Ministry of Agriculture Commune Management Bureau (1981a, 117, 120).

the Ministry of Agriculture reflects no poverty in rural Hunan (Table 4.9). Averaging at the county level may introduce some regional bias, obscuring relatively greater poverty in provinces where counties contain larger numbers of peasants. But until the Chinese release data on the geographic distribution of poor teams by county, the county-level data are the most useful available.

The report of the Ministry of Agriculture also suppresses all indication of the distribution of income within counties where per capita income is below the poverty line. The depth of poverty within Hopei Province indicates how far below the poverty line many teams are. In Hsingt'ai Prefecture, just south of Shihchiachuang in Hopei, there were six particularly poor counties in 1979, a year of record grain harvest in the province. Four of them also appeared on the official national list of chronically poor counties. In almost 5,600 production teams, or two-thirds of the total number in the six counties, annual per capita income and foodgrain rations in 1979 were below 50 yuan and 200 kilograms, respectively. In 1,047 teams, almost 20 percent, average annual per capita income was below 30 yuan. An unspecified portion of the teams had incomes of only about 15 yuan and consumed about 100 kilograms of collectively distributed grain a year. In what was apparently the poorest area in Kuangtsung County annual per capita income in one production brigade was only 13 yuan and grain consumption was 55 kilograms (Hsingt'ai Prefecture Communist Party Committee Office 1980).

The extent of chronic poverty for units as large as a county has far-reaching implications for any analysis of the capability of the Chinese government to meet basic needs of the rural population. As discussed above, the primary mechanism for providing a floor on the consumption levels of the poorest members of rural society is, in theory, to allow them to borrow indefinitely from their teams, largely in the form of grain and other staples. But the success of such a system in alleviating poverty is predicated on a particular cause of poverty – the shortage of labor power within individual households that are members of reasonably prosperous production teams. Under such conditions borrowing could provide an effective mechanism for smoothing out variations in consumption over the life cycle of a household. A family with several young children and aged grandparents and a relative shortage of labor could finance current consumption from internal borrowing. Such loans would be repaid subsequently when the children began to contribute to collective labor and the family's claim on collective income rose.

Borrowing from the production team is not a viable option where the average per capita quantity of food available for distribution is less than the minimum poverty standard.[22] Such units have accounted for a very significant share of production teams. In 1976, not a particularly poor harvest year by any means (Table 4.2), per capita collective income fell below 40 yuan in 24.2 percent of all production teams (Wang Han-chih 1980).

Maintenance of minimum consumption standards in chronically poor teams would thus appear to be dependent entirely on state redistribution of grain procured from relatively more advanced units. Yet as has already been shown in Chapter 2, the proportion of foodgrain procured by the state, over the long run, has declined, and the share allocated for redistribution within rural areas has fallen even faster. Moreover, when the data on rural relief expenditures (Table 3.8) are expressed in per capita terms, they are modest, well under 1 yuan per capita annually in both 1958–62 and 1976–77, the

years of peak rural relief programs. Even if these expenditures were successfully targeted on the poorest peasants, they would be quite small – for
example, 6 yuan per capita annually for the most deprived 150 million
peasants in 1976–77, an amount sufficient to purchase less than 30 kilograms
of grain from the state.[23] Beyond these modest relief expenditures residents
of disaster-stricken rural areas are eligible for short-term grain loans to
finance consumption (Ministry of Agriculture Policy Research Office 1982,
107). Although these loans are interest-free, they must be repaid within a
year, so it is not clear whether state loans generally are available to finance
consumption in chronically depressed areas. Part of the basic consumption
needs of peasants residing in chronically poor counties probably was met
from the declining quantity of foodgrains redistributed by the state, but the
magnitude of unmet needs is unknown.

Some examples of provision of redistributed grain by the state are available. For example, in 1979 widespread starvation in Hsingt'ai Prefecture
apparently was avoided by extensive borrowing from the state. In 1979 total
state credits granted to the six counties referred to above approached 55
million yuan, an average of 38 yuan per capita. An unspecified but presumably significant portion of these loans was used to finance current consumption, purchasing grain sold by the state.

But evidence on the overall efficacy of the state's system of loans and
resales of procured grain in alleviating rural poverty is not available. It is
simply not known whether the degree of state support provided in Hsingt'ai
in 1979 is typical of the support given to China's poorest counties. Hsingt'ai
Prefecture has locational advantages matched by few other poor areas. It
straddles the major north–south rail line reaching from Wuhan to Peking. It
is only a few dozen kilometers from the provincial capital in Shihchiachuang
and, perhaps more important, almost at the back door of the national capital. Whether similarly effective state support was provided in remote southwest Kweichow, where 14 million peasants live in forty-three chronically
poor counties, is not known.[24] Indirect evidence presented below suggests
that prior to the late 1970s the quantity of redistributed grains was small
relative to the magnitude of the chronically poor population.

Causes of chronic poverty

The causes of chronic rural poverty in China are not well understood, at
least in the West. That is not surprising given the preponderant impression
that China's rural development policies had raised the standard of living of
China's poorest rural residents. Actually, the levels of real income and

consumption of a significant portion of the rural population in the middle to late 1970s were as low or perhaps even lower than twenty years earlier. In some cases, including thirty counties in northwest China, per capita food consumption and income in the late 1970s not only were significantly below the levels of 1949 but even lower than the levels prevailing prior to the Sino–Japanese War (Ch'en Chang-ts'en 1980). Whether there was positive income growth in the 1950s or 1960s that was dissipated subsequently will be explored below.

Insight into the causes of rural poverty can be gained from a spatial analysis. Although chronic rural poverty is widespread, it is not random. As shown in Table 4.9, in 1977–79 there were hard-core poverty counties in nineteen provinces located in every region except the Northeast. While few provinces had no poor counties, chronic poverty was concentrated geographically. Sixty-five percent of the poor counties in 1977–79, for example, were in the first five provinces listed in Table 4.9. More useful for analytical purposes, rural poverty was concentrated in five geographic and climatic regions – the North China Plain (with seventy-one poor counties); Yunnan and Kweichow in the Southwest (sixty-six counties); the Northwest Loess Plateau (forty-eight counties); the southeast coast of Fukien Province (eleven counties); and Sinkiang Province (eight counties).[25] These five regions contained 204 chronically poor counties, more than 90 percent of the total.

Although tentative, an analysis of the geographic distribution of chronically poor counties supports the view that to a significant degree rural poverty in the late 1970s was policy-induced and not merely the consequence of resource endowments or other natural constraints. The hypothesis is supported by the rapid escape from poverty by some counties after 1978 as more economically rational cropping patterns were reintroduced and the burden of state taxation was reduced. The reemergence of more specialized production of nongrain crops was among the most critical elements since much poverty in the late 1970s was in areas that had engaged in specialized production in the 1950s. Lacking comprehensive evidence, I will discuss selected areas within several of the five major regions where chronic poverty was concentrated.

North China

A third of seventy-one chronically poor counties in north China in the late 1970s were in Shantung. Rural poverty in Shantung was highly concentrated. Twenty-two of the province's twenty-four poor counties were situated in four contiguous prefectures in the northwestern part of the province

– Hotse, Techou, Liaoch'eng, and Huimin (seat at Peichen).[26] Since more than half of the counties in these prefectures were chronically poor, poverty in these prefectures appears to have been widespread. In some years, such as 1978, the average collectively distributed income of all of the 20 million peasants in these four prefectures was 46 yuan, below the poverty line. In the same year average per capita income of 47 percent of the production teams was less than 40 yuan (Nan Chen-chung 1981), which in turn was equal to only 54 percent of average peasant income for all of China.

Widespread poverty in northwestern Shantung appears to be a phenomenon of recent origin. Although subject to considerable year-to-year variation, average annual per capita collectively distributed income in the province as a whole in 1956–57 was above the national average.[27] The northwestern prefectures of the province prospered in the 1950s when they were major cotton producers. They allocated, on average, 530,000 to 600,000 hectares to its production – over 20 percent of their total cultivated area and 70 to 80 percent of the province's cotton acreage. In 1956 three-fourths of all cotton procured by the state from Shantung originated in these four prefectures. Several counties in the region were famous for the high income derived from cotton production. Kaot'ang and Hsiachin counties in Liaoch'eng Prefecture were known as "Golden Kaot'ang" and "Silver Hsiachin" (Nan Chen-chung 1981). Hsiachin was among the most specialized cotton-producing counties in all of China in the 1950s. Fully a third of its sown area was devoted to cotton (Sun Ching-chih 1957, 127), about six times the share for the whole province (Table 2.3).

The economic decline of cotton-producing areas in Shantung dates from 1959–60. Because of the policy emphasis on cereal production, particularly the unwillingness or inability of the central government to supply grain procured elsewhere during the food crisis induced by the Great Leap Forward, the area sown to cotton declined sharply. At its nadir in 1961 cotton output in Hotse, Techou, Liaoch'eng, and Huimin fell to well under 10 percent of the average level of the 1950s. Large numbers of peasants survived the early 1960s by traveling to areas south of the Yellow River to barter their old clothes for grain (Nan Chen-chung 1981).

From a low point in the early 1960s cotton sown area and production increased as the goal of foodgrain self-sufficiency was partially relaxed. But after recovering to the peak level of output of the 1950s by 1965, cotton production stagnated for a decade as self-sufficiency in cereals was reemphasized. Although, as discussed in Chapter 2, Shantung had become a modest cereal exporter, on average, in 1970–78, that was achieved only through a distortion of resource allocation within the province. Exports were made possible by the increase in wheat production in the eastern portion of Shantung, the Liaotung Peninsula (Yent'ai and Ch'angwei prefectures), where yields in the middle of the 1950s were relatively high (Sun Ching-chih 1957, 135). The northwestern portion of the province, where wheat yields were initially less than two-thirds of those in the eastern part of the province, was driven away from its comparative advantage cropping pattern by the lack of external supplies of cereals and was reduced to abject poverty by 1977–78.[28]

Since 1978 northwest Shantung has experienced remarkable growth of agricultural output and income, based largely on a more rational cropping pattern, an infusion of state credit, increased trade – both in state and market channels – and an increase in the relative price of cotton. State loans and advance purchase payments in early 1980 to provide working capital totaled 54 million yuan – a critical infusion since, as was shown in Chapter 3, China's rural sector, particularly low-income regions, has been systematically undercapitalized. Second, cotton sown area in these four prefectures in 1980 expanded by 198,000 hectares to total 567,000 hectares (NCNA April 22, 1980, January 11, 1981; Chung I 1981, 15), almost equal to the 1956 peak of 587,500 hectares (Pai Ju-ping 1982, 15).

The expansion of cotton sown area was made possible by a state guarantee of adequate supplies of cereals for peasants who engaged in cotton production. Increased sales of state-procured grain in cotton-producing regions were authorized by a 1979 State Council decision allocating 480,000 (metric) tons of cereals and 1 million tons of urea for sale to cotton producers under specified conditions. Earmarking such supplies for sale to cotton producers was an advance over a 1978 State Council directive that endorsed the concept that cereal consumption of producers of economic crops should be no less than that of cereal producers in adjacent regions but provided no resources to ensure that that could be achieved (State Council 1978; State Agricultural Commission 1981, 20; Ch'en Yao-pang 1981, 28).

Under provisions of the new system of encouraging specialized production initiated in 1979, the Shantung Provincial Department of Agriculture specified that for producing units where deliveries of ginned cotton averaged 5 kilograms per capita, state resales of grain would make up any shortfall below the level of 182.5 kilograms in per capita distributed food grains. For each unit of sales in excess of 5 kilograms of cotton per capita the state would resell 1.5 units of grain up to the level of 190 kilograms. For every kilogram sold beyond 10 the state would sell an additional 4 kilograms of grain or 2 kilograms of chemical fertilizer, but beyond the level of 300 kilograms of grain per capita, only incremental fertilizer sales would be guaranteed (Cheng

Shou-lung 1980; Shantung Provincial Communist Party Committee Investigation and Research Office 1981, 16; Chung I 1981, 14–15). In 1980, the state sold 500,000 tons of grain and a million tons of nitrogenous urea fertilizer to cotton producers throughout China, including those in Shantung (Ko Ch'üan-lin 1981, 27).

Finally, increased cotton procurement prices discussed in Chapter 2 had a positive effect on peasant welfare. The quota procurement price for cotton increased by a third in north China between 1978 and 1980.[29] However, in the same period, the price of grain that cotton-producing peasants purchase from the state for their own consumption increased more than 20 percent. The cotton/grain price ratio thus rose only 8.4 percent in Shantung between 1978 and 1980.

The new arrangements had a remarkable effect on production and peasant incomes in the four Shantung prefectures. Peasant incomes increased from 46 yuan (less than two-thirds the national average) in 1978 to 51 yuan in 1979 and to 87 yuan (almost 10 percent above the national averge) in 1980.[30] Moreover, these increases were not achieved at the expense of internal reinvestment or loan repayments. Prior to distribution of income to members in 1980, teams in these four prefectures repaid 41.6 million yuan in loans borrowed prior to 1980, as well as 54 million yuan in 1980 loans, and set aside 375 million yuan in collective accumulation (reinvestment) funds (Shantung Provincial Communist Party Committee Investigation and Research Office 1981, 14–15). Finally, the gains in income and production were shared widely. Income of peasants in eighteen of the twenty-two counties on the chronic poverty list surpassed the 50-yuan level in 1980 (Ministry of Agriculture Commune Management Bureau 1981c). Cotton production in 1980 jumped to 409,000 tons, more than three-and-a-half times the level of 1979 and more than twice the peak historic production level of 1970. Per capita sales of ginned cotton to the state were 18.75 kilograms (*People's Daily*, 1981a). More significant, in 1980 Shantung reemerged as an important supplier of cotton to other regions, shipping out 247,500 tons. Planned 1981 exports were even higher, 385,000 tons (Pai Ju-ping 1982, 16).

Analyzing the sources of increased output and incomes after 1978 is complex. Weather is a source of short-run fluctuations in output. The widespread diffusion after 1979 of an improved cotton variety, Shantung no. 1, may also have been important (Shantung Science Commission 1981). More generous short-term credit to provide working capital also must have had a positive effect, or at least allowed other changes to affect production. I hypothesize, however, that like the case of sugarcane production in Fukien Province and Hsienyu County, guaranteed supplies of cereals were the most important stimulus to increased production and income. Empirically the hypothesis that increased specialization in production was due to trade restoration rather than changes in relative prices could be tested if we knew the shape of the transformation surface between cotton and grain. Then we would know whether an 8 percent change in the cotton/grain price ratio, in and of itself, would stimulate profit-maximizing peasants to increase their cotton sown area by more than 50 percent. If it would not, much of the increase in cotton sown area must have been due to simply the restoration of trading opportunities.

The above analysis of Shantung does not imply that all or even most of the rural poverty existing in the North China Plain in the late 1970s was policy-induced and thus easily ameliorated. Poverty in north Anhui, in the area known as Huaipei (referring to the area north of the Huai River), has been widespread since the latter half of the nineteenth century (Perry 1980) and persisted since 1949. The region's irregular rainfall is highly concentrated in the summer months, subjecting the plain to periodic devastating floods. Although one of the central government's most ambitious large-scale water conservation projects in the First Five-Year Plan was centered on the Huai River, irrigation developed very slowly. The share of cultivated land that was irrigated in the Huaipei region of Anhui rose from less than 1 percent in 1952 to about 3 percent by 1957 (Sun Ching-chih 1959b, 74). Nationally the share of irrigated land was far higher, 20 and 31 percent, respectively, in 1952 and 1957 (State Statistical Bureau 1960, 128, 130).[31] All ten counties in Fouyang Prefecture in northwest Anhui, with a population of almost 9.5 million, were chronically poor in 1977–79 (Ministry of Agriculture Commune Management Bureau 1981a, 120). Interestingly, these were the only poor counties in the entire province. Although poverty has been alleviated by policy changes in the past few years, the improvement has been far less marked than in Shantung. Six of the counties in Fouyang Prefecture remained below the poverty line in 1980 (Ministry of Agriculture Commune Management Bureau 1981c, 27). Poverty in this region of north China is rooted in long-standing problems of the natural environment rather than short-run policy failures. The rapid improvement after 1978 in the average income of almost 13 million peasants in western Shantung was facilitated by policy changes, but not all poverty in Huaipei will be so easily alleviated.[32]

Northwest

The Loess Platau encompasses 450,000 square kilometers in 211 counties in northwest China. Four provinces – Shensi, Kansu, Tsinghai, and Shansi –

and two autonomous regions – Inner Mongolia and Ninghsiahui – fall partly or wholly within this geographic region. Poverty in the Loess Plateau is concentrated in the middle reaches of the Yellow River where rainfall is both little and highly irregular. That area of 270,000 square kilometers includes 123 counties with a population of over 24 million (T'ung Ta-lin and Pao T'ung 1978a).

Poverty in the middle reaches of the Yellow River was endemic in the 1970s. In the last three years of that decade, 48 counties, 40 percent of the total in the area, were chronically poor. Their population exceeded 10.5 million, almost half of the 24 million in the region. The four provinces and two autonomous regions that fall partially or entirely in the Loess Plateau have 364 county-level administrative units. Of these, 49 were in the chronically poor category and all but one were located in the middle reaches of the Yellow River (Ministry of Agriculture Commune Management Bureau 1981a).

Poverty in these counties also was acute. In Kuyüan, a geographically large county in Ninghsiahui with a 1978 population of 490,000, average per capita income fell far below the poverty line. In 1977, a year of unusually low grain yields, per capita collectively distributed income was only 29 yuan and grain consumption from local production was only 100 kilograms (Sun Lin-fu, Ch'en Kuo-liang, and Chou P'ei-hua 1980, 33). In 1979, another poor harvest year, in Kuyüan Prefecture per capita peasant income was only 26 yuan and foodgrain distributed from collective production amounted to only 86.5 kilograms (Ministry of Finance Investigation Group 1981, 21). Kuyüan County is the largest of the five counties within the prefecture, so prefectural data for 1979 are probably a good reflection of the conditions in the county itself. Although Kuyüan has been the object of more press attention than most other parts of the Northwest, its poverty is by no means exceptional in the region. In 1979 in T'ungwei County in adjacent Kansu, per capita distributed income in 1979 was 23.5 yuan and grain distributed from collective production only 91 kilograms (Ministry of Finance Investigation Group 1981, 21).

State loans and relief funds and grain procured elsewhere that have been provided to Kuyüan and other counties in the Northwest usually have been sufficient to prevent mass starvation. State expenditures for relief and in support of agricultural production in Küyuan County totaled 92.18 million yuan between 1958 and 1979. In T'ungwei these expenditures totaled 46.51 million yuan. Although these appear to be large, their magnitude relative to the level of deprivation in the region may be low. On a per capita basis Kuyüan received 245 yuan, T'ungwei 185 yuan.[33] On an annual basis this was only 12 and 9 yuan, respectively. Finally, only part of these funds was allocated for current consumption; the remainder was allocated to agricultural fixed investment and working capital. Investment, including that financed from internal accumulation, must have been modest. A survey of 35 communes in Kuyüan County in the late 1970s revealed that agricultural fixed assets in Kuyüan averaged only 134,000 yuan per commune, only 4 yuan per commune member (Yü Kuo-yao 1980c, 28), 3.8 percent of the national average.[34]

Poverty in the Loess Plateau is particularly tragic because it appears to be partly policy-induced. Emphasis on grain production at the expense of traditional oilseed crops, animal husbandry, and forestry has contributed to peasant immiseration. Felling of forests and conversion of pasture lands to cultivated land has accelerated soil erosion and environmental degradation. Moreover, population growth in the region remains high relative to the rest of China, contributing further to declining per capita income standards.

Nowhere is immiseration more evident than in Kuyüan County. Kuyüan has always been subject to severe variations in grain output caused by yearly fluctuations in rainfall. In the 1950s, however, per capita grain production in the county was relatively high, and the county produced a diversified output mix that included edible vegetable oils and animal husbandry products. In 1949 per capita grain output was 414 kilograms (Chinese Academy of Sciences Economic Geography Research Office 1980, 366). During the 1950s per capita production reached a low of just below 250 kilograms in 1953 and a peak of 550 kilograms in 1956. Oilseed production was also important, as was animal husbandry. Production was not only for local consumption; significant quantities of meat, wool, and oil-bearing seeds were sold to the state. Although no data on the level of per capita peasant income for the 1950s are available, there is some evidence that consumption and income levels were moderately high. First, per capita foodgrain production throughout the First Plan was well above the national average, while grain taxes and procurements were modest, averaging 95,000 tons annually for the prefecture as a whole. Moreover, peasant household assets were significant – the average farm household in Kuyüan Prefecture in 1956 owned 2.5 large draft animals and 6 to 7 sheep (Ministry of Finance Investigation Group 1981, 21).

Mismanagement of agriculture ("promulgation of high production targets and blind commands"), perhaps compounded by poor weather, reduced per capita output of cereals during the Great Leap Forward. Starvation throughout Kuyüan Prefecture was widespread (Ministry of Finance Investigation Group 1981, 21) and the population of Kuyüan County declined in 1960 (Chinese Academy of Sciences Economic Geography Research Office 1980,

366). Famine deaths may reflect problems of distribution since at least in the county per capita output of foodgrains at the low point of 1960 was 240 kilograms, somewhat above the national average, as shown in Table 4.2. Grain output in Kuyüan County recovered rapidly after 1960 and averaged well above 300 kilograms per capita from 1962 through 1965, again well ahead of the national average (Academy of Sciences Economic Geography Research Office 1980, 366).

Per capita output of cereal as well as average per capita farm income, however, began a secular decline after 1967. It is possible that an adverse weather trend contributed to the decline. But even so, the decline was almost certainly accelerated by policy. A secular decline in the weather itself may be partially a consequence of policy, since destruction of the natural vegetation led to widespread erosion and desertification and ultimately to a destruction of the entire ecosystem (Smil 1980, 783). The pressure to raise grain output led to conversion of more than 60,000 hectares of pastureland to cropland in Kuyüan alone (Hsing Yen and Sun Shih-chieh 1980, 14). Thirteen communes in the county, more than a third of the total, by the late 1970s had no pasturelands remaining to support animal husbandry. Consequently, Kuyüan and other areas no longer had adequate draft animals for land cultivation. Production units in the region lack the resources to purchase tractors or are unable to afford diesel fuel or the costs of repairing and maintaining the equipment (Ministry of Agriculture Investigation Group 1981, 16). The number of sheep also declined, reducing peasant income previously derived from the sale of wool and meat.

The folly of expanding cultivated land in the region, where rainfall is barely sufficient to support grazing, is shown by the crop yields achieved. Much of the reclaimed land yields as little as 225 kilograms per hectare, less than one-tenth the average grain unit yields for all of China in 1975–78 (Agricultural Yearbook Compilation Commission 1981, 35). Excessive expansion of cultivated area in the region has accelerated the pace of soil erosion. Throughout the region an average of 5,000 to 10,000 tons of topsoil is eroded annually from every square kilometer of land, with the most severely affected losing 30,000 tons (Chinese Academy of Sciences Economic Geography Research Office 1980, 361).

Southwest China

Policy also contributed to acute poverty in Yunnan. Although not particularly well endowed, the province's agriculture flourished during the 1950s, partly on the basis of internal trade and specialization. Yunnan is climatically and topographically quite diverse, ranging from the tropical and semi-tropical regions in the South, to the warm central plateau region, to the more northern high plateau and mountainous regions. Yunnan's natural environment and agricultural production are among the most complex and varied of any of China's provinces (Sun Ching-chih 1960, 511).

Agricultural growth in the 1950s was based on specialization. Whereas total sown area grew moderately in the 1950s, area sown to economic crops – tobacco, sugarcane, cotton, rapeseed, and peanuts – soared fivefold from 62,600 to 326,000 hectares between 1949 and 1957 (Liu Shih-chiang 1980, 31; Central Intelligence Agency 1969). But up to 1957 Yunnan was one of the most rapidly developing regions of cereal production (Walker 1977b, 4) and annual per capita output was quite high, 327 kilograms, by the closing years of the First Plan, 1956 and 1957 (Liu Shih-chiang 1980, 31; Hsiyang Agricultural College 1980, 383). That was above the level of output of Szechuan, a major grain exporting province in the 1950s. But high transport costs meant that a proportionately much smaller share of output was exported (Hsiyang Agricultural College 1980, 383).

Internal trade in the province, however, flourished. The marketing rate for grain was quite high, particularly for a province with a relatively low rate of urbanization and small export volume.[35] Most of the grain tax and sales to the state must have been allocated to rural resales. Internal trade in grain was critical for tropical and mountainous regions where economic crops were concentrated. In the 1950s in hilly regions of the Hsishuangpanna Thai Autonomous Chou[36] on the border with Laos and Burma in southern Yunnan, grain production was sufficient for only 30 percent of local cereal consumption. The remaining 70 percent was acquired through internal trade with flatland regions within the province, where grain yields were relatively high, in exchange for nongrain crops such as tea, shellac, tropical fruits, and medicinal herbs (Liu Wen-wei 1980, 58; Yen Jui-chen 1981, 43). Although this trade was economically profitable even with poor transport conditions, transport in the region and links with the rest of Yunnan were improved during the First Plan when a major trunk highway to Hsishuangpanna was completed (Wang Chan-i 1981, 21). Internal trade contributed to increased incomes, for grain yields in these areas of specialized crop production were only about 60 percent of the area with which they were trading.

In the aftermath of the Great Leap Forward, the area sown to grains rose dramatically. The area sown to economic crops in Yunnan reached a low of 146,900 hectares in 1962, less than half the area of 1957, and then began to recover under the more liberal policies initiated in the early 1960s. Economic crop area in 1965, although up significantly to 241,400 hectares, was still far less than at the end of the First Plan.

After 1965, as internal trade was restricted and local foodgrain self-sufficiency and high grain output became the central policy objectives, economic crop area in the province fell to a low point of 156,700 hectares by 1969, about the same level as 1954. There was some recovery of economic crop area in the early 1970s, presumably reflecting the more moderate policies initiated at the North China Agricultural Conference where the momentum to generalize widely the provisions of the Tachai model, including grain self-sufficiency, was curtailed. By 1978 the area was 260,000 hectares, slightly above the level of 1965 but still well under that of 1957 (Liu Shih-chiang 1980, 31–2).

Most of the chronically poor counties in Yunnan Province in the late 1970s tended to specialize in nongrain crops in the late 1950s. That was particularly true of ten counties, almost half the provincial total of chronically poor counties, located in two contiguous prefectures, Wenshan and Hungho, in tropical southeastern Yunnan. These tropical regions, in response to the pressures to achieve grain self-sufficiency, raised the share of land allocated to grain. As late as 1978, after economic crop area had risen for almost a decade, 91.5 percent of their land was sown to grain and only 8.5 percent to economic crops (Liu Wen-wei 1980, 57).

The allocation of such a high percentage of sown area to grain in areas traditionally allocating a significant share of their land to nongrain crops appears to be explained by the low rate of marketing of cereals in the province.[37] The low marketing rate has constrained the pursuit of comparative advantage cropping, a major source of output growth prior to the late 1950s. Indeed, the loss of income-earning opportunities in these regions has been compared explicitly with the Sino–Japanese War years when Japanese occupation of southern Yunnan, Southeast Asia, and east China substantially curtailed the volume of the province's internal and external trade (Liu Wen-wei 1980, 58).

Summary

Although Chinese sources by the late 1970s began to discuss rural poverty far more explicitly than at any previous time in the Communist period, the dimensions of chronic poverty and its causes still are understood poorly. Evidence on the extent of poverty prior to 1977 is particularly scarce, so it is difficult to compare the magnitude of the problem with earlier years. Moreover, Chinese sources seldom provide intertemporal data for those regions where poverty was endemic in the late 1970s. Thus, it is difficult to differentiate between poverty of recent and historic origin. The absence of time series data is a serious problem because year-to-year fluctuations in weather still induce major fluctuations in farm output and income. Weather-induced declines in output have a more pronounced effect on farm income in China than they do in market economies because there is no partial offset to harvest shortfalls through higher prices for farm products. Flexible prices, which generally move upward in response to reduced levels of output, provide significant insulation from the income effects of weather-induced harvest declines in commercialized agriculture in market economies. Thus one-year observations of the magnitude of rural poverty in China are likely to either over- or understate the magnitude of the problem.

The data on chronic rural poverty in 1977–79 provide a partial basis for avoiding upward-biased estimates of the magnitude of rural poverty. Since that period includes what were, up to that time, the two all-time largest per capita grain harvests, 1978 and 1979, it is almost certain that these data understate the magnitude of chronic rural poverty in the 1960s and 1970s.

The county-level data, analyzed earlier, cast doubt on several widely held propositions regarding the state of rural conditions after almost three decades of Communist rule. First, they suggest that absolute deprivation was widespread. Although government loans and transfers may have prevented mass starvation, these programs certainly had not eliminated chronic malnutrition and had left wide variations in the level of life expectancy that are directly related to rural income and consumption. Second, the data suggest that a significant portion of rural China had not experienced any long-term income growth. Real per capita income levels of the poorest decile or quintile of China's rural population in the late 1970s were no higher than those of the mid-1950s.

Third, and more tentatively, the data suggest that government policy contributed to the immiseration of a significant portion of the peasantry. Policies that encouraged or even compelled the pursuit of local self-sufficiency in foodgrains squeezed out the gains from specialized production based on local comparative advantage. Thus poverty in the late 1970s was widespread in some regions that historically had enjoyed a comparative advantage in cultivation of nongrain crops or derived a larger-than-average share of their income from animal husbandry. Although some of these regions historically may have had relatively low incomes, in several cases, particularly in Shantung and Fukien, either relative prosperity based on specialized production prevailed as recently as the mid-1950s or income levels rebounded once the constraint of foodgrain self-sufficiency was eased. A greater familiarity with the relative levels of agricultural development by county in the 1950s might reveal counties similar to Kaot'ang, Hsiachin, Kuyüan, and Hsienyu where per capita farm incomes were relatively high in the 1950s but depressed by the mid-1970s.

Population and migration policy also has exacerbated rural poverty. The government has eschewed serious birth control efforts in rural areas inhabited by minorities. Because outmigration from rural areas is also prevented, relatively rapid population growth in minority-populated regions has depressed per capita income. In Kuyüan County, where one-third the population is Hui, population growth between 1949 and 1978 averaged 3.2 percent, a full percentage point over the national average (Sun Lin-fu, Ch'en Kuo-liang and Chou P'ei-hua 1980, 33). Moreover, although the national birth rate has fallen somewhat in response to birth control campaigns and perhaps (at least in urban areas) to rising incomes, improved opportunities for female employment, and decreasing housing standards, population growth has not slowed in minority-populated rural regions.

Finally, tax and procurement policy, at least until 1979, exacerbated rural poverty. In the 1950s the level of grain taxes and quota delivery sales of grain to the state were set so that producing units under normal weather conditions would have retained grain supplies sufficient to cover minimal consumption needs, as well as grains required for seed and animal feed. Thus, in principle, taxes would be progressive, absorbing relatively more where grain output was relatively higher. That principle was retained in 1958 when the agricultural tax was restructured. The central government specified average provincial tax rates that were higher where per capita output was relatively high. Thus agricultural tax rates ranged from a high of 19 percent in Heilungkiang to 13 percent in Sinkiang. Provincial authorities were instructed to set progressive rates within their provinces (Lardy 1978a, 125–7).

By the late 1970s agricultural tax policy was far less rational. That appears to be a consequence of the failure to adjust tax and quota sales of grain over time as agricultural and population growth varied widely across regions. Poorer production units had to buy grain from the state at the same time that they were struggling to meet their tax and basic quota delivery targets. Such transactions had an important income effect, since the bulk of such deliveries to the state were for zero-price grain – that is, tax – whereas repurchases were at the quota procurement price. The latter, as has already been noted, doubled between the mid-1950s and the mid-1970s. In Yünlung, one of the chronically poor counties in Yunnan, between 1971 and 1979 tax payments and quota deliveries totaled 42,420 tons. In the same period the county had to repurchase 23,290 tons of grain to maintain an average annual per capita consumption standard of only 125 kilograms of grain. In the best year, per capita consumption was only 148 kilograms, in the lowest 111 kilograms (Ministry of Agriculture Commune Management Bureau 1981a, 118–19). Since the bulk of deliveries to the state were for taxes, while purchases were at the procurement price, those transactions significantly depressed peasant income and consumption.

Rural poverty has been reduced through the restoration of trade and comparative advantage cropping patterns, higher prices for farm products, and tax reductions in the poorest regions. In early 1979, following a decision reached at the Third Plenum in December 1978, the Ministry of Finance promulgated a new regulation exempting production units from all grain taxes and reducing quota delivery targets in areas where annual per capita distributed grain was below a specified minimum level. Although the level nominally was to be specified by each province, the actual levels generally were 150 kilograms in wheat-producing areas and 200 kilograms in rice-producing areas (Chinese Communist Party Central Committee 1979, 7). In the grain year 1979–80 under the provisions of the regulation, grain taxes were reduced 18 percent, or 2,367,500 tons (Reporter 1980c), and quota deliveries cut by 383,000 tons (NCNA August 29, 1980). Although these amounts are small relative to national grain production, they are large relative to the consumption requirements of China's chronically poorest production units. In 1978, for example, the cumulative deficit in cereals in the 463,000 production teams where grain supplies fell below the 150–200-kilogram standard was 5 million tons (P'an Chih-fu 1980, 76). Because the tax and procurement reductions for these poor units were not one-year adjustments but were to be sustained for three years, and because a large share of the incremental retentions of grain were probably passed through directly to peasants in the form of collectively distributed grain, reductions in taxes and procurement had a large poverty-alleviating effect. They would meet the shortfall in the minimal consumption standards of about half of the least-well-fed teams in 1978. Tax reductions for the poorest producing units since 1978 have been one of the most important measures to reduce rural poverty.[38]

Despite these tax measures and the marked income gains noted earlier for some of the chronically poor counties, in 1981 there were still 211 counties where collective income fell below the poverty line (Table 4.8). And as in earlier years, a much higher portion of production teams were poor. In 1981 collectively distributed per capita income in 1.18 million teams, 19.9 percent of the total, was below the poverty line (Ch'en Fu-kuei 1982, 22). And as in earlier years, a substantial (though declining) portion of the poor counties fell in the chronically poor category and were concentrated geographically. Eighty-seven counties were chronically poor in 1981, down from 221 in 1979 and 165 in 1980 (Table 4.8), and of these 61 (70 percent of the total) were in the three provinces of Kansu, Yunnan, and Kweichow.

5

Prospects for reform

Agricultural production and peasant incomes in China both increased at an almost unprecedented pace in 1978–81. The only other periods of comparably rapid growth in the Communist era occurred in 1949–57 and the first half of the 1960s. These three periods share several common features. Most obviously, rapid growth was partly recovery in nature. Output in 1949 had been depressed by more than a decade of war, with its attendant disinvestment in land and disruption of internal trade. A sequence of poor harvests in 1959–61 caused by planning failures and reduced production incentives associated with the creation of communes set the stage for rapid recovery after 1962.[1] More than a decade of pressure on marketing and specialized production after 1966 set the stage for rapid growth after 1977.

Even after the recovery factor is recognized, however, it appears that the underlying trend of agricultural development was more rapid in these periods. A central hypothesis of this study is that greater reliance on price or indirect planning contributed to this superior performance.[2] The essential characteristics of price planning include increased specialization and marketing and fewer constraints on producers, whether the private farm households of the early 1950s or the production teams in later periods. Moreover, specialization occurred along lines of local comparative advantage so that improved allocative efficiency was an important source of growth.

Finally, state policy toward agriculture in each of these periods was less extractive than at other times. Thus agricultural growth was accompanied by improvements in peasant welfare and income. After land reform the state was able to transfer a significant portion of the surplus generated in agriculture to support industrial development. Yet the resources extracted from agriculture in this period appear to be somewhat less than those accruing to China's rural landlords in the 1920s and 1930s. Thus the net effect of land reform may have been, as Perkins (1975b) has suggested, to raise the living standard of most of the peasantry while allowing the state simultaneously to raise the investment rate and to allocate most investment to industry. Although the usual interpretation is that the Chinese followed a rather Stalinist policy in the First Five-Year Plan, peasant incomes rose in real terms. It is true, as we have seen in Chapter 3, that state investment in agriculture and in those branches of industry turning out agricultural producer goods was niggardly, but the taxation of the peasantry was light enough to allow significant reinvestment within the farm sector. That contrasts sharply with Soviet collectivization when there was massive disinvestment by the peasantry. Less extractive state policy confirmed by the Tenth Plenum of the Eighth Party Congress in 1962 was reflected in a one-third reduction in the direct agricultural tax, a reduction in the investment rate, and a substantial increase in agriculture's share of state investment (Table 3.6). Significantly, improved farm prices were another important source of income growth in the early 1960s, as they were again after 1977.

Yet after 1957 and again after 1966 reliance on price planning was reduced and rapid agricultural growth was truncated. What are the prospects that the policies stimulating agricultural growth since 1977 will be sustained? Although one might hypothesize that the absence of Mao Tse-tung, the chief instigator of the Great Leap Forward and the Cultural Revolution, would insure a continued role for prices in agricultural planning, the situation is more complex. Reluctance to rely on price planning, to pursue comparative advantage cropping, and to value adequately agriculture's potential contribution to economic growth seems deeply rooted in China's political and economic structure. Even since 1978, institutional arrangements unduly restrict the scope for reducing allocative inefficiency, and policy continues to inhibit agricultural growth. The persistence of these institutional arrangements and policy choices long after Mao's death suggests more fundamental problems.

Undervaluation of agriculture

Many of the policy changes confirmed at the Third Plenum of the Eleventh Party Congress in December 1978 appeared to reflect a more realistic view of the role of agriculture in economic growth. It is unclear, however, whether the changes were made primarily in response to the crisis of consumption discussed in Chapter 4 or because Chinese policy makers fundamentally abandoned their attitude of undervaluing agriculture. In many respects development policy continues to accord a much higher priority to urban industrial development than to rural growth.

State investment allocations indicate the ambivalence of policy. At the Third Plenum, agreement was reached to increase the share of state investment allocated to agriculture from its then 10 percent to the range of 15 to 18 percent within a few years (Chinese Communist Party Central Committee 1978, 154–5). State budgetary reports since 1978 present data in a discontinuous fashion that makes reliable year-to-year comparisons almost impossible. But it seems clear that the commitment of the Central Committee was abandoned within little more than one year. In 1980, for example, although government investment in agriculture rose slightly in absolute terms, its share of total investment appears not to have increased. Current expenditures on agriculture in the 1981 and 1982 budgets were less than in 1979 (Table 3.8). For the Sixth Five-Year Plan (1981–85) the planned share of agricultural investment, 6.1 percent, is lower than in any other period ("The Sixth Five-Year Plan..." 1982, K9).

Price policy also reflects the ambivalence of agricultural policy. At the Third Plenum agreement was reached to reduce by 10 to 15 percent the prices of machinery, fertilizers, and other agricultural producer goods sold by the state to peasants. These price reductions, which were to have been carried out in 1979 and 1980, were not implemented. Indeed, at a meeting of the National People's Congress in September 1980, a staid affair that usually fails to produce even a hint of criticism, a provincial delegate from Hupei castigated central government officials for their failure to follow through on the promised price reductions. The prices of some products had been raised, he charged (Hupei Delegates 1980). His charge went unanswered, at least in public, and State Statistical Bureau communiqués released in April 1981 and April 1982 tended to bear out the delegate's complaint – the official index revealed a 1 percent increase in the prices of agricultural producer goods in 1980 and a 1.7 percent increase in 1981 (State Statistical Bureau 1981a, 17; 1982a). The director of the Commodity Price Bureau has acknowledged raising the price of farm tools and semi-mechanized farm implements in late 1980 and early 1982 (Ch'ang Chih-p'ing 1982; 6).

On the other side of the ledger of state–peasant transactions, the state clearly has signaled that the prices of cereal crops will not be raised in the near future (State Agricultural Commission Investigation Group 1981, 37; Hu Yao-pang 1982, 18). The unwillingness to consider further price increases reflects the strong residual pro-urban bias of policy and a continued preference for a high rate of investment. A major constraint on further price adjustments is the growing budgetary burden of subsidized food for residents of urban areas and for nonagricultural rural residents. China, in that respect, is like other centrally planned economies where movement toward a rational farm-level price structure is inhibited by an explicit commitment to stable urban food prices (Johnson 1981).

The initial commitment to stable ration prices for staple foods was made in the early 1950s. Since the spread between the procurement price and the retail price of rationed cereals was in excess of 100 percent, more than enough to cover costs of processing, transportation, and distribution, the commitment posed little financial problem for the government. The profit margin on cereal transactions was reduced as procurement prices rose and retail urban prices remained unchanged. But as late as 1959, when procurement prices were about 15 percent higher than in 1953 (Lardy 1978a, 177), commercial profits on the purchase and resale of cereals were approximately 400 million yuan (Ministry of Food 1959, 278). It is likely that the procurement and resale of edible vegetable oils also was profitable.

Profits were reduced sharply as grain procurement prices rose by almost a third in 1961–62, while retail prices remained unchanged. In January 1965, to offset the losses on grain transactions, the Central Committee of the Chinese Communist Party and the State Council issued a joint decision raising the retail prices of rationed cereals (Tuan Chien-k'o 1981, IV-164). This price change, which was modest, was the first one in thirty years – at least, the first to be publicly announced. In Peking, for example, rice that sold for .296 yuan per kilogram in 1952 cost .304 yuan in 1978; wheat flour rose from .344 to .370 yuan per kilogram over the same period (NCNA July 22, 1978). A fair presumption is that most or even all of the retail price increases for wheat flour (7.5 percent) and rice (2.7 percent) between 1952 and 1978 occurred in 1965. No further price increases have been disclosed.

The relief this upward price adjustment provided to the budgetary deficit on food transactions was temporary, since procurement prices of cereals were increased about 15 percent in 1966.[3] Since then the state has incurred growing losses in its sale of rationed cereals and oils to the nonagricultural population. Losses must have been incurred in the early 1970s, although reports on their magnitude have not been published. Between 1974 and 1978 cumulative losses were 20.8 billion yuan or in excess of 4 billion yuan per year (NCNA November 5, 1979). That magnitude is usually compared with national income or with the population eligible for such subsidies. Subsidies for cereals and oils for urban and nonagricultural rural residents approached 2 percent of national income and in 1978 were 179.6 yuan per state employee, almost 30 percent of the average annual wage (Ching Lin and Lei Yang-lu 1981, 33).

Although consumption subsidies already were large by 1978, they have soared since because of the continued commitment to fixed ration prices, the increase in state quota and over-quota prices, and the larger share of deliveries to the state at higher over-quota prices. Financial losses on cereals and oils jumped to more than 6.8 billion yuan in 1979 (NCNA November 5, 1979), 10.3 billion yuan in 1980 (Ministry of Food Research Office 1981, 4), and 12.9 billion yuan in 1981 for cumulative losses in three years of more than 30 billion yuan (Yang Sheng-ming 1982). Losses in 1981 were two-tenths of 1 yuan per kilogram for cereals and 1.6 yuan per kilogram of edible vegetable oils (Yang Sheng-ming 1982). These subsidies accrue largely to urban residents and those living in rural areas classified as "nonagricultural" who receive state ration allotments of these commodities.[4]

The burden of food subsidies increased substantially in 1979 because they were extended to cover nonstaple foods. Following the rise in procurement prices for nonstaple commodities in 1979, the urban retail price was less than the procurement price for many commodities, most of which were not rationed. Naturally enterprising peasants found they could profit from buying products at retail and reselling them to the state (NCNA October 31, 1979; Liu Chou-fu 1979, 41).[5] The state's solution to the reverse-flow problem was to raise the retail prices of most nonstaple foods by about a third (China Communist Party and State Council 1979). However, to offset the price increases all state employees as well as retirees drawing state pensions have been awarded special 5-yuan monthly "nonstaple food allowances" since November 1979.[6] Outlays for this program amounted to 16 billion yuan in 1979–81 (Yang Sheng-ming 1982).

Food consumption of nonagricultural households is further subsidized in two important ways. First, even when calculations are based on the official exchange rate (1.7 yuan per U.S. dollar), which vastly overstates the value of the yuan, by 1981 the state began to incur losses on the sale of imported wheat that are not reflected in the data discussed above.[7] These losses, conservatively estimated – on the basis of the official exchange rate, at 600 million yuan in 1981, or more realistically estimated on the basis of the cost in terms of domestic resources of earning a U.S. dollar (2.29 yuan)[8] at 2.4 billon yuan – should be added to the subsidy of urban consumption since imported grains are sold almost exclusively to nonagricultural households.[9] Second, the state provides additional indirect subsidies of nonstaple foods, amounting to 2.8 billion yuan in 1981 (Liu Chuo-fu 1982, 34).

The magnitude of food subsidies for nonagricultural households in 1981 – about 25 billion yuan (Table 5.1) – can be judged in several ways. It represents one-quarter of total budgetary revenues for all levels of government. Alternatively, it can be judged as a share of the officially reported 1981 national income (Table 1.1) – 6.4 percent – or as a share of the wage bill for state workers and employees – 30.5 percent (State Statistical Bureau 1982a). By comparison, in the German Democratic Republic, where food subsidies

Table 5.1. *State subsidies of the food consumption of the nonagricultural population, 1979–81 (billions of yuan)*

	1979–81 (cumulative)	1981
Indirect subsidy of domestic cereals and edible vegetable oils	30.0	12.9[a]
Indirect subsidy of nonstaple foods	8.4[b]	2.8
Direct subsidy of nonstaple foods	16.0	7.5[c]
Indirect subsidy of imported wheat	.6– 5.3[d]	.6– 2.4[d]
Total	55.0–59.7	23.8–25.6

[a]Estimated on the basis of the cumulative amount and the reported subsidies of 6.8 and 10.3 billion yuan for 1979 and 1980, respectively.
[b]Estimated at three times the reported 1981 subsidy.
[c]Estimated. The direct subsidy program was not begun until November 1979; thus the bulk of the cumulative 1979–81 expenditures on this program were in 1980 and 1981.
[d]The unit price of wheat imported from the United States in 1981, $173 per ton (f.o.b. Atlantic Ports), plus freight of $36 per ton times the official exchange rate of 1.7 yuan per dollar yields a c.i.f. price of 355 yuan per ton. Port charges and domestic transport costs are estimated at 20 yuan per ton, and the milling rate is assumed to be 90 percent. I assume that the sale of milling by-products covers the cost of milling. The cost of flour milled from imported wheat is thus 417 yuan per ton. Since the domestic price of rationed flour is .370 yuan per kilogram and Chinese wheat imports were 12.66 million tons in 1981, losses are estimated at 600 million yuan. The same methodology applied to 1979 and 1980 using the wheat prices and the average official exchange rate prevailing in those years shows no losses incurred. A calculation similar to that described immediately above, using the domestic resource cost of earning a unit of foreign exchange, shows losses of 800 and 2,100 million yuan in 1979 and 1980, respectively. See notes 7 and 9 for further discussion of these estimates.
Sources: Yang Sheng-ming (1982), Liu Chuo-fu (1982, 34), Ministry of Food Research Office (1981, 4), United States Department of Agriculture (1982, table 17).

are large, subsidies were 10 percent of national income in the latter half of the 1970s. Subsidies amounted to 10 percent of state budget expenditures in 1976 in Hungary and 3 percent of the planned 1981 budget in Bulgaria. Poland is probably the most notorious case. Food subsidies soared during the 1970s and in 1980 were 17.6 percent of the wage fund (Johnson 1981, 196, 199).

Two refinements of these comparisons of Chinese food subsidies with those of Eastern Europe should be made. First, whereas the subsidies in other centrally planned systems take the form of low prices – that is, indirect subsidies – a significant share of the subsidies in China are direct, in the form of nonstaple food allowances, rather than low commodity prices. The

5-yuan monthly subsidy is a cash allowance, which, like wage payments, is allocated by consumers in a welfare-maximizing fashion.[10] But because the prices of nonstaple foods were raised substantially in 1979, there is no direct encouragement of consumption of these commodities. Second, the distortions in resource allocation caused by nonagricultural food subsidies are a function not only of the magnitude of the subsidy relative to national income but also relative to the share of the population receiving the subsidy. Chinese subsidies are concentrated on the 16–17 percent of the population eligible for rationed staples and subsidized nonstaples, causing greater distortion than in most of the Eastern European countries, where the share of population benefiting from subsidies is proportionately at least three to four times as large.[11] This greater distortion is reflected in the very high ratio of subsidies to the wage bill in China compared to the countries of Eastern Europe.

The central implications of food subsidies for nonagricultural households are distorted resource allocation and increased inequality in the distribution of income. Because the prices of staples have changed little since 1952 while the general cost of living index for state employees rose 20.8 percent by 1975 and 27.6 percent by 1979 (State Statistical Bureau 1981c, VI-23), the relative price of basic foods for consumers eligible for rationed commodities declined over the long run.[12] That, in turn, contributes to excess demand that is only partially curtailed through the rationing system. The administrative costs of managing a coupon rationing system for the 160 million or so individuals eligible for rationed grain and edible oils increase with the growing incentive individuals have to secure access to staples at a declining real cost.

The growing real subsidies available to state employees provide a major incentive for agriculturalists to become nonagricultural workers. Between 1978 and 1980, some 18 million agricultural workers became permanent state workers, not through meeting rigid state eligibility requirements but in large numbers by "going through the back door" (State Council 1981). The state seeks to limit the migration of labor from rural to urban areas and the conversion of household registrations from agricultural to nonagricultural status both because there are already large numbers of unemployed in the nonagricultural sector (Emerson 1982b) and because the large cost of subsidies for housing, medical care, intracity transportation, heat, food, and so forth that the state, rather than the hiring enterprise, must largely bear. The difficulties in controlling this flow of workers are reflected in urgent State Council directives (1981; 1982b). The Ministry of Public Security is charged with the major responsibility for controlling rural to urban migration and preventing the unauthorized conversions of registration status. But the Ministry of Food (since 1982 the Food Bureau of the Ministry of Commerce) and its local agencies in 1981 were empowered to carry out their own investigations. If irregularities in such conversions are uncovered that the Public Security Bureau does not rectify within a limited time, they have been enjoined to cut off the supply of rationed low-price staple commodities (State Council 1981).

A closely related problem arises in the apparently uncontrollable expansion of the number of rural residents employed in urban areas as temporary workers, as contract workers, or in the category of both worker and peasant. These forms of employment differ from permanent state nonagricultural employment since they enable state enterprises either to meet seasonal demands for construction workers, as in the system of contract work, or to evade state control of the magnitude of their labor force and to pay wages lower than those specified in state wage scales. Peasants working in any of these categories are not considered permanent state employees, and thus are not eligible for rationed food and other subsidies and must obtain their grain either on urban markets or directly from their native places (Andors 1980). At the end of 1980 there were 9.3 million peasants working in state-owned enterprises in these categories of nonpermanent employment (State Council 1981).

Differentials in food consumption between the nonagricultural and agricultural populations, discussed in Chapter 4, grew significantly between the mid-1950s and mid-1970s. Although that pattern was partly a consequence of trends in relative income levels, it probably was reinforced by the growing relative price wedge between these two groups. The prices of staple foods faced by nonagricultural consumers declined relative to other commodities, whereas those faced by agricultural consumers rose substantially. The official index of the prices of manufactured goods sold in the countryside, which in Chapter 3 was shown to reflect primarily prices of consumer goods, was unchanged between 1952 and 1976, while the price of grain, when it could be purchased, had increased 83.5 percent. Thus over time the relative prices faced by nonagricultural and agricultural consumers have changed substantially. But since food is a much larger component of the average consumption bundle than manufactured goods, growing food subsidies skew the distribution of consumption in favor of urban residents and the nonagricultural population living in rural areas.

The reform program instituted since 1977 has exacerbated long-standing problems and at the same time undermined the instruments of control that had been used to control population movements. The growing real value of subsidies increases both the disparity between the agricultural and the non-agricultural population and the costs of managing the coupon rationing system. Although the state has used its control of access to rations to try to control the expansion of the permanent workforce, growing real resources must be deployed to ensure the viability of that form of control. At the same time, the state has denied access to rationed staples to nonpermanent workers to control the flow of contract and temporary workers into urban areas. But the reopening of urban farmers' markets to provide greater incentives to peasants tends to undermine that form of control. In 1981 there were 2,919 farm markets in urban areas where staple commodities were sold without ration coupons (Hu Ch'iao-mu 1981, 195). Although the prices are quite high, typically two to three times the price of identical rationed cereals (Lardy 1982b), they are probably less than under the previous system in which such commodities were available only on black markets. Thus the state's control of the mobility and place of employment of peasants in the collective sector is in danger of erosion. Finally, in addition to fostering a growing gap between agricultural and nonagricultural workers, the new arrangements may lead to a two-class urban society: privileged permanent state employees with high wages, cheap food, and access to subsidized services and second-class temporary workers with lower wages, facing higher prices, and without access to subsidized services and perhaps not able to purchase certain bureaucratically provided services at any price. The usual rationale of the rationing system – that it provides access to basic commodities to all members of society – seems dubious since a significant share of the population living and working in urban areas for long periods of time are excluded.

The growing budgetary burden of food subsidies has long-term economic implications as well as the static allocative and distributive effects discussed above. Politically it has become more difficult to raise further state grain procurement prices because that would require even larger subsidies for the Ministry of Food that would come at the expense of other government expenditures. That constraint inhibits setting rational farm-level prices and increasing commercialization of Chinese farming. The political infeasibility of raising grain prices reinforces what seems to be the underlying tendency to revert to the use of quantity targets. Given the political infeasibility of rolling back procurement price increases for nongrain crops, quantity targets for grain sown area and output may be perceived as a substitute for higher grain prices.

Subsidies also inhibit the development of marketing. Since 1978 the Ministry of Food has been constrained in its ability to expand its purchases of cereals because its budgetary allocations have not been expanded sufficiently to cover both the subsidies necessary to maintain retail price stability and to expand purchases. Indeed, it appears that the implications of the 1979 price adjustments for the state budget were not systematically examined as part of the policy-making process. The Ministry of Finance was consulted only superficially and then late in the process (Oksenberg 1982, 191).

As a consequence, the policy of stimulating larger deliveries of cereals through higher prices simultaneously has been more expensive and perhaps less successful in quantity terms than originally hoped. The procurement agencies have been given substantially more funds than initially planned in order to cover the losses incurred due to the replacement of some tax grain with purchased grain (Table 3.2), higher purchase prices, and the increased share of deliveries at over-quota prices. But the share of output delivered to the state as taxes, quota deliveries, and over-quota deliveries has not increased (Table 2.1, column 1). Indeed, the absolute quantities purchased in 1979–81 rose only 5 million tons (metric tons throughout) or 10 percent on average compared to 1976–78, while cereal production in 1979–81 on average was 12 percent higher than in 1976–78 (Table 4.2). Thus although the usual objective of a two-tier price system is to promote increased deliveries to the state, in China both the quota and over-quota quotas were set so high relative to the quantities that would have been voluntarily delivered at prevailing quota and over-quota prices that raising the over-quota price by 40 percent did not stimulate any proportionate increase in deliveries to the state.[13]

The share of grain marketed, including sales to the state at negotiated prices and sales on rural and urban markets, did rise (Table 2.1, columns 2 and 3). Private transactions on markets were 5 million tons both in 1979 and 1980. State purchases of cereals at negotiated prices on rural markets rose from .215 million tons in 1977 to 3.25 million tons in 1978, to 5.25 million tons in 1979, and to 8.6 million tons in 1980 (Ministry of Agriculture Policy Research Office 1980, 30; Ministry of Food Research Office 1981, 13; Reporter 1980b). But the prices required to elicit such truly voluntary grain deliveries to the state were close or equal to the prices prevailing on rural markets, about twice the quota prices (Table 3.6).

Between 1978 and 1981 the nonagricultural population grew by at least 20 million,[14] increasing the demand for state-rationed grain. From the perspective of the state, although financial outlays on domestically procured cereals soared, the demand for rationed grain threatened to outstrip state supplies, and imports of cereals from the West increased after 1977, although per capita production in 1979–81 was 10 percent greater than in 1957 when China was a net cereal exporter.

Finally, the unwillingness to raise procurement prices increases the prospect that the state will move to curtail rural markets. Under the regulations promulgated in 1979 these markets are less constrained than at any time in recent history. But the state probably failed to anticipate that such wide differentials would arise and then persist between the increased quota and over-quota prices and rural market prices. The differential made procurement more difficult, despite regulations to offset the price advantage to peasants of rural market transactions (NCNA January 15, 1981). Under the more liberalized market rules peasants sought to dispose of their products on their own initiative rather than selling to the state. This situation is analogous to that faced in the latter part of 1956 and in 1957 when rural markets were liberalized in response to criticism by Ch'en Yün and others when those markets were curtailed in the process of collectivization. In the fall of 1957 the State Council decreed that more than a dozen agricultural commodities, including cereals, edible vegetable oils, cotton and other fiber crops, tobacco, and live hogs could no longer be sold on free markets even after the fulfillment of state delivery quotas but could only be sold to state purchasing agencies. The pricing arrangements for such transactions were not specified (State Council 1957b). Despite the decree, deliveries of grain to the state continued to decline in 1957 even as grain output rose (Table 2.1, column 1).

Comparative advantage, specialization, and productivity growth

Thus, the degree of commercialization of grain production was determined largely by bureaucratic policies. The magnitude of funds available for underwriting the losses sustained in grain marketing by the state determines the marketing rate. Moreover, there appears to be little discussion within the government bureaucracy, or even within the research institutes, of the appropriate degree of commercialization of agriculture. Authors may lament the low rate of marketing of cereals, but rarely suggest what an appropriate rate might be. Few even perceive that the short-run optimal rate depends on the tradeoff between gains from specialized production on the one hand and the costs of transportation and marketing on the other, and that, in the long run, one might compare the returns to investment that would reduce those costs with returns on alternative investments.

A widespread lack of understanding of the theory of comparative advantage is one reason the optimal degree of specialization is almost never discussed. Interestingly, the Chinese translation of David Ricardo's seminal work, *The Principles of Political Economy and Taxation*, first published in Peking in 1962 during a previous economic liberalization, was brought back into print in late 1976.[15] However, the book apparently is not part of the political economy curriculum in Chinese universities, and it is doubtful whether Ricardo's theory of comparative advantage is taught to aspiring bureaucrats trained in China's network of finance and economics institutes.[16]

A small core of officials do understand that productivity gains could be achieved through increased specialization. Foremost among these, at least as measured by published articles, is Yü Kuo-yao of the Policy Research Office of the Ministry of Agriculture. Yü has supported strongly the policy of supplying cereals to areas of commercial crop production. He argued in 1980 that if cotton planting areas in Nant'ung and Yench'eng prefectures in Kiangsu were supplied over a five-year period with 500,000 tons of grain, they would be able to increase their cotton sown area and raise cotton production by 200,000 (metric) tons. The foreign exchange savings that would follow from a 200,000-ton reduction in cotton imports would permit China to import 3 million tons of grain. In short, such an adjustment would be highly rational; an investment of 500,000 tons of grain would allow the import of 3 million tons of grain. Yü provided other examples as well. Greater imports of phosphate and urea fertilizers would lead to more-than-offsetting foreign exchange savings on imported grains (Yü Kuo-yao 1980b). Interestingly, after presenting examples of profitable reallocation of resources facilitated by foreign trade, Yü went on to argue in more general terms that similar productivity gains would be achieved through increased internal trade and specialization (1980b). Hsiang Nan, formerly a vice-minister of agricultural machinery and subsequently first Party secretary in Fukien Province, has made similar arguments (1980).

Yü and Hsiang, however, appear to represent a distinct minority. While comparative advantage is an increasingly used term, it is rarely understood. There is a widespread belief that, ceteris paribus, increased specialization cannot lead to simultaneous growth of both grain and nongrain output. That view is reflected in *Red Flag*, the Party's major monthly journal, as well as in the pages of *Economic Research*, published by the Economic Research Institute of the Academy of Social Sciences. Fang Yüan (1980) has defended the past policy of placing primary emphasis on grain production and recommended that development of nongrain crops be deferred until after the grain problem has been solved. Although he stops short of endorsing local self-sufficiency, Fang denies the prospect for accelerating growth through a transformation of the structure of agriculture. Others are more direct, expressing doubts about the entire concept of comparative advantage and maintaining that provincial self-sufficiency provides the only solution to China's food problem (Chi Chin-t'ien 1981, 62).

The ideal of self-sufficiency is still upheld, even below the provincial level. Teams that purchase grain are said to "rely on the state in order to eat," a phrase of apparent extreme opprobrium. A reduction in the number of production teams where the state sells procured grain a priori is still considered a sign of progress. The reduction in the number of teams purchasing grain by 210,000 in 1978 and 140,000 in 1979 was heralded on the front page of *People's Daily* as a sign of significant progress in agricultural modernization (NCNA August 29, 1980).

A lack of understanding of specialized production and increased marketing as a source of productivity growth is also evident in reporting of data on grain marketing. The most frequently cited data (often not so identified) are for the "net marketing rate," that is, total sales less the quantity resold to rural producers of nongrain crops, expressed as a portion of output. A low net marketing rate really only reflects the Party's long-run policy of restricting rural-to-urban migration and its short-term policy of meeting the cereal needs of 40 percent of the population of China's municipalities with imported grain (Wang Keng-chin 1979a, 37).[17] Resales of grain that do facilitate specialized production are less frequently mentioned.

Debate on the performance of agriculture reflects a similar widespread misunderstanding of the role of specialization and comparative advantage.

Criticism of more specialized production of nongrain crops was muted in 1979, when output of virtually every agricultural product rose, but was articulated forcefully after grain output fell slightly while other crops grew – cotton (22.6 percent), edible vegetable oils (19.5 percent) and so on – in 1980. The decline in grain production was primarily the consequence of weather-induced output declines in major producing regions, rather than the expansion of economic crops by 1.15 million hectares, which was less than 1 percent of grain sown area (Table 2.9). The single largest absolute decline in provincial grain production, 3.13 million (metric) tons (16.9 percent), for example, occurred in Hupei Province. But that was caused by poor weather that also depressed cotton output by 29.3 percent. Other Lower Yangtse producers, especially Kiangsu and Shanghai, had sharp drops in output of both cotton and grain. The single largest increase in cotton production, 370,500 tons or 222.1 percent, occurred in Shantung. That increase, as explained in Chapter 4, was the result of a more rational pattern of cropping within the province and improved production incentives, not the 18 percent increase in cotton sown area. The diversion of grain land to peanuts and cotton, about 260,000 hectares, occurred in regions of the province where grain yields were far less than average and is unlikely to explain more than a small portion of the 3.6 percent decline in the province's grain production. At first glance, Hopei Province might seem a stronger example supporting the advocates of renewed controls on grain sown area. In 1980 cotton output rose 113.8 percent, while grain output fell by 2.57 million tons (14.4 percent), second only to Hupei. But cotton sown area actually declined by 8,000 hectares (Appendix 2), and the 56,000 hectare increase in the area sown to oil-bearing crops was so small compared to the province's 1979 grain sown area of 7.762 million hectares that it cannot have significantly affected grain production (Agricultural Yearbook Compilation Commission 1982, 22, 31–3).

The national decline in grain output was attributed to reduced grain sown area. In December, when 1980 grain production estimates were available internally, a *People's Daily* editorial took up the issue, saying that acreage adjustments in 1979 and 1980 were sufficient: "From now on there should be some control for such readjustment so that, by and large, we can stabilize the grain acreage" (Editorial 1980b). That view was reiterated in the Party's journal, *Red Flag*, in early 1981. The article, entitled "It Is Necessary to Attach Great Importance to the Grain Problem," although giving nodding approval to policy changes initiated by the Third Plenum in 1978, charged that "the area of grain fields has been inappropriately reduced for developing cash crops. That tendency, if not stopped, will affect the development of the whole national economy. It is necessary to place grain production in a top position and keep the area of grain fields stable" (Liang Yen 1981, 25).

The theme of increased control of grain area was echoed in several provinces as well. For example, in Hunan and Shansi grain output declined while cotton output rose in 1980. In Hunan it was said that "agriculture should be restructured in light of local conditions and industrial crops should be developed under the premise of promoting grain production. However, we must not reduce the area sown to grain" (Hunan Provincial Service January 24, 1981). In Shansi production teams were exhorted by the provincial governor not to rely on income from industrial crop production to buy grain (Shansi Provincial Service December 20, 1980).

The lack of understanding of comparative advantage at the provincial level is also evident in the special agreements, discussed in Chapter 2, for state supply of foodgrains to promote specialized production in Hainan Island, Fukien Province, and Shansi Province. These arrangements are described as stopgap measures, necessary only in the short run and to be eliminated after a few years when self-sufficiency in grains is finally obtained. In short, the "small-scale self-sufficient peasant mentality," derided by advocates of comparative advantage cropping as an obstacle to progress, appears to afflict higher-level planners as well.

Several conclusions may be drawn from the press articles referred to above. First, the concept of sustained and growing intraregional and inter-regional trade in agricultural products as a means of facilitating specialized production and productivity growth still is poorly understood. Second, the bureaucrats responsible for agriculture still think primarily in terms of quantity controls. None of the authors who expressed concern that economic crop area had expanded too much suggested that the solution was to raise the price of grain relative to other crops. All explicitly or implicitly advocated quantity controls on the area sown to grain and to individual nongrain crops. Finally, the analysis of the tradeoff between grain and nongrain crop production is invariably too simplistic. Reductions in grain sown area are assumed to be the primary determinant of changes in aggregate grain output in the short run when disaggregation of the data at the provincial level suggests a more complex pattern. Similarly, analysis overlooks the effect of changes in relative prices on the allocation of labor and current inputs, particularly fertilizer, among alternative crops. The emphasis on controlling sown area presumably arises because bureaucrats can more easily measure and enforce the planned allocation of land than of current inputs. But that approach ignores the substantial effect on the relative growth of yields, and consequently on outputs of different crops, that is a consequence of the allocation among crops of nonland inputs, particularly fertilizers.

Transport

Commercialization allows gains from specialized production, but is constrained by costs of transport and marketing. Transport costs are as little studied in China as are gains from specialization. It appears, however, that China's transport system is a further obstacle to specialization. That is somewhat surprising given the extensive development of transport since 1949. Transportation and communications since the First Plan have persistently absorbed 15 to 20 percent of state investment outlays (Liu Hui, Li Ch'ün, and Ch'i Ming-ch'en 1981, 412), and by virtually every indicator the long-run growth of transport capacity has been rapid. The pace was particularly impressive in the 1950s, but progress has continued since. The highway network more than tripled from 81,000 to 225,000 kilometers between 1949 and 1957 and more than tripled again to 875,000 kilometers in 1980. The rail network grew from 22,000 to 30,000 kilometers between 1949 and 1957 and then to 51,000 kilometers by 1979. Air routes, though a minor contributor to freight transport, quintupled from 26,000 to 149,000 kilometers between 1957 and 1978. Only inland water routes expanded slowly. They doubled between 1949 and 1957, grew very slowly to 1965, and then declined (State Statistical Bureau 1981c, VI-18).

The increase in highway and rail lines understates the increase in transport capacity since the carrying capacity of many of the routes has increased. Diesel locomotives have begun to replace steam engines. Electrified rail routes did not exist in the 1950s, but by 1979 some 1,031 kilometers of the most important lines were electrified (Ministry of Railroads General Office 1981, IV-106). More of the road network is now composed of class A and B all-weather highways. Moreover, truck, railroad freight car, and locomotive production have all expanded. Railroad freight car production was only 7,300 units in 1957 and dropped to 2,900 in 1965. Subsequently production recovered, to 15,700 units in 1975 and 16,000 units in 1979. Truck production was 6,200 units in 1957 but 26,500 units in 1965, 77,600 in 1975, and 116,700 in 1979. Annual production of railroad locomotives almost doubled between 1957 and 1979 (State Statistical Bureau 1981c, VI-15).

Lengthened and improved transport routes and more transportation equipment are reflected in the growth of the volume of freight hauled by modern forms of road, rail, and water transport – the best single indicator of China's transportation development.[18] That grew from 76 to 181 million ton-kilometers between 1952 and 1957 and then to over 1 billion ton-kilometers in 1979. Average annual growth of freight haulage was 19.0 and 8.5 percent from 1952 to 1957 and from 1957 to 1979, respectively (State Statistical Bureau 1981c, VI-19).

The geographic distribution of transport routes also has improved, a priori raising the optimal degree of specialization in production. In 1950 only 19.5 percent of the rail network lay west of the Peking–Canton line. Rail lines were extended to Sinkiang, Tsinghai, Ninghsia, and Szechuan during the 1950s, and by 1979 the share of the network west of the Peking–Canton line was 45.3 percent (Ministry of Railroads General Office 1981, IV-105–IV-106). Similar measures of the change in the distribution of highways are not available, but indirect evidence points to improved distribution. Ninety percent of all communes were accessible by road by the late 1970s (Ch'eng Ying-hua 1981, IV-109). Progress in road construction is not limited to advanced provinces. The road network in Yunnan expanded from 4,700 kilometers in 1949, when two-thirds of the province's counties lacked roads, to 44,000 kilometers in 1979, a pace of development matching the national average (Yunnan Provincial Government General Office 1981, IV-300). In

Kweichow, among China's poorest provinces, the road network grew even more rapidly from 1,950 to 27,367 kilometers between 1949 and 1979, and 80 percent of the province's communes were accessible by road by 1979 (Chin Yen-shih 1981, IV-296)

Despite the improvement in the distribution of transport capacity and the rapid growth of transport volume, it is not certain that the costs of transporting agricultural products have declined since the mid-1950s. That, however, reflects state policy rather than an immutable law of nature. The density of the road network is still low – for example, substantially less than in India – and its quality is poor. In 1980 a quarter of the network consisted of unimproved roads (earth surface), and only 151,000 kilometers, less than 20 percent of the network, consisted of paved asphalt roads (Ch'eng Ying-hua 1981, IV-109). Truck manufacturing remains a lagging industry technologically. China's largest truck plant, Ch'angchun No. 1, was built with Soviet assistance in the 1950s. The plant produces primarily 4- and 4½-ton Liberation models, a copy of an early 1950s Soviet model, that in turn was a copy of World War II–vintage U.S. truck. Not only is the level of production low, but the ratio of vehicle weight to carrying capacity is relatively high and fuel efficiency is low. A large share of road freight is still hauled by donkeys and other animals, particularly in north China where water transport is relatively limited. China's rail system is inadequately developed to support agricultural specialization since a significant portion of its route structure was designed for and a large share of its capacity devoted to hauling coal from a few regions of concentrated production, particularly Shansi and Shensi. Development of inland water routes, traditionally a major form of transport for agriculture commodities, has lagged. Between 1965 (the peak year) and 1979 navigable inland waterways shrank by one-third, from 157,700 to 107,800 kilometers (State Statistical Bureau 1981c, VI-18). Parts of the Grand Canal in northern Kiangsu, for example, were no longer navigable by the late 1970s. Neglect of water transport is somewhat surprising since capital outlays, at least for renovation of existing routes, and operating costs are far less than for other forms of transport (Editorial 1981b).

Despite these continued glaring weaknesses improvements in the transport system could have been sufficient to reduce the costs of transporting agricultural commodities, thus increasing the optimal degree of specialization in agricultural production between the mid-1950s and the mid-1970s. Increased capacity, however, has not been allocated for the transport of food products. Indeed, the share of transport capacity allocated for agricultural products has declined substantially since the mid-1950s, when grain transport absorbed slightly more than 10 percent of all railroad freight hauled (Editorial 1956, 13). By 1979, foodgrains, perishable foods, and livestock combined accounted for less than 4 percent of rail freight. That is substantially less than in India, where such products account for 19 percent of rail freight (International Bank for Reconstruction and Development 1981, F: 46). More important, the development of the road network and organization of China's truck fleet, which are critical for the movement of agricultural products, have not fostered agricultural marketing. Truck tariff rates for distances under 50 kilometers and for distances of 50 to 100 kilometers are six and nine times, respectively, as great as railway rates. Thus a disproportionately large share of short-distance transport is by rail that is simply not available to most agricultural producers. Not only are tariff rates inappropriate, but the truck fleet is used very inefficiently. There is substantial excess capacity in the trucking fleet, largely because only 11 percent of all the vehicles are managed by transportation companies – that is, public carriers (Ch'eng Ying-hua 1981, IV-109). The great bulk of the fleet, particularly trucks, consists of own-account vehicles, almost all of which are allocated for nonagricultural use. These vehicles haul only the products of the enterprises to which they are attached. The large proportion of own-account vehicles means substantial empty running of vehicles, high operating costs, and road congestion. Few trucks, on the other hand, are owned and operated by agricultural producers and processors. Producers rely almost exclusively on small makeshift trailers pulled by field tractors. The entire inventory of heavy trucks in agricultural use in 1975 was only 39,585 (Ministry of Agricultural Policy Research Office 1982, 125), about 1 truck per 2,500 hectares of cultivated land.[19] There has been some improvement in recent years; by 1979 the inventory of trucks in agricultural uses had risen to 97,105.

Marketing arrangements

Underinvestment in marketing infrastructure parallels the neglect of agricultural transport, posing a further obstacle to increased specialization. The state marketing bureaucracy in many places lacks not only the transport but also the staff and the processing and storage capacity required to market the larger volume of commodities offered for sale by the peasantry (Yunnan Provincial Service September 16, 1981). The cold-storage facilities of the Ministry of Commerce, the agency responsible for the procurement and wholesale distribution of agricultural commodities, were only 1.31 million (metric) tons in 1980 (NCNA April 3, 1981). These constraints are critical because local rural periodic markets can only absorb a small fraction of the specialized output.

Private sales of agricultural products in rural markets are supposed to be limited to locally produced commodities that individuals can carry or pull, on foot or by bicycle, but not beyond neighboring communes. Urban private markets are accessible to only the very small proportion of peasants living in periurban areas. Rail transport of cereals is prohibited without prior authorization by the Provincial Grain Department, and transport by any means of grains and oils by individuals other than producers is prohibited (Kirin Provincial Service November 18, 1980). When local offices of the Ministry of Food have inadequate storage and virtually every household has surplus grain for sale, there is little prospect for selling the grain in periodic markets or moving it privately to more distant markets (Chung Yüan-ho 1980). Although grain can be stored privately or converted to animal protein through privately owned pigs or chickens, specialized producers of perishable commodities such as fruits and vegetables are less fortunate. When state agencies are unable to purchase these commodities, they frequently rot (Ch'en Pi-chiang 1979). Allowing peasants to sell perishables directly to urban consumers without going through local commercial departments (NCNA November 17, 1980) has alleviated this problem for peasants that are geographically close to such urban markets, but not for the vast majority of rural producers.

Because of the state's policy discouraging marketing and lack of investment in agricultural transport and marketing infrastructure, interregional output markets are still underdeveloped. State marketing of foodgrains across provincial lines, in 1978 and 1979, was quite limited (Table 2.2). Only in the cases of Fukien, Hainan Island, and Shansi, discussed in Chapter 2, and of cotton producers, discussed in Chapter 4, has the central government guaranteed extraprovincial supplies of foodgrains over the medium term.[20]

The state also froze, for three years beginning April 1982, both the level of resales of grain to rural producers of nongrain crops and the level of interprovincial cereal transfers (Ministry of Food Rural Procurement and Sales Bureau 1982; Reporter 1982a). The freeze reflects both the bureaucratic difficulties of operating a multiple-price procurement system and a desire to strengthen some types of quantity controls. The multiple-pricing system stimulated a vast unanticipated increased demand for cereals supplied by the state. Producers of cotton and oilseed crops sought to accelerate their deliveries of cotton and edible vegetable oils so as to earn over-quota prices on an ever-increasing share of their output, while seeking to satisfy their demand for cereals by purchasing grains from the state at the quota purchase price. Such a strategy would allow producers to take maximum advantage of relative price developments by, in effect, shifting the terms of trade in their transactions with the state. The state, to meet this incremental demand for cereals, given its policy of fixing quota deliveries, would have to purchase a growing quantity of cereals at above-quota prices only to resell these grains at the quota price. Thus it would be forced into transactions that would entail substantial financial losses, not only with urban consumers, but also with rural producers of noncereal crops. To ration its limited supplies of cereals the state has allocated incremental cereal supplies bureaucratically – for example, the 500,000 tons allocated annually to cotton producers, discussed in Chapter 4. Beyond this level producers of noncereal crops are to satisfy their incremental demand either by purchasing grains from the state at negotiated prices or by making purchases on the free market.[21] By freezing the level of resales the state is attempting to insulate itself from this surge of incremental demand for cereals.

The state is also reinforcing its authority to impose quantity controls on the production and delivery of noncereal crops. Under the freeze, grain-deficient provinces are not eligible for even their usual quantities of cereals from other provinces unless they have guaranteed that sown area of cotton, sugarcane and sugar beets, and vegetables has not surpassed assigned targets and that delivery quotas for fish, salt, timber, and animal products have been met. Thus the role of prices is eroded by the imposition of sown area targets.

Even the old system in which the state sought to supply cereal needs in the cases of natural disasters has been modified. The directive warns localities that cereal deficits caused by droughts, floods, and other natural causes must be solved on the basis of local resources. Central government supplies of cereals will be forthcoming, the directive warns, only in the case of large-scale disasters, and even then such deliveries must be repaid in kind in subsequent years (Reporter 1982a).

Moreover, the small-scale interprovincial barter agreements, discussed in Chapter 2, are unlikely to provide an effective substitute for an increased state role in interprovincial cereal marketing. These agreements are small in number and probably modest in their effect on efficiency. Although this quasi-market mechanism represents an important departure from self-reliance and may improve allocative efficiency, such improvements will fall short of those that could be achieved. That judgment is based solely on a priori logic, not empirical evidence. Because of extreme imperfections in information available, it is likely that barter agreements lead only to small local improvements in allocative efficiency rather than national optimization. Furthermore, it is not clear whether even limited agreements will be sustained.

What are the mechanisms by which bartered commodities are shipped interprovincially in nationally controlled transport systems? Do transactions of this type provide reliable supplies of foodgrains to specialized producers, or do supply uncertainties inherent in barter arrangements inhibit the degree of specialization to less than optimum?

Moreover, barter agreements may ultimately be curtailed by the state because they undermine the system of state procurement. In theory, producers can enter barter agreements only after compulsory state procurement quotas have been fulfilled. But since official procurement prices for some economic crops are far below the prices implicit in barter transactions, producers prefer to trade their output in quasi-market arrangements. Just as the state has rescinded certain opportunities in rural markets, freedom to enter into barter agreements may also be constricted because of the difficulty the state has in enforcing prior fulfillment of compulsory deliveries at below-market prices.

Effectively, then, the state has abdicated its role in facilitating, either directly or indirectly, an expansion of interprovincial trade. The decision to freeze state transfers, moreover, appears not to have been motivated by a weighing of the gains from specialized production against the costs of interregional distribution but rather by short-term bureaucratic exigencies that, in turn, grew out of the multiple-level pricing system. The barter agreements among producing units seem a poor substitute for long-distance state trade in agricultural commodities, given the constraints that effectively limit the character and volume of such barter arrangements. These new constraints on the interregional flow of cereals bear a strong resemblance to the ideal of local self-sufficiency, an ideal that although rejected in principle has returned as a matter of bureaucratic expediency.

Price policy

As discussed in Chapter 2, there is a strong a priori case for the use of price controls as the primary instrument to influence the allocation of inputs and the composition of output in agriculture. The advantages of price control have been recognized in the discussion of the role of the law of value that has flourished since 1978 and have been reflected in the more active use of price policy. Yet agricultural pricing policy seems to serve neither equity nor efficiency objectives.

Prices and the distribution of income

In a two-part pricing system fixed deliveries at a low quota price are the equivalent of a fixed rent that need not affect the distribution of income. In practice, China's dual price system effectively constitutes a regressive tax, one that makes the distribution of after-tax income (that is, income after deliveries are made to the state) more unequal than the pretax distribution. Since quota delivery targets are adjusted only at five-year intervals, the implicit proportional tax burden declines where the growth of output is sufficiently rapid to ensure that the over-quota price is received for a growing share of deliveries to the state. On the other hand, where output growth is less, the share of over-quota deliveries declines and the implicit tax burden rises. The practical significance of this theoretical possibility is well recognized by the grain procurement authorities. Describing the effects of disparate rates of growth of cereal output during the 1970s, they conclude, "The following situation developed: in some regions and in some communes and brigades the quantity of per capita grain sales to the state was large but the amount of income earned from sales at the over-quota price was very small. In other, poorer, regions where the pace of development had been very slow, they were not only unable to sell over-quota grain, but were even unable to complete their quota deliveries. In these regions the burden of state grain sales became extremely heavy" (Ministry of Food Research Office 1981, 32).

Prices and allocative efficiency

The efficiency gains associated with the shift from quantity to price controls presume that planners will be able to adjust prices with ease and that producers are free to respond. But adjustments of agricultural purchase prices still tend to be too infrequent and seldom based on an adequate appreciation of the magnitude of relevant supply and demand elasticities. Consequently, there is both a considerable degree of overshooting in the adjustment process and a persistence of quantity constraints. Pricing of hogs provides a graphic example.

In 1979 the state raised pig purchase prices by 26.4 percent, the first significant increase since 1965 (Appendix 3). To cover the increased procurement costs, the state also raised retail pork prices by about 30 percent. These price adjustments do not appear to have been based on reliable estimates of supply and demand elasticities and led to excess supply of pork. Deliveries to the state soared from 108 to 129 milllion live pigs between 1978 and 1979 (NCNA February 13, 1980; Ch'iu Yüan 1980). But the planners badly miscalculated the price elasticity of demand for pork in uban areas. Excess demand at the old retail price was repressed through pork rationing in most cities. After rationing was eliminated and retail prices raised, pork sales increased "only a little." The market was probably as far from a supply-and-demand equilibrium as before since the state purchased 8 million hogs more than it sold.

One response would have been to reduce the purchase price or lower retail prices. Retail price reductions or "sales" for pork were reported in some urban areas in 1979 and 1980, particularly at Chinese New Year and on May Day, but this was not sufficient to restore equilibrium (People's Daily Commentator 1980; Kirin Provincial Service August 29, 1980). Because the state was unwilling to reduce the newly increased purchase price for pigs, in areas where disequilibrium was most severe the bureaucrats responsible for the purchase and distribution of pork reinstituted quantity planning under the guise of "planned pig raising and planned pig procurement" (Ch'iu Yüan 1980). In some localities purchases were made by drawing lots (Ch'en Pi-chiang 1979). In short, state purchases were curtailed to reduce the disequilibrium between supply and demand. Rationing of sales was replaced by rationing of purchases that in turn encouraged peasants to cut back pork production to the level of "planned purchase." But when central authorities discovered that some localities had reverted to quantity planning, they criticized the responsible local cadres.

The Ministry of Commerce, the Ministry of Finance, and the General Commodity Price Bureau subsequently issued a joint circular reaffirming the higher purchase price for pigs and directing procurement agencies at the local level to buy all hogs offered for sale by the peasants (Ch'iu Yüan 1980). But since pig slaughtering, processing, transport, and cold-storage facilities are extremely limited, bureaucratic foot dragging on procurement probably continued. In November 1980 the Ministry of Commerce issued a new circular stating that "the procurement of hogs should not stop" (NCNA November 15, 1980). In practice, government hog purchases remained rationed (Crook 1982, 12).

This example suggests that the central government is somewhat inflexible in its use of prices to regulate supply and demand. Price adjustments for some critical commodities are too infrequent and when finally undertaken are not based on an appreciation of the likely magnitude of changes in demand and supply. Such inflexibility does not augur well for the use of price planning. If prices are set at disequilibrium levels, lower-level bureaucrats, as in the case of pig procurement, will implement informal rules and restrictions that essentially entail a return to quantity planning. That could reduce significantly the gains in allocative efficiency that might otherwise be achieved through specialization and undermine the intended incentive effect of higher prices. An unwillingness to make more frequent and less coarse price adjustments reduces the prospects for increasing efficiency. Prices that are fixed far from equilibrium may generate as much misallocation of resources as production planning.

Moreover, for cereals and other crops subject to procurement at multiple prices, price policy almost certainly impedes the efficient allocation of inputs used in farming. For cereals, for example, although a significant share of total sales to the state occurs at either the over-quota or the negotiated price, these sales constitute only a small share of total cereal output. In 1981, for example, when premium price deliveries reached a record level of 60 percent of all grain sold to the state, they constituted only 12 percent of cereal output.[22] More important, the earlier lengthy quotation from the Ministry of Food Research Office revealed that quotas have not been set to allow all producers to sell at the over-quota price. Since producers thus face marginal prices that vary by from 50 to 100 percent, there must be significant inefficiency in the allocation of farm inputs. If various forms of the responsibility system introduced since the late 1970s allow producing units to choose freely their level of input usage, the marginal product of fertilizer and other inputs may be much higher in units unable to sell at the over-quota price, compared to those selling at the over-quota or the negotiated price. But they would not increase their use of inputs since the marginal price they receive for their output is the lower quota price.

Evidence on price elasticities of supply and demand will accumulate, marketing infrastructure could be developed, and quota delivery targets for producing units could be adjusted, all of which would allow the realization of the efficiency gains associated with the shift from quality to price planning. A less optimistic interpretation is that the penchant for quantity planning is deeply rooted. Indeed, much increase in specialized production of nongrain crops has been planned and implemented by quantity targets, particularly for sown area. Not all changes can be interpreted as the response of newly liberated producers to changes in relative prices of various agricultural products. "Scientific" quantity planning is in vogue. Soil, hydrological, climatic, and biological surveys have become minor growth industries (Editorial, 1980d). These surveys are to form the basis for long-term land use planning or "zoning." The work is being carried out under the direction of the newly established National Commission for the Survey of Agricultural Resources and the Zoning of Agricultural areas chaired initially by Wang Jen-chung, vice-premier of the State Council and chairman of the State Agricultural Commission. Subordinate organizations have been established in each province and autonomous region and the three municipalities. The Survey of Agricultural Resources was the first item listed in the draft plan for National Science and Technology Development in 1978–85 (NCNA April 13, 1979).

The first national meeting of the National Commission was in April 1979.

After more than two years of survey work, undertaken in 70 percent of China's more than two thousand counties, an initial draft plan for provincial-level comprehensive agricultural zoning had been completed (Ho Tung-chiin 1981). In the fall of 1981 over a hundred thousand cadres and technical personnel in a fourth of China's counties were carrying out agricultural surveys and zoning work. The work also has absorbed large numbers of personnel of the State Bureau of Surveying and Cartography. These personnel, together with staff from the State Agricultural Commission, have established a National Land Resources Survey Office. The first major project completed in 1980 was the compilation of detailed topographical maps of the Erhsung River Valley in Kirin, the Sanchiang Plain in Heilungkiang, the Chiahsing Ningpo area of Chekiang, the Pearl River Delta in Kwangtung, and Chinchou Prefecture in Kwangsi. In 1981 the project was extended to the Poyang Lake district in Kiangsi, the Chianghan Plain in Hupei, and the Yellow River Ordos Bend in Inner Mongolia. All of these areas have been designated as commodity grain bases.

The fundamental objective of the surveying and cartographic effort is to "correctly lead agricultural production without issuing arbitrary orders" (NCNA April 13, 1979). The past mistake of promoting cereal production at the expense of other crops in regions not well suited to grain production has been recognized. But it is thought that specialization is best achieved not through allowing production units to make independent choices based on relative crop prices and the marketing choices they face, but through planning. Or as it is sometimes expressed by cadres at the local level, "accurate commands" are replacing "blind commands" (Butler 1981).

In short, one suspects that much of the improvement in allocative efficiency achieved after 1978 was a consequence of planned shifts in cropping patterns. Past distortions caused by quantity planning were so enormous that allocative efficiency could be improved by deemphasizing local grain self-sufficiency. However, given the continued substantial constraints on the information-processing capacity of planners at all levels, only gross distortions are likely to be removed in a planned fashion. The infinite variation in cropping conditions and microclimates will always be most readily apparent to producers. Unless they are given the opportunity to adjust freely their cropping patterns, allocative inefficiency is likely to remain pervasive.

Input markets

The efficiency characteristics of a system of price control in agriculture depend on the existence of relatively unconstrained markets for inputs in agricultural production. Although an analysis of these markets lies beyond the scope of this study, it appears that input markets are very imperfect. The level of usage of modern inputs in the recent past was (and perhaps still is) determined by political cadres, not through the profit-maximizing calculus of producing units. In some regions cadre pressure led to the use of more fertilizer than was economical at prevailing prices, and when such pressure was eased in the late 1970s, substantially reduced quantities of fertilizers were purchased.

At the macro level, there are widespread variations in the levels of use of purchased inputs even within the thirteen areas that have been designated "commodity grain bases" (Hsü Tien-shih and Hsi Shou-ying 1981). These regions have greater access to modern inputs, and their marketing rates are relatively high. On average these regions in 1979 utilized 544 kilograms of chemical fertilizer and 320 kilowatt-hours of electricity per hectare culti-vated area and marketed 27.6 percent of their grain output. Yet the varia-tion in input usage is relatively large compared to variations in yields. Heilung-kiang has thirty-one contiguous counties designated as a grain base, where the marketing rate in 1979 was 38.5 percent, about twice the national average and well above the average for commodity grain bases. Although the market-ing rate is high, yields and the utilization of purchased inputs are quite low relative to the two other grain bases in the Northeast, where the marketing rates are close to those achieved in the Heilungkiang grain base. In the Kirin grain base fertilizer application per unit of land was greater than four times and electric power almost two times than in Heilungkiang. Yet yields in 1979 were only 56 percent higher than in Heilungkiang. The disparities in Liaoning were even greater. Fertilizer applications and electric power usage were respec-tively almost twelve and more than five times per unit land area than in the Heilungkiang grain base, whereas yields were only 140 percent greater. Input usage also varies more widely than unit yields in the grain bases in the Middle Yangtse Plain, where the marketing rates are virtually identical. The Tungt'ing Lake area in Hunan utilized more than two-and-a-half times the quantity of electricity and two-thirds more chemical fertilizers than the grain base around the Poyang Lake District in neighboring Kiangsi, yet the unit yields are only a quarter greater. Without more data on the usage of other inputs it is impossi-ble to compare the production functions for grain in commodity grain bases that, like those within the Northeast or Middle Yangtse, are broadly compa-rable in climatic environment and cropping systems. It is possible that despite the large variation in input use compared to resulting yields, the marginal rates of return to inputs were equal. It is more likely, however, that output and marketings would be increased by reallocating input supplies.

Yet China's system of resource allocation, with its strong reliance on bureaucratic procedures, provides no mechanism for systematically allocating inputs so that the marginal rate of return is equalized across and within regions. Chemical fertilizers and other industrial inputs rather appear to be allocated in a somewhat arbitrary fashion at each level of the bureaucracy. This may be a consequence of large interprovincial variation in the level of industrial development and quasi-autarkic internal trade policies. Since Liaoning has been the major center of heavy industrial development for more than five decades, it produces considerably larger quantities of chemical fertilizer than Heilungkiang. Thus the variation in fertilizer usage is 12:1 in the grain base areas in the two provinces. Below the provincial level input supplies do not flow freely but continue to be allocated bureaucratically. The State Council has sought to overcome these constraints by forbidding internal trade embargoes on manufactured goods, but it is too soon to judge whether this will have any effect (State Council 1982a). As has already been discussed in Chapter 4, entitlements to purchase fertilizers are frequently contingent on meeting a number of widely varying side constraints so that the implicit price of inputs may vary widely, depending on the region, cropping system, and year. Under such conditions it is unlikely that marginal rates of return on inputs would be equalized.

Party control of rural China

The long-run prospects for sustaining and building on the reforms instituted since 1977 depend not only on a wider appreciation of the efficiency gains achievable through specialization, an expansion of the resources allocated to the transportation and marketing of agricultural products, and more effective use of price policy and liberalized input markets, but ultimately on the acceptance by the Chinese Communist Party of reduced control of rural China. But the reluctance of lower-level Party cadres to relinquish the increasing power they came to exercise after 1966 and the persistence of a major constituency within the Party for a heavy industrial development strategy thought to depend not on markets and more flexible prices, but ultimately on a more coercive extractive strategy in which the Party plays a major role organizing both rural production and deliveries to the state make the prospects for reduced Party control uncertain.

Opposition by intermediate- and lower-level cadres to the policies necessary to sustain increased specialization is not insignificant. Editorials in *People's Daily* revealed widespread opposition to vesting expanded authority in lower-level production units, to enhancing price incentives to stimulate production, and to reopening of rural markets (Editorial 1979, 1980b).

Party cadres reluctant to relinquish their administrative control of cropping patterns apparently opposed the Party's policy that "some peasants must get rich first." Consequently in many localities the implementation of price planning lagged.

Some comrades erroneously regard the difference in wealth arising from permitting some peasants to become well to do earlier than others as polarization, and thus they have not dared to implement boldly related policies. We have lagged far behind in implementing the policy of expanding the production team's decision-making power. Many localities have stubbornly held on to their power in planning crop sowing and planting and in handling and processing products. Some comrades fear that when the production team's decision-making power is expanded, they will no longer "exercise control." They have always relied on administrative orders and have never been good at promoting production with economic methods. (Editorial 1980b)

Superficially, it appears that the opposition of lower-level cadres to the reforms endorsed at the Third Plenum has been overcome. The share of rural units practicing some form of the responsibility system expanded from about 20 percent in 1980 to over 80 percent by 1981. Although the demise of some aspects of collective farming was quite sudden, the fundamental relationships between collective agriculture and the state have changed more slowly. Although peasants may enjoy marginally increased autonomy vis-à-vis the basic units of which they are members (usually teams), the teams must fulfill targets for sown area, quota and over-quota delivery of specified crops at fixed prices, and tax payments. Input supplies are still allocated through bureaucratic channels from the network of state-run supply and marketing cooperatives to the basic-level accounting units. The power of the rural bureaucracy has been modified less than the large increase in the share of land cultivated by households and small groups would suggest, since these smaller units remain embedded in a broader institutional structure that enhances the power of Party cadres.

At higher levels of the Party, opposition to a more liberalized agricultural development policy stems from several sources. There is, of course, a major Party constituency that for years has supported a development policy based on heavy industry. Partly that represents the self-aggrandizement of the extensive bureaucracy overseeing steel, coal, machinery, and other branches of heavy industry. Partly, too, this constituency's views appear to have been formulated primarily on the basis of exposure in the 1950s to what was then the pre-reform thinking in traditional Soviet planning. Perhaps as well there were others who supported a strategy based on the priority development of producer goods not out of self-interest or because of intellectual inertia but because of a belief that China's sovereignty depends, even in the short run, on incremental additions to its modern industrial and military base. The latter group may be aware of the economic costs of such a strategy, but may believe those costs are offset by the gains in China's international strategic position that accrue as a result of a larger heavy industrial base.

In the short run Teng Hsiao-p'ing, Ch'en Yün, Chao Tzu-yang, and others have reduced the influence of this coalition. At the Third Plenum of the Eleventh Central Committee in December 1978 they succeeded in scrapping the heavy-industry-oriented Ten-Year Plan (1975–85) that had been ratified at the Fifth National People's Congress in January–February 1978. In place of the plan to raise steel and machinery output they substituted Ch'en's program of "readjustment" that scaled back the planned rate of investment in favor of a program that simultaneously reduced the burden of direct and indirect taxation on collective agriculture and provided for an increased flow of government expenditures on agriculturally related programs. And they moved to enhance the rights of peasants in farming production decisions.

During the readjustment they sought to reduce further the role of the Party in the countryside by reestablishing the township (*hsiang*) as a level of government.[23] Township-level governments were abolished in most of China in the late 1950s when their functions were subsumed within the Party-dominated communes formed at that time. The reestablishment of the township is intended to curb further Party power over agricultural production. The commune is to remain in existence, but solely as an economic organization.

Whether even the reformist coalition will try to push through more fundamental reforms is uncertain. The field of vision of the reformers is broader than the dominant coalition of past decades, but still constrained. Moreover, the readjustment program has had its own short-run difficulties, many of which have been explored above, that have reduced the momentum of the reform in agriculture.

The fundamental constraints are suggested by the lack of response to a reform proposal made by Sun Yeh-fang (1978). Sun, a respected economist vilified during the Cultural Revolution for his support of the role of prices and profits in resource allocation, proposed that the state increase the direct tax (the grain tax, the cotton tax, and so on) by an amount sufficient to replace all of the government revenues generated indirectly through the system of compulsory deliveries at artificially established low prices, while simultaneously raising prices paid to farmers, perhaps even substituting market for state-set prices. Sun implicitly recognized that in a two-part pricing system fixed deliveries at the low price are the equivalent of a fixed rent that, in theory like other types of lump-sum taxes, does not distort resource allocation. But, he pointed out, even deliveries at the over-quota price impose an implicit tax since they are below market prices. This marginal tax reduces the incentive to apply labor and other current inputs since the marginal rate of return to peasants from the cultivation of products sold to the state is less than the marginal product.[24] Sun's proposal was dismissed as impracticable by government planners and elicited little response within the pages of *Economic Research*, a largely theoretical journal published by the Academy of Social Sciences.[25]

Since Sun's proposed direct tax program would generate revenues equivalent to the indirect taxes it would replace, opposition to it seems to stem from the political judgment that specifically identifying the magnitude of the agricultural tax burden is potentially explosive.

Compared to Sun's proposal, changes in price policy implemented in 1979 were timid. The system remains essentially one in which the state compels deliveries at artificially low prices. The higher over-quota premium price instituted in 1979 failed to increase the proportion of grain delivered voluntarily. Only about 2–3 percent of output is sold voluntarily to the state. But these transactions occur at negotiated prices explicitly tied to prevailing rural market prices that are about twice the quota price. This system is difficult to administer since, as in the 1950s, the state has to prohibit the sale of grain in each of 37,890 rural markets until quota and over-quota deliveries to the state have been fulfilled and has to prevent peasants from moving grain from areas where delivery quotas have not been fulfilled to regions where grain markets have been opened.

Similarly, the reformist coalition holds unswervingly to the sanctity of fixed prices for staple foods purchased by nonagricultural consumers. Even Ch'en Yün clings dogmatically to this policy. Ch'en is said to recognize that large state consumption subsidies are economically irrational but that raising food prices, even if part of a larger restructuring of the wage system, would create "chaos" – that is, urban political unrest – and is thus unacceptable (Teng Li-ch'ün 1981, 92).

Summary

Many analyses by Chinese authors condemn agricultural development policy since 1949, with the frequent exception of the First Five-Year Plan, which is now viewed as a brief golden era. These authors suggest that past decisions were somehow anomalous, reflecting the undue influence of a small "leftist" group. Once the errors of the past have been exposed sufficiently, these authors imply, the Party will be better able to design and implement appropriate policy.

This view is fundamentally flawed. As this study has shown, past policy was debated widely both in the public media and in closed meetings at the highest levels of the Party. Policy appears to reflect a consensual process, not the dictates of one man or a small group. Periodic fluctuations in agricultural pricing, credit, marketing, and investment policy attest to the ongoing character of the debate. The relatively slow pace of development of agriculture since 1949 was more the consequence of deliberate policy choice than of the aberrant influence of a small group.

Moreover, the fundamental shortcomings of agricultural development policy stem not from the Cultural Revolution, when the so-called leftists were in the ascendancy. They stem rather from the introduction of compulsory procurement of farm products in the fall of 1953 and the collectivization of agriculture in 1955–56. In theory, cooperatives can be designed to share most of the positive efficiency characteristics of private farming in a market system (Johnson 1980). In practice, in China the establishment of cooperatives provided unparalled opportunities for Party intervention in farm decision making. In some periods Party intervention was moderate, primarily taking an indirect form through price manipulation. But the use of price incentives rather than direct control always has had consequences for the rate and pattern of investment that have proven unacceptable to China's ruling coalition, whatever its composition. That coalition proclaims frequently its affinity for the peasantry but, except for brief interludes, has adopted policies that promote urban and industrial development, even at the expense of the vast majority.

Much current analysis within China seems flawed, too, in its belief that decollectivization can provide the basis for sustained growth of agriculture. The egalitarian forms of work assessment and distribution of in-kind and cash income that became widespread during the Cultural Revolution certainly reduced work effort and output. Agricultural growth since 1978 reflects the changes in incentives offered producers under the variant forms of the responsibility system, as well as the changes in prices, markets, and cropping patterns on which this study focuses. But the current Party line is to attribute rapid growth since 1978 primarily to changes in organization. At the same time the Party appears to be ambivalent regarding, or even retreating from, the commitments made in the late 1970s to reduce prices for agricultural inputs, to increase state investment in agriculture, to liberalize private marketing, and to increase intra- and interregional specialization. Yet it is the latter set of policies that offer the greatest hope of sustained growth of agricultural output and productivity. In the long run neither cooperative nor household farming is likely to provide sustained growth if confronted with distorted prices and restricted markets for inputs and out-puts. Whether the current policy ambivalence reflects the persistence of a pro-urban, pro-industrial bias even of the reform-minded coalition currently in power, or is a pause in a sustained program of reform, will become clear with time.

Appendixes

Appendix 1. *National cotton sown area, output, and yield, 1949–81*

	Area (× 1,000 ha)	Output (× 1,000 metric tons)	Yield (kg/ha)
1949	2,770	444.4	165.0
1950	3,786	692.5	180.0
1951	5,485	1,030.6	187.5
1952	5,576	1,303.7	232.5
1953	5,180	1,174.8	225.0
1954	5,462	1,064.9	195.0
1955	5,772	1,518.5	262.5
1956	6,255	1,445.1	232.5
1957	5,775	1,640.0	285.0
1962	3,497	1,062.9	217.5
1965	5,003	2,097.8	420.0
1966	4,925	2,366.8	472.5
1970	4,997	2,277.0	457.5
1973	4,942	2,561.8	517.5
1975	4,960	2,380.8	480.0
1976	4,929	2,055.5	420.0
1977	4,845	2,048.8	420.0
1978	4,866	2,167.0	442.5
1979	4,513	2,207.4	487.5
1980	4,920	2,707.0	550.2
1981	5,185	2,968.0	590.0

Sources: Agricultural Yearbook Compilation Commission (1981, 35, 36). *1980–81:* State Statistical Bureau (1982b, 139, 144).

Appendix 2. *Provincial cotton sown area and yields, 1957–80*

	1957		1977		1979		1980	
	Sown area (× 1,000 ha)	Yield (kg/ha)	Sown area (× 1,000 ha)	Yield (kg/ha)	Sown area (× 1,000 ha)	Yield (kg/ha)	Sown area (× 1,000 ha)	Yield (kg/ha)
Hopei	969	324	410	246	557	210	549	450
Hupei	583	390	—	—	578	775	592	534
Shansi	343	287	—	—	221	293	224	346
Sinkiang	114	447	—	—	161	308	181	437
Honan	875	205	—	—	555	360	627	648
Kiangsu	671	284	—	—	588	900	631	663
Shansi	321	322	—	—	250	420	242	334
Shantung	767	236	—	—	543	308	738	729
Liaoning	195	206	—	—	36	435	38	555

Sources: 1957: Table 2.3 for all but Liaoning; for Liaoning – *Committee on the Economy of China* (1969). *1977:* Hopei – Niu Jo-feng (1979). *1979:* Agricultural Yearbook Compilation Commission (1981, 107) except for Hupei, for which that source provides mutually inconsistent area, output, and yield data; Hupei yields from Hu Ch'iao-mu (1980, 102). *1980:* State Statistical Bureau (1982b, 31–2).

Appendix 3. *State quota procurement prices of selected farm products, 1952–79 (yuan per kilogram)*

	Wheat (grade 3)	Corn (yellow grade 2)	Rice[a] (grade 3)		Grain[b]	Cotton, ginned[c] (grade 3, 27 mm)		Peanuts, shelled	Rapeseed	Sugarcane	Sugar beet	Pigs
			Indica	Japonica		Central	North					
1952	.1630	.0944	.1134		.1192	1.7356		.3270	.2186	.0210	.0330	.5300
1957	.1786	.1116	.1236		.1332	1.7134		.3872	.3188	.0226	.0400	.7314
1962	.2348	.1506	.1650		.1802	1.7004		.6078	.4548	.0280	.0542	.9150[d]
1965	.2212	.1516	.1694		.1848	1.8404		.6078	.4548	.0300	.0546	.9416
1970	.2686	.1818	.1962		.2164	1.8558		.6078	.4548	.0300	.0546	.9488
1975	.2686	.1818	.1962		.2176	2.1160		.7600	.5600	.0346	.0600	.9886
1977	.2686	.1818	.1962		.2176	2.1160		.7600	.5600	.0346	.0600	.9886
1978	.2722	.1760	.1904	.2492	.2128	2.3048		.7600	.5606	.0346	.0600	.9892
1979	.3296	.2144	.2312	.2972	.2572	2.6552	2.7880	.9658	.7146	.0424	.0750	1.2506

[a] Through 1977 an average price of indica and japonica types.
[b] The average procurement price of wheat, corn, rice, millet, sorghum, and soybeans.
[c] Prior to 1979 the procurement price for cotton was uniform.
[d] For 1961.

Source: Agricultural Yearbook Compilation Commission (1981, 380–2).

Notes

1. The role of agriculture

1. The most widely accepted estimate shows that recovery to the level of per capita national income of the prewar period was complete by 1952 (Liu Ta-chung and Yeh Kung-chia 1965, 66, 122). Thus the tripling of per capita income represents real growth over the prewar period as well as over the 1952 baseline used here.

2. Each population census (1953, 1964, and 1982) has employed a different definition of the urban population. In the 1950s urban places included (1) cities that were the seat of a county or higher level of government administration; (2) places with a population of 2,000 or more, of which at least 50 percent was nonagricultural; and (3) places with a permanent population of between 1,000 and 2,000, of which at least 75 percent was nonagricultural that were centers of commerce, industry, education, health, or communication (Ni 1960, 3). Beginning in 1964 the concept of urban was narrowed to include only cities and towns with a population over 3,000 of which at least 70 percent was nonagricultural. Moreover, farmers living in suburban wards, who had previously been included, were excluded (State Statistical Bureau 1982b, 495). In 1982, at the time of the third national population census, a definition of urban was adopted that appears to be intermediate between the definitions in use in the 1950s and the one adopted in 1964. On the new definition, including both cities and towns (lower population limits not specified) but excluding farmers living in suburban wards, the midyear 1982 urban population was 206,588,582 or 20.0 percent of the population. On the same definition the 1964 urban population was calculated retrospectively to have been 127,103,041 or 18.3 percent (State Statistical Bureau 1982d, 21). Thus on a consistent definition there was little increase in the urban share of the population between 1964 and 1982.

3. Although it is not shown in Table 1.2, between 1957 and 1965 the urban population reached a peak of about 130 million in 1960–61 (Ch'en Yün 1961a, 128).

4. The industrial labor force figures used here and shown in Table 1.2 exclude rural small-scale enterprises operated at the level of brigade. Data have not been released for the years prior to 1977 that would allow the construction of an industrial labor force series that consistently included this portion of rural industry. Of the 16 million brigade-level enterprise employees in 1978 and 1979, some 9.7 million (61 percent of the total) were classified as industrial. (The others were in enterprises classified as agriculture [25 percent], communications and transportation [3 percent], construction [5 percent], and other [7 percent]). If workers in brigade-level collective industry are added to industry in 1979, its share of the labor force rises 2 percentage points to 15 percent. That adjustment does not change the conclusions drawn from Table 1.2. This adjustment excludes rural agriculturalists who work in state industry and construction in the off-peak agricultural seasons.

5. The rates of growth of industry and agriculture are measured in constant prices and in valued-added terms. Higher agricultural growth rates are cited fre-

quently, but they stem from inclusion of the years between 1949 and 1952 or the use of current prices or are calculated in terms of gross value. Because official data for 1949 are probably biased downward and because the initial years after 1949 were ones of rapid postwar recovery, value added in agriculture, measured in constant prices, grew at an average annual rate of 3.4 percent between 1950 and 1978 (Yang Chien-pai and Li Hsüeh-tseng 1980, 183). Because the prices used to value agricultural output have risen substantially over time, the rate of growth of value added measured in current prices is also substantially higher than the 2.3 percent cited in the text, 4.5 percent for the years 1952 through 1978 (Yang Chien-pai and Li Hsüeh-tseng 1980, 20). Also, the use of a gross value measure yields a higher rate of growth, even when measured in constant prices, since it fails to account for the increase in the use of inputs per unit of output. Between 1952 and 1978 the gross value of agricultural output grew by 3.3 percent annually, measured in 1970 constant prices (Yang Chien-pai and Li Hsüeh-tseng 1980, 183). The rate of growth of agriculture cited in the text, 2.3 percent, is the most appropriate since I wish to exclude both the years of rapid postwar recovery and the effect of rising prices and because I wish to take into account the increased use of inputs necessary to produce each unit of output.

6. Because of the great stress given to achieving high yield levels, local cadres have had an incentive to underreport new land brought under cultivation and to impose higher rates of usage of chemical fertilizer and other purchased inputs than would be warranted according to a purely economic criterion. The output produced on unreported land is included in production data, inflating reported unit yields. To reduce this incentive to utilize inputs inefficiently and to underreport sown area in 1980, the use of unit yields as a success indicator was abolished (NCNA October 24, 1980). However, the official data still underestimate the total cultivated area by about 20 percent (Agricultural Yearbook Compilation Commission 1981, 2). Even if the understatement of cultivated land were negligible in 1957 and as great as 20 percent two decades later, it would not change the major conclusion in the text below: that the man/land ratio has risen more rapidly in China than in other developing countries in East and South Asia. Moreover, the official data may understate China's population by as much as 10 to 20 percent.

7. Even internally the view that China's defense needs warranted an imbalanced growth strategy implicitly was rejected by Ch'en Yün, first in the mid-1950s, again in the early 1960s, and finally in the late 1970s. A collection of previously unpublished reports and speeches by Ch'en to various party and government meetings (including the Central Committee, the Politburo, and the Standing Committee of the Politburo) in the years 1956–62 reveals more clearly than ever before the profound debate within the highest levels of the leadership over the issue of balanced growth. An analysis of these materials and translations of the original texts are contained in Lardy and Lieberthal (1983).

8. The delineation of the agricultural and nonagricultural sectors is taken up explicitly in Chapter 3.

9. This study is more concerned with what might be called the external relationships of producing units than with the evolution of the internal organizational arrangements within the farm sector. There is no history here of land reform, the transition to socialized agriculture, and the subsequent evolution of the commune system. Among the many excellent studies of these topics the interested reader should consult are studies by Shue (1980), Crook (1975), and Stavis (1974).

2. Planning and allocative efficiency

1. The central advantage of price control is that planners can estimate the production function and thus the position of the marginal cost curve by collecting

information from a small random sample of producers. This enables them to set the appropriate single price to which each producing unit adjusts. Setting the appropriate $\hat{q}_i$, on the other hand, requires planners to have information on the production function of each producer. Between 1962 and 1979 i ranged between 4.5 and 5.6 million (Agricultural Yearbook Compilation Commission 1981, 5).

2. This assumes that producers under a price regime set their level of output after the values of the stochastic variables are known, whereas $\hat{q}_i$ are set prior to the time these values are known. More generally, if $\hat{p}$ and $\hat{q}_i$ are both set prior to the time the value of the random variable is known, the superiority of the price regime is preserved as long as producers make their output decisions on the basis of better information on the ultimate position of MC than is possible at the center. That would usually be the case simply because their production decisions would be based on more recent information than that available to planners.

3. For grain-deficient regions the slope of the transformation surface between grain and nongrain crops is much flatter, meaning that the opportunity cost of increased grain production, measured in terms of the nongrain output that must be foregone, is higher.

4. Increased budgetary outlays are necessitated because of the state's commitment to provide grain to urban consumers at a fixed nominal price. This is discussed in some detail in Chapter 5.

5. Data on peasant sales to the state are reported including and excluding soybeans, in terms of original, trade, or fine-grain weight, and on a calendar or grain year basis. Without painstaking analysis of all available reports, it is difficult to resolve these differences in reported data.

6. Buck (1937) does not provide direct data on marketing but rather farmers' allocation of each crop to consumption, seed, feed, sale on market, payment of land rent in kind, and so forth. The aggregate marketing rate can be derived by making an assumption about how landlords allocated the large share of the crops that they collected in kind as land rent. Perkins implicitly assumes that landlords market none of the crops they collected, and his resulting estimate of the marketing rate is 18 percent (1969, 157). His assumption, however, seems rather extreme since landlords' income was derived from marketing grain that they collected as rent. Consider rice, which was the largest single grain crop, comprising about 44 percent of total grain output in the farms in Buck's sample. A larger share of rice produced, 22 percent, was paid in land rent than any other single crop. (The next highest were sorghum, 5 percent, and wheat and corn, 4 percent each.) If landlords marketed half the rice they collected in land taxes, the aggregate marketing rate for the farms in Buck's study would be 23 percent; if landlords marketed 90 percent, the aggregate rate would be 26 percent. Taxes are not listed separately but implicitly are included in the share sold on the market so no additional adjustment is necessary to make the rate comparable to that for the 1950s. The hypothetical shares of rice "marketed" by landlords should be interpreted to include the taxes they paid.

7. Perkins estimates net transfers of grain, exclusive of soybeans, to be 1 to 1.5 million tons. On a gross basis transfers can be estimated, using his data, as 2.1 million tons, and adding soybean exports to international markets raises this to 2.9 to 3.8 million tons. G. William Skinner has argued that Perkins's estimate of interprovincial grain trade in the 1930s is implausibly low (Skinner 1977, 713). If Skinner's hypothesis is confirmed by future research, the analysis in the text overstates the increase in interprovincial marketing in the 1950s.

8. For discussions reflecting efforts to change the system of agricultural planning at the provincial level at that time see Sun Te-shan (1956) and Heilungkiang Provincial Planning Commission (1956).

9. Grain output data for 1958 may be less reliable than that for other years. In

the 1949–79 time series of cereal output published in the *Chinese Agricultural Year-book 1980* (Agricultural Yearbook Compilation Commission 1981) it is the only figure listed with only one nonzero digit. Perhaps the zeros listed for 1958 are significant digits, but given the disruption of the statistical system they may simply reflect uncertainty.

10. According to Ho Ch'eng and Wei Wen (1962, 14), grain could not be sold legally in these markets, even after state delivery targets were fulfilled. But such transactions appear to have been widespread, and rural market grain prices in the late 1970s are sometimes compared with the price levels prevailing in the first half of the 1960s. These comparisons suggest that state grain markets "*kuo-chia liang-shih shih-chang*," i.e., the traditional periodic grain markets that came under government control in late 1953, were also reopened or that grain sales in "free markets" (*tzu-you shih-chang*) or "rural markets" (*nung-ts'un shih-chang*), as they were called by the early 1960s, occurred in violation of the regulations, as they had from June 1956 through most of 1957.

11. The agricultural tax is assessed on the basis not of actual output but of "normal yields." Tax collections as a share of output are less than the nominal rate since "normal yields" when established in the early 1950s were less than actual yields and because the normal yield base rarely is adjusted. The agricultural tax is discussed further in Chapter 3.

12. I am referring not to brief visits to model communes but the opportunities for extended field research in rural areas that arose after 1978. Almost without exception the production teams or brigades to which Western scholars have been able to make repeated visits over a period of months (or in some cases years) or with which they have been able to live in situ have been characterized by levels of per capita income and rates of marketing substantially above average. While these research opportunities are of unusual value in many respects, they do not provide a basis for making general statements on average economic conditions in rural China.

13. Inner Mongolia was a net exporter of cereal crops in 1953 (Sun Ching-chih 1956, 28).

14. Based on reported 1979 cereal output of 5.1 million metric tons (Agricultural Yearbook Compilation Commission 1981, 101) and a population of 18.5 million (Hu Ch'iao-mu 1980, 70). Output declined by 22 percent in 1980 (Hu Ch'iao-mu 1981, 277), but rose by 20.1 percent in 1981 (Inner Mongolia Regional Service October 26, 1981, in FBIS November 12, 1981, R3).

15. Geometric growth rates calculated on the basis of absolute population data in the following sources: national – Table 1.1; provincial – Hu Ch'iao-mu 1980, 84; 1981, 43; State Statistical Bureau 1960, 11.

16. State subsidies for resettled urbanites are shown in Table 3.8. Two points deserve mention. First, the subsidies are modest relative to the numbers of persons resettled. Second, the bulk of the funds were used to subsidize consumption in the first year or so of resettlement and to subsidize local construction of housing. It is possible that some of the resettled population was assigned to state farms that received increased investment funds through the state budget that could be used to purchase fixed assets. However, the growth of employment in the state farm system, a little over 4 million nationally between 1957 and 1975 (Table 1.2, footnote *a*), seems modest compared to the 20 million or so who were resettled. Thus it seems likely that fixed assets per agricultural worker grew modestly at best in Inner Mongolia and Sinkiang.

17. This is difficult to show because we lack sown area data for the mid-1960s for Inner Mongolia. Between 1957 and 1979 grain sown area declined 5 percent from 4.229 to 4.0423 million hectares (Agricultural Yearbook Compilation Commission

1981, 100; Central Intelligence Agency 1969). It is likely that erosion in the 1970s offset earlier gains in cropped area. In Heilungkiang, which shares with Inner Mongolia both a concentration of state farms that are engaged primarily in land reclamation and a relatively low initial man/land ratio, but where husbandry is less important, sown area rose 20 percent between 1957 and 1979.

18. At the margin, of course, since producers would sell some output in rural markets after fulfilling state delivery quotas, cropping decisions would be influenced by prices farmers anticipated in these nonstate markets, as well as the fixed procurement price. Sale of cotton on rural markets was increasingly restricted after 1954. State purchases absorbed 80–90 percent of cotton production in 1957–58 and again in the mid-1970s. Nonetheless, the ability to sell grain privately in most years in the 1950s at a price substantially above that for state deliveries perhaps raised the marginal grain/cotton price ratio above the relative procurement price ratio.

19. Table 2.3 shows Shansi with a relative cotton yield that is slightly higher than that for Hopei. That is because Shansi grain output and yields in 1957 were lower than in any other year in the First Plan (Walker 1977b, table 1). Cotton output and yields were not depressed in 1957. In the mid-1950s, with normal weather in both provinces, relative cotton yields were higher in Hopei than in Shansi.

20. Barley and millet were the predominant cereal crops in Nant'ung and Yench'eng Prefectures, the major cotton-growing regions of Kiangsu (Sun Ching-chih 1959b, 30–34). In Hupei most cotton was grown in the Chianghan Plain, where rice was the predominant alternative crop (Sun Ching-chih 1958, 24–25).

21. When discussing interprovincial trade I use the word *export* to mean to ship out of a province.

22. That transfer of a million metric tons of cereals was in addition to the large quantities of cereals brought in from outside north China to feed the urban populations of Peking and Tientsin, the two largest cities on the North China Plain. Both these cities, while administratively separate, are geographically surrounded by Hopei Province.

23. Total cultivated area in north China suffered a long-term decline between 1957 and the late 1970s (Agricultural Yearbook Compilation Commission 1981; Central Intelligence Agency 1969). Whether this is due to growth of urban areas and industry, or whether north China has still not recovered from the extreme soil salinization in the early 1960s, due to the poorly designed irrigation projects of the Great Leap years, is not clear. But the decline in cotton-sown area in these regions was disproportionately large.

24. Sun Ching-chih (1959a, 170) states that sugarcane was grown on 17 percent of the county's arable land but it is likely that 6,700 hectares was 17 percent of sown area. If 6,700 hectares were 17 percent of arable land, total arable land in the county would have been 39,400 hectares. Arable land in the county in 1979 is given by Hsiao and Chang as 24,000 hectares. Since sown area in the whole province expanded slightly from 2.378 million hectares in 1957 (Central Intelligence Agency 1969) to 2.645 million hectares in 1979 (Agricultural Yearbook Compilation Commission 1981, 100), it is unlikely that sown area in Hsienyu County could have fallen by 40 percent between 1957 and 1979. Thus, I believe that sugar was sown on 17 percent of sown area. Since the multiple cropping rate in the province and presumably in Hsienyu as well was quite high (1.4 in 1957: Sun Ching-chih 1959a, 112, 115) and sugarcane matures in somewhat over a year, sugarcane as a share of cultivated area would be much higher than 17 percent.

25. The target was about equal to production when the plan was established. The quantity of sugarcane pressed in the 1975–76 crushing year, shown in Table 2.5 as 1976, was 900,000 metric tons, and production was probably 1.00 to 1.06 million

metric tons. Note that since the plan was announced in late 1975 and implemented beginning in calendar year 1976, its effect on the allocation of land and current inputs would not be reflected in output and yields until the 1976–77 crushing year and later. Thus the first data in Table 2.5 that reflect the new plan are those for the 1977–78 crushing year, shown in the table as 1978.

26. The tax exemption presumably was instituted to undermine the incentive for producers to refine sugarcane via native methods to avoid the high tax on sugar refined in state factories. As is discussed in Chapter 3, the tax and profit markup at the refining stage are equal to 145 percent of the costs of raw material and refining. One-and-a-half kilograms is equal to a little more than half of average per capita sugar consumption in 1976–77.

27. The decline in production between the 1966 and 1969 crushing years is so precipitous that I wonder whether it might not reflect the disruption of transportation systems during this violent phase of the Cultural Revolution as well as the official policy of local cereal self-sufficiency. After the army was called in to manage the rail system and restore order nationally in 1969, the decline in sugarcane production in Hsienyu was halted, but production stagnated through 1972.

28. Rice purchase prices rose 15.8 percent between 1965 and 1975 while the purchase price of sugarcane rose 15.3 percent. Between 1975 and 1979 the purchase price of rice and sugarcane rose 20.3 and 22.5 percent, respectively (Appendix 3). For the whole period the relative price of sugar rose less than 2 percent. As discussed in Chapter 3, specialized producers of noncereal crops purchase cereals from the state at a slight premium over the purchase price. Confirmation of this practice in the case of Fukien sugar producers in the wake of higher purchase prices in 1979 is contained in Hsü Chien-p'ing and Shih Wei-lian (1980, 21).

29. In summary, unit yields in metric tons per hectare evolved as shown below:

	1957	1978	1979	1980
National	38.9	38.5	42.0	47.5
Fukien	49.9	—	78.8	85.2
Kwangtung	42.6	39.7	41.7	—

The data for 1957 are from Table 2.4; national data for 1978 are cited in the text, for 1979 and 1980 they are calculated from data in tables 2.9 and 4.4; Fukien data are from Table 2.5; Kwangtung data for 1979 and 1980 are from Kwangtung Provincial Service (May 14, 1979).

30. The large volume of sugar imports reflected Ch'en Yün's strategy of putting high-priced candy on the domestic market to soak up the large excess urban purchasing power that was a consequence of an explosion of the nonagricultural labor force during the Great Leap Forward and a decline after 1959 in the production of manufactured consumer goods based on agricultural inputs (Ch'en Yün 1961d, 117).

31. Although the State Statistical Bureau (1982c) has released trade data in physical terms, I have relied on the estimates of the United States Department of Agriculture here as well as in my analysis of trends in cotton trade earlier in this chapter. Although the State Statistical Bureau report is the most comprehensive ever released, for sugar and cotton data are provided only for imports, not for exports. Since China was simultaneously an importer and exporter of these commodities in most years, trends in imports of these commodities are most meaningfully measured in net rather than gross terms.

32. Sown area of all sources of edible vegetable oils declined to a trough of 4.153 million hectares in 1962, compared to 6.932 million hectares in 1957. The output trough was in 1961 when production was 2.418 million metric tons, down from the peak of 5.085 million metric tons in 1955 (Agricultural Yearbook Compilation Commission 1981, 35, 36).

33. In 1956 and 1957 per capita cereal production in Heilungkiang was 541 and 523 kilograms, respectively, 77 and 74 percent greater than the national average. Exports to other provinces averaged 1.4 million metric tons a year between 1953 and 1957 (Donnithorne 1970, 28–30; Li Ssu-heng 1981, 56). By the 1970s Heilungkiang's relative productivity had declined. But production remained more than a third greater than the national average and Heilungkiang remained a cereal exporter, although on a reduced scale. For example, in 1979 the province exported 400,000 metric tons (Li Ssu-heng 1981, 56). Although production data are lacking for most of the 1960s, it seems safe to assume that Heilungkiang was relatively unconstrained by the self-sufficiency program.

34. As will be discussed in Chapter 3, the index of prices of manufactured goods sold in rural areas is fundamentally flawed by its virtual exclusion of producer goods. The judgment that the terms of trade of agriculture improved after 1977 is based on independent information on price trends for machinery, chemical fertilizers, and other commodities. Some of these price trends are discussed in Chapter 3.

35. A price increase of 24.7 percent between 1975 and 1978 can be calculated from data reported in Agricultural Yearbook Compilation Commission (1981, 378). Wu Leng (1980, 29) reports that the purchase price of soybeans was raised twice in 1976–79. The 1979 price increase was announced in State Statistical Bureau (1979b). The other increase was in 1978, according to Chi Lung and Lu Nan (1980, 46). Thus all of the increase between 1975 and 1978 probably occurred in 1978.

36. The two-part pricing system, which has a long history in Soviet agriculture, appears to have been used in some provinces prior to 1970, but apparently on a local option basis. The uniform 20 percent premium beginning in 1970 is given in Agricultural Yearbook Compilation Commission (1981, 382).

37. Rice sown area data in Table 2.9 do not show what portion is double-cropped. Conceivably the reductions in total rice sown area could be of single-crop rice (midseason rice). Actually, single-crop rice area expanded, so the shrinkage in total rice area understates the reduction in double-cropped rice. For example, in 1979 when total rice sown area fell 550,000 hectares, there was a separate report that early rice sown area had fallen 600,000 hectares (NCNA August 14, 1979).

38. Private rural sales appropriately are compared with state resales in rural areas since only a very small share of the grain sold on these rural markets is purchased by urban residents (Chang Li-fen 1980, 31).

3. Prices and intersectoral resource transfers

1. The analysis here is of "state farms" (*kuo-ying nung-ch'ang*) in the "state farm system" (*nung-k'en hsi-t'ung*). That includes only farms under the Ministry of State Farms and Land Reclamation (*nung k'en-pu*). The 2,047 such farms in 1979 included 990 specialized in the production of cereal, fiber, and other nongrain crops; 425 state animal farms; 160 plantations producing rubber and other tropical crops; 288 fruit and tea farms; 83 ginseng farms; and 101 farms in other unspecified categories (Agricultural Yearbook Compilation Commission 1981, 18). Excluded are

3,883 state forestry farms that were administered by the Ministry of Forestry and 880 state fish farms that were presumably administered by the Bureau of Aquatic Products. In 1957 there were almost 2,000 state farms under local governments cultivating 1.04 million hectares of land (Chao Kang 1970, 70), almost the same area as cultivated by farms administered by the Ministry of State Farms and Land Reclamation (Agricultural Yearbook Compilation Commission 1981, 5). Although the local state farm system expanded rapidly in the late 1950s, little information on these farms in recent years, to my knowledge, has been disclosed. Local state farms do not appear to be included in data on the state farm system. The military, Ministry of Public Security (secret police), Ministry of Civil Affairs (Min-cheng pu, prior to 1978 called the Ministry of Internal Affairs – Nei-wu pu) and other state organizations presumably also operate farms. State Statistical Bureau data on farm output and employment probably exclude these latter organizations.

2. A province-by-province listing of the number, though not the cultivated area, of state farms in 1979 is given in Agricultural Yearbook Compilation Commission (1981, 20).

3. The gross value of agricultural output of the state farm system in 1979 was 4.22 billion yuan (Agricultural Yearbook Compilation Commission 1981, 19), 2.7 percent of the gross value of agricultural output of the whole country, 158.4 billion yuan (State Statistical Bureau 1981c, VI-4).

4. In the 1953 54 grain year purchases increased by more than 11 million (metric) tons (Wu Shuo 1957, 25), implying that 1952–53 purchases were about 11 million tons (Table 3.2).

5. Total state purchases of agricultural and subsidiary agricultural products in 1978 were 55 billion yuan. Of this 13.36 billion yuan was grain, 23.00 billion yuan consisted of subsidiary and other products, and more than 19 billion yuan consisted of eight major commercial crops (including cotton, sugarcane, sugar beet, tobacco, hemp, and tea), animal husbandry products, and fish products (Special Commentator 1981). The discrepancy between the total of 55 billion yuan and the 46 billion yuan cited in other sources (Table 3.3) appears to be caused by price differences. The Special Commentator article, published in 1981, appears to have calculated 1978 purchases in the prices introduced in 1979, whereas the 46-billion-yuan figure is measured in the prices prevailing in 1978.

6. Between 1957 and 1978 the share of cotton output procured rose from 84.3 to 94.3 percent. Between 1958 (1957 data are not available) and 1978 the share of sugarcane and sugar beet rose from 70.1 to 89.2 percent (Agricultural Yearbook Compilation Commission 1981, 327).

7. In the 1950s, the major offset to higher income derived from rising procurement prices was the increased expenditures for agricultural products purchased by peasants from the state. For the years for which data are available the offset was usually one-third the gains from higher procurement prices (Data Office Statistical Work 1957c). In the 1950s grain resold in the countryside was priced at 8 percent over the procurement price in order to cover the costs of distribution and storage (Yao Yi-lin 1960, 16). The link between procurement and rural sale prices has persisted in most transactions and the price of resold grain rose sharply in the late 1970s (Liu Pao-chin 1981, 103).

8. In 1978, for example, net sales of grain can be estimated as gross sales of 31.7 million tons (Table 3.2) less repurchases of 15.3 million tons (Table 2.1) or 16.7 million tons or 6.6 percent of the 1978 grain harvest (output and deliveries all measured in trade grain). Ceteris paribus, a 20 percent increase in the price of grain (roughly the change in quota grain prices in 1979 – Appendix 3) would raise the cash value of the cereal harvest by 1.32 percent.

9. This can be inferred from data in Ministry of Agriculture Policy Research Office (1980, 43–4). Purchases of producer goods as a share of rural purchases of consumer goods and producer goods rose from 13.8 to 34.7 percent between 1957 and 1977. The denominator may include sales of consumer goods to the nonagricultural rural population, which may bias these shares somewhat, but the general trend is quite clear.

10. Production costs of 150 yuan per ton of urea output probably understate the real cost of capital. In state industrial enterprises production costs include only a modest depreciation charge, typically 5 percent, an understatement of the opportunity cost of capital even in an economy with very little price inflation. The approximate capital cost per ton of annual nutrient output in China's thirteen modern large-scale urea complexes is 650–730 yuan (Wong 1981, 17–18). That is inclusive of the costs of imported machinery and equipment, engineering charges, and an additional 80 to 100 percent for site construction and infrastructure costs. The 200 yuan per ton of urea or 434 (= 200 ÷ .046) yuan per ton of nitrogen of financial profits at the enterprise level, almost all of which undoubtedly accrue to the central government through the Ministry of Chemical Industry, suggest a rate of return on fixed capital of 60 to 70 percent (assuming the plants operate at designed capacity), in addition to depreciation charges already included in costs and the financial profits accruing to the provincial level and the commercial system. Using a shadow price for foreign exchange that was a multiple of the official exchange rate would reduce the calculated rate of return.

11. The analysis below is based on nitrogen in the form of urea. Ammonium sulfate, another source of nitrogen, in the late 1970s was considerably more expensive per unit of nutrient weight. Moreover, the domestic price of ammonium sulfate did not decline between the mid-1950s and 1980 and the price per unit of nutrient of ammonium sulfate in international markets is somewhat below that of urea. Thus the analysis in the text understates the overpricing of nitrogen. See the discussion in Lardy (1982b) for more details.

12. The marginal price of rice in 1976–78 was 1.3 times the quota price, or .255 yuan per kilogram. For the fixed urea price of .978 yuan per kilogram of nitrogen, the nitrogen/paddy rice price ratio was 3.8.

13. Between 1975 and 1979, when the complexes for which contracts were signed with foreign suppliers in 1972–74 were coming into production, nitrogen production (of all types, measured in terms of nutrient weight) rose 5.112 million tons (State Statistical Bureau 1981c, VI-15). The designed capacity of the thirteen imported plants totals 7.8 million tons of urea or 3.5 million tons of nitrogen. In 1979 all thirteen plants had been completed and ten were believed operating at capacity. See *China: International Trade Quarterly Review, Fourth Quarter 1979* (Washington, D.C.: National Foreign Assessment Center, 1980), p. 7. Thus 55 to 70 percent of the increase in nitrogen production over this period appears to be accounted for by the imported ammonia–urea complexes.

14. See note 6, Chapter 1.

15. Steven Butler reports substantial reductions in the use of chemical fertilizers by teams in Huolu County in Hopei Province where he carried out field research in the first half of 1980. These reductions were said to reflect efforts of producing units to raise their net income, not the result of shortages of supply.

16. Expansion of production capacity could have been based on either domestically produced or imported equipment. China has had the capacity to produce complete sets of equipment for large nitrogenous (urea) fertilizer plants since the 1960s (Wong 1981, 19).

17. This analysis focuses on nitrogenous fertilizers, ignoring evidence that relative

to nitrogen, phosphorous and potassium were in shorter supply. The pricing of these other nutrients, when supplied by chemical sources, is not analyzed here since production is very limited in quantity. From the perspective of intersectoral resource transfers nitrogenous fertilizers are far more important.

18. Adjustment for quality differences presumably would make the comparison even less favorable to the Chinese model.

19. Chang Ch'un-yin (1979, 71) reports that the ratio of the average to the quota price in 1976 was between 1.13 and 1.14. Since the premium over-quota payment was 30 percent, the share of purchases at the over-quota premium price must have been more than 43 but less than 47 percent.

20. Chang Li-fen (1980, 32) states that in 1978 and before, the over-quota share was one-quarter of sales to the state. Since it was about 45 percent in 1976, I presume that this figure refers to 1977 and 1978.

21. The marginal price had also dropped, although by a proportionately smaller amount. In 1981 the marginal price was 1.5 times the quota price or .3532 yuan per kilogram (for a weighted average of indica and japonica varieties). For the fixed urea price of .978 yuan per kilogram, the nitrogen/rice marginal price ratio was 2.8, a decline of about one-quarter compared to the ratio prevailing in 1976.

22. For data on trends in international rice prices I have relied on the World Bank publication *Commodity Trade and Price Trends* (Baltimore: Johns Hopkins University Press, 1981), p. 40. This source shows the world price of rice doubled between 1977 and 1981. The price of urea roughly doubled over the same period.

23. In the long run the stability of the system and the persistence of a weighted price above a single free market price also requires that the (absolute) elasticity of demand of the rich exceed the elasticity of supply of producers.

24. Assuming a milling rate of 70 percent.

25. The prices of rice in urban farmers' markets were substantially higher than those prevailing in rural markets. It isn't clear, however, whether the differential was due to quality variation, government restrictions on the marketing of grain by peasants in cities, or transport costs that are higher than for rural periodic markets. These urban market price data are analyzed in Nicholas R. Lardy (1982b).

26. Li Te-pin (1980a, 50) suggests that the price of cotton has fallen even more than in my analysis. He suggests that by 1977 the relative price of cotton in China was one-half the world price. Because my knowledge of quality variations and other sources of price variations is limited, I have in the text only compared trends in the cotton/wheat price ratios in China and in the world market. For world market prices I have relied on the World Bank Annual, *Commodity Trade and Price Trends* (Baltimore: Johns Hopkins University Press, 1981). A more detailed examination of the levels and trends in cotton prices in China and the world market would be useful.

27. A significant portion of the rise in raw cotton imports in the last half of the 1970s was to provide raw materials for textiles produced for the export market. Since the cotton was purchased and the cotton textiles sold in world markets, profitability on these transactions is unrelated to intersectoral resource flows.

28. Hsiao's data appear to be based on the 1978 procurement price for sugarcane and the 1978 retail price of refined sugar. Raw material costs of 314 yuan per ton are consistent with the 1978 procurement price of .0346 yuan per kilogram (Appendix 3) and extraction rate of about 11 percent (calculated from data on national sugarcane production in Table 4.4 and refined sugar produced from cane in the following note). The retail price of 1.54 yuan per kilogram is consistent with the range of prices of from 1.4 to 1.6 yuan observed by Western travelers in China in the first half of the 1970s. See Tong-eng Wang, *Economic Policies and Price Stability in China* (Berkeley, Calif.: Institute of East Asian Studies, 1980), p. 35. The price adjustments undertaken in 1979, including a 22.5 percent increase in the procurement price of sugar-cane and a substantial upward revision in the retail price, probably did not reduce the profitability of sugar processing and retail sale. This differentiates sugar from cotton textiles, for which retail prices have not been adjusted upward despite the three increases in the price of raw cotton in 1978–81.

29. Total refined sugar production in the 1979–80 refining season was 2.5 million tons, of which .37 million tons was derived from sugar beets and 2.13 million tons was derived from cane, according to Huang Hsiao-shan, the deputy head of the Food Processing Bureau of the Ministry of Light Industry (NCNA November 5, 1981). The estimate of profitability may be too high if "other costs" include inadequate provision for capital costs, although for sugar refining that may be a far less significant problem than the case of nitrogenous chemical fertilizer production discussed earlier in this chapter (note 10). The estimate is too low if the difference between the ex-factory and retail prices includes an additional profit or tax component. The original source does not identify the appropriate label for this 290-yuan-per-ton magnitude.

30. The rate of accumulation is simply investment in fixed assets and increased working capital expressed as a share of national income measured in the material product concept. Since some so-called non–material-producing branches of the service sector are excluded from this national income concept and because depreciation is understated, the rate of accumulation is a slightly upward-biased estimate of the more familiar concept of gross domestic investment as a share of gross domestic product.

31. The values of agricultural, subsidiary agricultural, and processed agricultural products (including textiles) exported from China were 65.4, 69.1, 74.3, 60.7, and 60.1 percent of total export value in 1962, 1965, 1970, 1975, and 1977, respectively (Ministry of Agriculture Policy Research Office 1980, 45).

32. The balanced growth criterion may be expressed

$$\frac{I_i}{\Delta_i} = \frac{I_a}{\Delta_a},$$

where I_i and I_a denote, respectively, investment in industry and agriculture and Δ_i and Δ_a denote the incremental output of industry and agriculture. Rearranging terms, this is equivalent to

$$\frac{I_i}{I_a} = \frac{\Delta_i}{\Delta_a}$$

The left side is equal to the ratio of the shares of investment in industry and agriculture. If i and a denote, respectively, the initial levels of output of industry and agriculture, the right side can be rewritten

$$\frac{\Delta_i / i}{\Delta_a / a} \cdot \frac{i}{a}$$

which is the ratio of the growth rates of industry and agriculture times the ratio of their initial shares of output. If the initial product shares are equal, the balanced growth criterion is simply the equality of the ratio of the investment shares and the ratio of the growth rates of the two sectors. When the shares are initially unequal, the balanced growth criterion is that the ratio of the investment share equal the ratio of the growth rates times the ratio of the product shares.

33. The growth rates cited are for the period 1952 through 1979, rather than 1978, but this does not affect significantly the long-run growth rates in the two sectors. The use of net rather than gross value measures of output growth is desirable because the gross value measure is subject to a number of distortions. See Field, Lardy, and Emerson (1975, 2–5) for a discussion of these problems in industry and Chapter 2 of this study for a discussion of these problems in agriculture. On a gross value measure, the average annual growth rates of the two sectors between 1952 and 1978 were 11.1 and 3.3 percent, respectively (Yang Chien-pai and Li Hsüeh-tseng 1980, 183) and the ratio of the growth rates 3.4:1.

34. The most comprehensive analysis of Chinese concepts of investment is contained in Shigeru Ishikawa's definitive study (1965).

35. For the First Five-Year Plan farmers' self-investment, 17 billion yuan, was four times budgetary investment in agriculture. For 1976–78 collective farm investment, 20.252 billion yuan (State Statistical Bureau 1982b, 195) was only 1.3 times state investment (Table 3.7). It is difficult to interpret the ratios of these two types of investment since, as discussed later in this chapter, state agricultural investment flows almost exclusively into large-scale water works, state farms, and other noncollective activities, whereas collective farm investment occurs within collective agriculture.

36. An analysis of the increased retention of depreciation funds after 1966 by state industrial enterprises has been undertaken by Barry Naughton, a graduate student in economics at Yale University.

37. This figure is exclusive both of financial expenditures on these water conservation projects undertaken by brigades and communes with nonbudgetary funds (so-called self-raised funds) and the value of labor contributed by peasants to these projects.

38. The Ministry of Aquatic Products was not created until 1956. The ministries of Forestry and Agriculture merged in 1970 and absorbed the Ministry of State Farms and Land Reclamation a year later. In 1979 these were split into three separate ministries. In 1979 the Ministry of Water Conservation and Electric Power was split into separate ministries, but in 1982 they were merged again. The evolution of the Ministry of Aquatic Products is less clear, but in 1979 it was listed as a bureau directly subordinate to the State Council. In 1982 it was reorganized, along with the Ministry of Agriculture and Ministry of State Farms and Land Reclamation, to form a new Ministry of Agriculture, Animal Husbandry, and Fishery. See *People's Handbook, 1979* (Peking: People's Daily Publishing House, 1980) and Chao Tzu-yang's report on the restructuring of the State Council delivered at the Twenty-Second Session of the Standing Committee of the Fifth National People's Congress (NCNA March 8, 1982).

39. Chinese statements show that the capital output ratio roughly doubled between 1952 and 1979. Conceptually one might want to discount for that portion of the rise that reflects the growing relative importance of more capital-intensive products, such as metallurgy and machinery, on the grounds that their rising shares reflect planners' choices regarding the rate of investment. Empirically this is quite difficult since it requires time series data on capital stock by branch of industry.

40. Increased investment in agricultural producer goods accounts for only 1.7 percentage points of the 8.4-percentage point increase in the share of heavy industrial investment.

41. The final approval for the purchase of these plants may have been given at a Central Party Work Conference convened in November 1978. It was at this meeting, at which Ch'en Yün made a major speech, that the proagricultural policies that were officially approved by the Party at the Third Plenum the following month and made public shortly after the Plenum was adjourned were pounded out. Three con-

tracts signed were for four ammonia plants, three from Japan and one from West Germany, in December 1978, and a fourth contract with a West German firm in March 1979. Although these projects were postponed as part of the central government's readjustment program, they subsequently were reinstated. The plants involved included a major synthetic ammonia plant at the Chekiang oil refinery in Chekiang Province; an ammonia-urea complex at the Urumchi Petrochemical Works Plant in Sinkiang with an annual capacity of 520,000 tons of urea; and two major plants at the newly established Shansi chemical fertilizer plant, one to produce 300,000 tons of synthetic ammonia annually and the other 900,000 tons of nitrophosphate fertilizer. See *China: International Trade Quarterly Review, Fourth Quarter, 1979* (Washington, D.C.: National Foreign Assessment Center), pp. 25, 26, and 28, and the NCNA communiqué of April 15, 1982, "Construction of Petrochemical Plants Resumed" in FBIS, April 16, 1982, p. K2.

42. The *Chinese Statistical Yearbook 1981* (State Statistical Bureau 1982b) has a complete time series for internal investment in collective agriculture for the years 1958 through 1981. Data for 1957 and 1974 through 1979 were also published in *Chinese 1980 Agricultural Yearbook* (Agricultural Yearbook Compilation Commission 1981, 382–3), and data for a few years were also included in *China's Basic Agricultural Situation* (Ministry of Agriculture Policy Research Office 1980, 103). Data in the latter two sources vary slightly from those reported in the *Statistical Yearbook*. I have relied in my analysis on the *Statistical Yearbook* data because they are the most complete and most authoritative. Also, careful comparison among the three sources and with other reports for specific years (Chao Jung 1980, 39; Chan Wu and Liu Wen-p'u 1982, 59; Reporter 1980a, 11; Tai Mao-an and Li Yu-hua 1980, 39; Wang Keng-chin 1979a, 37; 1979b, 20) clearly establishes that the internal investment data in the *Statistical Yearbook* are inclusive of additions to working capital. The inclusion of working capital is desired both because conceptually it is properly a part of internal investment and because the data for the 1950s are inclusive of working capital. Interestingly, the data also show that working capital shrank by several hundred million yuan annually in 1974–77 but grew by 1.2 and 2.3 billion yuan in 1978 and 1979, respectively.

43. For 1953–57 cumulative value added in agriculture was 181.259 billion yuan (Ishikawa 1965, 56). Farmers' self-investment was 17 billion yuan or 9.4 percent of value added. Farmers' investment was 4.757 billion yuan or 6.0 percent of value added in agriculture in 1970; 6.918 billion yuan or 7.0 percent of value added in 1975; 7.484 billion yuan or 7.0 percent of value added in 1978. Calculated from value added data in Yang Chien-pai and Li Hsüeh-tseng 1981. 103; *Chinese Statistical Yearbook 1981* (State Statistical Bureau 1982b, 20).

44. For example, in 1980 and 1981 the production of garden tractors averaged 208,500 units, down 35 percent from the average output of 320,000 units in 1977–79 (State Statistical Bureau 1982b, 227).

45. I follow the approach of Shigeru Ishikawa below in that the measure of bank-credit-financed investment is taken to be the increase in the volume of loans outstanding that are allocated for investment. Of course, this understates the relative role of bank credit since I should also include the return on investments in excess of the interest payments for the loans. But this procedure does not understate total investment because the return on investment in excess of interest payments flows into "net distributable (collective) income" (*tun shou-ju fen-p'ei*), which in turn is allocated to (a) taxes, (b) internal accumulation and reserves (i.e., collective farm investment), (c) public welfare funds, (d) other collective retentions, and (e) income distributed to commune members (Ministry of Agriculture Policy Research Office 1980, 102–4). Thus to the extent the rate of return on investments in excess of interest payments is

allocated to investment, it is included in internal accumulation. I use the word *potential* because it is possible that the increase in loans outstanding was used to finance consumption rather than investment.

46. During the First Plan, about 22 percent of loans was used to finance fixed investment, 13 percent was used to finance current production (i.e., working capital), and 24 percent was used to finance consumption (Ishikawa 1965, 170). There is some indication that the share used to finance consumption in the 1970s was somewhat less than in the 1950s. For example, in the first quarter of 1979 bank loans were allocated 45 percent for working capital (for purchases of seeds, chemical fertilizer, and diesel fuel), 37 percent for fixed investment (17 percent for financing purchases of agricultural machinery and 20 percent for investment in commune and brigade collective industry) (NCNA May 8, 1979). Although in 1981 over 40 percent of agricultural loans were made to individuals, that reflects the devolution of production management to the household level under the new responsibility system – not an increase in loans used to finance consumption. In the analysis in the text I assume that 80 percent of the increase in loans is allocated to investment, both fixed and working capital, for the years since 1957.

47. Estimated as about 80 percent of 180 million yuan per year.

48. The increase in loans outstanding was 2.28 billion yuan, of which about three-quarters was for nonconsumption purposes.

49. In addition to the People's Bank, including the Agricultural Bank of China, there is a system of rural credit cooperatives that accept deposits from and lend money to individual farmers and rural collective units. Data on credit provided through this system during the 1960s and most of the 1970s are extremely scarce. Since credit cooperatives appear to accept deposits from and extend loans to individuals and units entirely within the collective sector, I have not examined their role in the intersectoral flow of funds. For the late 1970s, however, the loan/deposit ratio in the agricultural credit cooperative system was very much lower than in the People's Bank, and credit cooperatives deposited substantial funds within the People's Bank. It is possible that the agricultural credit cooperative system is thus a mechanism for mobilizing agricultural resources for allocation to other sectors by the state.

50. The increase in total loans outstanding cited here exceeds that shown in Table 3.10 since it is inclusive of loans extended by credit cooperatives.

51. Yang and Li (1980) report that the figure for 1978 excludes fixed assets of collective agriculture in Kwangtung, Kansu, Tsinghai, and Tibet. Of these omissions only Kwangtung would be significant. Other sources, including the Ministry of Agriculture Policy Research Office (1980; 1982) and the Agricultural Yearbook Compilation Commission (1981), report the 84.9-billion figure without qualification as to geographic coverage.

52. Since agricultural fixed assets are the sum of the assets owned by basic agricultural accounting units, the exception to this would be the machinery and other assets of brigade and commune rural enterprises within brigades and communes that were also basic accounting units. In 1979 only 54 communes (of a total of 53,348) and 51,767 brigades (of a total of 698,613) were basic accounting units (Agricultural Yearbook Compilation Commission 1981, 6), so the inclusion of the assets of commune and brigade small-scale enterprises within the scope of agricultural fixed assets would be limited. This is another example where compilation of statistics reflects bureaucratic structure rather than function.

53. Industrial sector fixed assets are valued at original cost (State Statistical Bureau 1981c, VI-8). It is unlikely that scarce rural accounting manpower is devoted to maintaining accounts on the depreciated value of agricultural fixed assets. One uncertainty is the procedures used for writing off worn-out, obsolete, or uneconomic farm machinery. Another is whether assets include animal herds and, if so, how they are valued.

54. These figures are calculated on the basis of fixed assets in collective agriculture in 1977 and 1978, the size of the collective agricultural labor force, and the number of production teams. Fixed assets data are given in the text. The collective labor force is the agricultural labor force (Table 1.2) less an estimated 4.814 and 4.812 million state farm workers in 1977 and 1978, respectively. There were 4.805 and 4.816 million production teams in 1977 and 1978, respectively (Agricultural Yearbook Compilation Commission 1981, 5).

55. Chinese sources describe 15.5 billion yuan variously as the fixed assets of collective agriculture (Ministry of Agriculture Policy Research Office 1980, 58) and as the fixed assets of collective agriculture and the state farm system combined (Agricultural Yearbook Compilation Commission 1981, 339). The state farm system in 1957 was so small in absolute terms, with only 1.054 million hectares of cultivated land and 440,600 workers (Agricultural Yearbook Compilation Commission 1981, 5), respectively .9 and .2 percent of the totals for the country's agriculture as a whole (Tables 1.2, 1.3), that their inclusion or exclusion from the 1957 asset figures makes little difference to the analysis here. See note 1 of this chapter for a further discussion of the size of the state farm sector.

56. Ko Chih-ta (1980, 13) states that some of this 12 billion yuan was allocated to rural collective enterprises. These investments would not be reflected in the asset concept measured here except insofar as a few collective enterprises are under the management of basic accounting units (note 52). But most are not since they are run by brigades and communes that are not basic accounting units. Moreover, Christine Wong argues that state funds flow only to state-owned rural enterprises – that is, primarily those at the county and prefectural levels (1981, 24).

57. Eighty percent of the 7.06 billion yuan increase in loans outstanding over the period.

58. A significant share of collective farm investment may have been allocated to maintain existing assets rather purchasing new assets since even relatively advanced units retained depreciation funds less than 2 percent of the value of their fixed assets. I have not discussed structures, which typically have a longer life span than machinery and equipment, since I presume they constitute a very small share of farming assets.

4. Living standards and the distribution of income

1. Family budget surveys of the 1950s reported consumption only of major food items such as cereals and edible oils. Data on consumption of subsidiary foods and on total caloric intake were not reported.

2. The 1960 production level first was disclosed in *People's Daily* (Chang Ch'ing-wu 1979) and subsequently was confirmed in the *Chinese 1980 Agricultural Yearbook* (Agricultural Yearbook Compilation Commission 1981, 34). The most frequently cited earlier Western estimates of 1960 grain output are 160 million (metric) tons (Erisman 1975, 328) and 156 million tons (Field and Kilpatrick 1978, 372).

3. Data on foodstocks are very scarce. Moreover, not all of the data that have been reported represent the true year-to-year carryover. The Chinese in the 1950s and into the 1960s apparently used stocks on hand at the end of June (the end of the grain year) as a measure of the carryover since at that time the harvest of overwintering wheat in central and north China is well underway but state procurement of these crops has not yet begun. Thus the end-of-June stocks probably are a good measure of carryover of grain within the state system. Data on stocks held at the household and team level, including seed stocks that are not part of state inventories, are not available. Ch'en Yün in a report to a Central Work Conference in May 1961 (not available in the West until twenty years later) said state stocks at mid-year 1957 were 18.2 million tons, but were reduced substantially in 1959 and 1960 because of uncontrolled growth of the urban population during the Great Leap Forward. Ch'en reported that by the end of June, stocks would be 7.4 million tons, of which the carryover would be only 5.05 million tons (Ch'en Yün 1961a, 122–3). By the 1970s the end of the grain year and the date for measuring year-to-year carryover were shifted to the end of March. The number of draft animals declined 17 percent, from 83.82 to 69.49 million head, between 1957 and 1961. The number of pigs declined by 70.38 million or 48 percent in the same period (Agricultural Yearbook Compilation Commission 1981, 37–38).

4. For a survey of these data see Coale (1981).

5. Based on the incremental mortality rate of 14.6 per thousand times the 1960 population of about 660 million (Table 4.2).

6. Survey data show annual per capita vegetable consumption of commune members in 1978 and 1979 as 137 and 131 kilograms, respectively (State Statistical Bureau 1981c, VI-25). In 1955 annual per capita rural consumption was 88.6 kilograms (Data Office Statistical Work 1957a). Without more knowledge of the sampling process used in the 1978–79 survey it is unwise to presume that consumption rose.

7. The discussion above may understate the differences in consumption between the agricultural and nonagricultural population since the data on rural (*hsiang-ts'un*) may include the consumption of nonagricultural rural residents. Since they have incomes and access to rationed cereals (and probably oils) similar to state employees in urban areas, their consumption is probably greater than that of the agricultural population.

8. At the basic level in the countryside there was a close relationship between the All-China Federation of Supply and Marketing Cooperatives, the Ministry of Commerce, and the Ministry of Food. Although they each nominally had distinct functions, they each sometimes relied on the other to act on their behalf where they did not have their own local offices (Oksenberg 1982, 194). All three organizations were merged in the spring of 1982 to form a new Ministry of Commerce as part of a major restructuring and consolidation of the State Council (NCNA March 8, 1982).

9. As discussed in the footnotes to Table 1.1, the index of national income in constant prices is a composite of four indexes based on 1952, 1957, 1970, and 1980 constant prices. Prices of 1952 are used to measure growth in 1952–57, prices of 1957 to measure growth in 1957–70, prices of 1970 to measure growth in 1971–80, and 1980 prices to measure growth since 1980. Chinese prices, particularly those of 1952 and 1957, undervalue the slow-growing agricultural sector and overvalue the faster-growing industrial sector. Thus the growth of national income reflected in the index is more rapid than would be the case if prices of a later year were to be used to measure long-term growth. This is a familiar index number problem, but one that is more acute for China both because of the unusually large disparity in the sectoral growth rates and because of the substantial overpricing of industrial relative to agricultural products. Calculations by World Bank economists show that measuring growth since 1957 at the constant agricultural prices of 1980, which are about 35 percent higher than those of 1970, would reduce the annual growth of national income from 5.44 to 5.01 percent. An even lower rate, 4.60 percent, results from measuring Chinese growth in Indian prices, which no one has ever suggested favor agriculture (International Bank for Reconstruction and Development 1981, A:46). Even reducing

the growth rate by almost a percentage point, however, per capita national income increased by 70 percent between 1957 and 1978, still leaving a huge gap between the rate of growth of output and consumption.

10. At least one long-run constant price comparison for collectively distributed income at the provincial level has been released. In Honan Province collectively distributed income rose from 58.1 yuan in 1955 to 59.7 yuan in 1978 (Chao Hsiu 1981, 13).

11. Cash distribution to commune members was as follows: 1957–14.2 yuan; 1965 – 14.5 yuan; 1974 – 13.6 yuan; 1975 – 12.4 yuan; 1976 – 12.0 yuan; 1977 – 12.8 yuan; and 1978 – 13.6 yuan (Ministry of Agriculture Policy Research Office 1980, 105). In a subsequent report the Ministry of Agriculture Policy Research Office (1982, 202) provided identical data for the years through 1977 but reported cash income of 18.97 and 23.23 yuan for 1978 and 1979, respectively. The reason for the upward revision for 1978 was not explained, but there is an apparent discontinuity between the two series.

12. Interestingly, the same procedure cannot be applied to the data for years after 1978. The Chinese in 1979 began to value collectively distributed grains and other commodities at a set of internal accounting prices rather than the new, higher 1979 state purchase prices. In most localities the internal accounting price for products distributed in kind is the 1978 purchase price (Lu Hsüeh-i 1981, 80). The procedure apparently was followed so that collectively distributed income would reflect more accurately changes in real income, despite increases in purchase prices implemented in 1979. The number of localities that followed this procedure dropped in 1981, however, leading to a spurious rise in reported data on collectively distributed income (Chu Jung 1982, 2).

13. The increase in the direct consumption of grain by urban residents between 1957 and 1978 is somewhat puzzling for two reasons. First, since cereal rations are determined on the basis of age and occupation, it is not clear whether changes in the age and occupational composition of the workforce can explain the 10.5 percent growth of per capita consumption. Second, in most developing countries high-income urban residents consume fewer calories in the form of foodgrains than do rural residents, but more calories in the form of other vegetable foods and foods of animal origin. Indeed, this appears to have been the pattern in China in 1957 when rural direct grain consumption was higher than urban. The positive income elasticity of demand for directly consumed grain by urbanites between 1957 and 1978 probably reflects shortages in supplies of nongrain foods. After 1978, when a more diversified agricultural output mix was encouraged and the reopening and expansion of farmers' markets in cities increased the supplies of nongrain foods, urban residents were able to diversify their consumption somewhat. From the peak level of 1978, direct grain consumption declined by 8.4 percent by 1980 (Wu Shuo 1982, 52).

14. These subsidies are in addition to state budgetary expenditures for social, cultural, and welfare programs.

15. Food subsidies for the urban population are discussed in detail in Chapter 5.

16. Costs are calculated as the sum of management and maintenance outlays and amortization. Since amortization is calculated on the basis of a 50-year life (Peking Municipal Planning Commission 1981, 27), the cost measure probably understates the true economic cost of providing urban housing.

17. Grain distributed in kind is valued at quota procurement prices. Between 1966 and 1977 these prices were .2686 yuan per kilogram of wheat and .1962 yuan per kilogram of rice (a weighted average of japonica and indica varieties). The value of the annual minimum diet of wheat is thus 40.3 yuan, of rice 39.2 yuan.

18. The life expectancy data, reported in Jung Shou-te et al., (1981, tables 3 and

4), were derived from a large survey on cancer deaths undertaken by the Cancer Research Institute of the Chinese Academy of Medical Sciences.

19. Per capita distributed collective income for Kweichow was reported in "Our Country Has a Population of One Billion, Eight Hundred Million of Which Are Peasants," *NFJP*, February 16, 1981, p. 4. Life expectancy data reported in Jung Shou-te et al. (1981) did not include Kansu, Hupei, Kwangsi, Kwangtung, and Shantung. It is possible that life expectancy in Kansu, the province with the second lowest per capita distributed collective income in 1979 and the second greatest concentration of chronic rural poverty in 1977–79, was lower than in Kweichow.

20. Per capita distributed collective income in 1979 for these provinces was reported in "Statistics on the Per Capita Distributed Collective Income of Commune Members in a Portion of the Provinces and Municipalities," *PYT*, no. 8 (1980): 13.

21. If the distribution of income within these counties was normal and the average annual income was 50 yuan, half of the agricultural population of the chronically poor counties would be above the poverty line. Since the average level of annual income in each county was less than 50 yuan, the great majority of the agricultural population in these counties must have been poor.

22. Even poor teams would be able to meet the subsistence needs of their poorest members if they had adequate collectively held reserves that could be distributed in poor harvest years. There are very few data available to evaluate the magnitude of these reserves. My hypothesis is that in counties where average annual per capita collectively distributed income was routinely under 50 yuan, teams would be unable to accumulate significant reserves.

23. Calculated on the basis of the average weighted price of wheat, corn, rice, millet, sorghum, and soybeans in 1976–77 (Appendix 3).

24. By 1979–80, when interprovincial grain flows began to increase (see Table 2.2), transfers of cereal into Kweichow were 500,000 tons annually (Chu Jung 1981, 10; P'an Chih-fu 1980, 76).

25. The very limited extent of poverty in rural Kwangtung (3.9 percent of the province's agricultural population compared to 11.2 nationally) suggests that analyses based on interviews with refugees predominantly from areas proximate to Hong Kong may lead to an unduly optimistic assessment of both the rural income distribution and the extent of absolute deprivation in rural China. Parish and Whyte (1978, 76) reported that cash income per commune member in the teams they studied based on refugees averaged 2–3 yuan per month in the first half of the 1970s, two to three times the national average (note 11, this chapter). This suggests that peasants in Kwangtung Province were engaged in household sideline and private plot production to a greater extent than on average and that private rural marketing activities were less constrained than they appear to have been elsewhere. That may be a legacy of the historically high degree of commercial development of Kwangtung Province.

26. Shantung has a total of nine prefectures.

27. Per capita distributed collective income in Shantung was 51.9 and 34.5 yuan in 1956 and 1957, respectively (Ministry of Agriculture Commune Management Bureau 1981b, 13). That is equal to the national average for these two years (Table 4.6).

28. In 1953 wheat yields in Liaotung and northwest Shantung were .825 and .525 ton per hectare, respectively, 22 percent greater and 23 percent lower than the provincial average (Sun Ching-chih 1957, 131, 135). By 1976, after a decade of the policy of self-sufficiency, that relative productivity differential appeared to have widened. Wheat yields in Yent'ai were 2.80 tons per hectare (NCNA December 14, 1976, in SWB/FE/W915/A/11), and in Hotse, one of the four northwestern prefectures, only 1.35 tons per hectare (NCNA April 16, 1979, in FBIS April 19, 1979, p. O2).

29. Cotton purchase prices were raised 10 percent in 1978, 15 percent in 1979 (with an extra 5 percent supplement for north China producers, including Shantung), and 10 percent in 1980 (with an additional 5 percent supplement for north China (Ch'en Yao-pang 1981, 29). Thus in north China the cotton procurement price rose 50 percent from 1977 to 1980 and 32 percent between 1978 and 1980. I use 1978 as a base year, since that is the base year for the income figures. It should be noted that even after the three price increases of 1978–80 the price of cotton relative to wheat in north China was still less than in 1957.

30. Without a price deflator for goods purchased, it is impossible to disaggregate the increase in collective members' annual income from 46 to 87 yuan into real and price components. In principle the large increase in the price of grain purchased from the state should have been taken into account since these data, like those in Table 4.6, presumably are measured in a mixed set of prices with grain distributed in kind valued in old 1978 procurement prices. Since the prices of goods other than grain have not changed significantly, as a first approximation real income almost doubled.

31. The national standards for irrigated area were revised sometime after 1960, resulting in a downward revision in the area "effectively irrigated" to 18.5 and 24.4 percent, respectively, in 1952 and 1957 (Agricultural Yearbook Compilation Commission 1981, 345). The older data are repesented in the text since the criteria used in their compilation are comparable with the provincial data cited.

32. Rural poverty in Honan should be analyzed to see whether it is closer to the Shantung or Anhui cases. In 1977–79, twenty of Honan's twenty-six poor counties were in the Huaipei region, in prefectures adjoining Fouyang in Anhui. By 1980 only eight counties, four of which were in Huaipei, remained below the poverty line. Thus almost all of the large number of counties where per capita income rose above the poverty level were in the Huaipei area, facing natural conditions as unfavorable to agriculture as the counties in Fouyang Prefecture in Anhui. Unfortunately, there has been little press coverage of the Honan experience, so it is difficult to judge whether the improvement in per capita income is due to changes in cropping patterns, improved production incentives, tax reductions, or improved weather.

33. The population of Kuyüan County was about 270,000 in 1958 and 490,000 in 1978 (Chinese Academy of Sciences Economic Geography Research Office 1980, 366; Sun Lin-fu, Chen Kuo-liang, and Chou P'ei-hua 1980, 33). The Ministry of Finance Investigation Group report divides cumulative state expenditures over twenty-one years by the 1979 year-end population and states that per capita expenditures were 192 yuan, an understatement. My estimate is based on an average of the 1958 and 1979 populations. I do not have comparable population data for T'ungwei and so have assumed that the path of population growth was the same as in Kuyüan and inflated the reported per capita expenditures of 145 yuan by 28 percent (245 ÷ 192).

34. As discussed in Chapter 3, the agricultural fixed assets of China's communes in 1978 were 84.9 billion yuan. In the same year the commune population was 803.2 million (Agricultural Yearbook Compilation Commission 1981, 5). Per capita fixed assets thus were 106 yuan.

35. The urban share of the province's population was 7.4 percent in midyear 1953 and 7.9 percent in midyear 1958. In 1958 only four of China's twenty-four provinces were less urbanized (Lardy 1978a, 112).

36. Autonomous administrative units have been created in areas with significant minority (i.e., non-Han) populations. An autonomous *chou* administratively is equivalent to a prefecture.

37. The gross marketing rate (taxes plus procurement as a share of output) in 1978 in Yunnan was 15.6 percent (Li Ch'iao-nien 1980, 10). Another source (Yüan

Te-cheng 1981, 40) states that the marketing rate declined from 17.8 percent in 1957 to 9.6 percent in 1978. These rates refer to the net rate of marketing (taxes plus procurement less resales to peasants as a share of output) and cannot be used to infer anything about the extent to which state marketing policy facilitated or inhibited specialized production of noncereal crops.

38. The yuan value of the tax reductions has also been reported as 539.9 and 746 million yuan in 1979 and 1980, respectively (Ministry of Agriculture Commune Management Bureau 1981c, 26).

5. Prospects for reform

1. Adverse weather also contributed to reduced output in these years. Its relative importance is impossible to quantify. According to a Red Guard source, Teng Hsiao-p'ing attributed the failure of the Great Leap Forward 30 percent to weather and 70 percent to human error (Lieberthal 1976, 171). Data on sown area suffering from calamities and natural disasters show peaks in 1960 and 1961. For 1959, however, the area with severe weather-induced crop losses was less than in either 1956 or 1957 (State Statistical Bureau 1982b, 201).

2. An alternative hypothesis to explain the relatively rapid growth of agriculture through 1957 is that collectivization allowed significant economies of scale. An interesting analysis by Dennis Chinn (1980) seems to refute this view, at least for north China. In a model that simulated the formation of a collective from two villages in Anhui, he found that collectivization led to economies of scale only if there was no labor market. Under that condition, a binding labor constraint was eased through the formation of a collective in which labor could be allocated over the entire quantity of available arable land. Since rural labor markets were well developed prior to 1949, his simulation suggests that there were no economies of scale to be gained through collectivization.

3. Appendix 3 shows that the average price for grain rose 17 percent between 1965 and 1977. Chi Lung and Lu Nan (1980) state that "after 1966 the purchase price of grain was not raised for twelve years" (p. 46). Since Chi Lung has been identified as a staff member of the State Commodity Price Bureau, I presume that the article can be taken as authoritative. This implies that the price increase between 1966 and 1970 was all in 1966. It also implies that the 1 percent increase in the average grain procurement price between 1970 and 1977 was due to a slight change in the composition of grains purchased by the state rather than to a change in the price of any individual grain crop.

4. Since retail prices of grain and oils sold by the state to members of collectives rose in line with procurement prices, losses on agricultural resales are small. Most of the resales are of unprocessed grain procured within the same general vicinity, so processing and transportation costs are low and covered partially by the 8 percent markup over the procurement price that has usually prevailed. However, some peasants are eligible to buy grain at a unified selling price that is less than the procurement price, and the state also absorbs losses that arise because a significant share of purchases are at higher above-quota and negotiated prices while the highest rural resale price is tied to the quota price. In 1980 total losses on rural resale of cereals were 3 billion yuan (Ministry of Food Research Office 1981, 48).

5. The reverse-flow problem did not occur for all commodities. Peasants did not have ration cards to buy grain or oils in state shops, and the price of black market grain remained well above the procurement price, so there were no profitable transactions. Sugar was processed by the state while procurement was only of cane and beet sugar, so the problem did not arise there.

6. Nonstaple food allowances are also paid to some, but probably not all, workers in collective urban enterprises. Employees in state farms also are considered state employees and draw the same 5-yuan-per-month allowance.

7. The exclusion of losses on the resale of imported cereals is specifically stated in *People's Daily* (1981b) and Ministry of Food Research Office (1981, 4). The separate accounting for losses on imports probably reflects Chinese bureaucratic practices. The Ministry of Food and commercial departments absorb the losses on domestically procured products, whereas the losses on imported cereals presumably are absorbed by the state foreign trade apparatus. I am not including losses on the resale of imported cereals other than wheat, such as corn and soybeans, since the disposition of these commodities within China as between the agricultural and nonagricultural populations is not clear. By contrast, indirect evidence (note 17, this chapter) suggests that all wheat imports enter the predominantly urban rationing system. In the years 1979–81 wheat comprised 48 percent (in gross weight) of total cereal imports.

8. Kwangtung Economics Society (1981, 45) provides the average domestic resource cost of earning a U.S. dollar of foreign exchange for the country as a whole and for exports from Canton and a number of other major cities.

9. Estimates of losses on imported cereals are subject to error. Conceptually the major problem is to determine an appropriate exchange rate. I have used both the average official exchange rate prevailing in 1981 – 1.7 yuan per U.S. dollar – and the more realistic average domestic resource cost of earning a dollar – 2.3 yuan. It would be preferable to use a rate that reflects the marginal rather than the average domestic resource costs of earning a unit of foreign exchange. In early 1981 the exchange rate for decentralized enterprises that were allowed to make import and export decisions independent of the central state trade apparatus was pegged at 2.8 yuan to the dollar. That rate may reflect the Ministry of Foreign Trade's views of the opportunity cost of a unit of foreign exchange. If it were used in the calculations, losses on imported cereals would be 3.8 billion yuan in 1981 and 3.4 and 1.6 billion yuan in 1979 and 1980, respectively. These larger estimates of losses are not reflected in Table 5.1. Neither the Chinese nor the large multinational grain traders have disclosed wheat contract prices. I have used the unit price f.o.b. of wheat imported from the United States to make the estimates reflected in Table 5.1. Since most Chinese wheat imports are of a soft wheat comparable to that purchased from the United States, I presume that the average f.o.b. price of all Chinese wheat imports in each of the years 1979, 1980, and 1981 was equal to the United States unit price. Port charges and domestic transport costs are the values used by the World Bank in evaluating potential projects in China.

10. Conceptually one could argue that the 5-yuan supplement should be regarded as an across-the-board salary increase for all state employees and thus not include it in the discussion of food subsidies. However, since the supplement was tied explicitly to the increase in the prices of nonstaple foods in November 1979 (Chinese Communist Party Central Committee and State Council 1979), I regard the supplementary wage payments as an integral part of the food subsidy program.

11. The population eligible for rationed commodities includes those classified as urban and the nonagricultural labor force residing in nonurban areas. In 1980 they totaled about 160 million, 16.3 percent of the population (Li Ssu-heng 1981, 56; Special Commentator 1981).

12. The cost-of-living index is described as including both commodities purchased at fixed prices through the state retail network and purchases on nonstate markets,

where prices are higher. The commodity composition of this index, like that for sales of manufactured goods to collective agriculture (discussed in Chapter 3), is unknown. It is possible that the index is weighted primarily with fixed price commodities sold through the state commercial system and thus understates the cost-of-living increase faced by workers and employees.

13. The quota price of grain was raised 20 percent in 1979 and the premium for over-quota deliveries set at 50 percent. Thus the over-quota price in 1979 and subsequent years was 1.8 (= 1.2 × 1.5) times the quota price prevailing in 1978. Prior to 1979 the over-quota price was 1.3 times the quota price. Thus the over-quota price rose 38.5 percent (= 1.8 ÷ 1.3).

14. In addition to the 18 million individuals who converted their registration status from agricultural to nonagricultural, the natural rate of increase would have added about 1.7 million per year to the nonagricultural population in the late 1970s.

15. *Cheng-chih ching-chi hsüeh chi fu-shui yüan-li* (Peking: Commercial Press 1976).

16. The system of finance and economics institutes (*ts'ai-ching hsüeh-yüan*) dates from 1952 when it was adopted from Soviet practice. Initially comprehensive institutions of finance and economics were established in Wuhan, Shenyang, Shanghai, and Ch'engtu, but subsequently appear to have been established elsewhere as well. The curriculum of these institutions focuses on economic planning, statistics, public sector budgeting, etc. rather than the usual Marxian political economy. Graduates of these programs usually are employed in the state economic bureaucracy at the national, provincial, and local level rather than in universities or other educational institutions.

17. Wang states that "40 percent of the supply of cereals to municipalities (*ch'eng-shih*) comes from imported sources." Imports could not account for 40 percent of the food supply for the entire urban (*ch'eng-chen*) population, so clearly the municipal population is some portion of the urban population. The population of established municipalities (*she-shih ti ch'eng-shih jen-k'ou*) was 43 million and 78.954 million in 1953 and 1978, respectively. See Yen Chung-min and Ning Yüeh-min, "A Preliminary Study of the Development and Changes in the Special Characteristics of China's Urban Population," in *A Collection of Essays on Population Research*, Hu Huang-yung et al. (Shanghai: East China Teacher's College Press, 1981), pp. 20–38. If Wang's use of the word *municipal* follows that definition, his statement implies that about 30 million urban residents are dependent on imported cereals. That is consistent with the reported volume of imports and the total supply of grain available to supply a nonagricultural population of about 148 million in 1978.

18. The most important drawback of the measure is that it omits freight hauled by traditional means such as carts and wheelbarrows. An unknown portion of the rapid growth of modern means of transport during the 1950s reflects the replacement of traditional forms of transportation rather than growth of total transport turnover.

19. The national inventory of heavy trucks has not been published, but production in 1975 alone was 77,600 units (State Statistical Bureau 1981c, VI-15). It is not clear whether the term *agricultural use* implies that these numbers include trucks of the state procurement agencies and processing factories or are limited to producing units.

20. Fukien, Hainan, and Shansi were the only cases publicized in *People's Daily* and other periodicals and newspapers reaching the West. Moreover, they were the only cases discussed in the *Annual Economic Report of China (1981)* (Chang Szu-ch'ien 1981, IV-16).

21. Limits to the quantities of grain resold at the quota price to producers exist not only in the aggregate but also at the individual level. In Shantung grain resales to cotton producers are guaranteed only up to the point where per capita grain sup-

plies, including grain raised collectively and on private plots, reaches 300 kilograms. The state generally prefers to resell at higher negotiated prices where possible.

22. In 1981 total grain marketings were 68.46 million tons (Table 2.1, column 2). About 10 million tons were taxes (Table 3.2) and 5 million tons were private market sales (assuming conservatively that such transactions were the same as in 1980), implying that state purchases of quota, over-quota, and negotiated price grain were about 53.5 million tons. Sixty percent of state purchases in 1981 were at over-quota or negotiated prices (Wu Chen-k'un 1982). Sixty percent of 53.5 is 11.7 percent of national grain output (measured in terms of trade weight).

23. *Hsiang* is sometimes translated as "administrative village." "Township" is the term now used in English-language materials published in China.

24. This of course is analogous to the criticism that traditional share tenancy arrangements are inefficient. Because the marginal return to the tenant from the last unit of input is less than the marginal product of the input by the rate of land rent (output sharing), inputs are applied by tenants at a less than socially optimum rate. Steven Cheung (1969) and others have pointed out that with perfect information and no transactions costs, landlords will be able to stipulate the tenancy contract such that labor will be applied up to the optimum point.

25. The only published response to Sun's proposal I have seen was written by Yao Chin-kuan (1978). He didn't even refer to Sun by name but referred to a proposal by "some people" to "increase the purchase price of agricultural products to make them equal to their exchange value," while simultaneously increasing direct agricultural taxes "so that the state's budgetary resources would be unchanged" (p. 35). Yao criticized Sun's proposal on the ground that it would tend to increase income disparities in the countryside. But Sun's proposal was not tied to any particular tax structure. Moreover, as discussed earlier in this chapter, the dual price system used after 1970 appears to be regressive. Thus Yao's criticism of Sun's proposal seems misplaced.

References

The following abbreviations are used in the References:

AHSTHP	*An-hui shih-ta hsüeh-pao*
BR	*Beijing Review*
CCHK	*Che-chiang hsüeh-k'an*
CCHTT	*Ching-chi hsüeh tung-t'ai*
CCKH	*Ching-chi k'o-hsüeh*
CCKL	*Ching-chi kuan-li*
CCWT	*Ching-chi wen-t'i*
CCWTTS	*Ching-chi wen-t'i t'an-so*
CCYC	*Ching-chi yen-chiu*
CHCC	*Chi-hua ching-chi*
CHLT	*Chiang-han lun-t'an*
CHYTC	*Chi-hua yü t'ung-chi*
CKCCWT	*Chung-kuo ching-chi wen-t'i*
CKCJ	*Chung-kuo chin-jung*
CKLLYSC	*Chia-ko li-lün yü shih-chien*
CKSHKH	*Chung-kuo she-hui k'o-hsüeh*
CKTMP	*Chung-kuo ts'ai-mao pao*
CKYC	*Chung-kung yen-chiu*
CM	*Cheng-ming*
FBIS	Foreign Broadcast Information Service
FCJP	*Fu-chien jih-pao*
FCNYKC	*Fu-chien nung-yeh k'o-chi*
FTHP	*Fu-tan hsüeh-pao*
HC	*Hung-ch'i*
HH	*Hsüeh-hsi*
HHPYK	*Hsin-hua pan-yüeh k'an*
HHYP	*Hsin-hua yüeh-pao*
HPJP	*Ho-pei jih-pao*
HSYK	*Hsüeh-shu yüeh-k'an*
JKYC	*Jen-k'ou yen-chiu*
JKYCC	*Jen-k'ou yü ching-chi*
JMJP	*Jen-min jih-pao*
JMST	*Jen-min shou-tse*
JPRS	United States Department of Commerce, Joint Publications Research Service
KJJP	*Kung-jen jih-pao*
KMCCCHYKL	*Kuo-min ching-chi chi-hua yü kuan-li*
KMJP	*Kuang-ming jih-pao*
KSTW	*Kung-she ts'ai-wu*
KWYKP	*Kuo-wu yüan kung-pao*

KYSYHP	*Kuei-yang shih-yuan hsüeh-pao*
LS	*Liang-shih*
NCNA	New China News Agency
NCNHYHP	*Nan-ching nung hsüeh-yuan hsüeh-pao*
NFJP	*Nan-fang jih-pao*
NKTHHP	*Nan-k'ai ta-hsüeh hsüeh-pao*
NTKTTH	*Nung-ts'un kung-tso t'ung-hsün*
NYCC	*Nung-yeh ching-chi*
NYCCTK	*Nung-yeh ching-chi ts'ung-k'an*
NYCCWT	*Nung-yeh ching-chi wen-t'i*
PCTHHP	*Pei-ching ta-hsüeh hsüeh-pao*
PKCS	*Pai-k'o chih-shih*
PYT	*Pan-yüeh t'an*
SC	*Shih-ch'ang*
SCJP	*Szu-chuan jih-pao*
SHTCHYP	*Shan-hsi ts'ai-ching hsüeh-yuan pao*
SWB/FE/W	British Broadcasting Company, Summary of World Broadcasts, Far East Weekly Economic Report
TC	*T'ung-chi*
TCKT	*T'ung-chi kung-tso*
TCKTTH	*T'ung-chi kung-tso t'ung-hsün*
TCYC	*Ts'ai-ching yen-chiu*
TMCC	*Ts'ai-mao ching-chi*
TS	*Tu-shu*
TSYC	*Tang-shih yen-chiu*

The following Chinese newspapers and periodicals are cited in the References:

An-hui shih-ta hsüeh-pao (Journal of the Anhui Provincial Teacher's College)
Beijing Review
Che-chiang hsüeh-k'an (Chekiang Studies)
Cheng-ming (Contention)
Chi-hua ching-chi (Planned Economy)
Chi-hua yü t'üng chi (Planning and Statistics)
Chia-ko li-lün yü shih-chien (Price Theory and Practice)
Chiang-han lun-tan (Chiang and Han Forum)
China Daily
China Reconstructs
Ching-chi hsüeh tung-t'ai (Currents in Economic Studies)
Ching-chi k'o hsüeh (Economic Science)
Ching-chi kuan-li (Economic Management)
Ching-chi wen-t'i (Economic Problems)
Ching-chi wen-t'i t'an-so (An Exploration of Economic Problems)
Ching-chi yen-chiu (Economic Research)
Chung-kung yen-chiu (Research on Chinese Communism)
Chung-kuo chin-jung (Chinese Banking)
Chung-kuo ching-chi wen-t'i (China's Economic Problems)
Chung-kuo she-hui k'o-hsüeh (Chinese Social Sciences)
Chung-kuo ts'ai-mao pao (China's Finance and Trade Report)
Fu-chien jih-pao (Fukien Daily)
Fu-chien nung-yeh k'o-chi (Fukien Agricultural Science)

Fu-tan hsüeh-pao (Fudan University Bulletin)
Ho-pei jih-pao (Hopei Daily)
Hsin-hua pan-yüeh k'an (New China semi-monthly)
Hsin-hua yüeh-pao (New China Monthly)
Hsin kuan-ch'a (New View)
Hsüeh-hsi (Study)
Hsüeh-shu yüeh-k'an (Academic Monthly)
Hung-chi (Red Flag)
Jen-k'ou yen-chiu (Population Research)
Jen-k'ou yü ching-chi (Population and Economics)
Jen-min jih-pao (People's Daily)
Jen-min shou-tse (People's Handbook)
Kuang-ming jih-pao (Brilliant Daily)
Kuei-yang shih-yuan hsüeh-pao (Kueiyang Teacher's College Bulletin)
Kung-jen jih-pao (Worker's Daily)
Kung-she ts'ai-wu (Commune Finance)
Kung-yeh ching-chi kuan-li ts'ung-k'an (A Collection on Industrial Economic Management)
Kuo-min ching-chi chi-hua yü kuan-li (National Economic Planning and Management)
Kuo-wu-yüan kung-pao (State Council Gazette)
Liang-shih (Grain)
Nan-ching nung hsüeh-yuan hsüeh-pao (Bulletin of Nanking Agricultural College)
Nan-fang jih-pao (Southern Daily)
Nan-k'ai ta-hsüeh hsüeh-pao (Bulletin of Nankai University)
Nung-ts'un kung-tso t'ung-hsün (Agricultural Work Bulletin)
Nung-yeh ching-chi (Agricultural Economics)
Nung-yeh ching-chi ts'ung-k'an (A Collection on Agricultural Economics)
Nung-yeh ching-chi wen-t'i (Problems of Agricultural Economics)
Pai-k'o chih-shih (Encyclopedic Knowledge)
Pan yüeh t'an (Semi-monthly Forum)
Pei-ching ta-hsüeh hsüh-pao (Peking University Bulletin)
Shan-hsi ts'ai-ching hsüeh-yüan pao (Shansi Finance and Economics Institute Bulletin)
Shih-ch'ang (Marketing)
Social Sciences in China
Szu-ch'uan jih-pao (Szechuan Daily)
Tang-shih yen-chiu (Party History Research)
Ti-li chih-shih (Geographical Knowledge)
Ts'ai-cheng (Finance)
Ts'ai-ching yen-chiu (Finance and Economics Research)
Ts'ai-mao ching-chi (Economics of Finance and Trade)
Tu-shu (Reading)
T'ung-chi (Statistics)
T'ung-chi kung-tso (Statistical Work)
T'ung-chi kung-tso t'ung-hsün (Statistical Work Bulletin)

Agricultural Yearbook Compilation Commission. 1981. *Chinese 1980 Agricultural Yearbook*. Peking: Agricultural Publishing House.
　　1982. *Chinese 1981 Agricultural Yearbook*. Peking: Agricultural Publishing House.
Aird, John S. 1980. "Reconstruction of an Official Data Model of the Population of China." Unpublished manuscript. U.S. Bureau of the Census.

1982. "Recent Demographic Data from China: Problems and Prospects." In *China under the Four Modernizations*, selected papers submitted to the U.S. Congress Joint Economic Committee, pp. 171–223. Washington, D.C.: U.S. Government Printing Office.

Andors, Stephen. 1980. "Industry and Industrialization in Shulu County." Unpublished manuscript.

Boserup, Ester. 1965. *The Conditions of Agricultural Growth: The Economics of Agrarian Change under Population Pressure.* Chicago: Aldine.

Brown, Shannon R. 1981. "Cakes and Oil: Technology Transfer and Chinese Soybean Processing, 1860–1895." *Comparative Studies in Society and History,* 23(3):449–63.

Buck, John Lossing. 1930. *China's Farm Economy.* Chicago: University of Chicago Press.

1937. *Land Utilization in China.* Nanking: University of Nanking.

Butler, Steven B. 1981. "Price Scissors and Commune Administration in Post-Mao China." Unpublished manuscript.

Central Intelligence Agency. 1969. *Agricultural Acreage in Communist China, 1949–1968: A Statistical Compilation.* Washington, D.C.

Chan Wu. 1980. "A Correct Decision on the Development of Agriculture." *NYCCWT,* 8:2–8.

Chan Wu and Liu Wen-p'u. 1982. *Chinese Agriculture.* Peking People's Publishing House.

Chang Ch'iao-ling. 1981. "Readjust the Distribution of Agriculture Based on Comparative Advantage." In Hu Ch'iao-mu (1981, 274).

Chang Chih-yi. 1982 "A Discussion of Issues on Housing Rent." *CKLLYSC* 2:41–2.

Chang Ching-fu. 1979. "Report on the State's 1978 Final Account and the 1979 Draft State Budget." *HHYP,* 6:30–7.

Chang Ch'ing-wu. 1979. "Controlling Urban Population Growth." *JMJP,* August 21, p. 2.

Chang Ch'un-yin. 1979. "Problems in Reducing the Price Differential in the Exchange of Industrial and Agricultural Products." *HSYK* 5:68–72.

Chang Huai-tzu et al. *A General Survey of Population Theory.* Chengchou, Honan: People's Publishing House.

Chang Kuang-yu and Ch'iu Yung-sheng. 1980. "Why Are There So Many Rotten Vegetables in Beijing's Market?" *JMJP,* October 15, pp. 1, 4. In FBIS, October 16, p. R1.

Chang Kuo-fan. 1980. "Relative Prices and the Scissors Differential between Industrial and Agricultural Commodities." *CHLT,* 2:14–17.

Chang Li-fen. 1980. "The Limitations of the Law of Value in the Development of China's Grain Production." *SHTCHYP,* 4:6–10. Reprinted in *NYCC* 1981, 10:29–33.

Chang Liu-cheng. 1981. "A Short Explanation of Peasant Income and Consumption in China." *NYCCTK,* 4:43–7.

Chang Min-ju and Hsü Shu-keng. 1981. *Basic Knowledge of Agricultural Statistics.* Shihchiachuang, Hopei: People's Publishing House.

Chang Szu-ch'ien. 1981. "China's Agriculture in 1980." In Hsüeh Mu-ch'iao (1981, IV-11–IV-18).

Chang Tse-yü. 1982. "Urban Housing Rental." *BR* 41:27–8.

Chao Hsiu. 1981. "An Investigation of the Implementation of the Responsibility System in Honan." *NYCCWT,* 8:7–13.

Chao Jung. 1980. "How to Improve the Management of Team and Brigade Funds." *NYCCWT,* 4:39–40.

Chao Kang. 1970. *Agricultural Production in Communist China, 1949–1965.* Madison: University of Wisconsin Press.

1977. *The Development of Cotton Textile Production in China.* Cambridge: Harvard University, East Asian Research Center.

Chao Kuo-chün. 1960. *Agrarian Policy of the Chinese Communist Party, 1921–1959.* Bombay: Asia Publishing House.

Ch'en Chang-ts'en. 1980. "First the Food Problem of the Masses Must Be Solved." *KMJP*, April 27, p. 3.

Ch'en Ch'i-chen. 1982. "National Grain Procurement Exceeds the Plan Target." *CKTMP*, January 21, p. 1.

Ch'en Fu-kuei. 1982. "The Transformation of Poor Counties and Poor Production Teams in 1981." *KSTW* 7:22–3.

Chen Nai-ruenn. 1967. *Chinese Economic Statistics: A Handbook for Mainland China.* Chicago: Aldine.

Ch'en Pi-chiang. 1979. "We Must Consider the Peasants More." *JMJP*, September 8, p. 2.

Ch'en Po-yüan and Wang Min. 1978. "The Role of the Law of Value in Cotton Production." *KMJP*, December 9, p. 3.

Ch'en Yao-pang. 1981. "Develop the Comparative Advantage of Cotton Production in the Three Provinces of Hopei, Shantung, and Honan. *NYCCWT*, 6:27–31.

Ch'en Yün. 1955. "Problems Concerning the Unified Purchase and Unified Sale of Grain." *HHYP*, 8:50–4.

1956a. "Speech by Comrade Chen Yun." In *Eighth National Congress of the Communist Party of China,* vol. 2, *Speeches,* pp. 157–76. Peking: Foreign Languages Press.

1956b. "Manage Commercial Work Well." In Ch'en Yün (1981, 27–33).

1956c. "Ways of Dealing with Short Supply of Pork and Vegetables." In Ch'en Yün (1981, 14–19).

1959. "A Letter to Comrades in the Central Finance and Economics Small Group." In Ch'en Yün (1981, 93–6).

1961a. "Important Work on One Item Related to the Overall Situation." In Ch'en Yün (1981, 120–9).

1961b. "An Investigation of Rural Ch'ingp'u County." In Ch'en Yün (1981, 130–46).

1961c. "Accelerate the Development of the Nitrogenous Fertilizer Industry." In Ch'en Yün (1981, 108–15).

1961d. "Manage Foreign Trade Work Well." In Ch'en Yün (1981, 116–19).

1962. "The Present Economic and Financial Situation and Various Methods for Overcoming Difficulties." In Ch'en Yün (1981, 157–72).

1981. *Selected Manuscripts of Comrade Ch'en Yün, 1956–1962.* Peking: People's Publishing House.

Ch'eng Chao-jung. 1981. "A Superficial Discussion of China's National Situation and National Strength." *TC*, 1:18–20.

Cheng Chien-ho. 1982. "A Discussion of Price Subsidy Issues." *HHYP* 8:56–7.

Ch'eng Chih-p'ing. 1982. "Market Prices and the Standard of Living of Workers and Staff." *CKLLYSC* 4:1–7.

Cheng Chung-chieh. 1981. "An Investigation of the Prices of Medium and Small Farm Implements in Wuchiang County, Kiangsu." *CKLLYSC*, 4:41–4.

Cheng Po-ch'üan. 1980. "Several Opinions on Strengthening Grassland Construction." *NYCCWT*, 3:34–6, 4.

Cheng Shou-lung. 1980. "Bring Comparative Advantage into Full Play to Develop Cotton and Peanut Production." *NTKTTH*, 8:23–4.

Ch'eng Ying-hua. 1981. "China's Road Transportation." In Hsüeh Mu-ch'iao (1981, IV-109–IV-110).

Cheng Ying-ling. 1981. "Kwangtung's Decision to Raise Procurement Prices of Various Categories of Beans." *NFJP*, August 1, p. 1.

Cheung, Steven. 1969. *The Theory of Share Tenancy.* Chicago: University of Chicago Press.

Chi Chin-t'ien. 1981. "Summary of a Research Class on Developing Local Comparative Advantage." *NYCCWT*, 8:61–3.

Chi Lung and Lu Nan. 1980. "A Discussion of the Scissors Price Differential between Agricultural and Industrial Products." *HC*, 6:45–8.

Chi Pu. 1979. "North Kiangsu Surpasses Areas South of the Yangtse River, Double Crop Rice Surpasses Triple Crop Rice." *KMJP*, February 7, p. 1.

Chia Hsiu-yen. 1979. "Price Problems in China's Economic Readjustment and Reform." *NKTHHP*, 4:15–19.

Chiang Hsing-wei. 1980. "A Discussion of the Problem of the Scissors Price Differential between Industrial and Agricultural Products." *CCYC*, 4:73–6, 23.

Ch'in Nien. 1979. "Breeding Milk Goats Is an Important Way to Develop Resources for Dairy Products." NCNA, August 6. In FBIS, August 7, p. L12.

Chin Chi-ming. 1959. "The Flying Development of Agriculture in Kiangsu Province." *TLCS*, 6:244–7.

Chin Yen-shih. 1981. "A Survey of Economic Development in Kweichow Province." In Hsüeh Mu-ch'iao (1981, IV-296–IV-299).

Chinese Academy of Sciences Economic Geography Research Office. 1980. *A Treatise on China's Agricultural Geography.* Peking: Science Publishing House.

Chinese Agricultural Bank Rural Finance Research Office. 1981. "Chinese Rural Banking." In Hsüeh Mu-ch'iao (1981, IV-161–IV-162).

Chinese Banking Commentator. 1981. "Do a Good Job in Supervising Agricultural Appropriations, Support the High Speed Development of Agriculture." *CKCJ*, 1:13–15.

Chinese Communist Party Central Committee. 1962a. "Regulations on the Work of the Rural People's Communes." In *Documents of the Chinese Communist Party Central Committee*, vol. 1, pp. 695–725. Hong Kong: Union Research Institute, 1971.

1962b. "Resolution on Further Strengthening the Collective Economy of the People's Communes and Expanding Agricultural Production." In *Documents of the Chinese Communist Party Central Committee*, vol. 1, pp. 193–205. Hong Kong: Union Research Institute, 1971.

1970. "Approval and Distribution of a State Council Report on a Conference Concerning Chinese Cotton Production." In *Selected Legal Documents on the Policy of Unified Procurement and Unified Sale of Grain, Cotton, and Oil Seeds, 1951–April 1979*, p. 164. Peking: Chinese People's University Trade and Economics Department Materials Office, 1979.

1978. "Decisions on Some Problems in Accelerating Agricultural Development (draft)." *CKYC*, 13(5):149–62.

1979. "Decisions on Some Problems in Accelerating Agricultural Development, Adopted September 28." *HHYP*, 10: 140–50. In FBIS, supplement no. 32, October 25, pp. 1–18.

Chinese Communist Party Central Committee and State Council. 1956. "Directive Concerning Strengthening Production Leadership and Organization of Construction in Agricultural Producers' Cooperatives." *JMJP*, September 13, pp. 1, 3.

1959. "Directive on Organizing Rural Market Trade." In *JMST*, 1960, 380–1.

1979. "Decision to Raise the Retail Price of Major Subsidiary Food Products on November First and to Simultaneously Award Supplements to State Workers and Staff." *JMJP*, November 1, in *HHYP* 11:78–9.

Chinese Press Service. December 4, 1981. "Chao Tzu-yang Meets with the Szechuan Deputies." In FBIS, December 7, p. K7.

Ching Lin and Lei Yang-lu. 1981. "How to Reduce the Gap between Industrial and Agricultural Incomes in China." *NYCCTK*, 2:32–7.

Chinn, Dennis L. 1980. "Cooperative Farming in North China." *Quarterly Journal of Economics*, 94(2):279–97.

Ch'iu Yüan. 1980. " 'Planned Pig Raising' Should Be Postponed." NCNA Domestic Service, June 27. In FBIS, July 2, 1980, pp. L11–L12.

Chou Hui. 1980. "Chou Hui Addresses Inner Mongolia Standing Committee Meeting." Regional Service, August 10. In FBIS, August 14, pp. R3–R5.

Chou Po-ping. 1957. "The Policy of Unified Purchase and Unified Sale of Grain Shall Not Be Frustrated." *LS*, 7:1–4.

Chou Yung-shen and Wu Han-piao. 1980. "Develop Areas with a Comparative Advantage in Peanut Production, Raise the Production of Oil Sources." *NFJP*, June 30, p. 1.

Chu Ching-chih. 1958. *China's Grain Policy and the Work to Supply Grain to Cities and Towns*. Peking: Finance and Economics Publishing House.

Chu Jung. 1981. "Important Experiences and Lessons from the Last Thirty Years of Agricultural Development." *NYCCTK*, 4:5–12, 23.

1982. "Speech at the Third National Agricultural Cost Calculation Training Class." *KSTW* 8:2–9.

Chuan Han-sheng and Kraus, Richard A. 1975. *Mid-Ch'ing Rice Markets: An Essay in Price History*. Cambridge: Harvard University, East Asian Research Center.

Chung I. 1981. "What Does the Large Increase in Cotton Output in Shantung Mean?" *CCKL*, 7:14–16.

Chung Yüan-ho. 1980. "With No Way to Sell Their Surplus Grain Peasants Are Anxious." *NFJP*, October 25, p. 1.

Coale, Ansley J. 1981. "Population Trends, Population Policy, and Population Studies in China." *Population and Development Review*, 7(1):85–97.

Committee on the Economy of China. 1969. *Provincial Agricultural Statistics for Communist China*. Ithaca, N.Y.

Crook, Frederick W. 1975. "The Commune System in the People's Republic of China, 1963–1974." In *China: A Reassessment of the Economy*, a compendium of papers submitted to the U.S. Congress Joint Economic Committee, pp. 366–410. Washington, D.C.: U.S. Government Printing Office.

1982. "Report on an Agricultural Observation Trip to China, July 1982, Part I: Notes from Interviews with National and Provincial Officials." Unpublished manuscript. U.S. Department of Agriculture.

Data Office Statistical Work. 1957a. "Problems Concerning the Living Standards of Workers and Peasants." *TCKT*, 13:4–5, 24.

1957b. "The Basic Situation of Unified Purchase and Sale of Foodgrains in China." *TCKT*, 19:31–2, 28.

1957c. "The Changing Situation of the Scissors Price Differential between Industrial and Agricultural Products in China since Liberation." *TCKT*, 17:4–7.

Dernberger, Robert F. 1975. "The Role of the Foreigner in China's Economic Development." In *China's Modern Economy in Historical Perspective*, edited by Dwight Perkins, pp. 19–47. Stanford, Calif.: Stanford University Press.

Donnithorne, Audrey. 1967. *China's Economic System.* New York: Praeger.

1970. *China's Grain Output, Procurement, Transfers, and Trade.* Hong Kong: Economic Research Center, Chinese University of Hong Kong.

Eckstein, Alexander. 1977. *China's Economic Revolution.* Cambridge: Cambridge University Press.

Eckstein, Alexander, Kang, Chao, and Chang, John. 1974. "The Economic Development of Manchuria: The Rise of a Frontier Economy." *Journal of Economic History,* 34(1):239–64.

Editorial. 1956. "Improve Internal Grain Transport." 1956. *LS,* 4:12–13.

1979. "Leadership at All Levels Must Strictly Grasp Policies." 1979. *JMJP,* September 23, p. 1. In FBIS, September 25, pp. L8–L9.

1980a. "Conscientiously Solve the Urban Vegetable Supply Problem." 1980. *JMJP,* April 18, p. 4.

1980b. "Fully Develop the Potential of Party Policies." 1980. *JMJP,* May 14, p. 1. In FBIS, May 16, pp. L6–L8.

1980c. "Actively and Steadily Readjust the Internal Structure of Agriculture." 1980. *JMJP,* May 9, pp. 1, 2.

1980d. "Discover Natural Resources through Surveys and Do a Good Job in Agricultural Zoning." 1980. *JMJP,* August 5, pp. 1, 4. In FBIS, August 20, pp. L12–L15.

1981a. "Run Commune and Brigade Enterprises Well in the Course of Readjustment." 1981. *JMJP,* May 16, p. 1. In FBIS, June 2, pp. K19–K20.

1981b. "Actively Develop Water Transportation." 1981. *JMJP,* June 17, p. 1. In FBIS, July 29, pp. K15–K17.

Elvin, Mark. 1972. "The High-Level Equilibrium Trap: The Causes of the Decline of Invention in the Traditional Chinese Textile Industries." In *Economic Organization in Chinese Society,* edited by William E. Willmott, pp. 137–72. Stanford, Calif.: Stanford University Press.

1973. *The Pattern of the Chinese Past.* Stanford, Calif.: Stanford Univeristy Press.

Emerson, John Philip. 1982a. "The Labor Force of China, 1950–1980." Unpublished manuscript. U.S. Bureau of the Census.

1982b. "Urban School-leavers and Unemployment in China." Unpublished manuscript. U.S. Bureau of the Census.

Erisman, Alva Lewis. 1975. "China: Agriculture in the 1970s." In *China: A Reassessment of the Economy,* a compendium of papers submitted to the U.S. Congress Joint Economic Committee, pp. 324–49. Washington, D.C.: U.S. Government Printing Office.

Fang Ping-chu. 1962. "Problems in the Methodology of Compiling Commodity Prices Indices in a Socialist System." *CCYC,* 6:45–53.

Fang Yüan. 1980. "The Basic Task of China's Agricultural Modernization Is to Raise per Unit Yields." *CCYC,* 3:3–9.

Fei Hsiao-t'ung. 1957. "A Revisit to Kaihsienkung." *Hsin Kuan-ch'a,* nos. 11 & 12. In *Fei Hsiao-t'ung: The Dilemma of a Chinese Intellectual,* selected and translated by James P. McGough, pp. 39–74. White Plains, N.Y.: Myron E. Sharpe, 1979.

1979. "Szechuan: Calamity and Recovery." *China Reconstructs,* 1:59–63.

Fei, John C. H. and Ranis, Gustav. 1964. *Development of the Labor Surplus Economy: Theory and Policy.* Homewood, Ill.: Richard D. Irwin.

Field, Robert Michael, and Kilpatrick, James A. 1978. "Chinese Grain Production: An Interpretation of the Data." *China Quarterly,* 74:369–84.

Field, Robert M., Lardy, Nicholas R., and Emerson, John P. 1975. *A Reconstruction of the Gross Value of Industrial Output by Province in the People's Republic of*

China, 1949–73. Foreign Economic Report no. 7. Washington, D.C.: U.S. Department of Commerce.

Fisher, Franklin M., and Temin, Peter. 1970. "Regional Specialization and the Supply of Wheat in the United States, 1867–1914." *Review of Economics and Statistics,* 2:134–49.

Fu Shih-min. 1980. "Energetically Develop Edible Oil Materials from Trees." *CCWTTS,* 5:70–1.

Fukien Province Department of Agriculture. 1980. "Solve the Contradiction between Grain and Sugar, Develop Sugarcane Production." *NTKTTH,* 8: 24–5.

Fukien Provincial Academy of Agricultural Science, Sugarcane and Hemp Institute. 1980. "A Brief Discussion of the Development of Sugarcane Production in Fukien." *FCNYKC,* 6:37–40. In JPRS 77,878:21–7.

Fukien Provincial Service. December 21, 1978. "Fukien Crops." In SWB/FE/W1024/A/4. January 19, 1979. "Fukien Crops." In SWB/FE/W1024/A/4.
September 24, 1979. "Fukien Crops." In SWB/FE/W1053/A/17.

Fukien Provincial Statistical Bureau. 1981. "Communiqué on the Development of the National Economy in Fukien in 1980." *FCJP,* July 5, p. 2. In FBIS, July 21, O1–O7. 1982. "Communiqué on the Results of Implementing the 1981 Economic Plan in Fukien Province." *FCJP* July 8, p. 2.

Government Administrative Council. 1953a. "Directive Implementing Planned Purchase and Planned Supply of Grain." *HHYP* 1954, 4:158–9.
1953b. "Provisional Measures for the Management of Grain Markets." *HHYP* 1954, 4:159–60.

"Grain Allocation and Transportation Work." 1951. In *JMST.* Peking: Takung Publishers, p. 10.

Han Po. 1958. "Economize on Operating Expenditures in Agriculture." *CHCC,* 2:17–21.

Hayami, Yujiro, and Kikuchi, Masao. 1982. *Asian Village Economy at the Crossroads: An Economic Approach to Institutional Change.* Tokyo: University of Tokyo Press; Baltimore: Johns Hopkins University Press.

Hayami, Yujiro, Subbarao, K., and Otsuka, Keijiro. 1982. "Efficiency and Equity in the Producer Levy of India."*American Journal of Agricultural Economics* 4:655–63.

Heilungkiang Provincial Planning Commission. 1956. "Opinions Concerning Planning Work Following the Establishment of Agricultural Producer Cooperatives." *CHCC,* 6:11–13.

Heilungkiang Provincial Service. December 11, 1978. "Heilungkiang Crops." In SWB/FE/W1016/A/7.
August 14, 1979. "Heilungkiang Crops." In SWB/FE/W1046/A/13.

Ho Ch'eng and Wei Wen. 1962. "On Peasant Periodic Market Trade." *CCYC,* 4:11–15.

Ho Hsi-lan and Ch'en Yang-ts'ung. 1981. "Sugarcane Production Must Be Changed." *FCJP,* August 20, pp. 1, 4.

Ho Ping-ti. 1955. "The Introduction of American Food Plants into China." *American Anthropologist,* 57(2):191–201.
1956. "Early Ripening Rice in Chinese History." *Economic History Review,* 9(2):200–18.
1959. *Studies on the Population of China, 1368–1953.* Cambridge: Harvard University Press.

Ho Tung-chün. 1981. "State Agricultural Commission Carries out Zoning." NCNA, September 8. In FBIS, September 9, pp. K20–K21.

Hobsbawm, E. J., ed. 1980. *Peasants in History: Essays in Honour of Daniel Thorner.* Calcutta: Oxford University Press.

Hoffman, Charles. 1974. *The Chinese Worker*. Albany: State University of New York Press.

Hsiang Ch'i-yüan. 1981. "Chinese Economic Development and the Distribution of Income." In *Problems in Chinese Economic Development*, edited by Hsü Ti-hsin, pp. 47–70. Peking: Social Science Publishing House.

Hsiang Nan. 1980. "Beneath a Rich Harvest There Are Still Problems." *JMJP*, May 25, p. 2.

Hsiao Chuo-chi. 1980. "The Law of Price Movement in China." *Social Sciences in China*, 4:44–59.

Hsiao Hui-chia and Chang Jui-san. 1980. "Link up Sugar and Grain, Develop Comparative Advantage." *JMJP*, August 18, p. 2.

Hsingt'ai Prefecture Communist Party Committee Office. 1980. "An Investigation of the Poor Production Teams in Six Counties in Hsingt'ai Prefecture." *NYCCWT*, 8:32–5.

Hsing Yen and Sun Shih-chieh. 1980. "Report on an Inspection of Rural Ninghsia." *HC*, 22:10–14. In FBIS, December 11, 1980, pp. T2–T7.

Hsiung I. 1979. "Opinions and Suggestions on Cropping Systems in Southern Kiangsu." *JMJP*, March 17, p. 3.

Hsiyang Agricultural College. 1980. *Studies of Socialist Agricultural Economics*. Peking: Chinese People's University Publishing House.

Hsü Chien-p'ing and Shih Wei-liang. 1980. "Fully Develop Fukien's Comparative Advantage, Go All Out to Develop Sugarcane Production." *CKCCWT*, 4:17–22.

Hsü Ti-hsin. 1981. "Problems in China's Current Economic Readjustment." *CCYC*, 6:3–8.

Hsü Tien-shih and Hsi Shou-ying. 1981. "Develop Grain Commodity Bases Rapidly." In Hu Ch'iao-mu (1981, 275–6).

Hsü Tzu-hsin. 1982. "Fukien's Major Sugar Producing Region Strengthens the Concept of State Planning." *CKTMP*, April 8, p. 1.

Hsü Ya. 1981. "Grain Production and Diversified Economy Must Develop Simultaneously." *NTKTTH*, 3:18–19.

Hsü Yi-ming and Ch'en Ming-hsing. 1980. "Fukien Sugar Production Has Great Potential." *JMJP*, August 18, p. 2.

Hsüeh Mu-ch'iao. 1979. "An Arduous Thirty Years of Pioneering Work." *HC*, 10:40–9.

Hsüeh Mu-ch'iao, ed. 1981. *Annual Economic Report of China (1981)*. Overseas Chinese Language Edition. Hong Kong: Hong Kong Modernization Company.
    1982. *Annual Economic Report of China (1982)*. Overseas Chinese Language Edition. Hong Kong: Hong Kong Modernization Company.

Hu Chang-nuan. 1979. "A Discussion of the Problems of the Scissors Price Differential and the Overall Price Level." *CCYC*, 6:62–9.

Hu Ch'iao-mu, ed. 1980. *Chinese 1980 Encyclopedic Yearbook*. Peking and Shanghai: Chinese Encyclopedic Publishers.
    1981. *Chinese 1981 Encyclopedic Yearbook*. Peking and Shanghai: Chinese Encyclopedic Publishers.

Hu Huan-yong. 1947. "A New Cotton Belt in China." *Economic Geography*, vol. 23, no. 1: 60–66.

Hu Yao-pang. 1982. "Create a New Situation in All Fields of Socialist Modernization." *BR* 37:11–40.

Hunan Agricultural College. 1959. *Hunan Agriculture*. Peking: Higher Education Publishing House.

Hunan Provincial Service. January 24, 1981. "Hunan Promotes Increased Grain Production." In *FBIS*, 28 January, p. P9.

Hupei Delegates. 1980. "Opinions of Peasants on Current Policy." *JMJP*, September 11, p. 3.

Hupei Provincial Agricultural Economics Society. 1980. *Selected Essays on Agricultural Modernization from an Academic Discussion Meeting*. Wuhan: Hupei Publishing House.

International Bank for Reconstruction and Development. 1981. *China: Socialist Economic Development*. Nine Volumes; the Main Report and Eight Annexes A through F. Washington, D.C.

Ishikawa, Shigeru. 1965. *National Income and Capital Formation: An Examination of Official Statistics*. Tokyo: Institute of Asian Economic Affairs.

    1967a. *Economic Development in Asian Perspective*. Tokyo: Kinokuniya.

    1967b. "Resource Flow Between Agriculture and Industry: The Chinese Experience." *The Developing Economies*, vol. 5, no. 1:3–49.

    1979. "China's Economic Issues in 1980 and 1981: A Prospect." Unpublished manuscript.

Johnson, D. Gale. 1978. "International Prices and Trade." In *Distortions of Agricultural Incentives*, edited by Theodore W. Schultz, pp. 195–215. Bloomington: Indiana University Press.

    1980. "Agricultural Organization and Management in the Soviet Union: Change and Constancy." Unpublished manuscript. University of Chicago.

    1981. "Food and Agriculture of the Centrally Planned Economies: Implications for the World Food System." In *Essays in Contemporary Economic Problems: Demand, Productivity, and Population*, pp. 171–213. Washington, D.C.: American Enterprise Institute for Public Policy Analysis.

Johnston, Bruce F., and Kilby, Peter. 1975. *Agriculture and Structural Transformation: Economic Strategies in Late-Developing Countries*. New York: Oxford University Press.

Jung Shou-te, Li Chün-yao, Kao Jun-ch'üan, Tai Hsü-tung, Ts'ao Te-hsien, Li Kuang-yi, and Chou Yu-shang. 1981. "A Statistical Analysis of Average Life Expectancy of Inhabitants of China in 1973–75." *JKYCC*, 1:24–31, 17.

Kao Ping-k'un and Wang Huai-yang. 1979. "Thoroughly Understand the Principle of 'Planning Is Primary, Price Is Secondary.'" *CHLT*, 1:51–2.

Kao Yü-hsing. 1959. "In National Economic Activity We Must Make Great Efforts to Organize Transport Rationally." *CCYC*, 7:1–6.

Keng Chien-hua. 1981. "How Can We Calculate Whether the Rate of Increase in Budgetary Revenue Is Appropriate?" *Ts'ai-cheng*, 4:17–19.

Kiangsu Provincial Service. August 18, 1979. "Kiangsu." In SWB/FE/W1048/A/11.

Kirin Provincial Service. August 29, 1980. "Supplies and Marketing." In SWB/FE/W1106/A/6.

    November 18, 1980. "Kirin Issues Circular on Grain, Oil-bearing Crop Procurement." In FBIS, November 19, p. S3.

Ko Chih-ta. 1980. "Raise the Effectiveness of Financial Funds Used to Support Agriculture." *CCYC*, 2:12–18.

Ko Ch'üan-lin. 1981. "Improve the Purchase of Agricultural and Subsidiary Products, Accelerate Economic Adjustment." *CCKL*, 4: 26–28, 31.

Ku Chien-p'eng and Ku Chung-ch'eng. 1980. "Ku-yüan District Must Greatly Develop Large Animals." *JMJP*, February 20, p. 2.

Ku Wei-chin. 1979. "Develop Agriculture on the Principle of Comparative Advantage, Commune Members Collectively Become Rich, Increase Their Income." *JMJP*, February 2, p. 2.

Kuan Ta-t'ung. 1961. "On Peasant Periodic Market Trade." *HC*, 18:16–22.

Kuznets, Simon. 1961. "Economic Growth and the Contribution of Agriculture:

Notes on Measurements." *International Journal of Agrarian Affairs*, 3(2):56–75. Reprinted in *Agriculture in Economic Development*, edited by Carl Eicher and Lawrence Witt, pp. 109–19. New York: McGraw-Hill, 1964.

1971. *Economic Growth of Nations: Total Output and Production Structure*. Cambridge: Harvard University Press.

Kwangtung Economics Society. 1981. *An Economc Investigation of Kwangtung*. Canton: Kwangtung People's Publishing House.

Kwangtung Provincial Service. February 10, 1979. "Kwangtung Rural Tax Notice." In FBIS, March 1, p. H1.

May 14, 1979. "Kwangtung Crops." In SWB/FE/W1033/A/15.

Lardy, Nicholas R. 1978a. *Economic Growth and Distribution in China*. Cambridge: Cambridge University Press.

ed. 1978b. *Chinese Economic Planning: Translations from Chi-hua ching-chi*. White Plains, N.Y.: Myron E. Sharpe.

1982a. "Food Consumption in the People's Republic of China." In *China's Agricultural Economy*, edited by Randolph Barker. Boulder, Colo.: Westview Press.

1982b. "China's Agricultural Pricing Policy." Paper prepared for the International Bank for Reconstruction and Development.

1982c. "Comparative Advantage, Internal Trade, and the Distribution of Income in Chinese Agriculture." Paper prepared for the Trade and Development Workshop, Yale University.

Lardy, Nicholas R., and Lieberthal, Kenneth. 1983. *Chen Yun's Strategy for China's Economic Develoment: A Non-Maoist Alternative*. Armonk, N.Y.: M. E. Sharpe.

Li Ch'eng-jui. 1959. *A Draft History of the Agricultural Tax of the People's Republic of China*. Peking: Finance Publishing House.

Li Ch'eng-jui and Chang Chung-chi. 1982. "How to Perceive Changes in the People's Living Standards in the Last Three Years." *HC*, 8: 25–8.

Li Ch'eng-jui and Tso Yüan. 1979. "Firmly and Resolutely, and in a Down-to-Earth Manner Complete the Responsibility of the National Economic Readjustment." *CCYC*, 12:3–10.

Li Ch'iao-nien. 1980. "Seriously Develop Economic Research Work Based on Reality in Yunnan." *CCWTTS*, 1:7–13.

Li Erh-huang. 1979. "Is It True That Production Can't Be Increased through the Double Rice Triple Cropping System?" *KMJP*, June 20, p. 4.

Li Fu-ch'un. 1956. "Speech by Comrade Li Fu-chun." In *Eighth National Congress of the Communist Party of China*, vol. 2, Speeches, pp. 288–303. Peking: Foreign Languages Press.

Li Hsien-nien. 1956. "Speech by Comrade Li Hsien-nien." In *Eighth National Congress of the Communist Party of China*, vol. 2, Speeches: 206–224. Peking: Foreign Languages Press.

1957. "Report on the State's 1956 Final Account and the 1957 Draft State Budget." *HHPYK*, 14:16–28.

1958. "Report on Conditions of Implementation of the 1957 State Budget and the 1958 Draft State Budget." *HHPYK*, 5:3–12.

1959. "Report on the State's 1958 Final Account and the 1959 Draft State Budget." *HHPYK*, 9:20–3.

1960. *Report on the State's 1959 Final Account and the 1960 Draft State Budget*. Peking: Finance Publishing House.

Li Jui. 1982. "Reading P'eng Teh-huai's 'Account.' " *TS*, 4. In FBIS, April 16, pp. K5–K11.

Li Pin, Lu Yung-ch'ing, and Wang Feng-wen. 1981. "On Our Province's Experience, Lessons, and Ideas of Reforming the Planting System." *HPJP*, February 27, March 1, 2. In JPRS 78, 170:25–36.

Li Ssu-heng. 1981. "Points on China's Grain Situation." *NYCCTK*, 4:55–6, 36.

Li Te-pin. 1979. "The Problem of the Scissors Price Differential in the Exchange between Industrial and Agricultural Products in China since Liberation." *PCTHHP*, 4:2–9, 27.

———. 1980a. "Cotton Price and Cotton Production in China since Liberation." *PCTHHP*, 2:49–54.

———. 1980b. "The Problem of the Scissors Price Differential between Industrial and Agricultural Prices in China before the Anti-Japanese War." *CCKH*, 1:40–47.

Li Wen-chin and Chia Chih-shan. 1981. "Several Circumstances and Problems in the Economic Development of Shansi Province." *CCWT*, 5:37–41.

Liang Chao, Liu Hsiao-t'ieh, and Li P'u-mi. 1981. "An Investigation on Developing Kwangtung's Superiority in Sugarcane Production." *HC*, 2:26–8, 11.

Liang Hsiu-feng. 1981a. "China's Economic Achievements." *BR*, 40:18–23.

———. 1981b. "Correctly Draw the Lessons of Experience of the Three Years of the Great Leap Forward and the Five Years of Readjustment." *NYCCTK*, 4:19–23.

Liang Wen-sen. 1981. "Balanced Development of Industry and Agriculture in the Economy of China." In *Problems in Chinese Economic Development*, edited by Hsü Ti-hsin, pp. 3–25. Peking: Social Science Publishing House.

Liang Yen. 1981. "We Must Take the Grain Problem Very Seriously." *HC*, 5:24–6.

Lieberthal, Kenneth. 1976. *A Research Guide to Central Party and Government Meetings in China, 1949–1975*. White Plains, N.Y.: International Arts and Sciences Press.

Lin Kang. 1981. "China's Agricultural Backwardness Is the Root Cause of Its Rapid Population Growth." *JKYC*, 1:17–22.

Lin Shen. 1979. "The Inside Information on China's Economic Readjustment." *CM*, May, pp. 9–13.

Ling Yen. 1981. "On the Commercialization of Chinese Agriculture." *TCYC*, 3:31–7. In *NYCC*, 1981, 19:21–7.

Liu Chou-fu. 1979. "Readjust Unreasonable Prices in a Planned Way under the Premise of Price Stability." *HC*, 11:36–41.

———. 1982. "How Should We View Our Current Market Price Problems?" *HC*, 1: 33–6.

Liu Fang-yü. 1980. "A Discussion of the Position and Role of Consumption in a Socialist Society." *CCKH*, 1:14–20, 13.

Liu Hsien-kao. 1957. "Agricultural Production Planning Tables." *CHCC*, 4:30–3. Translated in Lardy (1978b, 179–89).

Liu Hsüan-huo, Han Hsien-ling, Hsin Te-hui, and Ku Yü-k'ai. 1982. "A Preliminary Discussion of a Development Strategy for the Huang, Huai, Hai [River] Area[s]." *NYCCWT*, 1:19–24.

Liu Hui, Li Chün, and Ch'i Ming-ch'en. 1981. "Redjusting the Direction of Capital Construction Promotes the Rationalization of China's Economic Structure." In *Research in Issues on China's Economic Structure*, edited by Ma Hung and Sun Shang-ch'ing, pp. 411–36. Peking: People's Publishing House.

Liu Jih-hsin. 1961. "An Inquiry into the Reform of China's Agricultural Planning System." *CCYC*, 7:17–23.

Liu Kuang-jung, Liu Huan-chen, and Cheng Chen-ju. 1979. *Agricultural Product Costs*. Peking: Agriculture Publishing House.

Liu Kuo-kuang and Wang Hsiang-ming. 1980. "A Study of the Speed and Balance of China's Economic Development." *Social Sciences in China*, 4:15–43.

Liu Pao-chin. 1981. "Several Current Problems in the Procurement of Agricultural and Subsidiary Products." *NCNHYHP*, 1:98–103.

Liu Shih-chiang. 1980. "Yunnan Agriculture and the Economics of Hill Regions." *CCWTTS*, 4:31–6.

Liu Sui-nien. 1980. "The Proposal and Implementation of the Eight-Character Policy of Readjustment, Consolidation, Filling-out, and Raising Standards." *TSYC* 6:21–33.

Liu Ta-chung and Yeh Kung-chia. 1965. *The Economy of the Chinese Mainland: National Income and Economic Development, 1933–1959.* Princeton: Princeton University Press.

Liu Wen-wei. 1980. "Problems in the Exploitation and Utilization of the Tropical Resources of Yunnan Province." *CCWTTS*, 6:56–61.

Lu Hsüeh-i. 1981. "The Trend toward Contracting down to the Household and a Problem That Should Be Clearly Understood." *NYCCTK*, 5:8–13. Reprinted in *NYCC*, 21:79–84.

Lu Shih-chien. 1979. "We Must Seek Truth from Facts When Reforming Cropping Systems." *KMJP*, September 11, p. 2.

Ma Yin-ch'u. 1958. "My Economic Theory, Philosophical Thoughts, and Political Standpoint." In *Ma Yin-ch'u's Selected Economic Writings*, vol. 2, pp. 196–274. Peking: Peking University Publishing House, 1981.

MacDougall, Donald. 1951. "British and American Exports: A Study Suggested by the Theory of Comparative Costs." *Economic Journal*, 61:697–724.

Mao Hsin-ts'ui. "Rural Trade Advances Briskly." In Hu Ch'iao-mu (1981, 220–1).

Mao Tse-tung. 1942. "Economic and Financial Problems in the Anti-Japanese War." In *Selected Works of Mao Tsetung*, vol. 3, pp. 111–16. Peking: Foreign Languages Press, 1967.

1943. "On Coalition Government." In *Selected Works of Mao Tsetung*, vol. 3, pp. 205–70. Peking: Foreign Languages Press, 1967.

1955. "On the Cooperative Transformation of Agriculture." In *Selected Works of Mao Tsetung*, vol. 5, pp. 184–207. Peking: Foreign Languages Press, 1977.

1956. "On the Ten Major Relationships." In *Selected Works of Mao Tsetung*, vol. 5, pp. 284–307. Peking: Foreign Languages Press, 1977.

1957. "On the Correct Handling of Contradictions among the People." In *Selected Works of Mao Tsetung*, vol. 5, pp. 384–421. Peking: Foreign Languages Press, 1977.

1960. "Reading Notes on the Soviet Text *Political Economy*." In *Long Live the Thought of Mao Tse-tung*. Taipei, 1969. Reprinted in *A Critique of Soviet Economics*, translated by Moss Roberts. New York: Monthly Review Press, 1977.

1966. "Speech to an Enlarged Politburo Meeting." In *Long Live the Thought of Mao Tse-tung*, pp. 634–640. Taipei, 1969.

Mason, Edward S., Mahn Je Kim, Perkins, Dwight H., Kwang Suk Kim, and Cole, David. 1980. *The Economic and Social Modernization of the Republic of Korea.* Cambridge: Harvard University Press.

Mei Fang-ch'üan. 1982. "How to Increase China's Cotton Production." *JMJP*, January 1, p. 3.

Mei Fang-ch'üan and Hsü P'ei-hsiu. 1979. "We Must Quickly Change China's Backward Cotton Production Situation." *KMJP*, December 15, p. 2.

Ministry of Agriculture Commune Bureau. 1980. "Several Problems in the Retention of Financial Depreciation Funds on Fixed Assets in People's Communes." *NTKTTH*, 1:28.

Ministry of Agriculture Commune Management Bureau. 1981a. "Poor Counties in China, 1977–79." *HHYP*, 2:117–21.

1981b. "Three Large Increases in Three Years in Production and Income." *CCKL*, 8:13–16.

1981c. "In 1980 One-Third of China's Poor Counties Changed Remarkably." *KSTW*, 8:24–7.

Ministry of Agriculture Investigation Group. 1980. "Opinions on Changing the Backward State of Agricultural Production in the Arid Regions of Kansu and Ninghsia." *NTKTTH*, 1:15–16.

Ministry of Agriculture Planning Bureau. 1958. *A Collection of Statistical Data on Agricultural Production in China and Other Major Countries.* Peking: Agricultural Publishing House.

Ministry of Agriculture Policy Research Office. 1980. *China's Basic Agricultural Situation.* Peking: Agricultural Publishing House.

1982. *An Outline of Agricultural Economics in China.* Peking: Agricultural Publishing House.

Ministry of Finance Investigation Group. 1981. "No Longer More of a Hindrance Than a Help, from Now On There Will Be Hope." *NTKTTH*, 1:21–3.

Ministry of Food. 1959. "Directive on Increasing Production and Economizing on Expenditures in the Red Flag Movement." In State Council Bureau of Legal Affairs, *Compendium of Laws and Regulations*, vol. 10, p. 278. Peking: Legal Publishing House.

Ministry of Food Research Office. 1981. *A Discussion of Policy on Procurement and Sales of Cereals and Oils in Rural Areas.* Peking: Finance and Economics Publishing House.

Ministry of Food Rural Procurement and Sales Bureau. 1982. "Purchased Grain May Not Be Used to Fulfill Procurement Tasks." *NTKTTH*, 3:45.

Ministry of Railroads General Office. 1981. "China's Railroad Transportation." In Hsüeh Mu-ch'iao (1981, IV-105–IV-109).

Ministry of Textile Industry Research Office. 1981. "China's Textile Industry." In Hsüeh Mu-ch'iao (1981, IV-46–IV-50).

Montias, John Michael. 1976. *The Structure of Economic Systems.* New Haven: Yale University Press.

1980. "On the Centralization and Decentralization of Economic Activities." Unpublished manuscript. Yale University.

Myers, Ramon H. 1970. *The Chinese Peasant Economy: Agricultural Development in Hopei and Shantung, 1890–1949.* Cambridge: Harvard University Press.

1978. "Wheat in China: Past, Present, and Future." *China Quarterly*, 74:297–333.

1980. *The Chinese Economy Past and Present.* Belmont, Calif.: Wadsworth.

Myint, Hla, 1975. "Agriculture and Economic Development in the Open Economy." In *Agriculture in Development Theory*, edited by Lloyd G. Reynolds, pp. 327–54. New Haven: Yale University Press.

Nan Chen-chung. 1981. "A Report from Northwest Shantung." *JMJP*, January 11, p. 2.

NCNA. July 30, 1954. "Sinkiang Cotton Is Allocated and Transported to Shanghai." *JMJP*, July 31, p. 2.

December 13, 1954. "The Successful Completion of Large-Scale Grain Allocation and Transportation Work." *JMJP*, December 14, p. 1.

December 6, 1973. "Szechuan." In SWB/FE/W755/A/9.

August 4, 1974. "Szechuan." In SWB/FE/W788/A/12.

August 24, 1976. "Kiangsu." In SWB/FE/W893/A/6.

December 28, 1977. "Fukien Crops." In SWB/FE/W963/A/5.

June 25, 1978. "Szechuan." In SWB/FE/W992/A/13.

July 22, 1978. "Commodity Price Bureau Official Explains Price Policy." In FBIS, July 26, p. E10.

September 27, 1978. "Szechuan Rural Economy Recovers." In FBIS, September 28, pp. J1–J3.

October 29, 1978. "Honan Crops." In SWB/FE/W1010/A/7.

December 3, 1978. "Farm Work in Inner Mongolia." In SWB/FE/W1012/A/7.

February 2, 1979. "People's Daily Stresses City Outskirts as Food Producers." In FBIS, February 6, p. E7.

April 13, 1979. "Agricultural Survey, Zoning Conference Held." In FBIS, April 16, pp. L8–L11.

May 8, 1979. "Agricultural Loans." In FBIS, May 16, p. L11.

July 1, 1979. "Effect of Increased Purchase Prices Noted." In FBIS, July 2, p. P4.

August 14, 1979. "Crops." In SWB/FE/W1046/A/12.

September 20, 1979. "State Council Announces November Cotton Conference." In FBIS, September 21, pp. L2–L3.

October 31, 1979. "Commodity Prices, Labor Bureau Officials Talk on Price Rise." In FBIS, November 5, pp. L5–L14.

November 5, 1979. "Commodity Prices and Peasant Income." In SWB/FE/W1059/A/2.

November 8, 1979. "Prices, Supplies of Vegetables Stable in Shanghai." In FBIS, November 9, p. O4.

December 8, 1979. "China Adopts Measures to Contain Cost of Living." In FBIS, December 10, p. L8.

December 27, 1979. "Crops." In SWB/FE/W1064/A/9.

January 13, 1980. "Fukien Crops." In SWB/FE/W1072/A/8.

January 23, 1980. "Finance for Farming." In SWB/FE/W1068/A/2.

February 13, 1980. "Supplies and Marketing." In SWB/FE/W1071/A/4.

March 2, 1980. "Supplies and Marketing." In SWB/FE/W1073/A/3–A/4.

March 10, 1980. "Szechuan Stresses Production." In FBIS, March 13, p. Q1.

April 22, 1980. "Shantung Local Development." In SWB/FE/W1081/A/10.

May 27, 1980. "More Sugarcane in Exchange for Incentive Grain, Greatly Increase Production of Sugarcane." JMJP, May 29, p. 1.

June 3, 1980. "State Council Issues Notice on Summar Grain, Oil Purchases." In FBIS, June 5, pp. L7–L8.

June 22, 1980. "Economic Cooperation across the Country." In SWB/FE/W/1093/A/2.

June 26, 1980. "Provinces Extend Area Sown to Industrial Crops." In FBIS, June 26, pp. L13–L14.

July 10, 1980. "Establish a Large-Scale Base for Comprehensive Testing and Research on Sugarcane." JMJP, July 14, p. 1.

July 31, 1980. "Cross-Country Economic Cooperation." In SWB/FE/W/1104/A/1–A/2.

August 27, 1980. "Shensi Constructs Grain, Cotton, and Oil Base Areas in the Kuanchung Plain and the Hanchung Basin." JMJP, August 29, p. 2.

August 29, 1980. "Last Year State Grain Taxes and Purchases Were Reduced by 5.5 Billion Chin." JMJP, August 30, p. 1.

October 24, 1980. "Central Organs' Circular on Agricultural Statistics." In FBIS, October 27, pp. L4–L5.

November 15, 1980. "Commerce Ministry Issues Circular on Market Supply." In FBIS, November 17, p. L10.

November 17, 1980. "Supplies and Marketing." In SWB/FE/W1111/A/2–A/3.

January 11, 1981. "Higher Peasant Incomes in Shantung." In SWB/FE/W1118/A/5–A/6.

January 15, 1981. "State Council Directive on Market Controls." In FBIS, January 16, pp. L7–L9.

January 21, 1981. "China's National Cotton Procurement Exceeds Fifty Million Dan for the First Time." JMJP, January 22, p. 2.

January 21, 1981. "Fukien Crops." In SWB/FE/W1127/A/10.

April 3, 1981. "Supplies and Marketing." In SWBFE/W1129/A/2.

April 20, 1981. "State Purchase Plans for Grain, Cotton Fulfilled." In FBIS, April 22, pp. K20–K21.

April 21, 1981. "Grain Prices on Rural Markets Have Dropped." *JMJP*, April 22, p. 1.

May 26, 1981. "China's Edible Vegetable Oil Reserves Reach an All-Time High Level." *JMJP*, May 27, p. 1.

July 3, 1981. "National Bank Statistics for 1980." *JMJP*, July 4, p. 2.

August 5, 1981. "Circular Issued on Agricultural and Sideline Goods." In FBIS, August 6, pp. K22–K24.

August 21, 1981. "Kwangtung Province Overfulfills Its Responsibility for Exports of Refined Sugar." *JMJP*, August 22, p. 1.

November 5, 1981. "State to Increase Output of Sugar in Current Season." In FBIS, November 6, pp. K13–K14.

March 8, 1982. "National People's Congress Standing Committee Decisions on Restructuring the State Council and Other Questions." In *BR*, March 15, pp. 5–6.

March 30, 1982. "People's Living Standards Rise in Three Years." In FBIS, March 31, p. K4.

June 7, 1982. "The State Council Approves and Distributes a Report of the Ministry of Commerce Requiring That Leadership Be Strengthened Everywhere." *JMJP*, June 8, p. 4.

NCNA Commentator. 1982. "Summary of a Rural Work Meeting." *JMJP* April 7, pp. 1, 4.

Ni, Ernest. 1960. *Distribution of the Urban and Rural Population of Mainland China, 1953 and 1958.* International Population Reports, series P-95, no. 56. Washington, D.C.: U.S. Bureau of the Census.

Niu Jo-feng. 1979. "Taking Grain as the Key Link or Suiting Measures to Local Conditions." *KMJP*, December 8. In *HHY*, 1980, 2:65.

Oksenberg, Michel. 1982. "Economic Policy Making in China: Summer 1981." *China Quarterly*, 90: 165–94.

Pai Ju-ping. 1982. "Readjust the Structure of Agriculture; Raise Economic Efficiency." *HC* 7:15–19.

P'an Chih-fu. 1980. "Important Existing Problems in China's and Kweichow Province's Economic Structure and Their Causes." *KYSYHP*, 4:26–31. Reprinted in *KMCCCHYKL*, 1981, 1:76–82.

Pao Kuang-ch'ien. 1980. "The State Cannot Assure Housing for All Urban Residents." *JMJP*, June 1, p. 2.

Parish, William L., and Whyte, Martin King. 1978. *Village and Family in Contemporary China.* Chicago: University of Chicago Press.

P'ei Yüan-hsiu, Liu Ping-ying, and Li Ping-chang. 1980. "An Inquiry into the Optimum Rate of Accumulation." *KMJP*, June 28, p. 4.

Peking Municipal Planning Commission. 1981. "How Large Are State Subsidies Relative to People's Consumption?" *Ts'ai-cheng*, 7:27–8.

People's Daily, 1980a. "China's National Economy Is Advancing Amidst Adjustment." May 2, pp. 1, 3.

1980b. "The Power of Our Policy Can Be Seen in Rural Markets." May 9, p. 2.

1980c. "This Year the National Grain Tax Exemption Is 4.7 Billion Chin." July 3, p. 1.

1981a. "Cotton Output and Procurement Have Exceeded the Highest Historical Levels." March 4, p. 3.

1981b. "Annual Financial Subsidies of More than 10 Billion Yuan to Stabilize the Selling Price for Grain, Cotton, and Oils Have Had a Beneficial Effect on the People." June 25, p. 1.

People's Daily Commentator. 1980. "Sell More Pork and Support the Continued Development of the Pig Raising Business." *JMJP*, July 11, p. 3. In FBIS, July 23, pp. L7–L9.

Perkins, Dwight. 1966. *Market Control and Planning in Communist China*. Cambridge: Harvard University Press.

   1969. *Agricultural Development in China, 1368–1968*. Chicago: Aldine.

   1975a. "Constraints Influencing China's Agricultural Performance." In *China: A Reassessment of the Economy*, a compendium of papers submitted to the U.S. Congress Joint Economic Committee, pp. 350–65. Washington, D.C.: U.S. Government Printing Office.

   1975b. "Growth and Changing Structure of China's Twentieth Century Economy." In *China's Modern Economy in Historical Perspective*, edited by Dwight Perkins, pp. 115–65. Stanford, Calif.: Stanford University Press.

Perry, Elizabeth J. 1980. *Rebels and Revolutionaries in North China, 1845–1945*. Stanford, Calif.: Stanford University Press.

Popkin, Samuel L. 1979. *The Rational Peasant: The Political Economy of Rural Society in Vietnam*. Berkeley: University of California Press.

Rawski, Evelyn Sakakida. 1972. *Agricultural Change and the Peasant Economy of South China*. Cambridge: Harvard University Press.

Rawski, Thomas G. 1977. *China's Republican Economy: An Introduction*. Unpublished manuscript. University of Toronto.

   1979. *Economic Growth and Employment in China*. New York: Oxford University Press.

Reporter. 1980a. "Scientific Research on Rural Banking Must Have a New Development." *CKCJ*, 2:10–12.

   1980b. "State Negotiated Price Procurement of Grain Exceeds Seven Million Tons in a Year and a Half." *NFJP*, October 10, p. 3.

   1980c. "This Year State Grain Taxes Have Been Reduced by 4.7 Billion Jin." *JMJP*, July 3, p. 1.

   1981. "Strengthen Farm Management, Raise Sugarcane Production." *NFJP*, May 19, p. 1.

   1982a. "State Council Decision on Guaranteeing Grain Procurement, Sales, and Transfers." *CKTMP*, March 20, p. 1.

   1982b. "Collectively Distributed Income of Chinese Peasants Rises Sharply." *JMJP*, September 16, p. 4.

Riskin, Carl, 1975. "Surplus and Stagnation in Modern China." In *China's Modern Economy in Historical Perspective*, edited by Dwight H. Perkins, pp. 49–84. Stanford, Calif.: Stanford University Press.

Roll, Charles R. 1975. "Incentives and Motivation in China: The Reality of Rural Inequality." Unpublished manuscript.

Rozman, Gilbert. 1973. *Urban Networks in Ch'ing China and Tokugawa Japan*. Princeton: Princeton University Press.

Schoonover, David M. 1979. "Soviet Agricultural Policies." In *Soviet Economy in a Time of Change*, a compendium of papers submitted to the U.S. Congress, Joint Economic Committee, vol. 2, pp. 87–115. Washington, D.C.: U.S. Government Printing Office.

Schran, Peter. 1969. *The Development of Chinese Agriculture, 1950–59*. Urbana: University of Illinois Press.

Schultz, Theodore W. 1964. *Transforming Traditional Agriculture*. New Haven: Yale University Press.

   ed. 1978. *Distortions of Agricultural Incentives*. Bloomington: Indiana University Press.

Sen, Amartya. 1981. *Poverty and Famines: An Essay on Entitlement and Depriva-tion*. Oxford: Oxford University Press.

Sha Ch'ien-li. 1959. "Brilliant Achievements in Grain Work." *JMJP*, October 25, p. 60.

Shabad, Theodore. 1972. *China's Changing Map: National and Regional Develop-ment, 1949–1971*. New York: Praeger.

Shansi Provincial Service. December 20, 1980. "Excerpts of Governor Luo Kui-po's Work Report." In FBIS, December 24, pp. R1–R2.

Shantung Provincial Party Committee Investigation and Research Office. 1981. "How Was Shantung Province Able to Achieve a Rich Cotton Harvest?" *HC*, 8:14–18.

Shantung Science Commission. 1981. "Popularizing Number One Spurs the Experi-ence of a Rich Cotton Harvest." *KMJP*, March 3, pp. 1, 3.

Shen, T. H. 1951. *Agricultural Resources of China*. Ithaca, N.Y.: Cornell University Press.

Shiba, Yoshinobu. 1975. "Urbanization and the Development of Markets in the Lower Yangtze Valley." In *Crisis and Prosperity in Sung China*, edited by John Winthrop Haeger, pp. 13–48. Tucson: University of Arizona Press.

Shue, Vivienne. 1980. *Peasant China in Transition: The Dynamics of Development toward Socialism*. Berkeley: University of California Press.

Sinkiang Regional Service. February 27, 1979. "Effective Use of Materials for Farm-ing." In SWB/FE/W1023/A/8.

"The Sixth Five-Year Plan of the People's Republic of China for National and Social Development, 1981–85." *JMJP*, December 13, pp. 1–4. In FBIS, December 20, pp. K5–K42.

Skinner, G. William. 1964–65. "Marketing and Social Structure in Rural China." *Journal of Asian Studies*, 24(1):3–43; 24(2):195–228; 24(3):363–99.

——— 1977. "Regional Urbanization in Nineteenth-Century China." In *The City in Late Imperial China*, edited by G. William Skinner, pp. 211–49, 707–15. Stanford, Calif.: Stanford University Press.

Slicher van Bath, B. H. 1963. *The Agrarian History of Western Europe, A.D. 500–1850*. Translated by Olive Ordish. London: Edward Arnold.

Smil, Vaclav. 1977. "Food Energy in the PRC." *Current Scene*, 15(6, 7):1–11.

——— 1980. "Environmental Degradation in China." *Asian Survey*, 20:777–80.

Special Commentator. 1981. "Straighten Out the Guiding Ideology of Economic Work." *JMJP*, April 9, p. 5.

State Agricultural Commission. 1981. "Actively Develop a Diversified Rural Econ-omy." *PYT*, 8:15–22.

State Agricultural Commission Investigation Group. 1981. "The Heavy Burden of Unified Procurement and Rising Production Costs Continuously Increases the Difficulties of Counties with High Grain Yields." *NYCCWT*, 3:35–7.

State Council. 1955. "Provisional Measures for the Unified Purchase and Unified Sale of Grain in Rural Areas." *HHYP*, 9:160–2.

——— 1956. "Directive Concerning the Increased Procurement Price for Rapeseed." In *A Compendium of Materials on Prices in Shanghai before and after the Revolu-tion*. Shanghai Economic Research Institute, Chinese Academy of Sciences and Economic Research Institute, Shanghai Academy of Social Sciences, pp. 594–5. Shanghai: Shanghai People's Publishing House.

——— 1957a. "Directive Concerning the Readjustment of Pig Procurement and Sales Prices." In State Council Bureau of Legal Affairs, *Compendium of Laws and Regulations of the People's Republic of China*, vol. 5, pp. 181–2. Peking: Legal Publishing House.

——— 1957b. "Regulations on the Restrictions on Certain Agricultural Products and Other Commodities Which Are Subject to Planned Purchase or Unified Purchase by the State." *HHPYK*, 18:207–8. Translated in *Economic Planning and Organi-*

zation in Mainland China, edited by Chao Kuo-chün, vol. 2, pp. 43–7. Cambridge: Harvard University, East Asian Research Center, 1963.

1978. "Notice on Several Policy Directives Concerning Cotton Production." In Agricultural Yearbook Compilation Commission (1981, 80–1).

1979. "Procurement Prices Are Raised for Eighteen Major Agricultural Products." *JMJP*, October 25, p. 1.

1981. "Directive on the Strict Control of the Flow of the Rural Labor Force into Cities to Work and the Conversion of Agricultural Population into Nonagricultural Population." *KWYKP*, February 10, 1982, pp. 885–7.

1982a. "Council Urges End to Sales Embargoes." *China Daily*, April 22, p. 3.

1982b. "Directive Strictly Forbidding Unhealthy Tendencies in the Work of Recruiting and Assigning State Workers and Staff." *KWYKP*, June 10, pp. 339–42.

State Statistical Bureau. 1960. *Ten Great Years*. Peking: Foreign Languages Press.

1979a. "Communiqué on Fulfillment of the 1978 State Economic Plan." *JMJP*, June 28, p. 2.

1979b. "The National Unified Procurement Prices for Grains and Oils Have Been Adjusted." SC, 2:1.

1980a. "Communiqué on Fulfillment of China's 1979 National Economic Plan." *BR*, 19:12–15, 20:20–4.

1980b. *Main Indicators, Development of the National Economy of the People's Republic of China (1949–1979)*. Peking: Statistical Publishing House.

1980c. "The Living Standards of China's Workers and Staff Have Increased." *KMJP*, December 31, p. 1.

1981a. "Communiqué on Fulfillment of China's 1980 National Economic Plan." *BR*, 19:23–7, 20:17–20.

1981b. "Our Country's Excellent Economic Situation Is Reflected in Four Important Indicators." *KMJP*, February 7, p. 1.

1981c. "Selected Economic Statistics Materials, 1949–1979." In Hsüeh Mu-ch'iao (1981, VI-3–VI-26).

1982a. "Report on the Results of the 1981 Plan Implementation." *JMJP*, April 30, pp. 2, 4.

1982b. *Chinese Statistical Yearbook 1981*. Overseas Chinese Language Edition. Hong Kong: Economic Reporter Publishing House.

1982c. "A Compilation of Materials on Chinese Economic Statistics." In Hsüeh Mu-ch'iao (1982, VIII-3–VIII-78).

1982d. "The 1982 Census Results." *BR*, 45:20–1.

Stavis, Benedict. 1974. *People's Communes and Rural Development in China*. Special Series on Rural Local Government, no. 2. Ithaca, N.Y.: Rural Development Committee, Cornell University.

Sun Ching-chih, ed. 1956. *Economic Geography of Inner Mongolia*. Peking: Science Publishing House.

1957. *Economic Geography of North China*. Peking: Science Publishing House.

1958. *Economic Geography of Central China*. Peking: Science Publishing House.

1959a. *Economic Geography of South China*. Peking: Science Publishing House.

1959b. *Economic Geography of the East China Region*. Peking: Science Publishing House.

1959c. *Economic Geography of the Northeast Region*. Peking: Science Publishing House.

1960. *Economic Geography of the Southwest Region*. Peking: Science Publishing House.

Sun I-min. 1956. "Strengthen the Leadership over the Free Market." *CHCC*, 12:5–8. Translated in *Extracts from China Mainland Magazines*, no. 77, April 19, 1957, pp. 14–20. Hong Kong: U.S. Consulate General.

Sun Lin-fu, Ch'en Kuo-liang, and Chou P'ei-hua. 1980. "An Exploration of the Policy for Agricultural Development in Kuyüan County." *NYCCWT*, 4:32–5.
Sun Ming. 1982. "New Problems Have Appeared in Grain Production in Suchou Prefecture." *HC*, 15:31–4.
Sun Pu. 1980. "What Does the Investigation of the Financial Resources of 637 Production Teams Explain?" *NTKTTH*, 12:12–13.
Sun Te-shan. 1956. "Several Opinions on Planning Work Following the Establishment and Improvement of Agricultural Producer Cooperatives." *CHCC*, 10:16–19.
Sun Wei-tsu. 1958. "Principles for Compiling Grain Circulation Plans." *CHCC*, 2:24–27.
Sun Yeh-fang. 1978. "We Must Boldly and Confidently Grasp Socialist Profit." *CCYC*, 9:2–14.
1981. "Strengthen Statistical Work, Reform the Statistical System." *CCKL*, 2:3–5.
Sun Yü-ch'i. 1979. "Use Economic Laws to Improve the Production, Supply, and Marketing of Vegetables." *JMJP*, January 17, p. 3.
Szechuan Provincial Service. May 21, 1980. "Szechuan Agricultural Production." In FBIS, May 22, p. Q1.
November 9, 1974. "Szechuan." In SWB/FE/W803/A/8.
Szechuan Statistical Bureau. 1980. "Communiqué on National Economic Development in Szechuan in 1979." *SCJP*, July 29, p. 2. In FBIS, August 29, 1980, pp. Q3–Q10.
1981. "Communiqué on the Development of the Province's National Economy in 1980." *SCJP*, May 24, p. 2. In FBIS, July 2, pp. Q2–Q11.
Tai Mo-an and Li Yu-hua. 1980. "Several Economic Problems in Agricultural Mechanization." *NYCCWT*, 1:36–9.
T'an Chen-lin. 1957. "A Preliminary Investigation of Chinese Peasant Incomes and Living Standards." *JMJP*, May 5, p. 3.
Tang, Anthony M. 1980a. "Food and Agriculture in China: Trends and Projections, 1952–77 and 2000." In *Food Production in the People's Republic of China* by Anthony M. Tang and Bruce Stone. Research Report 15. Washington, D.C.: International Food Policy Research Institute.
1980b. "Trend, Policy Cycle, and Weather Disturbance in Chinese Agriculture, 1952–78." *American Journal of Agricultural Economics*, 62(2):339–48.
T'ang Chen-yang and Wang Chang-hu. 1980. "Develop Hainan Island into a Base for Tropical Crop Production." *NFJP*, August 14, p. 2.
Teng Li-ch'ün. 1981. *Study How to Do Economic Work from Comrade Ch'en Yün*. Peking: Chinese Communist Party Central Party School Publishing House.
Ts'ai Hsin-i. 1981. "Profits and Losses of China's State Farms over the Years." In Hu Ch'iao-mu (1981, 295).
Ts'ai Yüan-yüan. 1979. "Specialization in Production in China's Agricultural Regions." *CCYC*, 11:30–5.
Tsou, Tang, Blecher, Marc, and Meisner, Mitch. 1982. "National Agricultural Policy: The Dazhai Model and Local Change in the Post-Mao Era." In *The Transition to Socialism in China*, edited by Mark Selden and Victor Lippit, pp. 266–99. Armonk, N.Y.: M. E. Sharpe.
Tsung Han. 1979. "Financial Problems in the Modernization of Chinese Agriculture." *HSYK*, 6:7–13.
Tu Ch'eng. 1980. "An Exploration of Problems of the Modernization of Chinese Agriculture." *AHSTHP*, 1:14–20.
Tuan Chien-k'o. 1981. "China's Price Situation." In Hsüeh Mu-ch'iao (1981, IV-164–IV-166).
T'ung Ta-lin and Pao T'ung. 1978a. "Problems in the Policy for Developing the Northwest Loess Plateau." *KMJP*, November 29, p. 3.

1978b. "Some Views on Agricultural Modernization." *JMJP*, December 8. In FBIS, December 18, 1978, pp. E10–E14.

United States Department of Agriculture. 1972. *Agricultural Trade of the People's Republic of China, 1935–69*. Washington, D.C.

1979. *Agricultural Situation: People's Republic of China, Review of 1978 and Outlook for 1979*. Washington, D.C.

1981. *Agricultural Situation: People's Republic of China, Review of 1980 and Outlook for 1981*. Washington, D.C.

1982. *China: Review of Agriculture in 1981 and Outlook for 1982*. Washington, D.C.

Walker, Kenneth R. 1964. "A Chinese Discussion on Planning for Balanced Growth: A Summary of the Views of Ma Yin-ch'u and His Critics." In *The Economic Development of China and Japan*, edited by C. D. Cowan, pp. 160–91. New York: Praeger.

1968. "Organization for Agricultural Production." In *Economic Trends in Communist China*, edited by Alexander Eckstein, Walter Galenson, and Ta-chung Liu, pp. 397–458. Chicago: Aldine.

1977a. "Grain Self-sufficiency in North China, 1953–75." *China Quarterly*, 71:555–90.

1977b. *Provincial Grain Output in China, 1952–1957: A Statistical Compilation*. London: Contemporary China Institute.

Wang Chan-i. 1981. "Highway Construction in China." *BR*, 45:21–3.

Wang Ch'eng-hsüan. 1981. "All Around Development in Production in Our Province's 1980–81 Sugarcane Pressing Season." *FCJP*, January 2, p. 1.

Wang Chia-liang, Chang Yüeh-jung, and Chang Ch'iao-lung. 1982. "Give Serious Attention to the Study of Land Problems." *JMJP*, April 9, p. 5. In FBIS, April 15, pp. K3–K6.

Wang Chien-ming. 1980. "A Discussion of the Three Great Advantages of Developing Sugarcane Production in Kwangtung." *NFJP*, July 11, p. 2.

Wang Feng. 1978. "Speed up Construction in Sinkiang." Sinkiang Regional Service, November 5, 1978. In FBIS, November 9, pp. M3–M7.

Wang Hai-tu. 1981. "A Preliminary Analysis of the Proportionate Relationship between Accumulation and Consumption in China." *CCHK*, 1:13–27. In *KMCCCHYKL*, 1981, 2:53–67.

Wang Hai-tu and Sun Lien-ch'eng. 1979. "We Must Protect the Material Benefits and Democratic Rights of the Collective Peasantry." *HSYK*, 3:1–8, 39.

Wang Han-chih. 1980. "The Experience of Several Rich Teams Relying on the Collective Economy to Become Rich." *JMJP*, October 26, p. 2.

Wang Hsiang-ch'un, Chiang Hsing-wei, and Ch'en K'un-hsiu. 1965. "Problems of Controlling Plans for Agricultural Production in China." CCYC, 3:33–9.

Wang Keng-chin. 1959. "An Appreciation of Several Points in Agricultural Planning Work." *CHYTC*, 14:15–21.

1979a. "The Rule in Socialist Construction Is to Respect Agriculture as the Foundation." CCYC, 12:36–8.

1979b. "Two Problems in the Development of Agriculture." *CCHTT*, 12:20–2.

Wang Kuang-wei. 1959a. "Strengthen Industry's Support of Agriculture." *HC*, 16:4–12.

1959b. "Agricultural Producer Goods Should Be Included in the Plan." *CHYTC*, 11:1–3.

Wang P'ing. 1981. "An Exploration of Issues Concerning the People's Livelihood in China." *KYCCKLTK*, 2:13–16. In *KMCCJHYKL*, 1981, 4:119–22.

Wang Ping-ch'ien. 1980. "Report on the State's 1979 Final Account, 1980 Draft State Budget, and 1981 Estimated State Budget." *JMJP*, September 13, pp. 3–4.

1981. "Report on the State's 1980 Final Accounts and the Conditions of Implementation of the State's 1981 Budget." *HHYP*, 12:28–34.

1982. "Report on the 1982 Draft State Budget." *CKTMP*, May 6, p. 2.

Weitzman, Martin. 1974. "Prices vs. Quantities." *Review of Economic Studies*, 41(4):477–91.

Wen Shao-hsing. 1981. "Reform the Method of Payment of Premiums for Over-Quota Grain Procurement." In Hu Ch'iao-mu (1981, 223).

Wiens, Thomas B. 1980. "Agricultural Statistics in the People's Republic of China." In *Quantitative Measures of China's Economic Output*, edited by Alexander Eckstein, pp. 44–107. Ann Arbor: University of Michigan Press.

Wong, Christine Pui Wah. 1981. "Rural Industrialization in the People's Republic of China." Paper prepared for the International Bank for Reconstruction and Development.

Wu Chen-k'un. 1982. "Several Issues in the Continued Reliance of Agriculture on Economic Planning." *JMJP*, May 27, p. 5.

Wu Leng. 1980. "Utilize Economic Laws, Develop Soybean Production." *NYCCWT*, 7:29–32.

Wu Shuo. 1957. "An Inquiry into the Grain Situation during the Transition Period." *LS*, 1:20–5.

1982. "Present Conditions, Trends, and Goals Regarding China's Food Problem." *NYCCWT*, 7:52–3.

Wu Yün-ch'ang. 1980. "Speed up Development of Agriculture in the Hsianghsi Minority Autonomous Region." *JMJP*, September 15, p. 3.

Yang Chien-pai. 1981. *On the Relations between Industry and Agriculture*. Peking: Social Science Publishing House.

Yang Chien-pai and Li Hsüeh-tseng. 1980. "On the Historical Experience of the Relations between Agriculture, Light Industry, and Heavy Industry in China." *CKSHKH*, 3:19–44 (English version in *Social Sciences in China* 2:182–212).

1981. "The Structure of Agriculture, Light Industry, and Heavy Industry." In *Research in Issues on China's Economic Structure*, edited by Ma Hung and Sun Shang-ch'ing, pp. 99–136. Peking: People's Publishing House.

Yang Hsün. 1980. "Seriously Sum up Historical Experiences, Change the Backward Features of Agriculture." *NYCCWT*, 1:12–17, 59.

Yang Jui-ch'un and Cheng Li-chih. 1979. "An Examination of the Double Rice Triple Cropping System as Seen from an Investigation of Agricultural Production Costs and Materials on the Distribution of Grain." *KMJP*, October 14, p. 2.

Yang P'ei-hsin. 1958. "How to Raise Funds for the Development of China's Agriculture." *CCYC*, 1:22–37.

Yang Sheng-ming. 1982. "Income, Commodity Prices, and Living Standards." *JMJP*, April 16, p. 5.

Yang T'ing-hsiu. 1981a. "The Advantages of Growing More Soybeans." *JMJP*, April 22, p. 3.

1981b. "A Discussion of China's 'Secret Weapon.' " *KJJP*, April 1, p. 4.

Yao Chin-kuan. 1978. "An Exploration of Several Issues in the Scissors Price Differential between Industrial and Agricultural Products." *CCYC*, 12:32–6.

Yao Hsien-kuo. 1981. "Cost, Price, and Value of Farm Products, Report of an Investigation and Calculation of Farm Costs for Chiating County." *FTHP*, 1:107–12.

Yao Yi-lin. 1960. "Ten Years of Commercial Work." In *A Compendium of Accomplishments in Ten Years of Commerce*, compiled by Ministry of Commerce Education Bureau and Commercial Economics Department of Chinese People's University, pp. 7–23. Peking: Ministry of Commerce Education Bureau Publishing House.

Yeh Chün. 1957. "An Inquiry into the Reform of China's Agricultural Planning System." *CHCC*, 2:14–16.

Yen Jui-chen. 1981. "A Discussion of the Mutual Relation between Grain Production and Diversified Economy." *NYCCWT*, 2:40–5.

Yohe, Gary Wynn. 1976. "Uncertainty and the Simultaneous Regulation of Complements, Substitutes, and Joint Products." Discussion Paper no. 72. Albany: State University of New York.

  1977. "Comparisons of Price and Quantity Controls: A Survey." *Journal of Comparative Economics*, 1(3):213–33.

  1978. "Towards a General Comparison of Price Controls and Quantity Controls under Uncertainty." *Review of Economic Studies*, 45(2) (148):229–38.

Yü Chin-man. 1979. "Problems in Agricultural Modernization from the Perspective of the Competition for Land between Grain and Sugar." *JMJP*, November 23, p. 3.

Yü Kuo-yao. 1980a. "Further Understanding of Problems in China's Agricultural Development Policy." *HC*, 5:28–30.

  1980b. "We Must Use Economic Methods to Readjust the Irrational Economic Structure of Agriculture." *KMJP*, January 17, p. 2.

  1980c. "An Investigation of the Agriculture of the Arid, Low-Yielding Regions of Central Kansu and Hsichi, Haiyuan, and Kuyüan Counties in Ninghsia." *NYCCW*, 1:26–8, 52.

  1980d. "Meat Production Must Be the Objective of Animal Husbandry Production." *KMJP*, June 7, p. 4.

Yü Yu-hai and Chou Ch'uan. 1980. "How to Achieve Self-sufficiency in Sugar in China." In FBIS, June 10, pp. L13–L14.

Yüan Te-cheng. 1981. "An Exploration of the Problems of Agricultural Modernization in Yunnan." *CCWTTS*, 2:39–43.

Yüeh Wei. 1958. "A Discussion of the Problem of Accumulation by Agricultural Producers Cooperatives." *HH*, 7:23–4.

  1981. "Questions Concerning the Production, Distribution, and Use of National Income." *CCYC*, 2:46–52.

Yunnan Provincial Government General Office. 1981. "A Survey of Economic Development in Yunnan Province." In Hsüeh Mu-ch'iao (1981, IV-300–IV-302).

Yunnan Provincial Planning Commission General Office. 1981. "An Analysis of the Important Sources of Increases in National Income in Yunnan Province." *CCWTTS*, 2:36–8.

Yunnan Provincial Service. September 16, 1981. "Yunnan Circular Urges Thrift in Grain Consumption." In FBIS, September 18, p. Q2.

Index

Academy of Sciences, 64
Academy of Social Sciences, 111, 219
    Institute of Agricultural Economics, 161
    Institute of Economics, 201
Agricultural Bank of China, 141–2, 236
Agricultural Cooperative Bank; *see*
    Agricultural Bank of China
Agricultural producer goods; *see* Producer
    goods in agriculture
Agricultural producers' cooperatives; *see*
    Producers' cooperatives, agricultural
Agriculture
    labor force employed in, 1, 3–4, 51
    production costs of, 43, 53–4, 86–8, 231
    rate of growth of ix, 3, 5, 52, 87–8, 92,
        129, 190, 223–4
    share of national income arising in, 2–3, 7
    share of national investment allocated to,
        6, 125, 129–30, 132–8, 143–4, 191, 192
    terms of trade with industry, 15, 19, 30,
        47, 101–3, 108–10, 112–19, 136, 191
Agriculture–industry
    commodity flows, 102–8, 122, 127, 190
    financial flows; *see* Capital investment,
        sectoral allocation of; Credit, agricul-
        tural; Taxation
    interactions, 5–6, 12–16, 30, 98–102
    see also Procurement
"Agriculture first" policy, 98, 107, 138
    see also Chinese Communist Party, Tenth
        Plenum of the Eighth Central Committee
        of
Aird, John S., 151, 152
All–China Federation of Supply and
    Marketing Cooperatives, 158, 217, 238
Allocative efficiency; *see* Planning,
    agricultural
Ammonium sulfate, price of, 113, 116
Amoy, Fukien, 69
Anhui Province
    poverty in, 166, 173, 180, 241
    rice trade of, 9

rural markets in, 11, 121–2
sesame production in, 75, 77–8
soybean production in, 75, 79
sugarcane production in, 73–4
Animal husbandry, 19, 32, 52, 54–57
    relative prices 89
    see also Hides; Meat; Northwest China;
        Pigs
Anyang County, Honan, 60–1
Aquatic products, 19, 20, 32, 133–4
    output of, 44, 52, 154–5
    relative prices of, 89
Arable land
    per agricultural worker, 3
    quantity of 3, 7–8

Balanced growth; *see* Concurrent growth
    strategy; Imbalanced growth
Bangladesh
    population–land balance in, 5
    relative nitrogen price in, 113
Barley, 59, 83, 227
Boserup, Ester, 11
Brigade-level enterprises; *see* Rural
    small-scale enterprises
Buck, John Lossing, 10–11, 33, 147, 148,
    225
Budget outlays for agriculture, 129–33
    see also Agriculture, share of national
        investment allocated to
Bulgaria, food subsidies in, compared to
    China, 195

Caloric consumption; *see* Food consumption
Canton Delta, grain trade of, 9, 67
    see also Pearl River Delta
Canton–Hank'ou (Yüeh-han) rail line, 33
Capital investment
    rate of, 12, 16–17, 42, 127, 190–1
    sectoral allocation of, 6, 15, 44, 98,
        126–7, 129–30, 192
    see also Farmers' self-investment

275

Oil-bearing seed crops
  international trade in, 76–7, 79–81
  procurement of, 107, 182
  output of, 44, 52, 92, 154–5, 202
  relative prices of, 31, 40, 44, 89
  sown area of, 74–6, 89–91, 229
  specialized production of, 52, 74–81, 93

P'anyü, Kwangtung, 73
Paochi Prefecture, Shensi, 96
Peanuts
  international exports of, 76
  introduction to China, 8
  relative price of, 31, 44, 249
  sown area, 90
  specialized production of, 52, 74–7, 93
Pearl River Delta, 73, 214
  see also Canton Delta
Peasant
  income maximizing behavior, 10–11, 18,
    19, 31, 40, 47, 58, 97, 139–40, 180,
    215
  income; *see* Income of peasants
  self-investment of; *see* Farmers'
    self-investment
Peasant markets; *see* Rural markets
Peichen, Shantung, 177
Peking–Canton (Ching-kuang) rail line, 205
Peking–Hank'ou rail line, 10, 59, 175
Peng Te-huai, 42, 152–3
People's Bank, 140–1, 236
  see also Agricultural Bank of China;
    Credit, agricultural
People's Daily, 202, 203, 216
Periodic markets; *see* Rural markets
Perkins, Dwight, 37, 190, 225
Philippines
  population–land balance in, 5
  relative price of nitrogen in, 113
Pigs
  output of, 44, 52, 149
  price elasticity of supply, 211
  procurement prices of, 40, 47, 211, 249
  state procurement of, 211–12
  see also Meat; Pork
Pin County, Shantung, 59–60
Planning, agricultural
  direct, 19–21, 37–8, 41–3, 46–8, 82, 204,
    212–14
  indirect, 18–19, 30–3, 38–40, 43–5, 57,
    88–92, 154, 190, 191, 210, 214
  see also Price versus quantity controls
Poland
  food subsidies in, compared to China, 195
Population
  migration, interregional, 67, 177
  rate of growth of, 3, 148, 187
  size of, 2, 4, 7, 149

see also Famine, deaths from; Life
    expectancy; Rural–urban migration; Urban
    population
Pork
  price elasticity of demand and supply,
    211–12
  rationing of, 158, 211
  see also Pigs; Meat
Potatoes, 156
  introduction to China, 9
Poultry
  consumption of, 156
Poverty, rural, x, 6–7, 71, 168–89
  alleviation of, 188–9
  measurement of, 169–70
  provincial distribution of, 173, 189
  sources of, 168, 174, 175–88
  see also Famine; Malnutrition; Rural relief
Poyang Lake, Kiangsi, 214–15
Price Bureau, 47, 110, 192, 212, 242
Price elasticities, 119–20, 126, 211–13, 232
Price indices
  problems in Chinese compilation of,
    102, 109–11, 161, 163, 229, 243–4
Price policy, 15–6, 18, 20, 31, 39–41, 44,
    47, 89–92, 94, 101–2, 112–28, 126, 128, 144,
    145, 146, 210–13, 218–20
  see also Agriculture, terms of trade
    with industry; Procurement prices;
    Subsidies
Price versus quantity controls, 21–7
Private plots, 19, 20, 41, 44, 46, 89,
    162
Procurement
  excessive, as a cause of poverty and rural
    starvation, 152–3, 187–8
  measurement of, 202, 225
  over-quota, 91–2, 118, 199, 213
  policy, 18, 30, 31, 39, 94, 105, 207–10
  quantity of foodgrains, 34–7, 50–1, 103–5,
    109, 127
  see also Procurement prices; Ministry of
    Food
Procurement prices, 19–20, 30–1, 40, 44,
    47, 72, 82, 89–91, 120–2, 161, 191,
    192, 193, 208, 211–13
  effect of multilevel on allocative efficiency
    and income distribution, 210–11, 218–19
  negotiated, 92, 199
  over-quota premium, 92, 112, 118, 137,
    145, 199, 209, 219
Producer goods in agriculture, 18, 106–7,
    110, 119
  allocation of, 38, 214–16
  investment in, 130, 136–7, 191
  prices of, 110–11, 118, 192
  subsidies of, 118–19
  see also Chemical fertilizer

Wuchang Plenum; *see* Chinese Communist
   Party, Sixth Plenum of the Eighth
   Central Committee of
Wuchiang County, Kiangsu, 117
Wuch'iao County, Hopei, 59–60
Wuhsi, Kiangsu, 139

Yang Chien-pai, 151
Yangtse Delta
   cotton production in, 10
   grain trade and commercial development
      of, 9, 31, 67, 96
   multiple cropping in, 83–4
   peanut production in, 8
   urbanization of, 9
   see also Middle Yangtse
Yangyung Commune, Kwangtung, 96
Yeh Kung-chia, 132, 147, 148
Yellow River, 55, 177, 181
   Ordos bend, 214

Yench'eng Prefecture, Kiangsu, 61, 201,
   227
Yent'ai Prefecture, Shantung, 178
Yingt'an, Kiangsi, 69
Yingk'ou, Liaoning, 67
Yü Kuo-yao, 201
Yuan, exchange rate, 194–5, 243
Yünlung County, Yunnan, 187–8
Yunnan Province
   evolution of cropping patterns in, 78,
      184–5
   foodgrain exports of, 184
   imports of vegetables oils, 78
   poverty in, 173, 176, 183–5, 189
   rapeseed exports, 78
   rapeseed production in, 75, 78
   sugarcane production in, 65
   transport development in, 184, 205